# A TREATISE

## ON THE

# AUGUSTINIAN DOCTRINE

## OF

# PREDESTINATION

By J. B. MOZLEY, D.D.

LATE CANON OF CHRIST CHURCH AND REGIUS PROFESSOR OF DIVINITY AT OXFORD

*SECOND EDITION*

Wipf and Stock Publishers
199 W 8th Ave, Suite 3
Eugene, OR 97401

A Treatise on the Augustinian Doctrine of Predestination
By Mozley, J.B.
ISBN: 1-59244-825-9
Publication date 8/26/2004
Previously published by E.P. Dutton, 1878

# CONTENTS.

| CHAPTER | PAGE |
|---|---|
| I STATEMENT OF THE ARGUMENT FOR PREDESTINATION | 1 |
| II. EXAMINATION OF THE ARGUMENT FOR PREDESTINATION | 15 |
| III. THE PELAGIAN CONTROVERSY | 46 |
| IV. DIFFERENT INTERPRETATIONS OF ORIGINAL SIN | 100 |
| V. AUGUSTINIAN DOCTRINE OF PREDESTINATION | 126 |
| VI. AUGUSTINIAN DOCTRINE OF GRACE | 148 |
| VII. AUGUSTINIAN DOCTRINE OF FINAL PERSEVERANCE | 179 |
| VIII. AUGUSTINIAN DOCTRINE OF FREEWILL | 195 |
| IX. SCHOLASTIC THEORY OF NECESSITY | 233 |
| X. SCHOLASTIC DOCTRINE OF PREDESTINATION | 259 |
| XI. CONCLUSION | 293 |
| NOTES | 321 |

# THE AUGUSTINIAN DOCTRINE

OF

# PREDESTINATION.

## CHAPTER I.

### STATEMENT OF THE ARGUMENT FOR PREDESTINATION.

THE design of this treatise is to give an account of S. Augustine's doctrine of Predestination, together with such comments as may be necessary for a due examination of, and judgment upon, it. Before entering, however, on S. Augustine's statements, some general description of the doctrine itself, its grounds, and its defences, will be necessary: and these will require special consideration, with a view to ascertaining their soundness and validity. This introductory matter will occupy the following chapter, in addition to the present one, in which I shall endeavour to give a general description of the doctrine.

A distinction must, in the first instance, be drawn between the predestinarian and the necessitarian or fatalist. The predestinarian and the fatalist agree, indeed, in the facts of the case, and equally represent mankind as acting necessarily, whether for good or evil, in distinction to acting by an original motion of the will. But the fatalist goes to philosophy for the reason of this state of things, the predestinarian to a truth of revelation; the former argues from the nature of things, the latter from a particular fact of which he has been informed by competent authority.

The fatalist takes the general ground that every event must have a cause; and applying it to the case of human actions, argues that just as the action must have a cause, so that cause, even if we say it is the will's own choice, must have itself a cause; this further cause another cause. Being thus provided with an unlimited series of causes in the case of every human action, while the past existence of the agent is limited, he extends this series backwards till it reaches a point at which it goes outside of the agent; who is consequently proved to have acted ultimately from causes over which he had no control.

There is another kind of necessitarianism, again, which takes for its basis, instead of a physical assumption, like the one just mentioned, a religious one—the attribute of the Divine power; and argues downwards from the First Cause, instead of backwards from human action. To the metaphysician who believes in a Creator or First Cause, and who contemplates man in relation to that Being, one great and primary difficulty presents itself in the question how a being can be a creature, and yet have freewill, and be a spring of action to himself, a self-moving being. Our very notion of cause and effect is of the cause as active, the effect as passive; and, therefore, if man is an effect, how is he an active being? A tool or instrument that we make, issues inert out of our hands, and only capable of that motion which the maker of it gives it. To make a machine is to cause the whole series of motions which it performs. Our idea of creation is thus at variance with the idea of free agency in the thing made. Man as a self-moving being and the originator of his own acts, is a first cause in nature; but how can we acknowledge a second first cause —a first cause which is an effect, a created originality?[1]

Of course the fact of moral evil is at once an answer to this line of argument; so far, at any rate, as to disprove the cogency and decisiveness of it. For unless we make

---

[1] If man be a self-determining agent, will it not necessarily follow, that there are as many First Causes (*i.e* in other words, as many Gods) as there are men in the world?— Toplady, vol. vi. p. 31. If I am an independent animal, I am also necessarily self-existent.—p. 45.

God the author of evil, moral evil must be referred to some original source other than God; in which case the attribute of the Divine omnipotence is seen to meet in the first instance with something counter to it; and so cannot be argued upon as if it were the whole of the truth in the question under consideration. But so far as we attend to this attribute exclusively, as is the fault with some schools, this is the natural argument from it.

The necessitarian thus believes freewill not only to be false, but to be impossible. On the other hand, the predestinarian cannot believe it to be impossible, because he admits, on the authority of Scripture, that the first man Adam, in the state in which he was created, had it.[1] He only believes that man has since the fall been deprived of it, and regards it as an historical fact, not an existing one. He is thus excluded, on this question, from the ground of philosophy, from the perfect and consistent theory of the fatalist, and draws his conclusion from the revealed doctrine of the fall.

But though predestinarians, as such, draw their conclusion from the particular sin of Adam, such a ground is so unsatisfactory to a philosophical mind, that few have, in fact, confined themselves to it. Some have dispensed with it altogether, and adopted the philosophy either of causes,[2] or of the Divine power: the latter being the ground of the supralapsarian, who asks how such a universal effect could follow from a particular sin, except by the will of God

---

[1] Augustine endows Adam with freewill: 'Potuit non peccare primus homo, potuit non mori, potuit bonum non deserere. Nunquid dicturi sumus non potuit peccare qui tale habebat liberum arbitrium.'—De Corr. et Grat. c. 12. 'Homo male utens libero arbitrio et se perdidit et ipsum.' Ench. c. 30. Lombard (L. 2. Distinct 24. 1.), Gotteschalus (Usher, p. 29.), and Calvin, follow Augustine: 'In his præclaris dotibus excelluit prima hominis conditio. . . . In hac integritate libero arbitrio pollebat homo.'—Instit. 1. 1. c. 15. Though the latter afterwards calls the notion of Adam's freewill 'frigidum commentum,' and asks why he should not have been the subject of a decree, as his posterity were: 'Atqui predestinatio velint, nolint, in posteris se profert. Neque enim factum est naturaliter ut a salute exciderent omnes unius parentis culpa. Quid eos prohibet fateri de uno homine quod inviti de toto humano genere concedunt.'—Instit. l. 3. c. 23.

[2] Edwards, On the Freedom of the Will.

ordaining it so, and so pushes back the ground of fact immediately to one of philosophical principle.[1] Others have, not without detriment to their consistency as reasoners, mixed the two grounds. The ground which S. Augustine adopted and which the Jansenists revived, was in the main that of Scripture, though the former joined to it occasionally that of philosophy[1]: the medieval predestinarians took in the main the ground of philosophy, mixing with it occasionally that of Scripture. The theory of necessity last described, was adopted under the name of 'the physical predetermination of the will' by this medieval school,[2] who maintained that there could be but one true cause of every event, all other causes being secondary and intermediate; and applying it to the case of human actions, explained that though they had a 'voluntary cause,' or a cause in the human will, this was only secondary and intermediate between the agent and the first cause; protecting this position from the consequence which it apparently involved in the case of evil actions, that God was the author of evil, by distinctions which it is not necessary here to state; yet the same writers referred to the fact of the fall as the ground of the doctrine of predestination.[3] Predestinarian preachers, again, guided half by sentiment and half by theory, are accustomed, though using the scriptural ground as their basis on this question, to speak of the doctrine of freewill as an insult to the Divine Power, which

---

[1] NOTE I.
At qui omnium connexionem rerumque causarum qua fit omne quod fit, fati nomine appellant; non multum cum iis de verbi controversia certandum atque laborandum est, quandoquidem ipsam causarum ordinem et quandam connexionem, summi Dei tribuunt voluntati.—De Civit. Dei, l. 5. c. 8.

[2] Jansen draws the distinction between the theory of the 'predeterminatio physica' of the will 'ex philosophia profecta,' and which 'defenditur a sectatoribus sancti Thomæ,' and the predestinarian doctrine of efficacious grace, which rests upon original sin. 'Predeterminatio physica necessaria statuitur omnibus agentibus ex vi causæ secundæ quæ essentialiter tam in operari quam in esse suo subordinatur primæ, a qua ad agendum præmoveri debet; Christi adjutorium nequaquam sed læsæ voluntati propter solum vulnus necessarium est.'—De Grat. Christi Salvatoris, l. 8. c. 1, 2.

[3] Ratio reprobationis est originale peccatum. Aquinas, vol. viii. p. 330.

is to mix the two grounds; for while the scriptural ground is one of fact, the argument of the Divine power is an abstract argument.

Assuming, however, the doctrine of the fall or original sin as the proper ground of the doctrine of predestination, how, it will be asked, is the one doctrine the reason and basis of the other? In the following way.

The doctrine of original sin represents the whole human race as in a state of moral ruin in consequence of the transgression of the first man, incapable of doing anything pleasing and acceptable to God, or performing any really good act[1]; that is to say, it represents the human race as without freewill. And such being the condition of man, the Divine mercy determines on his rescue out of it, on raising him from a state of ruin to a state of salvation. But how can the rescue of a ruined and powerless being be effected except by an absolute act of power on the part of the Deliverer? The subject of this rescue is supposed to be unable to do anything for himself; and therefore, if he is saved at all, he must be saved without any waiting for or depending upon his own individual agency.[2] It may perhaps be replied that, as God endowed man with freewill, or the power to act aright, as distinguished from a necessary virtue, at the creation; so when he raises him out of this state of ruin and slavery of the will, he may endow him again with freewill only, leaving the use which he may make of it to himself, as before. It may be said that this would be a true act of grace or favour on the part of God, and therefore that we need not suppose that in the act of delivering man out of the wretched and impotent state in which he is by nature, God does anything more than this.

---

[1] We have no power to do good works pleasant and acceptable to God, without the grace of God by Christ preventing us.—Art. x. Works done before the grace of Christ are not pleasant to God, . . . rather we doubt not but they have the nature of sin.—Art. xiii.

[2] So totally are we fallen by nature, that we cannot contribute anything towards our own recovery. Hence it was God's own arm which brought salvation. . . . . Conversion is a new birth, and resurrection a new creation. What infant ever begat itself? What inanimate carcase ever quickened and raised itself? What creature ever created itself?—Toplady, vol. iii. p. 363.

But though such a mode of acting on God's part does not involve any positive contradiction, it must be allowed to be at variance with our reasonable notions of the Divine dealings; for what is this but to institute the first dispensation over again, and repeat a trial which has been undergone once, and had its issue? Suppose a man carried away by a torrent, to master which he had proved himself unequal, would it be a reasonable or consistent act to take him out only to recruit his strength for a second resistance to it? So, after man in the exercise of freewill has fallen and lost freewill, is it not a mockery to save him by giving him freewill again? What will he do with the gift, but fall again? On such a mode of Divine dealing, the fall may be repeated indefinitely, and the Divine purposes for the salvation of man may remain in perpetual suspense, and never attain completion.

The principle, then, being acknowledged that God does not repeat His dispensations, it follows that a second dispensation cannot be the first one a second time instituted, but must be a different one in itself; divided substantially from the old one in the nature, character, and effect of the aid which it supplies to man for attaining salvation. A dispensation which left the salvation of man dependent on his will, was highly suitable as a first one; suitable alike to the justice of the Creator and the powers of the untried creature, and such as we should naturally expect at the beginning of things: but such having been the nature of the first, the second must, for that very reason, be a dispensation of a different kind, effecting its design not by a conditional, but by an absolute saving act.

And independently of all reasoning, the fact is plain from Scripture that the new dispensation differs substantially from the old in the nature of the aid which it supplies to man for attaining salvation. God is not represented in Scripture as repeating his dispensations, but as altering them according to the wants of man. The Gospel aid to salvation, then, is, in accordance with the fundamental difference in man's own state, fundamentally different from that which man had before the fall; and if funda-

mentally different, different in the way which has been just
mentioned. For whatever peculiarities of the second dispensation may be appealed to, if the grace of it depends
on the human will for its use and improvement, it is fundamentally a dispensation of freewill like the first one.

The Divine act, then, in the salvation of man being, as
the result of the doctrine of original sin, an absolute one,
effecting its purpose with infallible certainty, the rest of
the doctrine of predestination follows upon ordinary Christian grounds. It is confessed by all that, whatever God
does, He determines or decrees to do from all eternity; for
no one who believes properly in a God at all, can suppose
that He does anything on a sudden, and which He has not
thought of before. There is, therefore, a Divine decree
from all eternity to confer this certain salvation upon those
on whom it is conferred. And, again, it is universally admitted that only a portion of mankind are saved. But these
two admissions complete the doctrine of predestination
which is, that God has decreed from all eternity to save by
His absolute and sovereign power a select portion of mankind, leaving the rest in their previous state of ruin.

The doctrine of predestination being thus reduced, as
its essence or distinctive part, to an absolute saving act on
the part of God of which man is the subject, we have next
to consider the particular nature and character of this act.
The doctrine of predestination, then, while it represents
God as deciding arbitrarily whom He saves, and whom He
leaves for punishment, does not by any means alter the conditions on which these respective ends are awarded. His
government still continues moral—pledged to the reward
of virtue and punishment of vice. It follows that in ordaining those whom He does ordain to eternal life, God decrees
also that they should possess the qualifications necessary for
that state—those of virtue and piety.[1] And if God decrees
that particular persons shall be virtuous and pious men,

[1] They who are predestinated to life are likewise predestinated to all those means which are indispensably necessary in order to their meetness, entrance upon, and enjoyment of that life, such as repentance, faith, sanctification, and perseverance unto the end.—Toplady, vol. v. p. 251. Jackson mistakes the predestinarian position on this head.—NOTE II.

He necessarily resolves to bestow some grace upon them which will control their wills and insure this result. There are two main kinds of grace laid down in the schemes of divines, one, assisting grace, which depends on an original act of the human will for its use and cultivation, and which was therefore conferred on man at his creation when the power of his will had not been as yet tried; the other, effective or irresistible grace, given when that will has been tried and failed, and must have its want of internal strength supplied by control from without. The Divine saving act is the bestowal of this irresistible grace. The subject of the Divine predestination is rescued by an act of absolute power from the dominion of sin, dragged from it, as it were, by force, converted, filled with the love of God and his neighbour, and qualified infallibly for a state of ultimate reward.

Here, then, it must be observed, is the real essence and substance of the doctrine of predestination. Predestinarians do not differ from their opponents in the idea of eternal Divine decrees, which, though popularly connected with this system more than with others, belongs in truth to all theological systems alike. For the believer in freewill, who only admits an assisting grace of God, and not a controlling one, must still believe that God determined to give that assisting grace, in whatsoever instances He does give it, from all eternity. Nor do they differ from their opponents in the ground or reason of God's final judgment and dispensing of reward and punishment[1]; for this takes place in both schemes wholly upon the moral ground of the individual's good or bad character. But the difference between the predestinarians and their opponents is as to that act which is the subject matter of the Divine decree, and as to the mode in which this difference of moral character is produced; that is to say, the two schools differ as to the nature, quality, and power of Divine grace under the Gospel; one

---

[1] Vita æterna . . . gratia nuncupatur non ob aliud nisi quod gratis datur, nec ideo quia non meritis datur . . . Justitiæ quidem stipendium est, sed tibi gratia est, cui gratia est et ipsa justitia.—Aug. Ep. 194. n. 19. 21.

school maintaining that that grace is only assisting grace, depending on the human will for its use and improvement; the other, that it is irresistible grace. To the former school belong those who hold one interpretation of the doctrine of baptismal regeneration; who maintain the sacrament of baptism to be the medium by which the power of living a holy life is imparted to the previously corrupt and impotent soul; which power, however, may be used or neglected according to the individual's own choice.

The mode in which the doctrine of predestination is extracted from the doctrine of original sin, being thus shown, it may be added that, by thus reducing as we have done the former doctrine to its pith and substance, we evidently much widen the Scripture argument for it, extending it at once from those few and scattered passages where the word itself occurs, to a whole field of language. The whole Scripture doctrine of grace is now appealed to as being in substance the doctrine of predestination, because there is only the Divine foreknowledge to be added to it, in order to make it such. Scripture distinguishes in the most marked way between two covenants. The first was that under which mankind was created, and which ended at the fall. Its language was—This do, and thou shalt live. It endowed man with freewill, or the power to obey the Divine law, and in return claimed the due use of this power from him, the proper exertion of that freewill. The burden of obedience, the attainment of salvation, was thrown upon the man himself. And of this covenant the Mosaic law was a kind of re-enactment; not that the law was really a continuation of it, but it was so by a supposition, or as it may be called an instructive fiction, maintained for the purpose of exhibiting and proving the consequences of the fall. Man was addressed under the Mosaic law, *as if* he had the full power to love and obey God, and the issue of the attempt showed his inability; he was addressed as if he was strong, and the event proved his weakness. This was the covenant of works. The covenant of grace was opposed to it. But how could it be opposed to it, if under that covenant the salvation of man still continued, as before, dependent on his freewill?

If it be said that there was the addition of grace under the second covenant, given besides and for the support of freewill, and that this addition makes the distinction between the two covenants, the reply is obvious, that whatever addition of grace there may be under the second, no substantial difference is made out so long as the use of this grace remains dependent on the will. The burden of obedience is still thrown on the man himself in the first instance, and his salvation depends on an original act of choice, as it did under the first. Moreover, it has been always held that man had grace in addition to freewill, even under the first covenant.[1] Then, in what are the two opposed, except in the nature, quality, and power of that grace which they respectively confer, that in the one grace was, and in the other is not, dependent on any original motion of the will for its effect? The grace of the gospel issues in being an effective and irresistible grace, converting the will itself, and forming the holy character in the man by a process of absolute creation; according to such texts as the following: 'We are His workmanship, created in Jesus Christ unto good works, which God hath before ordained that we should walk in them[2];' 'It is God that worketh in us both to will and to do of His good pleasure[3];' 'According as God hath

---

[1] Bull 'On the State of Man before the Fall,' gives this as the doctrine of all the early Fathers.

Nam et tunc (cum natura erat integra et sana) esset adjutorium Dei et tanquam lumen sanis oculis quo adjuti videant, se præberet volentibus.—Aug. De Naturâ et Gratiâ, c. 48.

Quod fuerit conditus in gratiâ videtur requirere ipsa rectitudo primi status in quâ Deus homines fecit.— Aquinas Summ. Theol. Prima Q. 95. Art. 1. See NOTE III.

Hoc autem (the need of grace), nedum est verum propter depressionem liberi arbitrii per peccatum, verum etiam propter gravedinem liberi arbitrii naturalem qua ad principaliter diligendum se alligatur. —Bradwardine, p. 371.

Homini in creatione, sicut de angelis diximus, datum est per gratiam auxilium .... Non talis natura facta est ut sine Divino auxilio posset manere si vellet.'— Lombard, L. 2. Dis. 24.

Jackson objects to a supernatural original righteousness, on the ground that nature would not be corrupt by the loss of it. 'If the righteousness of the first man did consist in a grace supernatural, or in any quality additional to his constitution, as he was the work of God, this grace or quality might have been, or rather was, lost, without any real wound unto our nature.' —Works, vol. ix. p. 6.

[2] Eph. ii. 10.

[3] Phil. ii. 13.

dealt to every man the measure of faith[1];' 'Who maketh thee to differ from another? and what hast thou which thou hast not received[2]?' 'No man can come to Me, except the Father which hath sent me, draw him[3];' 'Who hath saved us, and called us with an holy calling, not according to our works but according to His own purpose and grace, which was given to us in Jesus Christ before the world began[4];' 'By grace, ye are saved through faith; and that not of yourselves, it is the gift of God[5];' 'By the grace of God I am what I am[6];' 'Of Him are ye in Jesus Christ, who of God is made unto us wisdom, and righteousness, and sanctification, and redemption[7];' 'If any man be in Christ, he is a new creature[8];' 'And I will give them one heart, and I will put a new spirit within you; and I will take away the stony heart out of their flesh, and will give them a heart of flesh.'[9] The ground of Scripture for the doctrine of predestination thus becomes a large and general one, consisting of a certain pervading language, instead of being confined to a few texts in which the word itself is mentioned, and which are popularly regarded as its ground; and the doctrine appears to be no more than the gospel doctrine of grace, with the addition of the Divine foreknowledge.

From the basis and structure of the doctrine of predestination, I now come to its defences. An arbitrary decree ordaining from all eternity, and antecedently to any difference of desert, some of the human race to eternal life, and others to eternal punishment, is in direct opposition to our natural idea of justice, and plainly requires a defence. And the defence given for it rests on the same article of belief out of which the structure of the doctrine arose—the article, viz., of original sin.

It is true, then, predestinarians say, that we do maintain an arbitrary decree, ordaining, antecedently to any difference of desert, the eternal salvation of some and punishment of others of the human race: but remember in what state this decree finds the human race. It finds the whole of the

[1] Rom. xii. 3.
[2] 1 Cor. iv. 7.
[3] John vi. 44.
[4] 2 Tim. i. 9.
[5] Eph. ii. 8, 9.
[6] 1 Cor. xv. 10.
[7] 1 Cor. i. 30.
[8] 2 Cor. v. 17.
[9] Ezek. xi. 19.

human race deserving of eternal punishment. This decree, then, does indeed confer gratuitous and undeserved happiness upon one portion of mankind; and to that nobody will have any objection; for it would indeed be a rigorous justice which objected to an excess of Divine love and bounty: but it does not do that which alone could be made matter of accusation against it, inflict gratuitous and undeserved misery upon the other. It simply allows the evil which it already finds in them to go on and produce its natural fruits. Had this decree, indeed, to do with mankind simply as mankind, it could not without injustice devote any portion of them arbitrarily to eternal punishment: for man has not, as man, any guilt at all, and some guilt is required to make his punishment just. But this decree has not to do with human nature simply, but with human nature under certain circumstances. Mankind are brought into a particular position before it deals with them. That position is the position of guilt in which the doctrine of original sin places them. Viewed through the medium of that doctrine, the whole human race lies before us, prior to the action of this decree upon them, one mass of perdition. This decree only allows a portion to remain such. Viewed through that medium, all are under one sentence of condemnation: this decree only executes this sentence upon some. But if it would be just to punish the whole, it cannot be unjust to punish a part. If two men owe us debts, we may certainly sue one. If all antecedently deserve eternal punishment, it cannot be unjust that some should be antecedently consigned to it. Or would we fall into the singular contradiction of saying that a sentence is just, and yet all execution of it whatever unjust?

The question of justice, then, is already settled, when man first comes under this decree; and the question which is settled by it is not one of justice at all, but one of Divine arrangement simply. The same human mass which, if innocent, would have been the subject of God's justice, becomes, when guilty, the subject of his will solely. His absolute sovereignty now comes in, and He hath mercy upon whom He will have mercy, and whom He will He hardeneth.

'Hath not the potter power over the same lump to make one vessel to honour, and another to dishonour?' Are we to complain of God's justice in some cases, because He shows mercy in others? To do so would be for the creature to dictate to the Creator. Man, guilty, has lost his rights, and falls under the jurisdiction of God's absolute and sovereign will, with which remonstrance is ridiculous.[1]

Such is the defence of the doctrine of predestination on the score of justice. Absolutely, or apart from any previous supposition, it is admitted to be unjust; but the defence is that it must not be considered absolutely, but in its real and intrinsic relation to another doctrine, which in theological order precedes it. If you think the doctrine unjust, it is said, it is only because you do not realise what the doctrine of original sin is, and what it commits you to. You go on really, and in your heart thinking the human mass innocent before actual sin, and therefore you are scandalised at the antecedent consignment of any part of it to punishment. But suppose it really guilty, as your creed represents it, and you will not be scandalised at it. Fix upon your mind the existence of real ill-desert antecedent to actual sin, and condemnation will appear just and natural. The first step mastered, the second has no difficulty in it.

The doctrine of predestination itself, and its defence on the score of justice, thus rest upon the one doctrine of original sin. There is another objection, however, made to it, which is met in another way; for this doctrine, it is objected, contradicts our experience and consciousness,

[1] Hic si dixerimus quanto melius ambo liberarentur; nihil nobis convenientius dicetur quam, O homo, tu quis es qui respondeas Deo? Novit quippe ille quid agat, et quantus numerus esse debeat primitus omnium hominum, deinde sanctorum, sicut siderum, sicut angelorum, atque, ut de terrenis loquamur, sicut pecorum, piscium, volatilium, sicut arborum et herbarum, sicut denique foliorum et capillorum nostrorum. Nam nos humanâ cogitatione adhuc possumus dicere, quoniam bona sunt cuncta ista quæ fecit, quanto melius illa duplicasset, et multiplicasset, ut multo essent plura quam sunt; si enim ea non caperet mundus nunquid non posset etiam ipsum facere quantum vellet ampliorem? Et tamen quantumcunque faceret vel illa plura, vel istum capaciorem et majorem, nihilominus eadem de multiplicandis illis dici possent, et nullus esset immoderatus modus.—Aug. Ep. 186. n. 22.

describing us as acting from an irresistible influence, either for good or evil; whereas we are conscious of will and choice, and feel that we are not forced to act in one way or another. But it is replied that this objection proceeds from a misapprehension as to the nature of this irresistible influence. The terms irresistible, necessary, and other like terms, imply, indeed, in their common use an inclination of the will which is opposed, and express a certain overwhelming power exerted upon the man, in consequence of which he is obliged to act against this inclination. But in the present instance these terms are, in defect of proper language for the purpose, used incorrectly, and express a power which inclines the will itself, in the first place, and does not suppose an inclination already formed which it contradicts. Between our experience and consciousness, then, and the exertion of such a power as this upon our wills, there is no opposition. Our consciousness is only concerned with the inclination of the will itself, beyond which we cannot by any stretch of thought or internal scrutiny advance, being obliged to stay at the simple point of our will, purpose, inclinations as existing in us. But the inclination itself of the will is the same, however it may have been originated; no difference therefore respecting its origin touches the subject matter of our consciousness. This question affects the cause, our consciousness is concerned only with the fact; these two, therefore, can never come into collision. And though in popular language such a grace would be spoken of as obliging a man to act in a particular way, as if it obliged him so to act whether he willed or not, operating as physical force does, independent of the will of the agent altogether; such a description of it is incorrect, and misses the fundamental distinction in the case. The agent is not caused by it to act in spite of his will, but caused to will.

This general description of the structure and defence of the doctrine of predestination will perhaps be sufficient as an introduction to the present treatise. Nakedly stated, the doctrine is simply paradoxical, and those who are acquainted with no more than the mere statement of it, are apt to feel surprise and perplexity how it could have been maintained by the pious and thoughtful minds that have maintained it. But it must be admitted that its paradoxical character is diminished, when we come to examine its grounds and construction. It happens in this case, as it does in many others, that the surprise which the conclusion produced is lessened by an acquaintance with the premisses, the steps by which it was arrived at.

Simplicity of system is a great object with one class of minds. The attribute of Divine power has also in many religious minds the position not only of important, but favourite truth. It is evident how acceptable on both these grounds must be a system which contrives in harmony with the facts of experience and the rule of justice, to secure the one great idea of the whole spiritual action of the human race being the pure creation of Almighty will. They are attracted by a conclusion which gives so signal a rebuke to human pride, and witness to Divine mercy, and embrace a doctrine which alone appears fully to set forth that man is nothing and God all in all.

## CHAPTER II.

### EXAMINATION OF THE ARGUMENT FOR PREDESTINATION.

WHEN particular truths of philosophy or religion are used as grounds to support conclusions which are repugnant to natural reason, there are two things for us to do. First, we have to examine if the reasoning upon these truths is correct, and if they really contain the conclusions which have been drawn from them; and, secondly, if this should be the case, we have to examine the nature of these truths, and the sense or manner in which we hold them; for if the truths themselves cannot be questioned, and yet the logical conclusions from them are untenable, there only remains for extricating ourselves from the difficulty, the consideration that these truths must have been held in some sense or manner which was improper; which impropriety in the manner of holding them has been the reason why, however certain themselves, they have led to such untenable results.

Let us take the case of philosophical predestination in the first place, or of predestination as resting on philosophical grounds, or what is ordinarily called necessitarianism or fatalism; and let us examine the nature of these grounds. It will be evident to any one at all conversant with philosophy, and who will summon to his mind a few instances of the different kinds of truth, to which it calls our attention, and which it assumes and uses in its arguments and speculations, that there are two very different kinds of truths upon which philosophy proceeds—one, of which the conception is distinct and absolute; the other, of which the conception is indistinct, and only incipient or in tendency. Of ordinary facts, such as meet the senses—of the facts of our internal consciousness, our own feelings and sensations, bodily and mental, we have distinct conceptions, so far at least, that these are complete and absolute truths embraced by our minds. On the other hand, there are various truths which we partly conceive and partly fail in conceiving; the conception, when it has begun, does not advance or come to a natural termination, but remains a certain tendency of thought only. Such are the ideas of substance, of cause, of infinity, and others which we cannot grasp or subject to our minds, and which, when we follow them up, involve us in the utmost perplexity, and carry us into great apparent contradictions. These, as entertained by our minds, are incipient truths, not final or absolute ones. In following or trying to follow them, we feel that we are in a certain right way, that we are going in a certain true direction of thought; but we attain no goal, and arrive at no positive apprehension.

In contemplating material objects, I encounter a number of impressions, such as hardness, softness, smoothness, roughness, colour, which are only qualities; but I cannot rest in them, but push on to some substance to which they belong, and from which it is absurd to imagine them apart.

But I cannot form the least idea of what substance is. I find myself only going in the direction of something which I cannot reach, which mocks all pursuit, and eludes all grasp; I have only a sort of idea of a confused something lying underneath all the sensible qualities of matter—that is to say, beyond and outside of all my real perceptions. And I am just as incapable of forming any idea of a spiritual substance or myself, though I am said to be conscious of it; for this plain reason, that it is in its very nature anterior to all my ideas.

Again, I have the idea of force or power, or, what is the same thing, of cause. After contemplating any event in life or nature I find myself going in thought beyond it, to consider how it came to pass; and this thought in me, once set going, tends, by some instinctive law, some constitutional motion inherent in it, in the direction of a cause of that event; something not merely antecedent to it, but which stands in such a relation to it, as that, in consequence of it, that event or thing exists. The intellect pushes on to this ultimate resting place, and satisfaction of its own indigenous want and desire. But while the movement *towards* a cause, or some kind of idea of one, is part of our rational nature, I find, on reflection, that I can form no distinct conception whatever of what a cause is. What is that of which existence is the necessary fruit and result? We can form no idea of what goes on previous to, and with infallible cogency and force for, producing existence. All this preliminary agency is so entirely hid from us, and our faculties so completely stop short of it, that it seems almost like an absurdity to us, that there should be anything of the kind. The order of nature puts before us an endless succession of antecedents and consequents, but in no one instance can we see any necessary connection between the antecedent and its consequent. The relation between the so-called cause and effect—the circumstance in a cause which makes it a cause, is wholly removed from my view. I see that fire melts metals and hardens clay, but I do not see why it does either; and prior to experience, I should have thought it as likely that these effects would have been reversed. The motion which one ball set in motion communicates to another, might or might not have taken place prior to experience. I see nothing in the first motion to produce the second, and can conceive no motion upon impact with as little contradiction as motion. Again, I look into myself, and observe my own motions, actions, thoughts. I find that by a certain exertion of the will, I can move my limbs, raise ideas, excite or suppress affections and emotions; but the nature of that power by which the will does this, is absolutely hidden from me. When I exert all my force to lift some weight or remove some barrier, I may seem at first to myself to have an inward perception of that force, and the manner in which it operates; but on examination, I find that I have only the idea of a motion of the will, and of a strain of the muscles which succeeds, not of any connection between the two.[1] I have looked around and within me then, and I do not see a cause anywhere. My reason, as surely as it leads me up to the truth, that there is a cause of things, stops at that point, and leaves me in utter perplexity and amazement as to what a cause is. It is a wonder, a mystery, an incomprehensible truth. My reason forces me towards the idea of something, of which I can give no more account to myself than I can of the most inexplicable article in a creed. What can be more astonishing than a power by which anything in nature *is*. Do all the mysteries of revelation—do even the wildest dreams of superstition ex-

---

[1] It may be pretended that the resistance which we meet with in bodies, obliging us frequently to exert all our force, and call up all our power, thus gives us the idea of force and power. It is this *nisus* or strong endeavour of which we are conscious, that is the original impression from which this idea is copied. But, first, we attribute power to a vast number of objects where we can never suppose this resistance or force to take place; to the Supreme Being, who never meets with any resistance; to the mind in its command over ideas and limbs. . . . Secondly, this sentiment of an endeavour to overcome resistance has no known connection with any event; what follows it, we know by experience, but would not know it *a priori*. It must, however, be confessed that the animal *nisus* which we experience, though it can afford no accurate or precise idea of power, enters very much into that vulgar inaccurate idea which is formed of it.—Hume, 'Enquiry concerning the Human Understanding,' sect. 7.

ceed it? What is it that prevents my reason from rejecting such an idea? Simply, that my reason gives it me—gives it me, though in that incipient and incomplete state from which this perplexity ensues.

Again, the idea of infinity is part of our rational nature. Particular times, spaces, and numbers, end; but we cannot possibly think of time, space, and number in general as ending. Any particular number is suggestive of further number. In two or three straight strokes I see a necessary capacity of multiplication, two, three, or any number of times *ad infinitum*. I imagine myself at the top of a high mountain, with the largest conceivable view all around me. I might know by geography that there are countries which lie beyond it on all sides, but I do not wait for that information. There is something in me by which I know antecedently, that the space is going on all the same as space, however differently it may be occupied, beyond my sight as within it. Having raised in my mind the largest picture of space I can, so that if I try to increase, I simply repeat it, I have still a sense of limitation. There is at the furthest line of the horizon an excess which baffles me, which is not included in the imagined space, or it would not be an excess, and which yet belongs and is attached to it and cannot be removed; an incipient beyond which must be endless, for the very reason that it begins; because this indefinable excess, for the very reason that it exists itself, must be succeeded by the like. It is the same with respect to time. Time, space, and number, then, do not end, but go on at the very last; that is the very latest perception we have of them, the last intelligence as it were; they are ultimately going further. They go onward, not only to the end (which particular portions of them do), but at the end—*i.e.* their utmost defined extent in our imagination; for their very nature is progressive; they are essentially irrepressible, uncontrollable, ever-growing, without capacity for standing still and subject to the absolute necessity of being continually greater and greater.

But while we find in our minds the idea of infinity, we

have no idea of what infinity is. I mean that we have no idea of an actual infinite quantity of anything. We apprehend so much of extent or number as we can measure or count, and can go on adding; but wherever we stop, we are on the margin of an infinite remainder, which is not apprehended by us. Imagine a large crowd increasing in all directions without end; it is obvious that such number is unintelligible to us; as much so as any mysterious article in a creed. Some idea of infinity we have no doubt, otherwise we should not be able to think or speak of it at all; and that seems to be more than a negative idea, as it has been asserted to be; for it is the idea of a progress, or going further, which is not negative, but positive; but it is no mental image or reflection of actual infinity.[1]

We find then a certain class of truths in philosophy of which we have only a half conception; truths which, as entertained by us, are only truths in tendency, not absolute, not complete. We are conscious of the germs of various ideas which we cannot open out, or realise as whole or consistent ones. We feel ourselves reaching after what we cannot grasp, and moving onward in thought towards something we cannot overtake. I move in the direction of a substance and a cause in nature which I cannot find: my thought reaches after infinity, but the effort is abortive, and the idea remains for ever only beginning. I encounter mysterious truths in philosophy before I come to them in religion, natural or revealed. My reason itself introduces me to them. Were I without the faculty of reason, I should not have these ideas at all, or derive therefore any perplexity from them. I should want no substance underneath my impressions; I should have no sense of an excess beyond the range of my eye: but reason creates these movements

---

[1] It is an oblique proof of the mysteriousness of infinite number, that it can be neither odd nor even. 'Nous connaissons qu'il y a un infini, et ignorons sa nature, comme nous savons qu'il est faux que les nombres soient finis; donc il est vrai qu'il y a un infini en nombre, mais nous ne savons ce qu'il est. Il est faux qu'il soit pair, il est faux qu'il soit impair; car en ajoutant l'unité, il ne change point de nature: cependant c'est un nombre, et tout nombre est pair ou impair; il est vrai que cela s'entend de tous nombres finis.—Pascal (éd. Faugère), vol. ii. p. 164.

CHAP. II. *Argument for Predestination.* 21

in my mind, and so introduces me to indistinct and mysterious truths within her own sphere.

And this, it may be remarked, is an answer to those who object to such truths in religion, and reject or put aside certain doctrines on the ground that they relate to subject-matter of which we can form no conception, and which, therefore, it is argued, we cannot entertain in our minds at all; cannot make the subject of thought, or therefore of belief. It is wrong to say that we are wholly unable to entertain truths of which we have no distinct idea; and those who suppose so have an incorrect and defective notion of the constitution of the human mind. The human mind is so constituted as to have relations to truth without the medium of distinct ideas and conceptions. The constitution of our minds makes this mixed state of ignorance and knowledge possible to us. Were the alternative of pure ignorance or pure knowledge necessary, it is evident that, as soon as we turn from sensible objects and mathematics, we should be in a state of absolute ignorance and unmixed darkness; we should not only be ignorant of the nature of many other truths, but should have no sort of idea what those truths were of which we were ignorant; we should be unable to think of or discuss them on that account, or even to *name* them. We should be cut off wholly from metaphysics, and all that higher thought and philosophy which have occupied the human mind in all ages. But this alternative is not necessary.[1]

With the general admission, then, of this class of truths in philosophy, we come to the grounds upon which philosophical predestination or fatalism is raised. We find these to be mainly two—first, the maxim that every event must have a cause, and, secondly, the idea of the Divine Power; the first being a physical, the second a religious assumption, but both alike forming premisses from which a scheme of absolute necessity in human actions is logically inferred.

[1] 'Nous sommes sur un milieu vaste, toujours incertains, et flottants entre l'ignorance et la connaissance; et, si nous pensons aller plus avant, notre objet branle, et échappe à nos prises; il se dérobe, et fuit d'une fuite éternelle: rien ne peut l'arrêter.'—Pascal. Locke and Hume both substantially admit the class of indistinct ideas.—NOTE IV.

To take first, then, the maxim that every event must have a cause. This is a maxim undoubtedly that approves itself to our understanding. If we see a body which has hitherto been at rest, start out of this state of rest and begin to move, we naturally and necessarily suppose that there must be some cause or reason of this new mode of existence. And this applies to moral events or actions as well as to events physical. Every action which is performed is undoubtedly a new event in nature, and as such there must have been some cause to produce it. Moreover, on the same principle that the action itself must have a cause, that cause must have another cause, and so on, till we come to some cause outside of and beyond the agent himself. The maxim, then, that there must be a cause of every event once granted, the conclusion of a necessity in human actions inevitably follows.

But though the maxim that every event must have a cause is undoubtedly true, what kind of a truth is it? Is it a truth absolute and complete, like a fact of sensation or reflection; or is it a truth indistinct, incipient, and in tendency only, like one of those ideas which have just been discussed? It is a truth of the latter kind, for this simple reason, that there is a contrary truth to it. When we look into our minds, and examine the nature and characteristics of action, we find that we have a certain natural and irresistible impression or sense of our originality as agents. We feel beforehand that we can do a thing or not as we please, and when we have taken either course, we feel afterwards that we could have taken the other, and experience satisfaction or regret, as may be, on that particular account. That our actions are original in us, is the ground upon which arise peculiar pleasures and pains of conscience, which are known and familiar to us. Could we really think that they were not, we should be without these particular feelings; we should not have a certain class of sensations which we know we have. We have, then, a certain sense or perception of our originality as agents, that an action is original in us, or has no cause.

This originality in human actions is, for want of better

language, sometimes expressed by what is called the self-determination of the will; and from this mode of expressing it persons have endeavoured to extract a *reductio ad absurdum* of the truth itself. For it has been said, 'If will determines will, then choice orders and determines choice, and acts of choice are subject to the decision and follow the conduct of other acts of choice;' in which case every act whatever of the will must be preceded by a former act, and there must therefore be an act of the will before the first act of the will.[1] But in the first place it is evident this is at the best an argument drawn from a particular mode of expressing a truth, and taking advantage of the inherent defects of language; and in the next place that it does not do justice even to the language; for however inconceivable self-motion strictly speaking may be, what we mean and, so far as we can, express by it, is one indivisible motion, not a relation of one motion to another, of something moving to something being moved, as is supposed in this argument, and is necessary to the force of it. The real question, however, at issue is, in whatever way we may express it, have we or have we not a certain sense of originality in our acts; that we are springs of motion to ourselves; that however particular motives and impulses from without may operate on us, there is a certain ultimate decision, which we can make either way, and which therefore when made, in one way or the other, is original. If we have, we have a certain sense or perception of action as being something uncaused, *i.e.* having nothing anterior to it, which necessarily produces it—a sense or perception which goes counter to the other, which was also admitted to exist in us, of the necessity of a cause for all events,

---

[1] Edwards 'On the Freedom of the Will,' part 2, sect. 1. Aquinas in arguing for the necessity of an external source of motion to the will (moveri ab aliquo exteriori principio) reasons in the same way. 'Manifestum est quod voluntas incipit velle aliquid cum hoc prius non vellet. Necesse est ergo quod ab aliquo moveatur ad volendum. . . . Et si quidam ipsa moverat seipsam ad volendum oportuisset, quod mediante consilio hoc ageret ex aliquâ voluntate præsupposita. Hoc autem est procedere in infinitum. Unde necesse est ponere quod in primum motum voluntatis voluntas prodeat ex instinctu alicujus exterioris moventis.'—Sum. Theol. p. 2, q. 9, art. 4.

actions included. Regarding actions in their general character as events, we say they must have a cause ; but in their special character as actions, we refuse them one: our whole internal feeling and consciousness being opposed to it. Here then are two contradictory instincts or perceptions of our reason, which we must make the best of, and arrive at what measure of truth a mixed conclusion gives. We certainly have both these perceptions, and one must not be made to give way to the other. However reason may declare for the originality of our acts, it says also that every event must have a cause ; again, however it may declare for a cause of every event, it says that our acts are original.

Metaphysicians on both sides appear to have undervalued the one or the other of these rational instincts or perceptions, according to their bias ; the advocates of freewill thinking slightly of the general instinct for a cause, the advocates of necessity thinking slightly of our perception, as agents, of originality. The former have simply dwelt on our inward consciousness of power of choice, dismissing the principle of causes, as if, however, it applied to other events, it did not apply to actions, being excluded from this ground *ipso facto* by this sense of the originality of our actions. But if the necessity of a cause of events is true at all, it must apply to actions as well as to other events ; and to suppose that it is *ipso facto* deprived of this application by this special sense of originality in the case of actions, is to assume that we cannot have two contradictory ideas ; which, according to what I endeavoured to show in this chapter, is a false assumption, and not true of us in the present imperfect state of our capacities, in which we may have, and have, imperfect opposing perceptions ; though it is of course absurd to suppose that this can be the case except in a very imperfect state of being, or that there can be *absolute* and *perfect* perceptions in opposition to each other. The latter, on the other hand, have regarded the principle of causation as the only premiss worth taking into account on this question, and have dismissed the sense of originality, as if it were a mere confused and blind sentiment, which, when examined, really spoke to nothing, and was found to issue in a mere cloud, or evaporate altogether. They have voted the one idea to be solid and philosophical, the other to be empty and delusive. But I cannot see how they are justified in thus setting up one of these ideas to the exclusion of the other. Express the idea of causation as you will, whether as the perception of an abstract truth that there *must* be a cause of all events, or simply as the observation of the fact, that all events *are* connected with certain antecedents as the condition of their taking place[1]—what is it, after all, but a truth so far as it goes, and so far as we perceive or observe it to be such? The reason desiderates a cause of anything that takes place, says one philosopher, putting it as the perception of an abstract truth; but this necessity is not to be acknowledged in any more unlimited sense than that in which it is perceived. In the case of events in nature, the axiom reigns supreme, and is not interfered with; but when we come to moral events or actions, it is there met by an innate perception—viz. that of originality which is just as rational as the other. Another philosopher says that we observe causation as a fact. We do; but though we observe it in nature, we do not certainly *observe* it in will; and observation can only speak to those cases to which it extends. The consideration of ourselves as agents presents another truth to us—viz. that of originality in our acts; and this instinct or perception must be taken into account as a philosophical premiss. How should we have the idea of the will as being self-moving and self-determining at all in the way in which we have it, unless there were truth in the idea? For nature does not deceive us and tell us falsehoods, however it may tell us imperfect truths. And though it may be said that all that we *mean* by the will's self-determination, is that we act with will as distinct from compulsion, however that will may have been caused; this is not true upon any natural test; for, put this distinction before any plain man, and he will feel it as an interference in some way with his natural consciousness, and will reject the idea of an externally-caused will, as not properly answering to his instinct on this subject. And if it

---

[1] The former is Edwards's, the latter Mr. Mill's position. NOTE V.

be argued that we cannot have this sense of originality or self-determination in the will, because all that we are actually conscious of is our will itself, the fact that we decide in one way or another, and not the cause of it, whether in ourselves or beyond us ; it is sufficient to say that this sense or perception of originality is not professed to be absolute or complete, but that it is still a sense or perception of a certain kind.  There is a plain instinct in us, a perception of a truth, in this direction ; and that being the case, to say that it is not apprehension and does not arrive at a positive conclusion or point, is to say no more than may be said of many other great ideas of our intelligent nature, such as that of substance, cause, infinity.

There being these two counter ideas, then, with respect to the necessity of a cause ; as on the one hand we demand a cause, and on the other reject it ; neither of these can be truths absolute and complete ; and, therefore, neither of them a basis for an absolute and complete theory or doctrine to be raised upon it.  So far as the maxim that there must be a cause of every event is true, so far it is a premiss for a scheme of fatalism.  But it is not true absolutely, and thus no absolute system of this kind can be founded upon it.  Did the fatalist limit himself to a conditional incomplete conclusion, *i.e.*—for this would be all that it would come to in such a case—to a mystery on this subject, no one could object.  But if he raises a definite scheme, his conclusion exceeds his premiss.

The same may be said of any absolute doctrine of Predestination drawn from the attribute of the Divine Power, or the idea of God as the cause of all things.  There is an insurmountable contradiction between this idea and that of freewill in the creature ; for we cannot conceive how that which is caused can itself be a first cause, or a spring of motion to itself.  And therefore the idea of Divine Power leads to predestination as its result.  But what is this truth of the Divine Power or Omnipotence, as we apprehend it ? Does it belong to the class of full and distinct, or of incomplete truths ?  Certainly to the latter, for there appears at once a counter truth to it, in the existence of moral evil which must be referred to some cause other than God, as well as in that sense of our own originality to which I have just alluded. The Divine Omnipotence, then, is a truth which we do not understand—mysterious, imperfect truth; and, therefore, cannot be used by the predestinarian as the premiss of an absolute doctrine, but only as that of an indefinite or conditional one.

The two ideas of the Divine Power and freewill are, in short, two great tendencies of thought inherent in our minds, which contradict each other, and can never be united or brought to a common goal; and which, therefore, inasmuch as the essential condition of absolute truth is consistency with other truth, can never, in the present state of our faculties, become absolute truths, but must remain for ever contradictory tendencies of thought, going on side by side till they are lost sight of and disappear in the haze of our conceptions, like two parallel straight lines which go on to infinity without meeting. While they are sufficiently clear, then, for purposes of practical religion (for we cannot doubt that they are truths so far as and in that mode in which we apprehend them), these are truths upon which we cannot raise definite and absolute systems. All that we build upon either of them must partake of the imperfect nature of the premiss which supports it, and be held under a reserve of consistency with a counter conclusion from the opposite truth. And as I may have occasion hereafter to use it, I may as well say here that this is what I mean by the distinction between absolute truths, and truths which are truths and yet not absolute ones—viz., that the one are of that kind which is distinct and consistent with other truth; the other of the kind which is indistinct, and especially such truth as has other truth opposed to it, and which is therefore obviously but half-truth.

I will add as a natural corollary from this relation of these two ideas, that that alone is a genuine doctrine of freewill which maintains such a freewill in man as is *inconsistent* with our idea of the Divine Power. There is a kind of freewill which is consistent with this idea. All men, whatever be their theory of the motive principle of, admit the *fact* of, the human will; that we act willingly and not like inanimate machines; nor does the necessitarian deny, that the human will is will, and as far as sensation goes free, though he represents it as ultimately moved from without. Here, then, is a sort of freewill which is consistent with the idea of the Divine Power. But this, as was above explained, is not such a freewill as meets the demands of natural consciousness, which is satisfied with nothing short of a characteristic of will, which comes into collision with our idea of the Divine Power—viz., originality.

Again, the objection against the doctrine of freewill, that it would remove human actions from the Divine Providence,[1] and so reduce this whole moral scheme of things to chance, has an immediate answer in the very nature of the truth as here described. Undoubtedly there is a contradiction in supposing that events really contingent can be foreseen, made the subjects of previous arrangement, and come into a scheme of Providence; and though this is sometimes met by the answer that the Divine foresight is the sight of the events as such, and not in their causes only, and that therefore contingent events can be foreseen by God as being events, which however future to us, are present to His eternal eye; it must be owned that such a foresight as this is a contradiction to our reason[2], and that

[1] If the will of man be free with a liberty *ad utrumlibet*, and if his actions be the offspring of his will, such of his actions which are not yet wrought, must be both radically and eventually uncertain. It is therefore a chance whether they are performed or no. . . . So that any assertor of self-determination is in fact, whether he mean it or no, a worshipper of the heathen lady named Fortune, and an ideal deposer of Providence from its throne.—Toplady, vol. vi. p. 90.

If it be said that volitions are events that come to pass without any determining cause, that is most palpably inconsistent with all use of laws and precepts; for nothing is more plain than that laws can be of no use to direct and regulate perfect accident.—Edwards ' On Freedom of the Will,' part 3, sect. 4.

[2] That no future event can be certainly foreknown whose existence is contingent and without all necessity, may be proved thus: it is impossible for a thing to be certainly known to any intellect without *evidence* . . . But no understanding, created or uncreated, can see evidence where there is none . . . But if there be a future event whose existence is contingent without all necessity, the future existence of the event is absolutely without evidence.—Edwards, ' On Freedom of Will,' part 2, sect. 12.

therefore an answer which appeals to it, to solve the contradiction of freewill to Providence, only gets rid of one contradiction by another. Allowing, however, the contradiction between Providence and freewill to remain, what comes in the way of argument from it? All imperfect truths run into contradictions when they are pursued. Thus, a great philosopher has extracted the greatest absurdities out of the idea of material substance; and the idea of infinity is met by the objection that all number must be either odd or even. In the same way freewill, when pursued, runs into a contradiction to Providence, but this does not show that it is false, but only that it is imperfect truth.

The same mode of treatment applies to the great principle of religion (substantially the same with that of the Divine Power) that God is the Author of all good, if used as a basis of an absolute doctrine of predestination. Undoubtedly from this principle the doctrine of irresistible grace follows; for according to it man derives all his goodness from a source beyond himself; and with this doctrine of grace, predestination. But what kind of a truth is this principle that God is the Author of all good? an absolute or an imperfect truth? Plainly the latter. There is, indeed, a principle of humility in our nature, whether belonging to us as fallen creatures, or necessary to the very relation of dependence implied in created being, which leads us to disown any source of good within ourselves. The enlightened moral being has an instinctive dread of appropriating any good that he may see in himself *to* himself. This is a great fact in human nature. Our hearts bear witness to it. We shrink from the claim of originating good. If the thought rises up in our minds, we put it down, and are afraid of entertaining it. As soon as we have done a good action, we put it away from us; we try not to think of it. Thus praise is a mixture of pleasure and pain: the first motion in our minds of pure pleasure is immediately checked by fear: we are afraid of the consciousness of being praised, and wish to cast it out of our minds. The general manners of society, the disclaiming of merit which always takes place as a matter of form, the readiness to give place to others, bear witness to a great principle of humility in human nature, by which it is ever ejecting the source of good from itself, and falling back on some source external and unknown. The act of prayer is a witness to the same principle; for we pray to God for moral and spiritual goodness, for conversion and renewal both for ourselves and others. Our very moral nature thus takes us out of ourselves to God, referring us to Him as the sole and meritorious cause of all moral action; while it takes upon itself the responsibility of sin. This constitutional humility, this fixed tendency of our minds to an external source of good, expressed in the formal language of theology, becomes the doctrine of irresistible grace, from which that of predestination immediately follows. But is there not a counter principle to this co-existing with it in our nature, a principle of self-appreciation and self-respect, whereby we are able to contemplate ourselves as original agents in good actions?

Let us turn now from philosophical to theological predestination, or to the doctrine of predestination as resting on scriptural grounds. It must, I think, be admitted according to the argument stated in the last chapter, that the predestinarian draws his conclusion naturally from the doctrine of original sin; while at the same time, that conclusion must be allowed to be repugnant to natural reason and justice. For there is no man of ordinary moral perception, who, on being told of a certain doctrine which represented God as ordaining one man to eternal life, and ordaining another to eternal punishment, before either had done a single act or was born, would not immediately say that God was represented as acting unjustly. There remains, however, for extricating us from this dilemma an examination of the sense and manner in which the church imposes, and in which we hold, the doctrine of original sin.

From the doctrine of the fall, then, which represents man as morally impotent, unable by nature to do any good thing, a lost and ruined being, the conclusion is undoubtedly a legitimate one, that if he is to be restored, he must be restored by some power quite independent of and external to him, or by that act of grace which divines call irresistible. But to what kind of truth does the doctrine of the fall belong? It is evident on the mere statement of it, that it is not a truth which we hold in the same manner in which we do the ordinary truths of reason and experience. Because it is met immediately by a counter truth. Mankind has a sense of moral power, of being able to do good actions and avoid wrong ones, which, so far as it goes, contradicts the doctrine of the fall. For so far as it is true that we *can* do what we ought to do, our nature is not fallen; it is equal to the task imposed upon it; and it is our own personal fault, and not our nature's, if it is not done. The conclusion, then, of the necessity of an irresistible grace to produce a good life, has in the doctrine of the fall not a complete, but an imperfect premiss, and must follow the conditions of that premiss. The doctrine of the fall is held under a reserve on the side of the contrary truth; the doctrine of irresistible grace, then, must be held under the same reserve. So far as man is fallen, he wants this grace; but so far as he is not fallen, he does not want it. One inference, then, from one part of the whole premiss lies under the liability to be contradicted by another from another part; and the legitimate issue is no whole or perfect conclusion, but only a conditional and imperfect one.

The predestinarian, however, neglects this distinction, and upon an imperfect basis raises a definite and complete doctrine. Or, which is the same thing, he does not see that the basis *is* imperfect. He does not consent to holding the doctrine of the fall with this reserve, but imagines he has in this doctrine a complete truth; and he proceeds to use it as he would any ordinary premiss of reason or experience, and founds a perfect argumentative structure upon it.

Thus much for the structure of the doctrine of predestination, as raised on the basis of original sin. And the same answer may be made to the defence of the justice of the doctrine on the same ground; to the argument that, inasmuch as all mankind deserve eternal punishment antecedently to actual sin, it cannot be unjust to consign a portion of them antecedently to it.

Undoubtedly the doctrine of original sin represents the whole human race as subject to the extreme severity of Divine wrath in consequence of the sin of Adam. It has two ways or forms in which it represents this. The doctrine is sometimes so expressed as to represent mankind as being actually parties to the sin committed by Adam, and so condemned, on a principle of natural justice, for a sin which is their own. All men are said to have sinned in Adam, and Adam, or the old man, is spoken of as the root or principle of evil in every human being. Sometimes it is so expressed as to represent mankind as punished, on a principle of vicarious desert, for the sin of their first parent, regarded as another person from themselves.[1] But whichever of these two modes of stating the doctrine of original sin is adopted, it is evident that in dealing with it, we are dealing with a mystery, not with an ordinary truth of reason and nature. If we adopt the former mode, it is contradictory to common reason, according to which one man cannot be thus the same with another, and commit a sin before he is born. If we adopt the latter, it is contradictory to our sense of justice, according to which one man ought not to be punished for another man's sin. Under either form, then, we are dealing with a mystery, and that which is described in this doctrine as having taken place with respect to mankind, has taken place mysteriously, not after the manner of common matter of fact.

And this distinction, it must be observed, is necessary not only to guard what we build upon the doctrine of original sin, but for the defence of the doctrine itself. This doctrine is sometimes called an unjust one, and this charge of injustice is sometimes met by an attempt to reduce and qualify the statement itself of the doctrine; as if it attri-

---

[1] Quanto magis prohiberi [a baptismo] non debet [infans] qui recens natus nihil peccavit, nisi quod secundum Adam carnaliter natus contagium mortis antiquæ primâ nativitate contraxit, qui ad remissam peccatorum accipiendam hoc ipso facilius accedit, quod illi remittuntur *non propria sed aliena peccata* (Cyprian, Ep. ad Fidum, 64. ed. Oxon.) The more common and recognised mode however of expressing the doctrine is that which represents mankind as having sinned in Adam, and having been parties in the act.—NOTE VI.

buted only negative consequences to the sin of Adam—a loss of perfection, a withdrawal of some supernatural aids. But such a qualification of the doctrine is contrary to the plain language of Scripture, as well as that of catholic writers. The proper defence of the doctrine is not a limitation of its statements, but a distinction as to the sense in which these statements are to be held. When this distinction has been drawn, objectors may exhibit as forcibly and vividly as they will the paradoxical nature of these statements; they gain nothing by doing so. We may be asked how it is possible that God should be angry with innocent infants, should condemn persons before they are born to the torments of hell and other like questions; but with the aid of this distinction it is easy to see that such objections suppose an entirely different mode of holding such statements from that which every reasonable believer adopts. We are not to measure these mysterious consequences of the sin of Adam by human analogies, as if the act of God in visiting the sin of Adam upon all mankind were like the act of a human monarch who punished a whole family or nation for the crime of one man. They are of the order of mysterious truths, and represent modes of Divine dealing which are beyond the sphere of our reason.[1]

Upon the premiss, then, contained in the doctrine of original sin, that all mankind deserve eternal punishment antecedently to actual sin, it is correctly argued that it cannot be unjust to consign a portion antecedently to it.

---

[1] Le péché originel est folie devant les hommes; mais on le donne pour tel. Vous ne me devez donc pas reprocher le défaut de raison en cette doctrine, puisque je le donne pour être sans raison. Mais cette folie est plus sage que toute la sagesse des hommes; *sapientius est hominibus.* Car, sans cela, que dira-t-on qu'est l'homme ? Tout son état dépend de ce point imperceptible. Et comment s'en fût-il aperçu par sa raison, puisque c'est une chose au-dessus de sa raison ; et que sa raison, bien loin de l'inventer par ses voies, s'en éloigne quand on le lui présente. —Pascal (éd. Faugères), v. ii. p. 106.

Nous ne concevons ni l'état glorieux d'Adam, ni la nature de son péché, ni la transmission qui s'en est faite en nous. Ce sont choses qui se sont passées dans l'état d'une nature toute différente de la nôtre, et qui passent notre capacité présente.—p. 369.

Jeremy Taylor loses sight of this principle of interpretation in his argument on Original Sin.—NOTE VII.

But it must be remembered what kind of a premiss this is. If it is a truth of revelation that all men deserve eternal punishment in consequence of the sin of Adam, it is a truth of our moral nature equally certain, that no man deserves punishment except for his own personal sin. And the one is declared in revelation itself as plainly as the other; for it is said, 'The soul that sinneth, it shall die: the son shall not bear the iniquity of the father, neither shall the father bear the iniquity of the son; the righteousness of the righteous shall be upon him, and the wickedness of the wicked shall be upon him.'[1] It is a truth, then, of reason and Scripture alike that no man is responsible for another's sin: and so far as this is true at all, it is universally true,[2] applying as much to the case of Adam's sin, as to that of any other man. For though God suspends the operation of general laws on occasions, such laws are only modes of proceeding in the physical world. Moral truths do not admit of exceptions. The premiss, then, on which we proceed in this question is a divided one; and if the predestinarian from one part of it concludes the justice of his doctrine, his opponent can, from the other, conclude the contrary. If the mystery of our responsibility for the sin of Adam justifies his scheme, the truth of our exclusive responsibility for our own sins condemns it.

Both in structure and defences, then, the doctrine of predestination rests on an imperfect premiss, and can only

[1] Ezek. xviii. 20.

[2] Jeremy Taylor's argument is sound so far as he insists that the case of original sin should not be treated as an *exception* to God's ordinary justice. 'When your lordship had said that "my arguments for the vindication of God's goodness and justice are sound and holy," your hand run over it again, and added "as abstracted from the case of original sin." But why should this be abstracted from all the whole economy of God, from all His other dispensations? Is it in all cases of the world unjust for God to impart our father's sins to us, unto eternal damnation; and is it otherwise in this only?'—Vol. ix. p. 383.

It is evidently wrong to treat the case of original sin as an exception, in one particular instance, to God's ordinary justice; for there can be no justifiable exception to the rule of justice. All God's acts must be just. It must be treated as a mystery, something unknown, and against which, on that account, we can bring no charge of injustice. For before we can call an act unjust, we must know what the act is.

be held as imperfect truth; for we cannot build more upon a basis than it can bear, and from what is conditional and incomplete extract what is absolute and determinate. But the predestinarian holds the premiss itself as complete and perfect, overlooking the contrary one to which it is opposed; and therefore raises upon it a complete and determinate doctrine. He does not consider, in the first instance, that the fall of man is, however clearly revealed to us, but one side of the whole truth as regards human nature; that it is mysterious, as distinguished from intelligible truth. He should revise the whole sense and manner in which he holds this doctrine.

To turn from reasoning to Scripture. Predestination comes before us in Scripture under two aspects, as a truth or doctrine, and as a feeling, and under both the conclusion is of that indeterminate character which has been described here as its proper and legitimate one.

1. The general conclusion of Scripture on this question, considered as a question of abstract truth, is indeterminate. There exists undoubtedly in Scripture, as was observed in the last chapter, a large body of language in which man is spoken of as a lost and ruined creature, and impotent by nature for good. And in this state he is pronounced to be saved by an act of Divine grace alone. And this language, as has been explained, is substantially the assertion of predestination; because we have only to add to it the acknowledged truth of God's eternal predetermination of all His acts, in order to make it such. And in addition to this general body of language, particular passages (such, especially, as the eighth and ninth chapters of the Epistle to the Romans) assert the express doctrine of predestination in such a way that we cannot escape from their force except by a subtle and evasive mode of explanation, which would endanger the meaning of all Scripture. The terms elect and predestinated in Scripture mean, according to their natural interpretation, persons who have been chosen by God from all eternity to be called, justified, or made righteous, and finally glorified.[1] But Scripture is two-sided on

[1] NOTE VIII.

this great question. If one set of passages, taken in their natural meaning, conveys the doctrine of predestination, another conveys the reverse. The Bible, in speaking of mankind, and addressing them on their duties and responsibilities, certainly speaks as if all had the power to do their duty or not, when laid before them ; nor would any plain man receive any other impression from this language, than that the moral being had freewill, and could determine his own acts one way or another. So that, sometimes speaking one way, and sometimes another, Scripture, as a whole, makes no assertion, or has no determinate doctrine on this subject.

To some persons, perhaps, such an estimate of the general issue of Scripture language on this subject may seem derogatory to Holy Scripture ; because it appears, at first sight, to be casting blame upon language, to say that it is self-contradictory; the form of such an assertion suggesting that the expression of something definite was aimed at, but that the language fell short of its aim. But it will not, upon consideration, be found that any such consequence attaches to this estimate of Scripture language. For though Scripture is certainly said not to be consistent, and, therefore, not to give support to a determinate doctrine of predestination, it is not said that the expression of any determinate doctrine was designed. And, therefore, the assertion made is not that Scripture has fallen short of an object which it aimed at ; rather, it is quite consistent with Scripture having most completely and successfully attained its object.

Were the nature of all truth such as that it could be expressed—that is, put into statement or proposition, to the effect that such is or is not the case, explicitness and consistency would be always requisite for language ; because real expression is necessarily explicit and consistent with itself. All intelligible truths—matters of fact, for example —are capable of expression ; and therefore, in the case of such truths, explicit statement is necessary, and contradiction is ruinous. But it is not the case that all truth *can* be expressed. Some truths of revealed religion cannot be stated without contradiction to other truths, of which reason or the same revelation informs us, and, therefore, cannot be stated positively and absolutely without becoming, in the very act of statement, false.

The truth of absolute predestination cannot be stated without contradiction to the Divine justice and man's free agency. It belongs, then, to that class of truths which does not admit of statement. It is an imperfect truth— that is, a truth imperfectly apprehended by us. There is a tendency, as has been said, to a truth on this subject, but this tendency never becomes a conclusion ; and an idea which is true, as far as it does advance, never does advance to any natural limit. The intellect stops short and rests in suspense, not seeing its way, and the line of thought, though it may admit of such a completion as will make it a truth, is not a truth yet, and cannot be made a proposition.

But with respect to this kind of truth which is only in tendency, and does not admit of statement, if anything is to be said at all, such contradictory or double language only can be employed as Scripture does employ on the subject of predestination. Consistent language would do more than, indeed the very reverse of what was wanted, inasmuch as it would state positively. Inconsistency could certainly be avoided by saying nothing at all, but that mode of avoiding inconsistency could not be adopted here, because there is a defective and incomplete truth to be expressed in some such way as is practicable. Something, therefore, is to be said. But to say something, and yet on the whole to make no positive statement, to express suitably such indeterminate truth, what is to be done but first to assert the truth and then by counter statement to bring round indefiniteness again ; thus carrying thought a certain way without bringing it to any goal, and giving an inclination and a direction to ideas without fixing them.

2. Predestination comes before us in Scripture as a feeling or impression upon the mind of the individual. All conscious power, strength, energy, when combined with a particular aim, tend to create the sense of a destiny—

an effect with which we are familiar in the case of many remarkable persons. A man who feels in himself the presence of great faculties which he applies to the attainment of some great object, not unnaturally interprets the very greatness of these faculties as a providential call to such an application of them, and a pledge and earnest of a successful issue. Thus, in proportion to the very strength and energy of his own will, he regards himself as but a messenger from, an instrument of, a Higher Power; he sees in himself but a derived agency, an impulse from without. It seems necessary that he should refer those extraordinary forces, which he feels working within him, to some source beyond the confines of his own narrow existence, and connect them with the action of the invisible Supreme Power in the universe. He is in a sense, in which other persons are not, a mystery to himself; and to account for so much power in so small and frail a being, he refers it to the unknown world in which reside the causes of all the great operations of nature. This is the way in which he expresses his own sense and consciousness of remarkable powers; he would have regarded an ordinary amount of power as his own, but because he has so much more, he alienates it, and transfers it to a source beyond himself. Thus heroes and conquerors in heathen times have sometimes even imagined themselves to be emanations from the Deity. But a common result has been the idea of a destiny, which they have had to fulfil. And this idea of a destiny once embraced, as it is the natural effect of the sense of power, so in its turn adds greatly to it. The person as soon as he regards himself as predestined to achieve some great object, acts with so much greater force and constancy for the attainment of it; he is not divided by doubts, or weakened by scruples or fears; he believes fully that he shall succeed, and that belief is the greatest assistance to success. The idea of a destiny in a considerable degree fulfils itself.

The idea of destiny, then, naturally arising out of a sense of power, it must be observed that this is true of the moral and spiritual, as well as of the natural man, and applies to religious aims and purposes, as well as to those connected with human glory. A strong will in moral things, a determination to resist the tendencies of corrupt nature, a sustained aim at the perfect life—this whole disposition of mind does, if recognised and contemplated in himself by the possessor, in proportion to its extent create a sense of a spiritual destiny; and the Christian in his own sphere, as the great man of the world in his, feels himself marked out for a particular work and the final reward which is to follow it. According to his calculation of his resources is his conviction that he shall attain his object; and from the calculation that he will, the sense that he is destined to succeed, almost immediately arises. Not that this result need take place in all Christian minds, for there are differences of natural character as well as of moral power which would affect it. Some minds are constitutionally more self-contemplative than others, and have before them their own condition and prospects, while others pursue the same actual course with less of reflection upon themselves as agents. So far, however, as a man thinks definitely of himself and of his own spiritual strength, and so far as the result of the inspection is satisfactory, this will be the result. He perceives in himself now that which must ultimately overcome, and looks forward to the issue as to the working out of a problem, the natural fruit of moral resources already in his possession. Nor need this result be confined to remarkable and eminent Christians. Whatever be the degree and standard of goodness before the mind, so far as a man definitely recognises in himself the capacity for attaining it, so far he will have the sense of being marked out for its attainment.

And it is evident that one whole side of Scripture encourages Christians in this idea. In the first place, without imposing as necessary, Scripture plainly sanctions and encourages that character of mind which is self-contemplative, or involves reflection upon self, our own spiritual state and capacities. The more childlike temper has doubtless its own praise; but the other is also set forth in Scripture as a temper eminently becoming a Christian. Indeed, placed as we are here, with an unknown future before us, of good or evil, and possessed by nature of the strongest self-love and desire for our own ultimate good, is it to be said for a moment, that we ought not to think of ourselves, our prospects, the object of our existence, and our amount of resources, the degree of our strength and ability to achieve it? Certainly, such a consideration is highly befitting our state, and suitable to a Christian man. And accordingly the New, as distinguished from the Old Testament, appears specially to encourage this peculiar tone of mind, and to direct men more to reflection upon themselves; it recommends a grave foresight, a prudential regard to our own ultimate happiness; it promotes a deep moral self-interestedness and spirit of calculation. The eye of the soul is turned inward upon itself to think of its own value, and estimate its own capacities, and prospects. 'Which of you intending to build a tower, sitteth not down first and counteth the cost, whether he have sufficient to finish it? Or what king going to war with another king, sitteth not down first and consulteth whether he be able with ten thousand to meet him that cometh against him, with twenty thousand.'[1] But if a man makes the estimate which is here recommended to him, and if he conscientiously finds it a favourable one—*i.e.* if he feels himself possessed of strong moral purpose and will, what is to prevent him from thinking that he is destined to the end, with a view to which the estimate is made? That he is marked out by Providence to build this tower and conquer this foe? History and experience show, that the human mind is so constituted as to receive this impression.

Accordingly, Christians are addressed in the New Testament upon this supposition. It is one of the first lessons which the Gospel teaches us, that the ends which earthly greatness proposes to itself, are but shadows of those to which Christians are called; that the conquest of sin is the true glory of man, and the heavenly his true crown. The Christian, therefore, is addressed as one predestined to eternal glory. He is encouraged to regard himself as a

[1] Luke xiv. 28, 31.

favourite of Heaven singled out from the world, and stamped from the very commencement of his course, with the token of future triumph. The resolution to obtain the spiritual crown is supposed to impart to him the same sense of a destiny, that the consciousness of a commanding mind imparts to the man of the world; and the life eternal is represented as an end assured to the individual before the foundation of the world. His life in this world is described as a passage, laborious and painful indeed, but still conducting him by a sure succession of steps to this end. It obstructs and postpones rather than involves any real hazard to his spiritual prospects; the goal is pledged, and he has only to go forward till he reaches it, putting aside the hindrances as they arise. Life is to him a purgatorial rather than a trial state, purifying him by affliction, and exercising him by conflicts, through all which, however, he passes steadily onward with the seal of God upon him, marking him infallibly from the very beginning as His own. Nor is this position confined to a few eminent saints, but supposed to be the position of all Christians, who, whatever be the differences among themselves, are all saints in comparison with the world around them. This is the natural construction of the language of S. Paul; and as this idea of a destiny is the result of, so in its turn it strengthens, the moral energies of the Christian. The conviction that he is marked out for a heavenly crown, elevates and inspires him in the pursuit of it.

This is 'the godly consideration of predestination,' recommended in the seventeenth Article of our Church. The sense of predestination which the New Testament encourages is connected with strength of moral principle in the individual; the Christian being supposed always to be devoted to his calling, so much so that he is even by anticipation addressed as if he were dead to carnal desires, and in the enjoyment of the new and heavenly life. But no idea can be more opposed to Scripture, or more unwarrantable, than any idea of predestination separated from this consciousness, and not arising upon this foundation; the notion of the individual that, on the simple condition which he cannot violate, that of being the particular person which he is, he is certain of salvation. It is not to the person simply as such, but to the person as good and holy, that eternal life is ordained. Does a man do his duty to God and his neighbour? Is he honest, just, charitable, pure? If he is, and if he is conscious of the power to continue so, so far as he can depend on this consciousness, so far he may reasonably believe himself to be predestined to future happiness. But to suppose that a man may think himself predestined, not as being good, but as being, whether good or bad, himself, is a delusion of the devil, and the gross fallacy of corrupt sects, that have lost sight, first of duty, and next of reason, and have forgotten that the government of the world is moral. The doctrine of predestination is thus, in effect, a profitable or a mischievous doctrine, according to the moral condition of those who receive and use it. It binds and cements some minds, it relaxes and corrupts others. It gives an energy to some, a new force of will, bringing out and strengthening high aims; it furnishes an excuse to others, already disinclined to moral efforts, to abandon them, and follow their own worldly will and pleasure.

The above remarks will supply a ground for judging of the doctrine of assurance; assurance being nothing else but the sense of predestination here spoken of. It is evident, in the first place, that assurance ought not to be demanded as a state of mind necessary for a Christian; for it can only arise legitimately upon a knowledge of our own moral resources and strength; and there is nothing to compel a Christian to have this knowledge. He may innocently be without it. He may do his duty without reflecting upon himself as an agent at all; and if he does think of himself, he may innocently make an erroneous estimate of his own strength. It sometimes happens that at the time of trial a man finds that he has more strength than he counted upon, and is surprised at his own easy victory. Nor should it be forgotten that the principle of humility in man is one which tends to an under-estimate of his own power and resources; and though to carry it to this extent is not perfection in respect of truth and knowledge, yet our moral nature is so fine and intricate, that it must be owned that, in the case of many minds, there is a sort of perfection in this very imperfection: and one would not wish them to estimate themselves correctly; if they did, we should feel the absence of something, and a certain indefinable grace which attached to them would be missed. This is one of those results which flow from the variety which marks the Divine creation and constitution of the world, whether physical or moral. Some characters are designed to raise our affections on one plan, others on another; some are formed to inspire what is commonly called love, others respect, principally; both being only different forms of the scriptural principle of love. These are diversities of His instituting who is Himself incomprehensible, and who has made man a type in some measure of Himself; with a moral nature which cannot be reduced to one criterion of right, but which attains perfection in different forms, and satisfies our moral sense, under modes which we cannot analyse, but to which that moral sense responds. For human goodness is not a simple thing, but a complex; nor is it a measurable, but an indefinable thing; attaining its perfection often by seeming excesses, incorrectnesses in the latter, and faults transmuted by the medium of the general character into virtues. The stronger mind confides in, the more amiable one distrusts, itself. Both are good according to their respective standards, and therefore, on a principle of variety, such difference is desirable. It is desirable also, on another ground—viz. that different instruments are wanted by Providence to execute its designs in the world. Large and difficult objects can only be achieved by men who have confidence in themselves, and will not allow obstacles to discourage them; and a sense of destiny helps these men. The tie, on the other hand, of mutual confidence, is aided by self-distrust. Did none confide in themselves, there would be none to command; but those who do so, are at the same time constitutionally slow to obey.

Accordingly the doctrine of assurance does not necessarily go along with the doctrine of predestination, because it does not follow that if a particular person is predestined to eternal life that therefore he should have the inward sense or feeling that he is. The Divine decree may be conducting him by sure steps all his life through to final glory, and he may not be aware of it ; for the only condition necessary to being one of the elect, is goodness ; and a good man may act without contemplating himself at all, or, if he does, he may distrust himself. Predestinarians accordingly, both Augustine and his school, and modern ones, have disowned the doctrine of assurance, so far as it is maintained in it that assurance is necessary for a Christian.[1]

Secondly, assurance separated from a good life, and the consciousness of resolution to persevere in it, is unreasonable and wicked. Thirdly, assurance united with both of these and arising upon this foundation, is legitimate.

The sense or feeling, then, of predestination is, as has

[1] As to what follows in your letter, concerning a person's believing himself to be in a good state, and its being properly of the nature of faith; in this there seems to be some real difference between us. But perhaps there would be none, if distinctness were well observed in the use of words. If by a man's believing that he is in a good estate, be meant no more that his believing that he does believe in Christ, love God, &c.; I think there is nothing of the nature of faith in it; because knowing or believing it depends on our immediate sensation or consciousness, and not on Divine testimony. True believers in the hope they entertain of salvation, make use of the following syllogism, *whosoever believes shall be saved. I believe, therefore, &c.* Assenting to the major proposition is properly of the nature of faith, because the ground of my assent to that is Divine testimony, but my assent to the minor proposition, I humbly conceive, is not of the nature of faith, because that is not grounded on Divine testimony, but on my own consciousness. The testimony that is the proper ground of faith is in the word of God, Rom. x. 17., 'Faith cometh of hearing, and hearing of the word of God.' There is such a testimony given in the word of God, as that 'he that believeth shall be saved.' But there is no such testimony in the word of God, as that such an individual person, in such a town in Scotland or in New England, believes. There is such a proposition in Scripture, as that *Christ loves those that love Him*, and therefore this every one is bound to believe or affirm. Believing thus on Divine testimony is properly of the nature of faith, and for any one to doubt of it, is properly of the heinous sin of unbelief. But there is no such proposition in the Scripture, nor is it any part of the gospel of Christ, that such an individual person in Northampton loves Christ.— Edwards, 'On the Religious Affections,' Letter 2. to Mr. Gillespie.

been shown, both sanctioned and encouraged in the New Testament. But while this is plain, it is also obvious that this is only one side of the language of the New Testament. There is another according to which all Christians, whatever be their holiness, are represented and addressed as uncertain, and feeling themselves uncertain, of final salvation. They are exhorted to 'work out their own salvation with fear and trembling';[1] to 'give diligence to make their calling and election sure';[2] and S. Paul himself the great preacher of predestination, who, if any, had the right to feel himself ordained to eternal life, and who said that there 'was laid up for him a crown of righteousness,'[3] also tells us of his careful self-discipline, 'lest that by any means when he had preached to others, he himself should be a castaway.'[4] Indeed to anyone who will fairly examine the nature of this feeling of destiny which we have been considering, and how far and in what mode it is entertained, when it is entertained rationally, it will be evident that it is not by any means an absolute or literal certainty of mind. It is not like the perception of an intellectual truth. It is only a strong impression, which however genuine or rational, and, as we may say, authorised, issues, when we try to follow it, in obscurity, and vanishes in the haze which bounds our mental view, before the reason can overtake it. Were any of those remarkable men who have had it, asked about this feeling of theirs, they would confess it was in them no absolute perception but an impression which was consistent with a counter feeling of doubt, and was accompanied by this latent and suppressed opposite in their case.

Whether regarded, then, as a doctrine, or a feeling, predestination is not in Scripture an absolute, but an indefinite truth. Scripture has as a whole no consistent scheme, and makes no positive assertion; it only declares, and bids its readers acknowledge, a mystery on this subject. It sets forth alike the Divine Power, and man's freewill, and teaches in that way in which alone it can be taught, the whole, and not a part alone of truth.

[1] Phil. ii. 12.   [2] 2 Peter i. 10.   [3] 2 Tim. iv. 8.   [4] 1 Cor. ix. 27.

## CHAPTER III.

#### THE PELAGIAN CONTROVERSY.

FROM a general introductory statement and examination of the argument of predestination, I turn now to the history and formation of this doctrine as exhibited in S. Augustine's writings. And as the Augustinian scheme of predestination rests upon the basis of original sin, the inquiry will suitably commence with an account of the latter doctrine. I shall therefore devote the present chapter to a general sketch of the Pelagian controversy :—First, the mode in which it arose ; secondly, the main arguments involved in it ; and, thirdly, its bearing upon the leading doctrines of Christianity. Antagonist systems moreover throw light upon each other, and an inquiry into the doctrines of S. Augustine will be aided by a previous account of the system of Pelagianism.

I. It may seem at first sight unnecessary to inquire into the mode in which the Pelagian controversy arose, because it appears enough to say that one side maintained, and another denied, the fall of man. But the doctrine of the fall though substantially, did not expressly or by name, form the original subject of dispute, but was led up to by a previous question.

It has been disputed whether the Augustinian system was a reaction from the Pelagian, or the Pelagian from the Augustinian. Historical evidence favours the latter assertion.[1] But the dispute, whichever way decided, is not an important one. The controversy between these two was contained in an elementary statement of Christian doctrine, which, as soon as it came to be examined intellectually, was certain˙ to disclose it. The language by which the Christian church has always expressed the truths of man's freewill and Divine grace has been, that the one could do no good thing without the aid of the other, *nihil bonum*

---

[1] NOTE IX.

*sine gratiâ.* This formula satisfied the simplicity of the primitive church as it has satisfied the uncontroversial faith of all ages; and no desire was felt for further expression and a more exact truth. But it is evident that this state of theology on this subject could not last longer than the reign of a simpler faith. When minds began to reason upon this formula and analyse it logically, it lost its finality, and the combination of grace and freewill divided into two great doctrines of an absolute power of freewill and an absolute power of grace.

For was the grace here asserted to be necessary for doing any good thing, a grace which assisted only the human will or one which controlled it? If it was the former, it depended on some action of the human will for being accepted and used, which action therefore could not be said without contradiction to be dependent upon *it*. Assisting grace, then, must be used by an unassisted will, and there must be some motion of the human will for good to which Divine grace did not contribute, but which was original and independent in the person who accepted and availed himself of that grace. Take two men who have both equal grace given to them, but of whom one avails himself of this grace, while the other does not. The difference between these two is not by the very supposition, a difference of grace; it is therefore a difference of original will only; and in one there has been a self-sprung, independent act for good, which there has not been in the other. But how great, how eventful a function thus attached to the unassisted human will? It decided the life and conduct of the man, and consequently his ultimate lot, for happiness or misery. That difference between one man and another in consequence of which one becomes a child of God and daily grows in virtue and holiness, and the other becomes a servant of sin, is no difference into which grace even enters, but one of natural will only. Indeed, was not the unassisted human will, according to this doctrine, more than a real agent, the chief agent in the work of virtue and piety? For the general sense of mankind has, in the case of any joint agency, assigned the part of chief agent to the one that uses and turns to account the action of the other. If one man furnishes another with the means and resources for any undertaking, and the other applies them to it, both indeed contribute action; but the latter is the chief contributor, and would, in ordinary language, be called the doer of the work. Thus to the act of learning a teacher and a learner both contribute, the one by giving information, the other by apprehending it; but the act of learning is the learner's rather than the teacher's act. Apply this distinction to the case of the human will using the assistance of Divine grace for the work of a holy life. While the giver and the user of that assistance are both agents in that work, the user is the principal one.[1] In cases where the use of means, if supplied, takes place easily and as a matter of course, the result may be properly referred to the supplier rather than the user of them. But the act of the will in using grace is no easy or matter-of-course one, but involves much effort and self-denial.

The combination of grace with freewill thus issued in the assertion of an independent freewill on the one hand, while this logical result was avoided on the other, only by a recourse to the opposite extreme. It was seen that an assisting grace could only be protected by making it something more than assisting, and that the will must have the credit of the unassisted acceptance and use of it, unless it were controlled by it. The original formula, therefore, issued on this side in the doctrine of a controlling and irresistible grace; and upon these two interpretations of the primitive doctrine rose, with their respective accompaniments and consequences, the Pelagian and Augustinian systems.

Pelagianism then started with the position, that, however necessary Divine assistance might be for a good work as a whole, there was at the bottom a good act or move-

[1] 'Nam quando ad eundem actum liberum concurrunt plura sine quibus libertas agendi in actum suum exire non potest, non illi causæ tribui debet exercitium actus aut voluntatis, *sine qua* non potest fieri, sed illi quæ nutu suo totam machinam ad motum impellit, aut otiosam esse sinit.'—Jansen, De Grat. Christi, p. 935.

## The Pelagian Controversy.

ment, which the human will was able to and must perform without Divine assistance. And this position supplies the clue to the solution of the Pelagian's apparently contradictory language about grace. The Pelagian asserts the ability of nature at one time; he asserts the necessity of grace at another.[1] Now his opponent explained this apparent inconsistency, by saying that by grace he meant nature; that he used the word dishonestly in a sense of his own, and only included in it the natural will and endowments of man, which, as being Divine gifts, he chose to call grace.[2] And, in the same way, he was charged with meaning by grace only the outward means of instruction and edification, which God had given to man in the Bible and elsewhere, as distinct from any inward Divine influence. This is the explanation of the Pelagian grace, as *Lex et Natura*, which we meet so often in S. Augustine. But with all deference to so great a name, I cannot think that this adverse explanation is altogether justified by the language of the Pelagians themselves. A verbal confusion of nature with grace is undoubtedly to be found there; nor is such a confusion in itself unpardonable. In one sense nature *is* grace; freewill itself, and all the faculties and affections of our nature being the gifts of God; while, on the other hand, grace may not erroneously be called nature, inasmuch as when received, it becomes a power which we have, and which belongs to us; especially acting, as it does, too, through the medium of our natural faculties, our conscience, and good affections. And in this sense of nature, the Pelagians asserted that nature was able to fulfil the law—*Posse in naturâ*[3]—a statement, which so understood, is no

---

[1] Anathemo qui vel sentit vel dicit gratiam Dei non solum per singulas horas, aut per singula momenta, sed etiam per singulos actus nostros non esse necessariam.— Pelagius ap. Aug. De Grat. Christi, n. 2. He repeats the same statement often.—De Grat. Christi, n. 5. 29. 33.; Contra Duas. Ep. 1. 4. n. 13. On the other hand he says, *Passe in naturâ*, velle in arbitrio, esse in effectu locamus.—De Grat. Christi n. 5.

[2] De Naturâ et Gratiâ, n. 12. 59.; De Grat. Christi, n. 3.

[3] To the objection of the Catholic, 'Protest quidem esse, sed per gratiam Dei,' Pelagius replies, ' Ego ne abnuo qui rem confitendo, confitear necesse est et per quod res effici potest; an tu qui rem negando, et quicquid illud est, per quod res

more than a truism; nature comprehending, in this sense of the word, all the moral power, from whatever quarter, of which a man is possessed, grace included. Again, the Pelagian, in his explanations of grace and its operations, certainly dwells most commonly on the outward helps which revelation and Providence afford to man in the path of obedience. But while he is so far open to the charge of his opponent, it does not appear that he limits the idea of grace, either to nature in the sense of the powers with which man was originally endowed at his creation, or to the outward helps of the Divine law. On the contrary, he includes in it those internal Divine impulses and spiritual assistances commonly denoted by the word.[1] This is the natural interpretation of his language; nor is there anything in his argument, as a controversialist, to require the exclusion of such grace. The Pelagian maintained the power of the human will; but if he admitted the need of the Divine assistance at all to it, as he did in the shape of the created affections, and general endowments of our nature, there was no reason why he should limit such assistance to that creative one. The distinction of prior and posterior, grace creative and grace assisting the creature already made, was of no importance in this respect. There was no difference, again, in principle between inward and outward grace; and any one who acknowledged Divine assistance, by means of instruction, warning, and exhortation addressed to us from without, would have no difficulty in acknowledging it in the shape of spiritual incitement and illumination carried on within. The clue, then, to the solution of the Pelagian's apparently contradictory language respecting grace, is rather to be found in the logical necessity there was for an unassisted act of the human will, in accepting and using Divine assistance. Admitting Divine grace to be wanted, but regarding the use of it as

efficitur procul dubio negas . . . Sive per gratiam, sive per adjutorium, sive per misericordiam, et quicquid illud est per quod esse homo sine peccato potest, confitetur, quisquis rem ipsam confitetur.'—De Naturâ et Gratiâ, n. 11.

[1] 'Sanctificando, coercendo, provocando, illuminando.'—Op. Imp. 1. 3. c. 106. 'Dum nos multiformi et ineffabili dono gratiæ cœlestis illuminat.'—De Grat. Christi, c. 7.

independent of grace, claiming some real power for unassisted nature, though not all, he was led into a double and inconsistent language, which sometimes asserted the necessity of grace, and sometimes the ability of nature alone.

Indeed, it is clear from the argument of the book *De Gratiâ Christi*, that, whatever objection Augustine may raise to the Pelagian doctrine of grace, on the ground that grace in it only means *Lex et Natura*, his main objection to that doctrine is, not that it maintains an external grace as distinguished from an internal, or a grace creative as distinguished from additional to created nature, but that it maintains a grace which depends entirely on an independent act of the will for its acceptance and use, as distinguished from a grace which supplies that act and secures its own use. Pelagius defines what the function of grace in his idea is, and he confines it to that of assisting the power of the natural will—*possibilitatem adjuvat*[1]; the phrase supposes a foundation of independent power in the will, to which grace is an addition. Augustine, on the other hand, says it is more than this, and condemns this definition as insufficient and insulting to the Divine Power. This is the question, then, to which the whole argument is substantially reduced, and on which the whole book hinges; and it is one concerned, not with the circumstances, so to speak, of grace, as the other distinctions were, but with its substantial nature, its relation to the human will;

---

[1] 'Nos sic tria ista distinguimus, et certum velut in ordinem digesta partimur. Primo loco posse statuimus, secundo velle, tertio esse. Posse in naturâ, velle in arbitrio, esse in effectu locamus. Primum illud, id est, posse, ad Deum proprie pertinet, qui illud creaturæ suæ contulit: duo vero reliqua, hoc est, velle et esse ad hominem referenda sunt, quia de arbitrii fonte descendunt. Ergo in voluntate et in opere bono laus hominis est; imo et hominis et Dei, qui ipsius voluntatis et operis possibilitatem dedit, quique ipsam possibilitatem gratiæ suæ adjuvat semper auxilio.'—Pelagius de Lib. Arb. apud Aug. de Grat. Christi, n. 5.

Thus Julian: 'Adsunt tamen adjutoria gratiæ Dei quæ in parte virtutis nunquam destituunt voluntatem: cujus licet innumeræ species, tali tamen semper moderatione adhibentur, ut nunquam liberum arbitrium locopellant, sed præbeant adminicula, quamdiu eis voluerit inniti; cum tamen non opprimant reluctantem animum.'—Op. Imp. l. iii. c. 114.

whether that relation is one of dependence upon the will for its use, or not.[1] This is the ultimate difference between the two; and it must be seen, that it does make *all* the difference in the nature and quality of Divine grace.

The charge against the Pelagian that he held human merit always to precede grace, appears to be alike without satisfactory foundation. He disowned the position himself[2], nor was it necessary for his argument. Grace is, indeed, sometimes taken in a final sense, for the designed effect of assisting grace; and stands for an ultimate spiritual habit, as when we speak of the graces of the Christian character, the grace of charity, and the like; and in that sense, if the human will is to have any share in the matter, grace must be the consequence in part of human merit. As the crown of human efforts, it supposes such efforts having been made. But it would be absurd to maintain that grace, in the sense of *assisting* grace, requires a previous effort of the human will for obtaining it, and that the individual must show goodness before he receives the Divine assistance to be good. All Christians allow that such grace is given to sinners in the very depth of their sin, and in order to draw them away from it: nor does the admission at all affect the Pelagian position of the independent power of the will; for this would be exerted in the acceptance and use of such grace. I will add that this distinction between the grace which crowns and that which stimulates the efforts of the will explains

---

[1] Bradwardine and Jansen thus understand the Pelagian doctrine of grace: 'Non enim existimandum est solam legem atque doctrinam esse possibilitatis adjutorium. . . . Pelagiani motus indeliberatos bonos sub gratiâ complexi sunt: nam sive motus illos a Deo conditos inseri, sive mente per istam gratiam pulsata, ulterius naturaliter a corde proficisci decernerent, eorum causam Deum adjuvantem esse sentiebant.' Jansen, De Grat. Christi, p. 127. NOTE X.

[2] 'Ostendit quomodo resistere debeamus Diabolo, si utique subditi simus Deo, ejusque faciendo voluntatem divinam mereamur gratiam.' —Pelagius ap. Aug. De Gratia Christi, c. 22. Augustine argues incorrectly from this passage that Pelagius holds that merit *must* precede grace; whereas he only says it *may*,—that grace may be obtained by merit, or good works. On the other hand Pelagius at the Synod of Diospolis 'damnavit eos qui docent gratiam Dei secundum merita nostra dari.'—De Grat. Christi, c. 3., and Ben. Ed. preface, c. 10.—Nor is there anything in the Pelagian statements to show that assisting grace was considered to wait till human merit earned it.

the apparently contradictory language used by divines to explain the combination of freewill with grace; sometimes the commencement of the spiritual life being attributed to the human will and its completion to grace, and sometimes its completion being attributed to the human will and its commencement to grace. Under both modes of speaking, the power of the human will is secured: but under the one the will uses an assisting, under the other it earns a crowning grace.[1]

Thus apparently sound and forced upon reason by the necessity of the case, this position of an ultimate unassisted strength in the natural will, was, nevertheless, the root of all the errors, the extravagances, and the impieties of Pelagianism. It was a position logically true, indeed, and such as could not be denied without admitting the alternative of irresistible grace or necessitarianism. Nor had it been maintained with due modesty and reserve, as being one side of the whole mysterious truth relating to human action, would it have been otherwise than orthodox. But to maintain absolutely and definitely an ultimate power in the human will to move aright independently of God, was a position untrue, and shocking to natural piety; a separation of the creature from the Creator, which was opposed to the very foundation of religion. And to proceed to argue upon such a truth, and develop it, as if it were a complete and ascertained premiss, upon which a system could be erected, was to mistake its nature, and to run at once into obliquity and error. But this was what the Pelagians did.[2] For from this position the conclusion was

---

[1] The general language of the Pelagians allows an initiative grace (provocans, excitans), and maintains a crowning will: 'Quod possumus bonum facere illius est qui hoc posse donavit; quod vero bene agimus nostrum est.'—De Grat. Christi, c. 4. The Semipelagians speak of an initiative will and a crowning grace: 'Priorem volunt obedientiam esse quam gratiam, ut initium salutis ex eo qui salvatur, non ex eo credendum sit stare qui salvat, et voluntas hominis divinæ gratiæ sibi pariat opem.'—Ep. Prosperi inter Aug. Ep. 225. 'Quod enim dicitur. *Crede et salvus eris*; unum horum exigi asserunt, aliud offerri; ut propter id quod exigitur si redditum fuerit, id quod offertur deinceps tribuatur.'—Ep. Hilarii apud Aug. Ep. 226. Julian the Pelagian speaks of a certain state of perfection as a crowning grace: 'ut hoc ipsum non peccare præmium censeamus.'—Op. Imp. Contra Jul. l. 2. c. 166.

[2] 'Quod possumus omne bonum facere, dicere, cogitare, illius est qui

immediately drawn that every man had the power of fulfilling the whole law. The will was able to make use of grace; but every man, as the Divine justice required, had sufficient grace given him. For confining sometimes, as a matter of language, the term grace to such higher grace, or grace *par excellence*, as was given under the gospel,—such grace as facilitated goodness rather than was necessary for it[1]; the Pelagians held really that every one had in the sense of natural or other endowments, providential aids, spiritual impulses, sufficient Divine assistance or grace to enable him to do his duty. Every man, therefore, having sufficient grace, and the absolute power to use it, had the power to fulfil the whole law.

The doctrine of the perfectibility of man in this life was held, indeed, by the opponents of Pelagius, as well as by himself, but upon a totally different ground from that on which he based it. Augustine maintained that no limits were to be put to the power of Divine grace; but that it might please God in a particular instance so to control and direct all the motions of a human will, that the person might even in this life become perfect.[2] The admission, however, is made with much hesitation; he confesses such a case would be a miracle, as being contrary to all the established laws of the operation of grace; and, what is most important, he rests the possibility of it solely upon the ground of grace, or the Divine power. Pelagius, on the other hand, naturalised this perfectibility, making it part of the constitution of man, and drawing it from the

---

hoc posse donavit: *quod vero bene vel agimus, vel loquimur, vel cogitamus nostrum est*, quia hæc omnia vertere in malum possumus.'—Pelagius, ap. Aug. De Gratiâ Christi, n. 5.

[1] 'In omnibus est liberum arbitrium, æqualiter per naturam, sed in solis Christianis juvatur a gratiâ.' —Letter of Pelagius to Innocent, ap. Aug. de Gratiâ Christi, n. 33.

'Ideo Dei gratiam hominibus dari ut quod facere per liberum jubentur arbitrium facilius possint implere per gratiam.'—Pelagius de Lib. Arb. ap. Aug. Epist. 186. n. 35.

'Sed formidantes multitudinem Christianam, Pelagianum verbum supponitis, et quærentibus a nobis, quare mortuus sit Christus, si natura vel lex efficit justos; respondetis ut hoc ipsum facilius fieret, quasi posset, quamvis difficilius fieri tamen, sive per naturam sive per legem.'—Op. Imp. Contra Jul. 1. 2. c. 198.

[2] NOTE XI.

essential power of the human will.[1] However rare, therefore, its attainment might be, perfection, upon his system, was attainable by everyone: indeed some he asserted had actually attained it: an assertion from which S. Augustine shrank. The possibility admitted in theory, his practical belief withdrew the admission, and bound man, as long as he remains in this mortal state to sin, obliged to cry with the Apostle 'who shall deliver me from this death?' and by the simple profession of 'having no sin' infallibly convicted of falsehood and pride.

The original position respecting the will thus led immediately to the other great question: and we find ourselves thrown at once on the great subject of the Pelagian controversy. Such a doctrine of the power of the human will was evidently opposed to the doctrine of the fall: for such a will was evidently not a corrupt, but a sound will, inasmuch as it could perform its proper function. It may be doubtful, therefore, whether Pelagius in the first instance meant to attack the catholic doctrine of the fall; he certainly showed reluctance to come into express collision with it, and resisted the logical strain upon him: his attitude was at the first a defensive rather than aggressive one, as if, provided the church would let him hold what he considered to be the plain facts of human nature, he did not wish to interfere with any received doctrine: and his answers at the Synod of Diospolis[2] are perhaps too

[1] 'Ante omnia interrogandus est qui negat hominem sine peccato esse posse, quid sit quodcunque peccatum, quod vitari potest, an quod vitari non potest. Si quod vitari non potest, peccatum non est; si quod vitari potest, potest homo sine peccato esse quod vitari potest. . . . Iterum quærendum est peccatum voluntatis an necessitatis est. Si necessitatis est, peccatum non est; si voluntatis est, vitari potest. . . . Iterum quærendum est, utrumne debeat homo sine peccato esse. Procul dubio debet. Si debet, potest; si non potest, ergo nec debet; et si nec debet homo esse sine peccato, debet ergo cum peccato esse; et jam peccatum non erit, si illud debere constiterit. Aut si hoc etiam dici absurdum est, confiteri necesse est debere hominem sine peccato esse, et constat eum non aliud debere quam potest. . . . Iterum quærendum est quomodo non potest homo sine peccato esse, voluntate an natura. Si natura, peccatum non est; si voluntate, perfacile potest voluntas voluntate mutari.'—Pelagius ap. Aug. De Perfectione Justitiæ, c. 2. 3. 6.

[2] Benedictine Editor's preface to Augustine's Antipelagian Treatises, c. x.

summarily attributed to duplicity rather than a real indisposition to advance beyond his original statements, though his disciple Celestius had been bolder. But the assertion of such a freewill as Pelagius asserted was in itself a denial of the fall, and therefore necessarily carried him, whatever his direct intention at first was, to the express denial of that doctrine. And thus the question assumed that shape in which it has come down to us in the Pelagian controversy.

II. With this introduction, then, I come to my second head, and shall endeavour to state in succession, and with such explanation as may be necessary, the main positions and arguments involved in that controversy ; and which may be conveniently placed under three general heads— the power of the will, the nature of virtue and vice, and the Divine justice.

1. The first and most obvious argument against the doctrine of the corruption of human nature, was contained in that power of the will which has been just now described. Here nature seemed to bear testimony to its own competency, and the doctrine of its corruption to be contradicted by a plain fact ; for we are conscious of freewill, power of choice, and self-determination. The Pelagians appealed to these instinctive convictions, and pointed out their contrariety to the doctrine of a captive and corrupted nature. Nor was their argument unsound had they been content to direct it against an absolute doctrine of human corruption and captivity. But they pressed it too far and lay more weight upon it than it could bear. They fancied themselves in possession of the whole ground because they had this sense of freedom on their side. But S. Augustine could appeal, on the other side, to a representation of human nature, which carried with it its own evidence, and met a response in the human heart—'To will is present with me, but how to perform that which is good I find not. For the good that I would I do not, but the evil which I would not that I do. . . . I see a law in my members, warring against the law of my mind, and bringing me

into captivity to the law of sin.'[1] The sense of freedom is a true part of human nature; but there is also, on the other side, a sense of captivity: and as Pelagius appealed to one side of our consciousness, Augustine appealed to the other.

The conscience of every enlightened man, as all confess, bears witness to the presence of sin. But—more than this—the enlightened conscience bears witness to a certain impossibility of avoiding sin altogether. It is true we are conscious of freewill, and feel we have the power of doing right and abstaining from wrong on each occasion. Nay, the very sense of sin depends upon this sense of the power to avoid it; for we do not feel responsible for what we cannot help. But with this sense of freedom there is also a certain sense of necessity—a perception that sin is not wholly avoidable in this present state of our nature. We cannot imagine an enlightened conscience in which there would not be this inward sense: no good man could ever

---

[1] 'In medium procedit homo ille qui clamat, "Non quod volo facio bonum, sed quod nolo malum hoc ago."'—Op. Imp. l. 6. c. 18. 'Qui per legem quam vidit in membris suis repugnantem legi mentis suæ et captivantem se sub lege peccati, clamat, "Non quod volo," &c. Si habet liberum arbitrium, quare non facit bonum quod vult?'—L. 3. c. 112. Augustine, assuming this captivity as an evident fact, proves original sin from it: 'Nam si peccatum non pertransisset, non omnis homo cum lege peccati quæ in membris est nasceretur.'—L. 2. c. 63. 'Homo qui non cogitas ubi sis, et in diebus malis tanquam in bonis cæcus extolleris; quando erat liberum arbitrium, nondum homo vanitati similis factus erat.'—L. 3. c. 110. 'Qui dicit, "Quod nolo malum, hoc ago," responde utrum necessitatem non habeat.'—L. 5. c. 50. 'Non ei possibilitatis inanitas, sed necessitatis inerat plenitudo.'—L. 5. c. 59.

The Pelagians interpreted this text as referring to the force of custom, 'Ille enim in membris legem consuetudinem malam vocabat, quæ ab eruditis etiam seculi dici solet secunda natura.'—Op. Imp. l. 1. c. 69. An interpretation which Augustine turned against them, as committing them to the admission that sin might be necessary, and yet real sin, and so to the principle of original sin. 'Nam et ille qui dicit, "Non quod volo, ago," certe secundum vos necessitate consuetudinis premitur: hanc autem necessitatem, ne liberum auferatis arbitrium, eum sibi voluntate fecisse contenditis, et tale aliquid in naturâ humanâ factum esse non creditis.'—L. 4. c. 103.; also l. 1. c. 105.; l. 4. c. 91. 'The body of this death was interpreted of the guilt of past sin.' 'Quis me liberavit a reatu peccatorum meorum quæ commisi, cum vitari potuissent.'—Op. Imp. l. 1, c. 67.

possibly think that he could be without serious sin in this world. This sense of a law working for evil in our nature is a consequence and a part of goodness; and conscience witnesses to opposite perceptions which it cannot harmonise. Experience, indeed, shows the great improbability of perfection in this life, but the enlightened conscience speaks to its impossibility, because it sees a law of our present nature to which it is opposed. Experience shows that men never have been perfect, but not that they could not be: but the enlightened conscience would, upon the mere hearing of some or other human being who was perfect, justify the setting down the assertion as in itself absurd and incredible; containing, according to the Scriptural criterion, its own refutation, 'If we say we have no sin, we deceive ourselves, and the truth is not in us.' But what is this but a sense of necessity on the side of evil; for if it is simply absurd that the state of man in this life should not be sinful, it must be necessary that it should be.

From this sense of freedom on the one side, and of captivity on the other, proceeds that mixture and opposition in our nature, that whole ambiguous state of mind of which man is so deeply conscious in moral action; that subtle discord in the will; that union of strength and weakness. Take the case of any action above the standard of ordinary practice that a man may propose to himself to do; with what a mixture of feelings does he approach it? He feels, on the one hand, that he is certainly *able* to do it, and can exert a force over himself sufficient for the purpose; and he prepares for the turning point of a resolve under this impression. On the other hand, the level of ordinary practice pulls him down, and the weight of habit rests upon him. Nature falls back, the will is unnerved, and invincible repugnance and disinclination contradict his natural sensations of moral power. He doubts the sincerity of these sensations, as if, however innate, they were specious and deceptive. Can he, then, really do the good act? Has he freewill or not? He alternates between both impressions, unable to deny his freedom, yet apparently unable to use it, feeling no constraint, yet inferring from the difficulties of the case some unfelt one, existing too deep in nature for actual apprehension, and only showing itself in its effects. Such is the inward struggle of the imperfect moral agent described by St. Paul.

Take, again, the known power of custom over the will. A man under the most inveterate bad habit, has on every successive occasion the *feeling* of a power to do the action opposed to it. However long and uniformly he may have acted on the side of his habit, the very next time he has to act he appears to himself to be *able*—though it be no more than naked, bare, ability—still able, I say, to do what he has never yet done. But it is evident that such an idea of power is not to be taken as a certain exponent of the fact. There is an idea of power, indeed, which represents faithfully the reality, a conscious strength of purpose, which is generally the result of moral preparation. But this is altogether a distinct sort of conviction from that mere sense of bare ability to do a thing which is now referred to.

The sense of freedom then in our nature, with whatever force and vividness it may appeal to us, is not to be relied upon absolutely, as if it represented our whole state. A larger insight into ourselves, a general survey of facts, modifies the result of the impression, and does not sanction the profession of absolute power. But the Pelagian relied upon this sense of bare ability, as if it were an infallible footing for the most complete conclusion, and betrayed that want of due and circumspect distrust which never forsakes the true philosophical mind, that knows how nature abounds in pitfalls to catch the unwary; and, however considerate of, is ever jealous of, appearances. He trusted with blind confidence a single impression and instinct, so blindly indeed, as to put aside the plainest facts, when they interfered with it.

For nothing can show more strongly the reckless and hasty faith, which the Pelagians reposed in this one impression, than that they supported it against the most palpable facts connected with nature and habit; arguing, that sin not being a substance, but only an act which took place and was then over, could not by any amount of repetition affect this power and impair freewill[1]; but that a man after any amount and duration of sin, had as much freewill as ever. The reason was that, as I have just stated, the sense of *bare ability* continues in spite of any length of habit; on which sense the Pelagian absolutely relied. But this was not a reasonable, but a fanatical[2] doctrine of freewill; a gross delusion, belonging to that class and rank of absurd ideas upon which corrupt and fantastic sects arise; forsaking the broad, inclusive ground of truth for some narrow conceit, some one notion to which everything gives way, and which, losing by such exclusiveness all its original share of truth, becomes a shadow and a lie. This was a departure from the first principles of morals, as attaching no consequences within the soul itself to moral evil, which is thus represented as passing off, and leaving no trace behind. The moral being incurred, indeed, the external consequence of liability to punishment, but was not in himself impaired by sin; remaining the same as before. But it is the internal consequences of sin, which fasten the idea of sin, as being such, upon us, and make us regard it as the real evil it is. Take away these consequences, and sin is little more than a shadow which just rests a moment on the soul, and is then gone. It ceases to be a serious thing, it ceases to

[1] 'Liberum arbitrium et post peccata tam plenum est quam fuit ante peccata.'—Julian ap. Op. Imp. l. 1. c. 91. 'Nos dicimus peccato hominis non naturæ statum mutari sed meriti qualitatem, id est et in peccato hanc esse liberi arbitrii naturam, per quam potest a peccato desinere, quæ fuit in eo ut posset a justitiâ deviare.'—c. 96. 'Primo eo disputandum est quod per peccatum debilitata dicitur et immutata natura. Unde ante omnia quærendum puto quid sit peccatum, substantia aliqua, an omnino substantia carens nomen, quo non res, non existentia, non corpus aliquid, sed perperam facti actus exprimitur. Credo ita est. Et si ita est quomodo potuit humanam debilitare vel mutare naturam quod substantia caret.'—Pelagius ap. Aug. De Nat. et Grat. n. 21. 'Materiam peccati esse vindictam, si ad hoc peccator infirmatus est ut plura peccaret.'—n. 24.

[2] It was perhaps an ironical charge against the Pelagians that they held 'etiam parvulos propria per liberum arbitrium habere peccata. . . . Ecce inquiunt, Esau et Jacob intra viscera materna luctantur, et, in nascuntur, alter supplantatur ab altero, atque in pede præcedentis manu consequentis et tenentis inventa, perseverans quodammodo lucta convincitur. Quomodo ergo in infantibus hæc agentibus, nullum est vel ad bonum vel ad malum propriæ voluntatis arbitrium, unde præmia sive supplicia meritis præcedentibus subsequantur.'—Ep. 186. n. 13.

CHAP. III.     *The Pelagian Controversy.*     61

be sin; its very substance is that part of it which survives the act, and its continuance is its existence. The Pelagian, then, secures his unqualified freewill at the cost of the very rudiments of morals; his theory would injure the moral tone of any mind that received it, and its natural effect, if it spread, would be a relaxation of the religious standard, and a lowering of the sense of sin in the world; showing how impossible it is to carry one truth to an excess without impairing another. Those who will not allow the will to be the less free for any amount of sin must accept the alternative, that sin has very little effect,—with its natural corollary, that that which has so slight an effect cannot be a very serious matter itself. And thus an unlimited freewill can only be maintained by abandoning the sanctity of moral principle.

2. The argument respecting the will was succeeded, in the Pelagian controversy, by the argument respecting the nature of virtue and vice. How could there be such a thing as hereditary sin? sin transmitted from father to son, and succeeded to by birth? How were moral dispositions involved in the operations of nature?[1] This appeal to reason was properly answered by an appeal to mystery—an answer, however, which was needlessly perplexed by too minute attempts to define the mode of the transmission of sin?[2] The explanation of a mystery cannot really advance beyond the statement of it, but the too subtle explainer forgets his own original admission and the inherent limits

[1] 'Amentissimum est arbitrii negotium seminibus immixtum putare.' —Julian, Op. Imp. l. 6. c. 9. 'Injustum est ut reatus per semina traderetur.'—L. 3. c. 11. 'Habuerunt ergo parvuli voluntatem non solum antequam nascerentur, verum etiam antequam proavi eorum generarentur; et usi sunt electionis arbitrio, priusquam substantiæ eorum semina conderentur. Cur itaque metuis dicere, in eis tempore conceptuum eorum esse liberam voluntatem, qua peccatum non trahant naturaliter sed sponte committant; si credis eos hodie conceptos ante tot secula habuisse sensum, judicium, efficientiam voluntatis.'—L. 4. 104.

[2] Op. Imp. l. 6. c. 22.; l. 2. c. 123.; l. 4. c. 90—104., l. 6.; c. 9—23. An elaborate attempt at an explanation of this difficulty, by the analogy of bodies, quæ afficiendo transeunt, non emigrando (l. 5. Contra Jul. Pel. n. 51.), concludes thus: 'Sic et vitia cum sint in subjecto ex parentibus tamen in filios, non quasi transmigratione de suo subjecto in subjectum alterum, sed affectione et contagione pertranseunt.'

of his task, and imagines himself solving what is inexplicable.

But the question of transmitted or hereditary sin gave place to the larger question of *necessary* sin. Sin was represented, in the doctrine of the fall, as attaching to human nature, *i.e.* as necessary. But was not this opposed to the self-evident truth, that sin must be voluntary?[1] To deserve properly praise or blame, must not a man be a free agent? and was he a free agent if he could not act otherwise than as he did? The Pelagian thus adopted, as a plain maxim of reason, and a fundamental truth of morals, the position that virtue and vice derived their essential characteristics from the power of the individual beforehand to choose the one or the other; *possibilitas utriusque partis*; that an act of the will, to be good or bad, must be a decision out of a neutral or undecided state.[2] The Pelagian controversy thus took up the question of the conditions of virtue and vice; whether virtue or vice were consistent with necessity or repugnant to it, whether they involved in their own nature the trial of the will or not.

The Pelagian, then, as the above statement shows, expressed himself unguardedly on this question, and exposed himself immediately to the irresistible answer of S. Augustine, that, on the ground he adopted, he must be prepared to deny all goodness to the angels in heaven, to the saints in glory,[3] and even to God Himself. The impossibility of sinning belonged to the Divine Being as His nature, and to the saints and angels as a privilege and reward; and therefore were contingency, or the absence of necessity,

[1] 'Naturale nullum esse peccatum potest.'—' Si est naturale peccatum non est voluntarium.'—' Voluntas necessitati non potest admoveri.'—'Non potest velle antequam potuerit et nolle.'—'Suum non est si necessarium est.'

[2] Julian: 'Inculco liberum arbitrium nec ob aliud datum esse, nec intelligi in alio posse, quam ut nec ad justitiam, nec ad iniquitatem, captiva aliquis voluntate rapiatur.' Augustine: 'Libra tua quam conaris ex utraque parte per æqualia momenta suspendere, ut voluntas quantum sit ad malum, tantum etiam sit ad bonum libera.'—Op. Imp. 1. 3. c. 112. 117. 'Sic definis liberam voluntatem, ut nisi utrumque, id est, et bene et male agere possit, libera esse non possit.'—L. 3. c. 120.

[3] 'Accedere nobis debet virtus major in præmio, ut malam voluntatem sic non haberemus, ut nec habere possemus. O desideranda necessitas!'—Op. Imp. 1. 5. c. 61.

essential to goodness, neither God, nor the angels, nor the saints would be good.

Thus easily and summarily refuted, however, his argument involved a mixture of truth and error. So much must be conceded to the Pelagian, that the trial of the will is the necessary condition of the highest kind of virtue that comes within our cognisance and experience. Of the Divine Nature, as being beyond our comprehension, we cannot speak, though we know that it must be infinitely good, while it must also be without trial. But the assertion is true of the moral creature in this present state. For whatever may be the sweetness of the good affections,—even though we could imagine them from the first in full possession of the mind, and so powerfully moving it, that it felt no inclination to act otherwise than as they dictated; even though we could imagine such an uninterrupted flow of virtue from a source of feeling,—such a result could not bear a comparison with the victory of the will. The good affections are aids and supports to goodness; aids and supports indeed not casual or adventitious, but permanent, and belonging to our nature; yet having the effect of saving pain and effort. But in trial we have to act without this aid. For though even the will itself cannot be said to act without affection, inasmuch as *some* love of what is good appears to enter as an ingredient into any decision in favour of it, we are properly said to act from the will as distinct from the affections, in the case of trial; such trial being in truth caused by the balance of the affections being on the side of evil. Trial, therefore, throws the man upon himself in a deep and peculiar sense. He is reduced to the narrowest condition, and with all the excesses of a bountifully constituted nature cut off, sustains from ultimate conscience and the bare substance of the soul, the fight with evil. But such a combat tests and elicits an inner strength which no dominion of the good affections, however continuous, could do. The greater the desertion of the moral being, and his deprivation of aids, the deeper appears his fidelity; the triumph is greater in proportion to the scantiness of the means with which it is gained;

and in this adoption of, this cleaving to, barren good, is a depth of affection, a root of love, contrasted with which, all the richness of the untried affections is a poor and feeble offering to God.

But though trial is the necessary condition of the highest kind of goodness in this life, it is not the necessary condition of all goodness. It is evident that we recognise and feel toward, as goodness, certain moral states and dispositions which have not been the result of trial, but are altogether natural. We may see this in a very low degree even in the case of animals of the gentler, more generous, and confiding character who engage our affections in consequence, and towards whom we instinctively feel as possessing a kind of goodness. But the good natural dispositions of moral beings deserve a serious consideration.[1] For though it may be doubted whether these dispositions are ever sustained entirely without trial of the will, and though we may not be able to tell in a particular case, whether what appears to be the man's natural disposition has not been formed in part by early trial and past moral acts, still the general sense of mankind acknowledges what are called good natural dispositions; that some persons have by nature a good bias in one or other direction, are amiable, courageous, truthful, humble naturally, or have a certain general happy conformation; that they have, that is, by nature, not only the power to act in a certain way, but the disposition so to act already formed within them; a *habit* implanted, or, as the schoolmen say, *infused*, in distinction to being acquired by acts. But it would be absurd to say that such dispositions as these were not virtues, and that such natural goodness was not real goodness. We feel towards persons who possess such dispositions as persons of a particular character, which character is good; nor do we do this on even the imaginary supposition that they have acquired it for themselves, the existing moral

[1] 'Cur non annuimus esse quosdam natura misericordes, si natura quosdam non negamus excordes? Sunt enim nonnulla congenita, quæ in ætate qua usus incipit esse rationis, sicut ipsa ratio, incipiunt apparere.'—Op. Imp. l. 4. c. 129.

state being the thing we attend to independent of any source from which it may have sprung. The system of trial and probation under which we are placed is thus to some extent a modified one; not throwing us wholly upon ourselves, to work our way up to the virtuous character by the power of the mere will, but more or less, and in portions, *endowing* us with it, and producing in us to begin with the ultimate forms of moral being.

And it is proper, as a further answer to the Pelagian confined idea of virtue, to add, that no exact limit is, to the eye of reason apparent, to the operation of such a power of infusing virtue into the human soul. It would undoubtedly be something like a contradiction to suppose that the distinctive effect of trial could be obtained without trial as the cause, and it must be granted that there must be some ultimate difference in favour of that virtue which is, over that which is not, the effect of trial. But there is no other apparent goal to an untried virtue. We know that a certain excitement of the feelings produces a pleasure in virtue, and that particular circumstances, junctures, appeals from without, act with an exciting power upon the feelings, kindling zeal, enthusiasm, and love. But this being the case, it is impossible to say to what extent this system of impulse and excitement existing in our constitution might be carried; what duration these conditions of mind are in themselves capable of, and whether they might not be made, by Divine power applying a fit machinery and succession of exciting causes, permanent. We only know that such a system would not serve that particular end for which the present system of trial is designed.

But the Pelagian was further wrong. As trial is not the necessary condition of all goodness, so it is not the necessary condition of the highest kind of goodness *always*. The system of probation points according to the reason of the case, to its own termination. It is designed for an end; but the end, when attained, implies the cessation of the means. There is a plain incongruity in the perfected being remaining still dependent on a contingent will, and exposed to moral risk; *i.e.* being for ever on his trial. A time must come, then, when this will cease, when there will be no more deciding between good and evil, when that power of choice which makes our virtue here will be over, and the goodness of the moral creature will be necessary goodness, from which he will not be able to depart for evermore.

And this consideration is much confirmed by another. The trial of the will is undoubtedly the condition here of the highest kind of virtue; but it must be admitted at the same time that it produces this virtue in an incipient and elementary stage. A distinction must be made between trial itself and its effects. The undergoing of trial is the intensest moral act we know of; but when we leave the primary stage of resistance made, strength manifested, and difficulty overcome, and look for the results, we are disappointed. Virtue, which is the result of this process, and arises wholly from effort or self-discipline, is deficient in its crowning characteristic—its grace, or what moralists call its beauty. It betrays effort, conscious aim and design; is practised with too much apparent system and method; it wants ease and naturalness; and is more or less hard, formal, and artificial, and to a spectator unattractive, which it is not its proper nature to be. Thus, take a person of an ambitious and assuming habit of mind originally, who has come to the resolution to cultivate humility; how little progress does he appear to make in the task compared with the sincerity of his intentions. Whatever acts he may do in conformity with his design, and however he may succeed in imposing on himself a certain general line of behaviour, something is wanting to animate it; the vital spirit keeps aloof, and some envious influence from original temper still works below to mar the growth of discipline. Compare this acquired virtue with the natural virtue of humility as seen in any one of a gentle and humble disposition by nature, how imperfect, how abortive, does the result of human effort appear by the side of the Divine gift? Were present effects alone to be considered, it were better to be simply shone upon by the creative grace of God, and without labour of our own to receive straight from His hands an unearned virtue. And this poverty in acquired virtues arises from the very fact that they are acquired, from the very manner of their growth and formation. It is essential to perfect virtue that it should be truly natural and part of ourselves; and self-discipline, care, and culture, much as they can do, cannot make a nature. For though custom is called a second nature to express its great power, it only in truth renders natural or easy to us the original act which it adopts. And therefore if this act is one of self-control, or resistance to evil, it only renders resistance to evil easy, not goodness itself natural. Custom, in short, improves a character upon its own basis, but does not give a new one, or make a man what Scripture calls a new creature. Nor, in fact, do we see it perform even this inferior function perfectly. For it must be asked, with all the correcting force of custom, where do we see in the world what may, in a thorough sense, be called renovation of character? Nor do I mean an eradication wholly of wrong tendencies, but even a complete and successful suppression of them existing. A serious fault originally attaching to a character assumes in some persons subtler forms and a more discreet and politic bearing, and is finely trained and educated rather than really resisted. In others it meets a resistance; but where is it suppressed, so that, after a life of self-improvement, we do not see it? The possibility of true moral renovation is a truth of faith rather than of experience.

But such being the defects inherent in the system of trial, if virtue is ever to be perfect and what it ought to be, it must be removed from this basis altogether. It must in a future state become in a way indigenous in us. It must become a nature, an inspiration, a gift; be cut away completely from the ground of effort; and be like what we call natural goodness here, though with this important difference, that it will have been *produced* by trial. That is, to become what it ought to be, it must become necessary.

The highest and the perfect state of the will, then, is

a state of necessity; and the power of choice, so far from being essential to a true and genuine will, is its weakness and defect. What can be a greater sign of an imperfect and immature state of the will than that, with good and evil before it, it should be in suspense which to do? That it should take the worse alternative is its prostration; but that it should be even undetermined is weakness. Even with the good action done, does not a great sense of imperfection attend the thought that it was but an instant ago uncertain whether it would be done or not? And, as we dwell in recollection on the state of our will previous to its decision, in that interval of suspense in which we might have acted in one way or another, does not so unsteady and indeterminate a source of action interfere even with the comfort of certainty which is derived from the action as being done? Is not the circumstance that it was but just now uncertain whether it would be done or not a surviving reflection upon the agent? Was it a sort of luck that he did it? And would he do it again if tried again?

We have indeed at first an idea that the power of choice is that which ennobles and dignifies the will, and that the will would be an imperfect one without it: but this arises from a misconception. The power of choosing good or evil is indeed that which ennobles the will of man as compared with the lower wills of the brute creation; but it is not therefore the perfection of man's will. If we imagine it to be so, we appear to attach this value to it, for this reason, viz., because a power in the will of determining itself either way is *power*, and we suppose power to be an advantage. But power is not itself an advantage. In our ordinary mode of speaking, indeed, we regard it as such; because we ordinarily associate power with an advantageous subject-matter, or think of it as the power to do things which are advantageous to ourselves. But power in itself is neither an advantage nor the contrary, but depends entirely on its object, or that which it has the power to do, for being the one or the other. The power to do that which is injurious to oneself is a disadvantage, inasmuch as it involves the chance of injury; and the power to do evil is the power to injure oneself. Such power has no more an advantage as *power* than it has as *liability*. It is true that, when the subject-matter of power is good, then the power to accomplish it has an excellence as power; that is to say, it is an additional advantage that the good which happens to us is from ourselves, and not from an external source. And on this ground the attribute of power as belonging to the Supreme Being is an excellent attribute: it being an excellence that the good which He enjoys comes from Himself, and not from any other source.

The actions, again, which the good will perform in a future state of necessity will not be the less good on that account, and because they do not proceed from a power of choice. It is true that in one sense a good act which proceeds from the exercise of a power of choice is more meritorious than one which proceeds from a will acting necessarily right. If we measure the merit of an action by the degree in which it is in advance of the general condition of the agent, then undoubtedly an action which proceeds from a will determined necessarily to good has no merit, because it is simply on a level with, and not at all in advance of such a will. On the other hand, an action which proceeds from a will which has to exert a power of choice in order to compass it, has merit, because it is in advance of such a will; inasmuch as the certainty of an action done is an advance upon the mere power of doing it. But it is evident that that which is here spoken of is not the positive merit of an action, but only a relative one; its merit as compared with the condition and ability of the agent. A will which acts of necessity for good is the very strongest will on the side of good; and therefore, compared with the ability of this agent, a good act is a *little* result. A will which has to exert a power of choice, and use struggle and effort, is a weaker will; and therefore a good action, as compared with the ability of this agent, is a *greater* result. The superior merit, then, of a good act, in this case, is arrived at by comparing it with the weakness of the agent; in the same way that the merit of a work of art is sometimes arrived at by comparing it with the inferiority of the instrument by which it was executed. It is a merit, therefore, which tells against the perfection of the will, and not in its favour. The act, as such, if we can separate the act from the will, is more meritorious; but that very superior merit of the act is gained at the cost of the will, from which it proceeds. The act is better because the agent is worse.

What has been said of natural or necessary goodness may be said of natural or necessary evil. Amid the obscurity which attaches to this class of questions, something to which mankind had borne large testimony would be relinquished in denying the existence of bad natural dispositions. And the system of trial points as much to a necessary evil state as it does to a necessary good one as its termination. It must be added, that the law of custom unhappily produces much nearer approaches in this life to a necessary state in evil than it does to the same in good; furnishing a proof of the compatibleness of a necessary with a culpable or sinful state, to which Augustine often appeals in defending the doctrine of original sin against the Pelagian objection on that head.[1]

The rational doctrine, then, of voluntariness, *i.e.* how far the trial of the will is involved in the nature of virtue and vice is a modified one. Freewill and necessity have both their place in it, nor does it oppose the necessary to

[1] 'Consuetudo fructus est voluntatis, quoniam ex voluntate gignitur, quæ tamen id quod agit, negat se agere voluntate.'—Op. Imp. l. 4. c. 103. The admission of Julian, 'Evenire hominibus affectionalem qualitatem, atque ita inhærescere, ut .aut magnis molitionibus, aut nullis separetur omnino,' and the Pelagian interpretation of the text *Quod nolo malum hoc ago*, on the ground of custom, were thus turned to the account of original sin. 'Ac per hoc etiam secundum vos peccandi necessitas unde abstinere liberum non est, illius peccati pœna fuit, a quo abstinere liberum fuit.'—L. 1. c. 105. ' " Dicis quod contrarium sit necessitas et voluntas, ita ut se mutua impugnatione consumant ; " inde nos arguens quod " alterum alterius subdamus effectui, dicentes necessitatem de fructibus voluntatis exortam," cum videas necessitatem consuetudinis fructum esse manifestissimum voluntatis. Nonne quod tibi impossibile visum est, "sua se voluntas multiplicatione delevit, et statum proprium operata mutavit," quæ multiplicata necessitatem consuetudinis fecit.'—Op. Imp. l. 4. c. 103.

the voluntary. But the Pelagian adopted an extreme and unqualified doctrine on this head; throwing everything upon the direct choice or exertion of the will, and separating absolutely the necessary from the voluntary. Virtue, in the heavenly state, then, could be no virtue in his eyes, because it had ceased to require effort and choice. He allowed, so far as his language went, no room for an ultimate and perfect state, and established an eternal restless contingency in the moral world. Not, however, to fasten this extreme meaning upon his language, which was perhaps hardly intended, inasmuch as the Pelagian nowhere denies the received doctrine of a future state; and understanding him only to mean that a man could not be good or bad in this life except by his own individual choice, his position is still a narrow and one-sided one. The general sense of mankind is certainly on the side of there being good and bad natural dispositions, and we attach the idea of goodness to generous excitements and emotions, which do not arise from any effort of the will but spontaneously. The Christian doctrine of grace which makes goodness a divine gift or inspiration is thus fully in accordance with the instincts of our nature, while the Pelagian doctrine, which reduces all virtue to effort and discipline, is felt as a confinement and an artificial limit in morals.

There are, however, two distinct questions properly involved in this subject; one, whether the trial of the will is, as opposed to implanted dispositions, essential to the nature of virtue or vice; the other relating to the determination of the will on its trial,—whether its self-determination is necessary to the nature of virtue and vice as distinct to its determination from without. The Pelagian thought it essential that, for this purpose, the will should determine itself, that virtue and vice, in order to be such, must be of our own originating. S. Augustine maintained a goodness and a sinfulness to which the will was determined from without. Both these positions are true, if held together, and both false if held apart.

3. To the questions of the power of the will, and the

nature of virtue and vice, succeeded the question of the Divine justice.

The doctrine of original sin described all mankind as punished for the sin of Adam, deriving a positive sinfulness, and even a necessity to sin, a slavery, and a captivity from it. But how was it consistent with justice that one man should be punished for the sin of another; that mankind should be created guilty, and derive from one particular act committed before they were born a positive necessity to sin?[1] The objection of the Pelagian was met in two ways; first, by an appeal to mystery; and, secondly, by an appeal to facts.

1. The objection that it was contrary to the Divine justice to punish one man for the sin of another was met by an appeal to mystery, and the answer that the Divine justice was incomprehensible. And this was a sound and proper answer, but the form in which it was put was not wholly faultless.

For it is one thing to say that the Divine justice is incomprehensible, and another thing to say that the Divine justice is different from human justice; or that we are to have a different idea altogether of justice as a human and as a Divine characteristic. In saying that the Divine justice is incomprehensible we make no assertion about it at all, and therefore do not establish any contradiction between it and our natural ideas of justice. Having conceived of it, so far as we conceived of it at all, as the ordinary natural quality so called, we only cease at a certain point to form any conception about it. But to say that the Divine justice is different from human is to confuse our moral notions altogether. Pressed by the Pelagian with the strong testimonies in Scripture to the rule of natural justice, that no man should be punished except

[1] 'Ais credere te quidem conditorem Deum, sed malorum hominum . . . . et Dei sanctitati informationem sceleris appulisti. Creat igitur malum Deus et puniuntur innocentes propter quod fecit Deus; imputat hominibus crimen manuum suarum Deus; et quod persuasit diabolus tenuiter, solerter et perseveranter fingit et protegit et format Deus. Et fructum ab homine bonitatis reposcit, cui malum ingenuit Deus.'—Julian, ap. Op. Imp. l. 3. c. 124. *et seq.*

for his own sins, S. Augustine properly appealed to another set of texts which represented God as visiting the sins of the fathers upon the children[1], and showed that Scripture asserted an incomprehensible as well as a natural justice. But he further proceeded to explain away these assertions of the rule of natural justice itself, as intended to apply to human, not to the Divine conduct. The rule laid down in Deuteronomy, that the 'fathers shall not be put to death for the children, neither the children for the fathers, but every man for his own sin[2],' was interpreted as applying to human judges only, not to God, who was altogether free from such an obligation.[3] And the natural rejoinder of the Pelagian, that God was not less just than He wanted man to be, was overruled by the argument, that God did many things which it would be wrong for man to do.[4] But such an argument was fallacious. The Being who gave life has a right to take it away, and the supremely good Being has a right to praise Himself; but the difference in the rightfulness of such acts in the case of God and man is not any difference of the moral law by which God and the creature act, but a difference in their respective positions, which justifies these acts in God, and not in the creature. Indeed, the chapter in Ezekiel applies the rule

[1] Op. Imp. l. 3. c. 30.
[2] Deut. xxiv. 16.
[3] Augustine: 'Aliter mandavit homini, aliter judicavit ipse.'—Op. Imp. l. 3. c. 33. Julian: 'Si quæ sunt justa a nobis fieri velit, et ipse faciat quod injustum est: justiores nos, quam ipse est, cupit videri; imo non justiores, sed nos æquos, et se iniquum.'—Julian, ap. Op. Imp. l. 3. c. 24.
[4] 'Hoc quidem præceptum dedit hominibus judicantibus, ne pater pro filio, vel filius pro patre moreretur. Cæterum judicia sua Deus non alligavit hac lege.'—Op. Imp. l. 3. c. 12. 'Non est legis suæ prævaricator Deus quando aliud facit Deus ut Deus, aliud imperat homini ut homini?'—c. 23. 'Facit enim Deus aliquando contra quæ facienda mandavit. Nec opus est ut multa commemorem. Mandavit homini Scriptura dicens "non te laudet os tuum" (Prov. xxvii. 2), nec tamen dicendus est arrogans aut superbus, cum se innumerabiliter laudare non desinit.' —c. 22. 'Hoc judicium Deus hominum voluit esse non suum, qui dixit, Reddam peccata patrum in filios. (Deut. v, 9.) Quod etiam per hominem fecit, quando per Jesum Nave non solum Achan, sed etiam filios ejus occidit; vel per eundem, filios Canaanorum etiam parvulos damnavit.'—c. 30. 'Quis enim homo justus sinit perpetrari scelus quod habet in potestate non sinere? Et tamen sinit hæc Deus.'—c. 24.

of natural justice directly to the Divine conduct, and represents God as asserting of Himself, that He punishes no man except for his own sins, and so gives no ground whatever for such a distinction. But this declaration was not allowed its obvious interpretation, as stating a universal law of the Divine dealings, but only a special prophetical one, as alluding to the Divine mercy under the Gospel dispensation and the covenant of grace,[1] under which the effect of original sin, the punishment of mankind for the sin of their first parent, was removed.

But the punishment which all mankind suffered for the sin of Adam was punishment of a peculiar kind; because it was not only pain but sin, and not only sin but captivity to sin and inability to do any good thing. This worst and strongest penalty, then, attaching to the sin of Adam, was defended by an appeal to a remarkable law of God's judicial administration, discernible in his natural providence, and specially attested by Scripture; the rule, viz. of punishing sin by further sin, *peccatum pœna peccati*,— a rule which, in the present instance, only received a mysterious application, as being extended to the case of a mysterious and incomprehensible sin.

S. Augustine argued, then, that original sin was real sin in the being in whom it resided; and being such, was justly punishable by the abandonment of the person guilty of it, to sin; that the natural man, therefore, could not plead his want of moral power as any excuse for his sins, any more than a man in common life, who had contracted a bad habit, could plead the dominion of that habit as such an excuse. That bad habit might be so strong that he could not help committing the sins to which it inclined

[1] 'Hæc per Ezechielem prophetam promissio est novi Testamenti, quam non intelligis, ubi Deus regeneratos a generatis si jam in majoribus ætatibus sunt, secundum propria facta discernit.'—Op. Imp. l. 3. c. 38. '"Si *dicetur* amplius parabola": . . . non arguit quia *dicebatur*, sed permittit ubi non dicatur . . . . "*Non dicetur in Is. rael*" recte diceres, si veros Israelitas regeneratos videres in quibus hoc non dicetur.'—c. 39. 41. Jeremiah xxxi. 21—32. is adduced to confirm this interpretation. '*In diebus illis* non dicent ultra. Patres comederunt,' &c.—c. 84. See Contra Jul. Pel. l. 6. n. 82.

him; but he was responsible for those sins, in that he was responsible for their cause. In like manner, man was responsible for the sins which in the state of original sin he could not avoid, in that he was responsible for original sin itself.[1]

Two difficulties, however, presented themselves to the application of such a law to the case of original sin. In the first place, though it is true that all sin, so far as it is indulged, predisposes the mind to further sin, or creates a sinful habit, this effect is in proportion to the amount of such indulgence; and it is only extreme indulgence that produces an uncontrollable habit, or a loss of freewill: whereas the sin of our first parents, to which this extreme effect was attached, was but a single sin, and not apparently a heinous one. But the sin of our first parents, it was replied, was neither a single nor a light one. The outward act was but the consummation of a course of inward sin, self-pleasing, pride, and departure from God. And, even were its subject-matter light, the sin itself was disobedience; the more wanton, that there was no strength of passion as yet in man's nature to excuse it. Who would measure the greatness of a first sin as being the first, a departure from created rectitude, the primary act of the will for evil, to which no previous evil predisposed? But the subject-matter was only externally light, not really, being not a mere fruit of a tree, but good *out of* their existing state of union with God, which was grasped at; showing a greediness for which God did not suffice; and that alien good being, moreover, the presumptuous position

---

[1] 'Sed vos ista peccata ex illis venire peccatis quæ nulla necessitate commissa sunt, in illo saltem conceditis, qui dicit, "*Quod nolo malum hoc ago.*" Qui enim, ut istam patiatur necessitatem, non nisi peccandi consuetudine premitur, procul dubio priusquam peccaret, nondum necessitate consuetudinis premebatur. Ac per hoc, etiam secundum vos, peccandi necessitas unde abstinere liberum non est, illius peccati pœna fuit a quo abstinere liberum fuit, quando nullum pondus necessitatis urgebat. Cur ergo non creditis tantum saltem valuisse illud primi hominis ineffabiliter grande peccatum, ut eo vitiaretur humana natura universa, quantum valet nunc in homine uno secunda natura?'—Op. Imp. l. i. c. 105.

of being gods themselves—a pride which was the very counterpart of our Lord's humility, who emptied Himself of a Divinity which was His right, while they grasped at a divinity to which they had none.[1]

But, however serious the sin of our first parents might be, a much greater difficulty presented itself in the question how individuals could be responsible for a sin to which they were not themselves personally parties. But this difficulty was overruled by an appeal to the doctrine of original sin itself, which rested upon Scripture, and the very foundation of which was, that all men had in some sense sinned in Adam. This was, indeed a mystery, and beyond our comprehension, but faith accepted it as true; and if true, the basis which this argument required was supplied to it. Such an explanation was only the application to a mysterious subject-matter of a law, which we recognise as just in that sphere of providence which comes under our knowledge. We see the justice of the law that sin hardens the heart, as applied to the case of actual sin because we know the sin; we see a justice in such sin, long indulged, leading to actual slavery and loss of freewill: but the justice of this law as applied to the case of original sin was a mysterious and incomprehensible justice, that which is its subject-matter being a mysterious and incomprehensible sin.

When S. Augustine, however, left the ground of mystery for that of reasoning, he adopted doubtful positions. The appeal to the Divine foreknowledge of men's evil lives, in spite of which He creates them, as a defence of a creation

---

[1] 'In occulto autem mali esse cœperunt, ut in apertam inobedientiam laberentur.'—De Civit. Dei, l. xiv. c. 13. *et seq.* 'Quantum malum sola inobedientia.'—De Gen. ad literam, l. 8. c. 13. 'Noluit homo inter delicias paradisi servare justitiam.'—De Pecc. Merit. et Remiss. l. 2. n. 55. 'Quid avarius illo cui Deus sufficere non potuit.'—In Ep. Joannis ad Parthos, Tr. 8. n. 6. 'Rapere voluerunt divinitatem, perdiderunt felicitatem.'—In Tr. 68. n. 9. 'Tanto gravius peccavit quanto ibi major non peccandi facilitas erat, ubi vitiata natura nondum erat.'—Op. Imp. l. 2. c. 189. 'Tanta impietate peccavit quantam nos metiri atque æstimare non possumus.'—Ibid. l. 3. c. 65. 'Illius natura quanto magis sublimiter stabat, tanto magis graviter occidit. . . . . Peccatum quanto incredibilius, tantó damnabilius.'—Ibid. l. 6. c. 22. See Bull on the State of Man before the Fall, vol. ii. (Oxford ed.) p. 64.

under a necessity to evil, was plausible [1]; but there is plainly a difference between exposing men to the risk, and subjecting them to the certainty of moral evil, and that evil in some cases eternal. The issue being alike foreseen in both cases; in the one the sinner has had the opportunity of a better issue given him, and has therefore only himself to blame for the worse one; in the other he has had no such opportunity. The appeal to God's natural providence and his support and nourishment of evil men in the world as an analogous case to the creation of men as evil, was still more incorrect.[2]

2. The objection to the punishment of mankind for the sin of Adam, on the score of the Divine justice, was answered by an appeal to facts; an appeal which divided into two great heads—the fact of sin, and the fact of pain.

First, how were we to account for the fact of sin, as it

---

[1] 'Ut quid creat quos impios futuros et damnandos esse præscivit.'—Op. Imp. l. 1. c. 48., vid. 119. 121; l. 5. c. 13.

The argument, however, with a modification, may claim the more recent authority of Archbp. Whately, who says: 'We should be very cautious how we employ such weapons as may recoil upon ourselves . . . Why the Almighty does not cause to die in the cradle every infant whose future wickedness and misery, if suffered to grow up, He foresees, is what no system of religion, natural or revealed, will enable us satisfactorily to account for.'—Essays on S. Paul, p. 88. But is there not some confusion of thought in this argument? As stated by S. Augustine, it is in *form* absurd. For the difficulty in the constitution of things which he sets against that of reprobation, or creating a being to be eternally miserable, is this, that God foresees men's evil lives and their judicial result, and *yet* creates them. But if God foresees men's evil lives, He by the hypothesis creates them, and it would be a contradiction that He should not. Facts cannot first be foreseen, and then because they are foreseen be prevented. Archbishop Whately, however, relieves the argument from this absurdity, by making foresight to be the foresight " of men's future wickedness and misery *if suffered to grow up.*" But what can be meant by the foresight of events which, by the very supposition, may not take place? This alleged difficulty, then, in the constitution of things, cannot be stated without a great absurdity and contradiction; whereas the difficulty of God creating a being to be eternally miserable is as plain and simple a one as can be conceived.

[2] 'Sic creat malos quomodo pascit et nutrit malos.'—De Nupt. et Conc. l. 2. n. 32, 33. Julian: 'Quod pascit Deus etiam peccatores, benignusque est super ingratos et malos pietatis est ejus testimonium non malignitatis. . . . Vide ergo quam nescias quid loqueris, qui de exemplo misericordiæ voluisti crudelitatem probare.'—Op. Imp. l. 5. c. 64.

met us in the world—the universal depravation and corruption of mankind? could we account for this by chance, or the contingent action of each man's freewill? Or did it not at once point to some *law* in our nature, on the same principle on which, in the physical world and common life, whenever we see a uniform set of phenomena, we refer them to some law?

The argument, however, for original sin derived from the prevalence of actual sin in the world, though undoubtedly sound and unanswerable, requires some caution and discrimination in the use of it. And in the first place it must be observed that, when we examine this argument, we find, that upon a nearer view it divides into two distinct arguments, depending upon two different kinds of reasoning. One is the argument simply of cause and effect. On the principle that every event must have a cause, actual sin must have a cause anterior to itself, from which it proceeds: and for the same reason that this cause is wanted itself, another cause is wanted for *it*, and so another and another in succession, till we arrive at some origin or first cause of sin. But this origin of sin cannot be in the Divine will, it must therefore be in the human; which ultimate and original evil in the will is what is signified by original sin.

This argument, then, for original sin, does not at all depend on the amount of actual sin in the world, but would be just as valid on the supposition of one sin, as on that of universal; original sin *itself* following from the simple fact of actual, though its universality depends on the universality of actual. And the validity of this argument depends on the validity of the general argument of cause and effect, or upon the truth of the axiom, that every event must have a cause,—an axiom which I discussed in the last chapter, when I defined the degree and measure of truth which belonged to it. It will be enough to say here of this *rationale* of original sin, that it is a wholly philosophical, as distinguished from a scriptural one; because, in representing original sin as anterior to all actual sin, it represents it as anterior to the sin of Adam, and as much the condition of man at his first creation as it ever was afterwards.[1]

The other and the more common argument, is the argument of probability,—that it is contrary to the doctrine of chances, that every one of those innumerable millions that have lived in the world should have been a sinner, if such sin had depended on the mere contingency of every individual's freewill; such a universal fact evidently proving the existence of some law of sin in our nature. But the correctness of this argument for original sin depends on the sense in which we understand sin in the preliminary statement, that every one of the human race has been, and is, a sinner.

If by sin is meant here the absence of perfection only— that every man that has ever lived has done something wrong in the course of his life, there appears to be nothing, even in a universal faultiness of the human race, in such a sense, more than may be accounted for on the principle of each man's contingent will, or that requires the operation of a law. For, considering the length of human life, the constant succession of temptations in it, and their variety, the multiplicity of relations in which a man stands to others, all of which have to be fulfilled in order to constitute him faultless, is there anything very remarkable in the coincidence that every man should, on some occasion or other in his life, have diverged from the strict duty? If, on the one hand, it may be said, that out of so great a number of individuals as there have been in the world some few perfect men might have been calculated upon; on the other hand, it may be said that, with so vast a number of trials, we could not calculate any one's universal success under them. The chances in favour of cases of perfection which the number of individuals in the world presents, are met by the chances against it, contained in the number of trials in the life of each individual.

But if by sin we understand not only a loss of perfection,

[1] Mr. Coleridge, in his 'Aids to Reflection,' adopts this *rationale* of original sin, and discusses it with his usual mixture of obscurity and power. *See* NOTE XII.

but positive depravity, certainly the general fact of sin in this sense cannot be accounted for on the mere principle of contingency. Supposing ourselves calculating beforehand the result of the action of freewill in the human race, we should have no more right to calculate on general depravity and wickedness as the result, than on general piety and virtue. Undoubtedly there is this important distinction between vice and virtue, that vice is pleasant, and virtue painful at the time ; and it may be thought perhaps that, in making any calculations beforehand as to the conduct of mankind, we should be justified in expecting that the generality would do what was easiest at the time. But if anyone will examine the real ground on which he forms this expectation, he will find that he forms it upon the experience of the result, and not upon any ground of antecedent calculation. He sees that this is the general way in which mankind act, and, therefore, he imagines himself expecting it beforehand. But it is evident that, in calculating the conduct of mankind beforehand, we should have no more right to calculate on a general preference of present to future interests, than on a general contrary preference. The choice that freewill would make in the matter would be as probable one way as another.

Understanding sin, then, in the sense of depravity and wickedness, the general fact of human sinfulness in this sense certainly requires some law of sin in our nature as its explanation; such a law as is asserted in the doctrine of original sin. But while such a fact must be allowed as a proof of the doctrine of original sin, it must at the same time be remembered, that the assertion of general depravity and wickedness is a very grave assertion to make respecting the human race. It is an assertion, however, which rests on a ground of actual observation and experience, confirmed by the authority of Scripture, and is true in two different ways.

First, every man is depraved in the sense of having vile, selfish, and proud desires, which have a certain power over him, and occupy and fill his mind with sufficient strength and frequency to constitute a depraved condition of mind. A certain tendency to evil is indeed no more than what is necessary to constitute a state of trial, and does not show depravity or corruption in the moral being. But it is evident that evil desire, in the degree in which it exists in human nature, is more than such a tendency as this, and is in itself a disease; inasmuch as men feel it as something sinful in itself, independent of its gratification. Test even the best of men, with this strength of evil desire residing in him, by a perfect standard, and it must be seen that he is a corrupt being, whom we can only think of at all as good by a kind of anticipation, regarding this as a transient condition of mind, of which he is one day to be relieved. In the sense, then, of having concupiscence, which hath of itself the nature of sin, *all* mankind are depraved.

Secondly, the *generality* of mankind are depraved in the sense of actual bad life and conduct; as the former was a fact of inward experience, this latter being a fact of observation. The wickedness of the generality of mankind was acknowledged even by the heathen, and has been generally admitted. It is proved, therefore, in the only way in which a general fact admits of being proved, viz. by large general and consentient observation; observation, moreover, which, when once made, keeps its ground, and meets with comparatively little contradiction. It is, moreover, strongly asserted in Scripture, which refers to it, however, as a known and ascertained fact, rather than professes to reveal it in the first instance. Such being the case, it is evident, even supposing particular persons should say that their own observation had been otherwise, that their individual testimony is no counterbalance to the general observation of mankind. And though the reluctance of all persons to form judgments upon their relations, friends, and acquaintances may be appealed to, as counter-evidence on this subject, it should be remembered that a judgment of charity does not supersede that of observation.

Secondly, the defence of the doctrine of original sin, on the ground of fact, from the objection urged on the score of the Divine justice, appealed straight to the great fact of pain and misery in the world. How was this to be accounted for? It could not be accounted for on the ground of men's actual sins, because it was evidently a part of the present constitution of nature, and in the case of infants preceded actual sin. Anyhow, then, we were in a difficulty with respect to the Divine justice; for if we gave up the doctrine of original sin, there was nothing to account for this fact, and the charge of injustice could be brought against God for an undeserved infliction of pain.[1]

The argument, however, which infers sin from pain, should be used with caution; we do not know enough of the whole scheme of things to decide whether, distinct from judicial grounds, pain may not be necessary simply as a preparation and training for a higher state of existence. That kind of pain which is involved in effort and the overcoming of difficulty we do not naturally regard as at all of necessity judicial; and S. Augustine exceeds the limits of a common sense judgment, when he appeals to the slow and gradual growth of the understanding in man, the imbecility of infancy, and the difficulties which accompany the progress of education, as evidences of the Divine wrath.[2] But pain of the positive and acute kind certainly suggests

[1] S. Augustine, in Op. Imp. l. 1. c. 92., l. 2. c. 89. 104. 116. 124. 139. 144., l. 3. c. 7. 48. 89. 95. 154. 198., l. 5. c. 1., l. 6. c. 7. 9., and *passim*, refers to the general fact of human misery as a proof of original sin: 'Teste ipsa generis humani miseria peccatum originale monstratur.'— L. 3. c. 89. 'Constat mala hujus vitæ quibus plenus est mundus Manichæos cum Catholicis confiteri: sed unde sint hæc non utrosque idem dicere: quod ea Manichæi tribuunt alienæ naturæ malæ, Catholici vero et bonæ et nostræ; sed peccato vitiatæ, meritoque punitæ.'—L. 6. c. 14. 'Si parvuli sine ullius peccati merito premuntur gravi jugo, iniquus est Deus.'—L. 2. c. 124. 'Si ergo nulum esset in parvulis ex origine meritum malum, quicquid mali patiuntur esset injustum.'—L. 3. c. 204.

[2] 'Sed illi parvuli nec flerent in paradiso, *nec muti essent, nec aliquando uti ratione non possent*, nec morbis affligerentur, nec a bestiis læderentur . . . . nec surgentes in pueritiam domarentur verberibus, *aut erudirentur laboribus.*'—Op. Imp. l. 3. c. 198. 'Omnibus cogenita est quædam tarditas mentis, qua et hi qui appellantur ingeniosi, non sine aliqua laboris ærumna, vel quascunque artes, vel eas etiam quas liberales nuncupant discunt . . . . Si in paradiso aliquid discereter, quod illi vitæ esset utile scire, sine ullo labore aut dolore id assequeretur beata natura, vel Deo docente vel seipsa. Unde quis non intelligat in hac vita etiam tormenta discentium ad miserias hujus sæculi, quod ex uno in condemnationem propagatum est, pertinere.'—L. 6. c. 9.

a judicial source; nor can we reflect on the dreadful forms of misery and the diseases, bodily and mental, which attach to human nature, without being led instinctively to the idea of some moral evil residing in that nature. It admits perhaps of a doubt, whether the overwhelming nature of present pain, whether as a sight or feeling, does not disorder us as judges on such a question; nor can we say for certain that, supposing ourselves to be looking back from the immense distance of a happy eternity upon the pains of this mortal life, the greatest amount of these might not appear so small in comparison with the happiness which had succeeded them,[1] that they might be regarded, *then*, as a simple preparation for and introduction to futurity, and accounted for on that ground, superseding the judicial one. The common spectacle of human misery, however, has, in fact, impressed the religious portion of the world in all ages, Christian or pagan, in the latter way; and the general feeling of mankind has connected it with some deep though undefined root of sin in the human race.

Thus maintained and defended on the several grounds of the power of the will, the nature of virtue and vice, and the Divine justice, the Catholic doctrine of original sin adopted, as an account of the existence of evil, a middle ground between two extreme theories on either side, which prevailed in the world. According to the Manichean theory, evil was an original substance in nature, coeval with the Divine. It was therefore an ineradicable, unconquerable thing; for though some triumph over the *Gentes tenebrarum* was talked of, a part of the Divine nature was irrevocably polluted in the contest. The practical meaning of this theory was, that the world was a mixture; that good and evil had gone on together in it from all eternity, and would to all eternity continue to do so; that things were what they were, and that there was no altering them;—much the view taken by practical worldly men, who cannot persuade themselves to believe that there is such a thing as

[1] ‘'Εσλῶν γὰρ ὑπὸ χαρμάτων
Πῆμα θνάσκει παλίγκοτον δαμασθὲν

"Οταν Θεοῦ μοῖρα πέμπῃ
'Ανεκὰς ὄλβον ὑψηλόν.'
PINDAR. *Olymp.* 2.

pure good, the whole of experience going so much against it, and therefore virtually disbelieve in Him who is absolute goodness. The other extreme theory was the Pelagian, which accounted for the universal corruption of the world simply upon the ground of each individual's will; and the practical tendency of the Pelagian, as of the Manichean theory, was to carelessness and indifference; attributing too slight a power to sin over the liberty of the will, and so lowering our idea of the nature of sin; as the other gave it too much, and so abandoned us to it. Between these two theories the Church has taken the middle line, denying evil to be original in the universe, but asserting it to be original in our present nature; giving it a voluntary beginning but a necessary continuance, and a descent, when once begun, by a natural law. This mixture and balance of voluntariness and necessity makes up the doctrine of original sin; and the practical impression it leaves, is that of the deep and awful nature, but not the dominance of sin. And thus S. Augustine was enabled, in answer to the Pelagian charge of Manicheanism, to appeal to his doctrine as a safeguard against that system. The facts of the world drove the Manichean into blasphemy and a denial of the Divine omnipotence; but the doctrine of original sin accounted for these facts in a way which saved at once the Divine justice and the Divine power. It attributed evil, moral and physical, to the wilful act of man; thus separating it from the essence of his nature, and dislodging it as a substance in the universe, while it accounted judicially for the pains of this present life.[1]

III. The main arguments of Pelagianism being stated[2], it remains to notice the bearing of this system upon the Catholic doctrines of the Original State of man, the Incarnation, and the Atonement.

1. Scripture represents the original state of man as one of innocence and goodness, and as blessed with a cor-

[1] Op. Imp. l. 3. c. 170—177. 186.; l. 4. c. 2.; l. 5. c. 30. 56.; l. 6. c. 7. 9.
[2] For the mode in which the Pelagian interpreted the texts of Scripture bearing on the doctrine of original sin, see NOTE XIII.

responding happiness. He comes from the hands of his Maker an upright being, and he is placed in the garden of Eden, where he is surrounded with all that can please the senses and satisfy the mind of a creature thus constituted. And revelation is here confirmed by general tradition. The legend of the golden age goes back to a primitive state of our nature, in which it was both good and happy.

Such an original moral disposition of man again involves a certain measure of stability and strength in the formation of it; such a character implies a certain degree of depth, with which it is stamped upon human nature. It may be said that a being is good till he has sinned; and that, consequently, if he is endowed simply with freewill at his creation, he is created a good being. But it may be doubted whether freewill of itself, and prior to its determination to good, can be called goodness[1]: at any rate, the possession of it alone affords no reason for a state of goodness. lasting beyond the first moment of creation; and therefore we are evidently intended to regard man's original state of uprightness as something more than the mere state of freewill. Man's uprightness, however, being this farther state, whatever we may call it; the support and continuance of this state depended upon freewill in a being not yet perfected but on his trial. It thus became an object of attention in Catholic theology to define, under this balance of considerations, with as much accuracy as the subject admitted of, what was the condition of Adam before the fall, in respect of goodness on the one side, and liability to sin on the other.

On the one hand, then, it was determined that Adam could not have concupiscence or lust, *i.e.* the direct inclination to evil; that positive appetite and craving for corrupt pleasure which is now the incentive to sin in our nature; for this would be to make no difference between man unfallen and fallen. There was no positive contrariety as yet between the flesh and the spirit; and the inward struggle, which is now the normal condition of man, was alien to a

[1] An rectus erat non habens voluntatem bonam sed ejus possi- bilitatem?—Op. Imp. 5. 57. *See* NOTE XIV.

nature made harmonious and at peace with itself.[1] On the other hand, Adam must have had a tendency of some kind toward evil, in order to be in a state of trial at all.[2] There remained, then, the conclusion, of an indirect or distant tendency to evil in Adam. A regular and formed virtuous habit of mind, or, as S. Augustine calls it, *a good will*, implanted in him to begin with by God, intervened between him and sin, and stood as a barrier against any strong and disturbing force of temptation. Suppose a tendency to evil in man, with simply freewill to resist it, and that tendency is at once a strong power and force in his nature; but suppose, together with that tendency to evil, and coeval with it, a formed and set habit and disposition of the whole soul to good—suppose, in short (allowing for necessary distinctions), a *character* equal to a virtuous character which it has taken time and effort to acquire, existing in man as the gift of God, at the moment of his creation[3], and it is at once evident that the evil tendency in his nature is at a very great disadvantage; because it starts with a loss of position, and opposes an antedated strength, a created precedence, and an implanted growth of goodness. Evil thus begins its course under a righteous oppression, which confines its movements and keeps it at a distance from the centre of human life and feeling; its invitations are faintly heard from the extremities of nature, a solid intervening formation of good intercepting them before they arrive at a forcible and exciting stage; and sin, yet unknown to conscience, accompanies human nature, like a dream, with languid and remote temptations, while good occupies the active and waking man. Such a state may be partially understood from the ordinary case of any one who has acquired virtuous habits of any kind. These habits do not

---

[1] 'Hæc discordia carnis et spiritus in paradiso, si nemo peccasset, absit ut esse potuerit.'—Op. Imp. l. 4. c. 37.

[2] 'Quasi non potuerit Deus hominem facere voluntatis bonæ, in qua eum tamen permanere non cogeret sed in ejus esset arbitrio sive in ea semper esse vellet, sive non semper, sed ex illa se in malam nullo cogente mutaret, sicut et factum est.'—Op. Imp. l. 5. c. 61.

[3] 'Illa itaque perfectio naturæ quam non dabant anni sed sola manus Dei, non potuit nisi habere voluntatem aliquam, eamque non malam.'—Op. Imp. l. 5. c. 61.

exclude a man from trial, for, however firmly rooted, they have still to be sustained by the effort of the will. Still, in the case of confirmed virtuous habits, this effort is an easy and unconscious one, not anxious or laborious; the person, though not out of the reach of evil, is separated at a considerable interval from it, and, under the safeguard of his habit, a serene precaution has to defend him from distant danger, rather than positive fear from a near and immediate one. In the same way, only more perfectly than in any case of habit of which we have experience, the first man was protected from sin by an implanted holy disposition of mind, and habitual inclination to good imparted to him at his creation. His trial lay in having to sustain a divinely bestowed defence against sin, rather than engage in direct conflict with it; and a tranquil precaution, not inconsistent with the happiness of paradise, against a remote issue on the side of evil, had it been adequately maintained, would have effectually preserved him.[1] He had by his created disposition a pleasure in goodness; and that pleasure naturally preserved him in obedience without the need of express effort. But though thus held to obedience by the persuasive tie of an adequate pleasure and delight, man was not without an indefinite principle of desire in his nature, which tended to pass beyond the bounds of present happiness in quest of more. Thus, in common life, persons happy after a human measure in their present situation and resources, still carry about with them a general sense of a capacity for greater happiness, which is without much difficulty kept under and controlled, by the mind simply sustaining a proper estimate of the resources in its possession and applying a just attention to the enjoyment of them; but which may be allowed to expand unduly, till it impels the man to a trial of new and dangerous sources of pleasure. Happy within the limits of obedience, Adam was still not out of the reach of a remote class of invitations to advance beyond the precincts of a sacred sufficiency and make trial of the unknown. But the happiness with

[1] 'Pœnæ illius devitandæ quæ fuerat secutura peccatum, tranquilla erat cautio non turbulenta formido.'—Op. Imp. l. 6. c. 14.

which God had connected his duty could have easily, with the aid of an unpainful caution of his own, mastered the temptation.[1] Thus, in some calm interval, produced by sight or sound, or by some cheering or tranquillising news, or arising in the mind he knows not how, a man enjoys, amid the business, anxiety, and turmoil of the world, a brief repose and happiness within; which does not, however, while it removes to the distant horizon for the time the evils and the pains of life, altogether put them out of sight. Behind him are the sorrows and misfortunes of the past, before him those of the future. He is not unconscious of either; but they yield to the reign of the present hour, which disables and unsubstantiates, though it does not suppress them. The fulness of present peace occupies the mind, excluding the power of realising anything which is not in harmony with it; and evil is only seen as a distant shadow, hovering on the outside of things, a feeble and inert phantom belonging to another world than our own, which cannot come near enough to hurt, or penetrate within the sphere of solid things. So, from some inland scene is heard the distant roar of the sea, or from some quiet country spot the noise of the neighbouring city; the sounds are heard, but they affect the mind altogether differently than if they were near. They do not overwhelm or distract, but rather mingle with the serenity of the scene before us.

This implanted rectitude or good habit it was which made the first sin of man so heinous, and caused that distinction between it and all the other sins which have been committed in the world. For the first sin was the only sin which was committed against and in spite of a settled bias of nature toward good; all the sins which have been committed since have been committed in accordance with a natural bias toward evil. There was therefore a perversity in the first sin altogether peculiar to it, and such as made it a sin *sui generis*. S. Augustine is accordingly exact in

[1] 'Bonæ igitur voluntatis factus est homo, paratus ad obediendum Deo, et præceptum obedienter accipiens, quod sine ulla quamdiu vellet difficultate servaret.'—Op. Imp. l. 5. c. 61.

distinguishing the motive to the first sin as being *a depraved will* as contrasted with concupiscence or lust; by a depraved will meaning a perverse opposition to the good will established in the first man, a voluntary abandonment of the high ground on which he stood by nature, a violation of his own created inclination to good.[1] A kind of horror attaches to the falls of saints, when those who have maintained a high and consistent course of holiness commit some deep sin. Such sins are like unaccountable convulsions in nature, and our moral instincts immediately draw a distinction between them and common sins. The peculiarity, however, of the sin of Adam, exceeded that of any sin of fallen man, in that it was the sin of man unfallen.

It may be added, that such an inspired good habit or disposition of man as first created is part of the tradition of the golden age. A certain disposition is described in that legend as being that of the whole human race at the commencement of its existence—an original moral formation, like the creation of the race itself,—and it is described as continuing some time;—a disposition involving general goodness and uprightness, love, gentleness, serenity, content. So suitable has it seemed even to the unenlightened human mind that the morning of a world of moral beings should arise in light and purity,—that the creation fresh from the Divine hands should shine with the reflection of the Divine goodness, and bear the stamp of a proximity to God,—that the will of man as first created should not be neutral or indeterminate, but disposed to good. Nor have the definitions of Catholic theology, however elaborate and subtle in form, diverged in substance from the ground of general tradition and natural ideas.

Scripture and common tradition thus assert a paradisal life as the original state of man. But the Pelagian, in denying the fall, rejected Paradise; as he would not admit

[1] 'Præcessit mala voluntas, et secuta est mala concupiscentia . . . Voluntas cupiditatem, non cupiditas voluntatem duxit.'—Op. Imp. l. 1. c. 71. 'Voluntatem ejus prius fuisse vitiatem venenosa persuasione serpentis, ut oriretur cupiditas quæ sequeretur potius voluntatem quam resisteret voluntati.'—Ibid. l. 6. c. 14.

original sin, he could fall back on no antecedent state of innocence. He robbed human nature of the glory, the freshness, and the beauty of its first creation, reduced the primitive to the level of all that succeeded it, and fixed the present facts of the world as the standard of our nature. He made this existing state of sin and pain coeval with the commencement of things; and S. Augustine taunted his opponents with the 'Pelagian Paradise.'[1] Human nature in the midst of trials looks back with consolation to the paradisal state as a sign that pain is the accident and happiness the law of our being; and were the rest of the Old Testament silent, a future state was still preached to the Jew in the first chapter of Genesis; but the Pelagian cut off both the retrospect and the pledge. The paradisal age was to him nothing more than the first age of the world, when science, art, and the refinements of life had not yet arisen, and man was simpler than he was afterwards, only because he was more rude. He took the same view of it that a human philosopher would take who pictures to himself the primitive state of man simply as a state anterior to civilisation[2], and contrasts it with the law, system, and social growth of a more advanced age.

And, together with the paradisal life in general, the created goodness of the first man fell to the ground. The idea of created virtue jarred with the Pelagian theory of freewill, according to which virtue was no virtue at all, unless a man acquired it for himself. An original gift of righteousness was thus dismissed as a contradiction, and

---

[1] 'Naturam humanam a Deo bono conditam bonam magno inobedientiæ peccato fuisse vitiatam, Catholica fides dicit. Sed vos qui hoc negatis, quæso, paulisper Paradisum cogitate. Placetne vobis ut ponamus . . . innumerabiles morbos, orbitates, luctus, etc. Certe si talis paradisus pingeretur nullus diceret esse paradisum, nec si supra legisset hoc nomen conscriptum: nec diceret erasse pectorem, sed plane agnosceret irrisorem. Veruntamen eorum qui nos noverunt, nemo miraretur, si adderetur nomen vestrum ad titulum, et scriberetur. *Paradisus Pelagianorum.*'—Op. Imp. l. 3. c. 154. Vide l. 3. c. 95. 147.; l. 6. c. 25. 27. 28.

[2] 'Homines fuisse primitus nudos, quia ad solertiæ humanæ operam ut se tegerent pertinebat, quæ nondum in illis fuit.'—Contra Jul. Pel. l. 4. n. 81.

Adam at his creation was considered to be in the same condition as every other man that has been born, and to have had the same struggle of the flesh and spirit.[1]

2. The Pelagian doctrine had an important bearing on the doctrine of the Incarnation, in regard to the manner in which our Lord was, according to that economy, subject to temptation and trial, and exposed to the approaches of sin. Scripture says that our Lord was in all points tempted like as we are. But the Church has not considered it consistent with piety to interpret this text to mean that our Lord had the same direct propension to sin that we have, or that which is called by divines concupiscence.[2] Such direct appetite for what is sinful is the characteristic of our fallen and corrupt nature; and our Lord did not assume a corrupt, but a sound humanity. Indeed, concupiscence, even prior to and independent of its gratification, has of itself the nature of sin[3]; and, therefore, could not belong to a perfect Being. Our Lord had all the passions and affections that legitimately belong to man; which passions and affections, tending as they do in their own nature to become inordinate, constituted of themselves a state of trial; but the Church has regarded our Lord's trial in the flesh as consisting in preserving ordinate affections from becoming inordinate, rather than in restraining desire proximate to sin from gratification. So mysterious a subject precludes

---

[1] 'Quod miserrimum bellum introducere conaris in illius beatissimæ pacis et libertatis locum.'—Op. Imp. l. 5. c. 8. 'Nos autem dicimus tam beatum fuisse illum hominem ante peccatum, tamque liberæ voluntatis, ut Dei præceptum magnis viribus mentis observans, resistentem sibi carnem nullo certamine pateretur, nec aliquid omnino ex aliqua cupiditate sentiret, quod nollet.'—L. 6. c. 14. 'Addo ad bonitatem conditionis Adæ quod in eo caro adversus spiritum non concupiscebat ante peccatum: tu autem qui talem dicis carnis concupiscentiam qualis nunc est, in paradiso futuram esse, si nemo peccasset, talemque in illo fuisse et priusquam peccaret; addis ejus conditioni et istam miseriam per carnis spiritusque discordiam.'—C. 16.

[2] 'Christus ergo nulla illicita concupivit, quia discordiam carnis et spiritus, quæ in hominis naturam ex prævaricatione primi hominis vertit, prorsus ille non habuit, qui de Spiritu et Virgine non per concupiscentiam carnis est natus.'—Op. Imp. l. 4. c. 57.

[3] Malum esse quamvis mente non consentiente, vel carne tamen talia concupiscere.—Op. Imp. l. 5. c. 59.

all exactness of definition; yet the Church expressed a substantial truth of morals, as well as one of faith and piety, when she guarded the person of our Lord from the too near approaches of sin. Desire discloses, on a nearer examination, different moral complexions, and at a certain stage is seen to be no longer a neutral thing. Our Lord, therefore, had not the whole of desire assigned to Him, but only that earlier stage of it which is consistent with a sound nature; and, together with a true trial, a true sinlessness was provided for.

But S. Augustine had to contest this whole question with the Pelagian in the instance of our Lord, as he had contested it before in the instance of Adam. The Pelagian who attached concupiscence to man in Paradise, saw no reason against attaching it to the humanity assumed by our Lord. Intent on effort exclusively as the test of goodness, he argued that it was this very strength of desire which constituted the force of trial; and that, therefore, the great merit of our Lord's obedience was destroyed by supposing Him to have been without it.[1] Moreover, He was our Model, as having been subjected to the same trials; but if His desires were weaker than ours, His temptation had been less, and the force of His example was less with it.[2] But, it was replied, that a state of mind which kept off the approach of sin was a higher one than that which resisted it near; that the merit of our Lord's obedience

---

[1] Julian: 'Non qui virtute judicii delicta vitasset; sed qui felicitate carnis a nostris sensibus sequestratæ, cupiditatem vitiorum sentire nequivisset.' Augustine objects to this mode of stating the Catholic position. 'Sensisset enim si habuisset; non enim sensus ei defuit quo eam sentiret, sed voluntas adfuit qua non haberet.'—Op. Imp. l. 4. c. 48. And he observes that if, according to Julian's argument, the merit of virtue lay in conquest, it would follow that where the virtue was greatest, the passions must be strongest; which would lead to a blasphemous conclusion in the case of our Lord. 'Ecce quod Christo conaris importare insane. . . . . . Tanto quippe in eo continentia spiritus major est, quanto majorem carnis concupiscentiam coerceret.'—C. 52.

[2] 'Nunquam commemorationem fecisset exempli: quem enim hominibus ostenderet imitandum, si illum externæ carnis natura discrevisset. . . Quanto ei rectius diceret ægritudo peccantium et securitas coactorum; "cum valemus omnes recta consilia præbemus ægrotis; tu si sic esses, aliter longe longeque sentires."'—Op. Imp. l. 4. c. 86, 87.

was the perfect one of a triumphantly sustained distance from evil[1]; and that the force of example did not depend on the identity of trial, but on the goodness of the example itself, as was evident from the injunction in Scripture to imitate God.[2] It must, indeed, be remarked, on this reply, that Scripture rests the force of our Lord's example expressly on the ground that His trial was like our own. The Pelagian, therefore, was right in insisting on this similarity. But he proceeded to argue from it upon the principles of ordinary logic, and his conclusion degraded our Lord's humanity, and endangered that balance of truths on which the doctrine of the Incarnation rested. The doctrine of our Lord's Divinity modifies the truths connected with His humanity in this way, that He who was both God and man cannot be thought of even as man exactly the same as if He were not God. And the truth of our Lord's trial and temptation, among others, is in this sense a modified one. To carry out, therefore, the conception of a human trial to the full in the instance of our Lord, without respect to other truth, was to trench on his Divinity. To the idea of trial, and of example on the ground of trial, pursued exclusively, the next idea is that of peccability, and the next that of simple manhood. It was consistent with such ten-

---

[1] 'Dicimus eum perfectione carnis, et non per carnis concupiscentiam procreata carne, cupiditatem non habuisse vitiorum. . . . Illius virtus hæc erat eam non habere ; nostra virtus est ei non consentire.' —Op. Imp. l. 4. c. 48. 'Sic igitur Christus abstinuit a peccato, ut abstineret etiam ab omni cupiditate peccati : non ut ei existenti resisteret, sed ut illa nunquam prorsus existeret.'—C. 58.

[2] 'Neque negare debemus ejus excellentiam, neque propter hanc excellentiam nos excusare, ut non eum pro modo nostro studeamus imitari.'—Op. Imp. l. 4. c. 89.

'Quid enim, homo multum loquens et parum sapiens, si dicerent homines Christo, Quare nobis jubetur ut imitemur te ? Nunquid nos de Spiritu Sancto et Virgine Maria nati sumus ? Postremo nunquid tanta nobis esse virtus potest quanta, tibi est, qui ita homo es, ut etiam Deus sis ? Ideone non debuit sic nasci ut hominibus eum nolentibus imitari talis excusatio daretur ? Sicut nobis ipse Patrem proposuit imitandum, qui certe homo fuit. . . . . Nec dicunt ei, Tu propterea hoc potes quia Deus es. . . Non itaque ideo debuit natus de Spiritu Sancto et Virgine Maria habere concupiscentiam, qua cuperet mala, etsi ei resistendo non faceret, ne dicerent ei homines, Habeto prius cupiditates malas, et eas vince, si potes, ut te imitari nostras vincendo possimus.'—Op. Imp. l. 4. c. 87.

dencies in Pelagianism that our Lord did not stand forth as the one sole example of perfect obedience in that system; but only one, though the principal one, of a succession of perfect men that had appeared in the world—extending from Abel and Enoch to Simeon and Joseph, the husband of Mary.[1] An extreme idea of freewill and human perfectibility was in truth inconsistent with a sound doctrine of the Incarnation, not admitting of such a singularity in our Lord's life and character as that doctrine involved.

The Pelagian, indeed, in retaliation for the charge of degrading our Lord's humanity, charged his opponents with unsubstantiating it, and threw back upon them the name of Apollinarists, as, with a difference of temptation, not assigning to our Lord the same humanity which other men have, and so denying His true assumption of our nature. But it was replied that our Lord took on Him the nature, but not the sin of man. He even charged his opponents with Manicheanism, as denying that Christ had assumed our flesh; but the same answer was made, that the flesh was assumed, but not the corruption. He discovered, again, in the Catholic representation of our Lord's trial in the flesh, a combination of both heresies modified—a semi-Apollinarism in a soul imperfectly connected with the flesh, a semi-Manicheanism in a flesh imperfectly connected with the soul of our Lord. But it was replied, as before, that the soul of Christ had perfect connection with the flesh, but not with its corruption.[2]

---

[1] De Natura et Gratia, n. 42.
'Incarnatio Christi justitiæ fuit forma non prima sed maxima, quia et antequam Verbum caro fieret, et in Prophetis et in multis aliis sanctis fulsere virtutes.'—Op. Imp. l. 2. c. 188.

[2] Julian: 'Hic igitur ut adsit toto animo lector admoneo: videbit enim Apollinaristarum hæresim, sed eam Manichæi per te adjectione reparari. Apollinaris primo talem incarnationem, Christi induxisse fertur, ut diceret solum corpus de humana substantia assumptum videri, pro anima vero ipsam fuisse deitatem. Quod posteaquam cœpit tam rationis quam evangelii attestatione convelli . . excogitavit aliud unde ejus hæresis, quæ perdurat hactenus, nasceretur; et dixit animam quidem humanam in Christo fuisse sed sensus in eo corporis non fuisse, atque impassibilem eum pronuntiavit universis extitisse peccatis.'—Op, Imp. l. 4. c. 47.

'Certe hanc vim in disputando Apostolus non haberet si secundum Manichæos et eorum discipulos Traducianos, carnem Christi a na-

## 3. The Pelagian Controversy.

**3.** Pelagianism was fundamentally opposed to the doctrine of the atonement; for no atonement was wanted if there had been no fall. And this was the chief obstacle between the Pelagian and a sound doctrine of the Incarnation. The design of the Incarnation was to remedy the effects of the fall; apart from which object, it could only be held as an isolated fact, and, without place or significancy, had no root in the system.

The Pelagian, however, in superseding the atonement fundamentally, retained some scattered fragments of the doctrine. The relation of Christ, as Redeemer, to the whole race of man, was abandoned in that doctrine of freewill which represented all men as able to fulfil, and some as having fulfilled, the whole law, without any other aids than such as were attached to the system of nature. This position was a contradiction to a universal atonement. But though the Pelagians did not regard the assisting grace, which that event procured, as necessary for everybody, or the pardoning grace as wanted by all, they attached an advantage and benefit to the one, and maintained a general need of the other. The grace of which Christ was the source rendered the fulfilment of the law, though possible without it, easier, and was a valuable, though not a necessary assistance; while the great mass of mankind stood in need of the atonement for the pardon of actual, though not of original sin. But the force of the Christian atonement lies in its interest to mankind as one corporate whole, and that interest being one of absolute need. To deny the universal necessity of the atonement, therefore, was to give up the doctrine. As advantageous to any, essential to some, the grace of Christ was a Pelagian fiction, accommodated to a theory opposed to it, and maintained as a

turæ nostræ communione distingueret.'—Op. Imp. l. 6. c. 33.

Augustine, in reply, distinguishes between the Apollinarist statement, *Christum non habuisse corporis sensus*, and his own, that those senses *non contra Spiritum concupisse* (l. 4. c. 47.); and as against the Manicheans, he says, 'Manichæi non sunt, qui carnem Christi a naturæ nostræ communione distinguunt, sed qui nullam carnem Christum habuisse contendunt. . . . Dimitte illos . . . quia nobiscum carnem Christi etsi dissimiliter confiteris. Nec nos enim eam a naturæ atque substantiæ carnis nostræ, sed a vitii communione distinguimus.'—Op. Imp. l. 6. c. 33.

feeble show of orthodoxy. The separation of renovating from pardoning grace, again, was a blow at the integrity of Gospel grace. Pardoning grace was necessary for any one who had sinned, because the sin was a past fact which could not be undone; but the renovating or assisting grace of Christ was not necessary, however advantageous to him, because the future sin could be avoided by nature alone. These two graces go together in the Divine scheme, and belong to the same act of the Divine mercy.

Out of one extreme statement at the commencement, Pelagianism thus expanded into a large body of thought, incomplete indeed, but having one general stamp, and developing more and more, as it came out, the original difference from Catholic truth; passing from the human will to higher mysteries, and upon the basis of exalted nature threatening the truth of the Incarnation.

The philosophical fault of Pelagianism was, that it went upon ideas without considering facts—in the case both of freewill and the Divine justice. The abstract idea of freewill is that of a power to do anything that it is physically possible for us to do. As man had freewill, then, the Pelagian argued that he had this power; and that any man, therefore, could fulfil the whole law and be perfect. But what we have to consider in this question, is not what is the abstract idea of freewill, but what is the freewill which we really and actually have. This actual freewill, we find, is not a simple but a complex thing; exhibiting oppositions and inconsistencies; appearing on the one side to be a power of doing anything to which there is no physical hindrance, on the other side to be a restricted faculty. It is that will which S. Paul describes, when, appealing to the facts of human nature (the account of which, as referred to the sin of Adam, is a matter of faith, but which are themselves matters of experience), he describes a state of divided consciousness, and a sense of power and weakness. But the Pelagian did not possess himself properly of the facts of human nature, and, committing the same fault in morals that the mediæval philosophers did in science, he argued upon an abstract idea, instead of examining what the faculty, as we experienced it, really is; and an absolute freewill, which was a simple conception of the mind, displaced the incomprehensible actual will, the enigma of human nature, the mystery of fact.

The Pelagian's argument respecting the Divine justice proceeded in the same way upon an idea without considering facts. It was founded indeed upon the true natural idea of justice in our minds; and so far no fault is to be found with it. Nor was this a mere abstract idea. But he did not take into consideration with it the facts of the existing constitution of things. We find a severe law of suffering in operation in this world previous to the existence of the individual; which law, therefore, can hardly be said to be, in a *comprehensible* sense, a just one. Our moral nature, then, and the existing constitution of things, being at variance on the question of the Divine justice, we arrive at the conclusion that the Divine justice is incomprehensible. But the Pelagian attended simply to the idea of justice in his own mind, and ignored the facts on the other side. The doctrine of original sin, then, which is in truth nothing but an *account*, though a revealed one, of these facts, was not wanted by him. He did not attend to the difficulty, and therefore wanted no solution. This doctrine was therefore, in his eyes, a mere gratuitous theory, which needlessly and wantonly contradicted the truth of the Divine justice.

But the primary fault of Pelagianism was the sin against piety contained in its fundamental assertion, as explained at the commencement of this chapter, of an ultimate movement of the natural will to good, unassisted by God. However logical a result of the admission of the freedom of the will, the absolute assertion of this position was false, because its premiss was an imperfect one; and it was contrary to piety, the religious mind feeling an insurmountable check and prohibition against calling any good movement purely its own, and appropriating it to the exclusion of God. But the Pelagian ventured on this act of appropriation.

Raised upon a basis thus philosophically and religiously

at fault, Pelagianism was first an artificial system, and next of a low moral tendency.

It wanted reality, and was artificial in assigning to man what was opposed to his consciousness and to what he felt to be the truth about himself. The absolute power of man to act without sin and be morally perfect was evidently a fiction, based on an abstract idea and not on the experienced faculty of freewill. And when he followed with a list of men who had actually been perfect moral beings, Abel, Enoch, Melchisedek, and others, he simply trifled; and showed how fantastic, absurd, and unsubstantial his position was. Human nature is too seriously alive to the law of sin under which it at present acts, not to feel the mockery of such assertions.

The system, again, had a low moral tendency. First, it dulled the sense of sin. Prior to and independent of action there exists a state of desire which the refined conscience mourns over; but which is part of the existing nature as distinguished from being the choice of the man. Hence the true sense in which the saints have ever grieved, not only over their acts, but over their nature: for, however incomprehensible, they have felt something to be sinful within them which was yet coeval with them. But the Pelagian, not admitting any sin but that of direct choice, would not see in concupiscence anything but a legitimate desire, which might be abused, but was in itself innocent. In disallowing the mystery of evil he thus impaired his perception of it; he only saw nature in that to which the acute conscience attached sin[1]; and gave him-

[1] 'Naturalem esse omnium sensuum voluptatem, testimonio universitatis docemus ... Concupiscentia cum intra limitem concessorum tenetur affectio naturalis et innocuus est.'—Op. Imp. l. 1. c. 71.

The particular difficulty attaching to concupiscence as sin, and yet unavoidable, Julian exposes with logical acuteness, which does not, however, still answer the real argument upon which this sort of sin rests, which is that of inward feeling and conscience. 'Quod vero posuisti, legem quidem peccati esse in membris nostris, sed tunc habere peccatum quando consentimus; tunc vero solum prœlium suscitare quando non consentimus, et indicere miseriam pace turbata; quis non prudens pugnare perspiciat? Nam si lex peccati, id est, peccatum, et necessitas peccati membris est inserta naturaliter, quid prodest non ei præbere consensum, cum propter hoc ipsum quod est, necesse sit

self credit for a sound and practical standard of morals, as opposed to a morbid and too sensitive one. The doctrine of perfectibility encouraged the same tendency in the system, demanding a lower moral standard for its verification.

And the same narrowness of moral basis which dulled the sense of sin, depressed the standard of virtue. The Pelagian denied virtue as an inspiration and gift of God, confining his idea of it entirely to human effort and direct choice. But the former conception of the source of virtue was necessary to a high standard of virtue itself. If we are to rely on what general feeling and practical experience say on this subject, virtue needs for its own support the religious *rationale*, *i.e.* the idea of itself as something imparted. There must be that image and representation of it in men's minds, which present it less as a human work than as an impulse from above, possessing itself of the man he knows not how; a holy passion, and a spark kindled from the heavenly fire. It is this conception of it as an inspiration that has excited the sacred ambition of the human mind, which longs for union with God, or a participation of the Divine life, and sees in this inspiration this union. Virtue has thus risen from a social and civil to a sublime and intrinsic standard, and presented itself as that which raised man above the world, and not simply moulded and trained him for it. This conception has accordingly approved itself to the great poets of the world, who have in their ideal of man greatly leaned to the inspired kind of virtue. So congenial to the better instincts even of the unenlightened human mind is the Christian doctrine of grace, while, disconnected with this ennobling conception, morality has sunk down to a political and secular level. Nor is there any justice surer than that by which the self-sufficient will is punished by the exposure of its own feebleness, and rejected grace avenged in a barren and impoverished form of virtue. Those schools

subire supplicium? Aut si est lex quidem peccati, sed quando ei non consentio non pecco, inestimabilis potentia voluntatis humanæ, quæ (si dici permittat absurditas) cogit ipsum non peccare peccatum.'—Op. Imp. l. 1. c. 71.

that have seen in the doctrine of grace only an unsound enthusiasm, and have aimed at fortifying the ground of morals by releasing it from this connection, have not improved their moral standard, but greatly lowered and relaxed it. With a dulled sense of sin, a depressed standard of virtue, Pelagianism thus tended to the moral tone of Socinianism, and the religion which denies the Incarnation. The asceticism of its first promulgators and disciples could not neutralize the tendencies of a system opposed to mystery and to grace, and therefore hostile at once to the doctrinal and the moral standard of Christianity.

The triumphant overthrow of such a school was the service which S. Augustine performed to the Church, and for which, under God, we still owe him gratitude. With all the excess to which he pushed the truth which he defended, he defended a vital truth, without which Christianity must have sunk to an inferior religion, against a strong and formidable attack. He sustained that idea of virtue as an inspiration to which the lofty thought of even heathen times ever clung, which the Gospel formally expressed in the doctrine of grace, and which is necessary to uphold the attributes of God and the moral standard of man.

## CHAPTER IV.

### DIFFERENT INTERPRETATIONS OF ORIGINAL SIN.

THE doctrine of the fall of man has been always held as a fundamental doctrine in the Church; and all Catholic writers have witnessed to the truth, that the first man came from the hands of God an upright creature, that he fell from that uprightness by voluntary transgression, and that he involved in his fall the whole of his posterity. But the different ways in which this doctrine has been held involve a discussion of some length and difficulty, to which I shall devote this chapter.

The language in which the primitive Church expresses this doctrine distinctly asserts two things. The early fathers, in the first place, clearly held that the sin of Adam did not stop with itself; they speak of the race and not of the individual only, with reference to it; and the universal terms of 'man,' 'mankind,' 'the soul,' leave no doubt as to their belief that human nature was in some way or other affected by that sin.[1] Secondly, when we examine what this universal consequence was, we find that it is called apostacy, captivity, corruption, and death.[2] These are metaphorical expressions, indeed, and convey no precise and accurate meaning, but they plainly signify something more than a privation of higher good, and something more than a mere tendency to positive evil. This tendency existed before the fall, and no mere increase of it could have brought it up to the natural meaning of these terms; which must therefore be taken to signify positive moral evil, and to indicate, as the doctrine of the early fathers, the positive sinfulness of the whole human race in consequence of the sin of Adam, that is to say, the doctrine of original sin.

But as Scripture reveals this consequence of the sin of Adam, so natural reason certifies, on the other hand, that nobody can sin but by his own personal act, and that one

---

[1] Justin Martyr: Τὸ γένος τῶν ἀνθρώπων ὁ ἀπὸ τοῦ Ἀδὰμ ὑπὸ θάνατον καὶ πλάνην τὴν τοῦ ὄφιος ἐπεπτώκει.—Dial. cum Tryph. c. 88.

Irenæus: Hominem (the *race*) absorberi magno ceto.—Adv. Hær. 3. 22.

Tatian: πτέρωσις γὰρ τῆς ψυχῆς τὸ πνεῦμα τὸ τέλειον, ὅπερ ἀπορρίψασα διὰ τὴν ἁμαρτίαν ἔπτη ὥσπερ νεοσσὸς, καὶ χαμαιπετὴς ἐγένετο.—Ad Græc. c. 20.

Athanasius: Ἡ ψυχὴ ἀποστᾶσα τῆς πρὸς τὰ καλὰ θεωρίας.—Contra Gentes, 4.

Basil: Ἐκακώθη ἡ ψυχὴ παρατραπεῖσα τοῦ κατὰ φύσιν.—Hom. Deus non Auctor Mali, s. 6.

Of the same generic sort are the expressions, ἡ πρώτη γένεσις (Justin. Apol. l. 61.), ἡ παλαιὰ γένεσις (Tatian, contra Græc. c. 11.).

[2] Dominabatur nobis *apostasia*.— Irenæus, Adv. Hær. 5. 1.

Quos in eadem *captivitate* (Adam) generavit.—3. 34.

Per priorem generationem *mortem* hæreditavimus.—5. 1.

*Vitium* originis. Naturæ *corruptio*.—Tertullian, De Anima, c. 41.

Nativitatis sordes.—Origen, Hom. 14. in Luc.

man's guilt cannot be transferred to another. This truth of natural reason mingled intimately in the statements of the early fathers with the truth of revelation; so intimately indeed, that often no definite meaning can be extracted from them. Two opposite truths are expressed together, and side by side.[1] The consequence is, that persons accustomed to the later theological statements of this doctrine have been often dissatisfied, when they have gone to examine the earlier one, and have set down the writers as not full believers in it. But the truth is, such mixed and double statements more faithfully express the truth than single-sided ones drawn out in either direction would, because they express the whole truth, and not a part of it. What appears to be ambiguity is comprehensiveness, and is a merit and perfection, and not a defect. Nor, on the same grounds on which the early fathers are charged with a disbelief in this doctrine, could Scripture itself be acquitted.

But it was not in accordance with the nature of the human mind to allow these great truths respecting the moral condition of man to go on thus mixed and united. Theology began soon to draw out each separately; and this mixture parted into two great doctrinal views or schemes, of which the earlier took the side of the natural truth, the later of the revealed. The earlier fathers, without negativing their witness to the true doctrine of original sin as expressed in Scripture, and handed down in the Church, wrote as theologians with a strong bias in favour of the natural truth; and gave it, in their scheme of philosophy and doctrine, a disproportionate expansion. Instead of leaving the truth of revelation in its original mystery and contradiction to human reason, as individual thinkers they modified and limited it, so as to be consistent with reason; while a later school went to the other extreme, and developed the revealed truth at the expense of the natural.

But an account of the doctrine of the fall will require

[1] NOTE XV.

as an introduction some account of the state from which this was a fall, *i.e.* of man's original righteousness.

The original righteousness of man, then, is universally described in ancient writers as partly natural, partly supernatural. It was natural in this respect, that it proceeded from the exercise of a natural freewill and power of choice. It was supernatural in this respect, that certain supernatural gifts, in addition to freewill, were required for it. These gifts could not produce righteousness unless his natural will first consented to use them; nor could his will, however sound, without the inspiring assistance of these gifts; and grace was necessary for the righteousness of man upright as well as of man fallen.

Such a doctrine, however, requires some explanation with respect to two points. First, how could it be maintained with a consistent meaning that supernatural assistance was necessary towards fulfilling the Divine precepts, if man had naturally freewill? For we mean by freewill, it may be said, the power, supposing the opportunity, of doing or abstaining from any actions whatever; and therefore, whatever impulse and facility might be given to right action by supernatural assistance, the *power* to act would not depend upon it. But to this objection it may be replied that, however we may define freewill in words as such a power, we do not mean that it is such a power abstracted from all stimulus or motive supplied to our nature from other quarters. Thus, in the sphere of common life, a man with freewill has the power to do his duty to his parents, relations, and friends; but he has not this power independently of certain affections implanted in his nature over and above his will. Such questions as these cannot be treated satisfactorily, on account of the great defects and obscurity both in our conceptions of our own nature and the language in which we express them. But, upon the most correct idea we can form of what the will is, and what the affections are, it would seem that neither of them could, without the other, enable us to fulfil our duties in common life. The benevolent affections incline us indeed to benevolent acts; but, unless supported by the will, they yield to selfish considerations, and produce no fruits. The will, in like manner, does not enable us to perform laborious services in our neighbour's behalf without the stimulus of the affections. Nor, did it even enable us to perform the external acts, could it therefore enable us to perform our whole duty; such duty involving something of love and affection in the very performance of it.

There is, then, something defective in the will as a source of action; and this defect existed in the will of the first man, however sound and perfect that will might be; because it is a defect inherent in the will itself, and not attaching to it as a weak and corrupted will only. As therefore, for fulfilling the relations of common life we require the help of certain natural gifts, such as the natural affections plainly are, being received from God at our creation; in the same way the first man, to enable him to perform the spiritual relations assigned to him, required the aid of certain gifts supernatural, or such gifts as come under the head of grace.

But, in the second place, granting that these gifts were necessary for the first man, it may still be asked, why call them supernatural? They were not supernatural as being Divine gifts; for in that case our natural affections would be supernatural gifts. Nor were they supernatural as being additions to his created state; though, had they been, they would not have been supernatural, because they were thus additional. Is not this, then, it may be asked, an arbitrary distinction? How can the nature of a man be defined but as that assemblage of faculties and affections, higher or lower, with which God endows him? and how can we therefore, out of this whole assemblage, single out some as natural, others as supernatural?

In answer to this objection, it may be enough to say, that when the fathers speak of these gifts as supernatural, they do not seem to mean that they were above human nature itself, that nature being whatever it might please God by His various gifts to make it, but above human nature as adapted to that order of things in which it is at present placed—this visible order of things or the world.

A world is below or on a level with any set of affections, according as it manifests or does not manifest the final objects of them. The world in which we are manifests or presents to our sight the final object of the social affections, viz. man; this world, therefore, is not below, but on a level with the social affections. But the final object of the spiritual affections is not man, but God; and this world, though it proves to the understanding the existence of, does not manifest or present to our sight, God. This world is, therefore, below the spiritual affections; *i.e.* the spiritual affections are above this world. The heavenly world cannot be carried on without these; for in heaven is what divines call the *Visio Dei*, the sight of God; and therefore the supreme visible Inhabitant of that world, and omnipresent as He is supreme, would want attention and regard without them. But, though absolutely needing the social affections for its maintenance, this world can be carried on and its affairs conducted without the aid of the spiritual; which, as being more than necessary for its maintenance, are therefore above it; that is to say, are above nature, or supernatural.[1]

Such being the composition of man's original righteousness, the earlier fathers held that the fall deprived him of these supernatural gifts, but left him a fundamentally sound nature, while Augustine maintained, together with the loss of these supernatural gifts, an entire corruption of his nature as the consequence of the fall.

To account for the rise of a particular school of thought is a superfluous task, when all that we are concerned with is the school itself; and a task often more perplexing than

---

[1] Man may be considered in a double order or relation. 1. In relation to the natural, animal, or earthly life. And so he is a perfect man that hath only a reasonable soul and a body adapted thereunto; for the powers and faculties of these are sufficient to the exercise of the functions and operations belonging to such a life. But, 2. Man may be considered in order to a supernatural end, and as designed to a spiritual and celestial life; and of this life the Spirit of God is the principle; for man's natural powers and faculties, even as they were before the fall, entire, were not sufficient of themselves to reach such a supernatural end, but needed the power of the Divine Spirit to strengthen, elevate, and raise them thereunto.—Bull, 'On the State of Man before the Fall,' vol. ii. p. 87.

useful. Some reasons, however, are perhaps discernible in the circumstances of the early Church for the supremacy of a milder interpretation of the doctrine of original sin. The writers of that age were, in the first place, more imbued with gentile thought than those of a later era; and the Church, on its first entrance into the world, was both more dependent on and less suspicious of the world's philosophers. It was more dependent on them, because it was as yet without an established literature of its own; it was less suspicious of them, because it did not stand in so strong an antagonistic relation to the world without, as it subsequently did when that world had been longer tried, and had shown—that portion of it which remained without— greater obstinacy in rejecting the Gospel. Earlier Christianity regarded the gentile world more as a field of promise; and saw in it the future harvest rather than the present foe. Nor is it to be forgotten, that the principal writers of that age themselves, Justin Martyr, Clement of Alexandria, and others, came from the ranks of gentile philosophy, and retained in their conversion the intellectual tastes of their former life. The early Church thus adopted a friendly tone toward gentile philosophy, and acknowledged sympathies with it. But such sympathies could not but raise the estimate of the natural state of man; for they were themselves a tribute of respect to the fruits of human thought and feeling in that state.

Another reason for the milder interpretation of original sin in the early Church was the great prominence then given to the doctrine of the Logos, *i.e.* to the contemplation of our Lord as the wisdom or reason of the Father, and as such the source of wisdom and enlightenment to the human mind;—the aspect in which he is set forth in the opening of St. John's gospel. The early fathers, partly from a peculiar sympathy with it as philosophers,—partly from an acquaintance with the Platonic doctrine of a Logos, which bore some resemblance to and appeared to be a heathen anticipation of the true one,—and partly to fortify a controversial position against the Gnostics, whose boast of a peculiar inward illumination imparted by their philosophy was thus met on its own ground, gave a conspicuous place to this character of our Lord. The result was, without any intention on their part, some loss of pre-eminence to our Lord's office of Victim and Expiator. The doctrine of the Logos divided a theological attention, which was afterward given more wholly to the doctrine of the atonement. And this position of the atonement would naturally affect the position of the doctrine of original sin.

But, whatever were the reasons, an earlier school represented man's nature as continuing fundamentally sound after the fall, and laid down, as the consequence of that event, a state of defect and loss of perfection as distinguished from a state of positive corruption. Man was deprived of impulses which elevated his moral nature; but still that moral nature remained entire and able to produce fruits pleasing in their measure to God. And though it was admitted that all mankind were, as a matter of fact, positive sinners, such positive sin was not regarded as the necessary consequence of original, but referred to the free-will of each individual, who could have avoided it, had he chosen;[1] all that original sin had entailed as of necessity and beyond the power of man to avoid, being a state of defect.[2]

Such an estimate of the effects of the fall, as it was partly produced by, in its turn produced, a more favourable view of the moral condition of that large proportion of

[1] Τὸ αὐθαίρετον τῆς ἀνθρωπίνης ψυχῆς—τὸ αὐτεξούσιόν—τὸ αὐθαίρετον ἀδούλωτον πρὸς ἐκλογὴν βίου — αἵρεσις μεταβολῆς αἰτία — προαίρεσις ἐλεύθερα—τὸ ἐφ' ἡμῖν—ἀφ' ἑαυτοῦ ἑλόμενος τὸ ἀγαθόν — αὐτοκρατής.—These expressions occurring in the early fathers (Justin Martyr, Irenæus, Clement of Alexandria, Athenagoras, Tatian, Cyril) are applied to man fallen as well as unfallen. 'All the Greek fathers,' says Hagenbach, 'maintain the αὐτεξούσιον of the human soul.' The early westerns are no less explicit: Homo vero rationabilis et secundum hoc similis Deo, liber in arbitrio factus et suæ potestatis, ipse sibi causa est, ut aliquando quidem frumentum, aliquando autem palea fiat.—Irenæus, l. 4. c. 9. Id quod erat semper liberum in homine et suæ potestatis.—C. 29. I give below Tertullian's elaborate statement of man's freewill. No distinction, as regards the *will*, appears to have been made between man fallen and unfallen, but man as such is spoken of as having it.

[2] Bull, 'On the State of Man before the Fall,' describes the loss of the *supernatural* gifts as the consequence which the early fathers annexed to the fall.

mankind which had been in no way relieved from them,—
the heathen world. It may be considered doubtful to what
precise extent S. Clement of Alexandria, the earlier schools'
great exponent on this question, represents the sentiments
of the actual early Church at large upon it. He acknowledges in his writings the existence, and answers the objections, of a part of the Church that did not agree with him.[1]
But it is difficult to judge of the size or importance of this
part; and a great writer is in later ages legitimately supposed, in the absence of express evidence to the contrary,
and if tradition has attached authority to his name, to
represent the mind of his age.

Clement of Alexandria, then, on this subject, takes what
may be called the natural view of the facts which meet his
eye. He acknowledges the noble affections, the moral
virtues, even the religious acts, of the heathen as real and
genuine, only as not reaching so high a standard as those
of the Christian. The authority of Scripture is claimed,
and the Apostle is cited as saying that 'the uncircumcision
kept the righteousness of the law.'[2] There was a first purification of the soul, which resulted in abstaining from evil;
a second, which advanced to positive goodness.[3] Attention
is drawn to the moral lessons of heathen poets, to the
labours of lawgivers,[4] to the ascetic fruits of the Buddhist
and Brahman religions,[5] to the worship which Athens igno-
rantly paid to the true God.

But the philosophy of the heathen, as the highest effort
of their moral as well as intellectual faculties, their discipline of life and school of perfection as well as guide to

[1] Οἱ πολλοὶ δὲ, καθάπερ οἱ παῖδες τὰ μορμολύκια οὕτως δεδίασι τὴν Ἑλληνικὴν φιλοσοφίαν, φοβούμενοι μὴ ἀπαγάγῃ αὐτούς.—Potter's ed. v. ii. p. 780. Ναὶ φασὶν γεγράφθαι, πάντες οἱ πρὸ τῆς παρουσίας τοῦ κυρίου, κλέπται εἰσὶ καὶ λησταί.—Vol. i. p. 366.
[2] Strom. l. 1. c. 19.
[3] Ibid. l. 6. c. 7.
[4] Ibid. l. 1. c. 14, 15.
[5] Ἰνδῶν τε οἱ Γυμνοσοφισταὶ, ἄλλοι τε φιλόσοφοι βάρβαροι. Διττὸν δὲ τούτων τὸ γένος, οἱ μὲν Σαρμάναι αὐτῶν, οἱ δὲ Βραχμᾶναι καλούμενοι· καὶ τῶν Σαρμανῶν οἱ Ἀλλόβιοι προσα- γορευόμενοι, οὔτε πόλεις οἰκοῦσιν, οὔτε στέγας ἔχουσιν, δένδρων δὲ ἀμφιέννυνται φλοιοῖς, καὶ ἀκρόδρυα σιτοῦνται, καὶ ὕδωρ ταῖς χερσὶν πίνου- σιν, οὐ γάμον, οὐ παιδοποίαν ἴσασιν, ὥσπερ οἱ νῦν Ἐγκρατηταὶ καλούμενοι. Εἰσὶ δὲ τῶν Ἰνδῶν οἱ τοῖς Βούττα πειθόμενοι παραγγέλμασιν ὃν δι' ὑπερ- βολὴν σεμνότητος εἰς Θεὸν τετιμή- κασι.—Strom. l. 1. c. 15.

CHAP. IV.     *of Original Sin.*     109

truth, was the great fact which influenced Clement on this question, and which elicited his greatest admissions, both as to the reality and the source of heathen goodness. Heathen philosophy, then, was, in his view, a reaching forward to Divine truth and a reflection of it. It only taught, indeed, comprehensible and not mysterious truth; but the one prepared the way for the other. Heathen philosophy was the forerunner of the Gospel,[1] and, as being so excellent a thing, it could have no other source than a Divine one. Philosophy was the great gift of God to the gentile world; and the less perfect law and the more perfect law came both from the same Fountain Head.[2] And though some called its truths stolen ones, or attributed them to the devil, or to nature as their teacher; still philosophy, if it had stolen its truths, had them; the devil, if he taught

---

[1] Ὀρέγεται τῆς θείας ἐπιστήμης, οὐδέπω δὲ τυγχάνει.—Strom. l. 6. c. 7. The true Gnostic or Christian alone attained this knowledge: Ὁ γνωστικὸς δὲ ἐκεῖνος, τὰ δοκοῦντα ἀκατάληπτα εἶναι τοῖς ἄλλοις, αὐτὸς καταλαμβάνει· πιστεύσας ὅτι οὐδὲν ἀκατάληπτον τῷ υἱῷ τοῦ θεοῦ.—L. 6. c. 8. But the heathen philosophy supplied the elements of the Divine: Διὸ καὶ στοιχειωτάτη τίς ἐστιν ἡ μερικὴ αὕτη φιλοσοφία τῆς τελείας ὄντως ἐπιστήμης ἐπέκεινα κόσμου περὶ τὰ νοητὰ, καὶ ἔτι τούτων τὰ πνευματικώτερα ἀναστρεφομένης.—c. 8. Προκατασκευάζει τὴν ὁδὸν τῇ βασιλικωτάτῃ διδασκαλίᾳ.—L. 1. c. 16. Ἀλλὰ συλλαμβάνεταί γε τῷ λογικῶς ἐπιχειρεῖν ἐσπουδακότ. ἀνθάπτεσθαι γνώσεως.—c. 20. Καίτοι ἐν πολλοῖς τὰ ἐοικότα ἐπιχείρει καὶ πιθανεύεται φιλοσοφία· ἀλλὰ τὰς αἱρέσεις ἐπιῤῥαπίζει.—c. 19. Καὶ κατ' ἔμφασιν δὲ καὶ διάφασιν οἱ ἀκριβῶς παρὰ Ἕλλησι φιλοσοφήσαντες διορῶσι τὸν Θεόν.—c. 19. Παῦλος ἐν ταῖς ἐπιστολαῖς οὐ φιλοσοφίαν διαβάλλων φαίνεται, στοιχεῖα τοῦ κόσμου ταύτην ἀλληγορῶν, στοιχειωτάτην τινὰ οὖσαν, καὶ προσπαιδείαν τῆς ἀληθείας.—Strom. l. 6. c. 8.

[2] Θείαν δωρεὰν Ἕλλησι δεδομένην.—Strom. l. 1. c. 2. Ἀγωγὸν δὲ τὸ ἐραστὸν πρὸς τὴν ἑαυτοῦ θεωρίαν, παντὸς τοῦ ὅλον ἑαυτὸν τῇ τῆς γνώσεως ἀγάπῃ ἐπιβεβληκότος τῇ θεωρίᾳ. Διὸ καὶ τὰς ἐντολὰς ἃς ἔδωκεν, τάς τε προτέρας τάς τε δευτέρας ἐκ μιᾶς ἀρυττόμενος πηγῆς ὁ κύριος, κ. τ. λ.—L. 7. c. 2.

Ἔστι γὰρ τῷ ὄντι φιλοσοφία μέγιστον κτῆμα, καὶ τιμιώτατον Θεῷ.—Justin Martyr, Dial. c. 2. Though in the *Cohortatio ad Græcos*, he disparages Pagan philosophy, while he acknowledges its possession of some truths, such as the unity of the Deity as taught by Plato; which, as well as his doctrine of ideas, however, he considers him to have got from the Scriptures which he saw in Egypt; the latter from the mention of the pattern shown to Moses on the mount.—Ad Græc. c. 21. *et seq.*

Ea quidem quæ ad sapientes seculi de veritatis scientia pervenerunt, Deo revelante pervenerunt; sed dum aut vanæ gloriæ student, aut adulantur erroribus vetustis, aut metu principum refrenantur, damnationis suæ ipsi judices fiunt.—Origen, in Rom. i. 18., vol. 4. p. 471.

them, had taught the truth; and there was but one Author of nature, *i.e.* God.[1]

But gentile philosophy is not only referred to Divine inspiration generally as its source, but especially to our Lord as the Logos; being a fragment of that truth which afterwards issued from the Incarnate Word as an harmonious whole.[2] The estimate of the heathen world thus gained another important step; and natural goodness, once admitted to belong to it, did not rest simply such, but rose above nature and claimed affinity with grace. The dispensation of Paganism, so far as it contained truth, was but a lower part of one large dispensation, which our Lord, as the Divine Reason, had instituted and carried on for the enlightenment of the human race, and of which the Gospel was the consummation; heathens and Christians were, though in a different measure, still alike partakers of that one 'Light that lighteth every man that cometh into the world;' and all mankind, as brought into union and fellowship by that common participation, formed one religious society and communion—one Church.[3]

---

[1] Οὐ τοίνυν ψευδὴς ἡ φιλοσοφία, κἂν ὁ κλέπτης, καὶ ὁ ψευστὴς κατὰ μετασχηματισμὸν ἐνεργείας τὰ ἀληθῆ λέγῃ.—Strom. l. 6. c. 8. Ὁ κλέπτης ὅπερ ὑφελόμενος ἔχει ἀληθῶς ἔχει, κἂν χρυσίον ᾖ, κἂν ἄργυρος, κἂν λόγος, κἂν δόγμα.—Strom. l. 1. c. 20. Εἰ δὲ (ὁ διάβολος), ὥς ἄγγελος φωτὸς προφητεύει, ἀληθῆ ἄρα 'ρεῖ.—L. 6. c. 8. Εἴτ' αὖ φυσικὴν ἔννοιαν ἐσχηκέναι τοὺς Ἕλληνας λέγοι, τὸν τῆς φύσεως δημιουργὸν ἕνα γινώσκομεν.—L. 1. c. 19.

[2] Οὕτως οὖν ἥ τε βάρβαρος, ἥ τε Ἑλληνικὴ φιλοσοφία τὴν ἀΐδιον ἀλήθειαν σπαραγμόν τινα, οὐ τῆς Διονύσου μυθολογίας, τῆς δὲ τοῦ Λόγου τοῦ ὄντος ἀεὶ Θεολογίας πεποίηται· ὁ δὲ τὰ διῃρημένα συνθεὶς αὖθις, καὶ ἑνοποιήσας, τέλειον τὸν Λόγον ἀκινδύνως εὖ ἴσθ' ὅτι κατόψεται, τὴν ἀλήθειαν.—Strom. l. 1. c. 13.

[3] Πάντες αὐτοῦ οἱ ἄνθρωποι· ἀλλ' οἱ μὲν κατ' ἐπίγνωσιν, οἱ δὲ οὐδέπω·

καὶ οἱ μὲν ὡς φίλοι, οἱ δὲ ὡς οἰκέται πιστοί· οἱ δὲ ὡς ἁπλῶς οἰκέται· ὁ διδάσκαλος οὗτος ὁ παιδεύων μυστηρίοις μὲν τὸν γνωστικὸν, ἐλπίσι δὲ ἀγαθαῖς τὸν πιστὸν, καὶ παιδείᾳ τῇ ἐπανορθωτικῇ δι' αἰσθητικῆς ἐνεργείας τὸν σκληροκάρδιον. . . . οὗτός ἐστιν ὁ διδοὺς καὶ τοῖς Ἕλλησι τὴν φιλοσοφίαν, διὰ τῶν ὑπερδεεστέρων ἀγγέλων. . . . Ἤτοι γὰρ οὐ φροντίζει πάντων ἀνθρώπων ὁ κύριος· καὶ τοῦτο, ἢ τῷ μὴ δύνασθαι πάθοι ἄν· ὅπερ οὐ θεμιτόν· ἀσθενείας γὰρ σημεῖον· ἢ τῷ μὴ βούλεσθαι δυνάμενος, οὐκ ἀγαθὸν δὲ τὸ πάθος. . . . ἢ κήδεται τῶν συμπάντων· ὅπερ καὶ καθήκει τῷ κυρίῳ πάντων γενομένῳ· σωτὴρ γάρ ἐστιν· οὐχὶ τῶν μὲν, τῶν δ' οὔ.—Strom. l, 7. c. 2.

Ὡς οὖν συγκινεῖται καὶ μικροτάτη σιδήρου μοῖρα τῷ τῆς Ἡρακλείας λίθου πνεύματι, διὰ πολλῶν τῶν σιδηρῶν ἐκτεινομένη δακτυλίων, οὕτω καὶ τῷ ἁγίῳ πνεύματι ἑλκόμενοι, οἱ μὲν ἐνά-

The interpretation of original sin, again, as a privation of higher good rather than a positive state of sin, affected the punishment which was assigned to it. The penalty of the fall was exclusion from Paradise, and with it exclusion from that state of blessedness for which the life in Paradise was a preparation.[1] Had man kept the commandment given to him, he would have been allowed to continue in a state of earthly felicity till his obedience had been tried; he would then have migrated by no process repugnant to nature, but by an easy and painless one, provided by God for this purpose, from an earthly to a heavenly Paradise. His disobedience excluded him from both these states. But both the earthly Paradise and the heavenly one were states of higher good; one of lower good was still left open to him, as the reward of such virtue as he was still capable of reaching.

The distinction between the natural and supernatural life, it is to be remembered, is a distinction between the two states themselves, and not between the dates of them, whether now or in futurity. It is one drawn from their respective inherent characteristics, which are not affected by the order of time. Christian association indeed identifies the supernatural with future life, the natural with present; because the future life at which, as Christians, we aim is a supernatural one; but the two ideas are not identical. The future eternal world of the Pagan, the Mahometan, and the savage is a natural order of things, and even an inferior one of that rank. A much higher and more moral eternity may be conceived, which would still be, according to the distinction which has been laid down on this subject[2], a natural one. Such an eternity was, according to early theology, open to man in a state of ori-

ρετοι, οἰκειοῦνται τῇ πρώτῃ μόνῃ, ἐφεξῆς δ' ἄλλοι μέχρι τῆς τελευταίας. —L. 7. c. 2.

Athanasius (De Incarn. c. 12) appears to speak of the heathen as in a certain sense under the same dispensation as the Jews; as having the power πατρὸς λόγον γνῶναι from the works of nature; the prophets sent by God to the Jews having been sent for their sake as well.

[1] Tatian, Ad Græc. c. 20. ἐξωρίσθησαν οἱ πρωτοπλασταὶ ἀπὸ τῆς γῆς μὲν, ἀλλ' οὐκ ἐκ ταύτης, κρείττονος δὲ τῆς ἐνταῦθα διακοσμήσεως. See Bull, On the State of Man before the Fall, p. 67.

[2] P. 105.

ginal sin, though shut out from a supernatural or heavenly one;—the penalty of which sin was therefore, as regards a future life, made a privation only, and not a positive punishment. As regards the present life, the exchange of pain, labour, and sorrow for the happiness of Paradise was indeed in itself positive punishment. But if transient pain leads to an eternity of happiness, even of the natural kind, the existence of the creature is on the whole a good to him, not an evil. And therefore, however it may have pleased God to lighten the state of trial in the first instance, and even to make it painless and happy, a painful trial is, as the means to so valuable an end, not otherwise than a good.

The assignment of such a punishment to original sin was in substance the doctrine of a middle state; and early theology may be considered as having pointed to such a state as the final condition of the heathen and unbaptized. In saying this, however, I give what theology before the time of S. Augustine upon this subject as a whole comes to, rather than any definite doctrine that was held. If we examine the particulars of the early Church's view, or what was said at different successive times on this subject, these will appear mainly under the three following heads :—

I. The statements of the three first centuries bearing on the question are principally confined to a general acknowledgment of real goodness existing among the heathen; such an acknowledgment as immediately suggests future reward as the necessary result, under God's moral government, of such goodness ; but without any reference, express or implicit, to such a result. These statements, however, assume occasionally a greater significance in this direction, and appear to include without expressly mentioning, a future state of reward. The Logos or Son of God is, according to Clement, not only the Teacher and Light of all mankind in different degrees, but the Saviour of all; dispensing His bounty, in proportion to their fitness for it; to the Greeks and barbarians a lesser, to the faithful and elect a greater share ; to all, according to the measure in which He has dispensed His gifts, and the use made of them, awarding a higher or a lower rank in the universe.[1] And an express allusion to a future life is made in the application to the heathen of the passage in Hermas relating to the salvation of just men before the law, bestowed by means of a baptism after death.[2] But while a proportionate eternal reward, in the case of the heathen, is pointed to, no positive line is as yet drawn between the heathen and the Christian states in eternity. One state with different ranks in it is rather suggested, and all good men considered Christians in their degree are admitted to one common, though variously arranged, kingdom of heaven.[3]

II. But, secondly, the concession to the heathen of some state of happiness after death not being abandoned, we find, in course of time, the opinion established in the Church, that original sin did exclude from that place of supernatural happiness which was called the kingdom of God, or the kingdom of heaven. Origen, while he pointedly claims for heathen goodness some eternal reward, and so applies the text 'Glory, honour, and peace to every man that worketh good, to the Jew first, and also to the Gentile,' at the same time excludes the heathen, as being still under original sin, from the kingdom of heaven.[4] The Pelagians, with a doctrine which did not support, or rather opposed such a conclusion, deferred to an established distinction, and excluded the unbaptized, whom the Church at large regarded as under the guilt of original sin, though they themselves acknowledged no such sin in the first

---

[1] Βελτίονα ἀπολαμβάνειν ἐν τῷ παντὶ τὴν τάξιν.—Strom. l. 7. c. 2.

[2] Ὡς Ἄβελ, ὡς Νῶε, ὡς εἴ τις ἕτερος δίκαιος.—Strom. l. 2. c. 9.

[3] Τὸν Χριστὸν. . . . λόγον ὄντα, οὗ πᾶν γένος ἀνθρώπων μετέσχε· καὶ οἱ μετὰ λόγου βιώσαντες χριστιανοί εἰσι, κἂν ἄθεοι ἐνομίσθησαν· οἷον ἐν Ἕλλησι μὲν Σωκράτης καὶ Ἡράκλειτος, καὶ οἱ ὅμοιοι αὐτοῖς· ἐν βαββάροις δὲ Ἀβραὰμ καὶ Ἀνανίας, καὶ Ἀζαρίας, καὶ Μισαὴλ, καὶ Ἠλίας, καὶ ἄλλοι πολλοί.—Justin, Apol. l. 46., Ben. ed.

[4] 'Quod (Rom. ii. 10) de Judæis et Gentibus dicit, utrisque nondum credentibus. Potest enim fieri . . ut Græcus, i.e. Gentilis justitiam teneat. . . . Iste licet alienus a vita videatur æterna, quia non credit in Christo, et intrare non possit in regnum cœlorum, quia renatus non est ex aqua et Spiritu, videtur tamen quod per hæc quæ dicuntur ab Apostolo, bonorum operum gloriam, et honorem, et pacem perdere penitus non possit.'—In Rom. ii. 10., vol. iv. p. 484.

instance from which such guilt could arise, from this state of happiness. The text, 'Except a man be born of water and of the Spirit, he cannot enter into the Kingdom of God,' was, indeed, considered to settle this question, and that in two ways: first, as deciding that no one in a state of nature could enter into the Kingdom of God; secondly, as deciding that the only means by which the penalty of nature was removed was the rite of baptism. An exception was made in favour of those who died accidentally, before partaking of this sacrament, having shown faith and repentance; and especially in favour of martyrs. But no supposition of a subsequent extraordinary Divine mercy, and extraordinary means, was allowed in favour of the rest, who were all, heathen and unbaptized infants alike, considered as cut off for ever from the remission of original sin, and so as excluded eternally from the kingdom of heaven.[1]

III. A state of happiness after death, which is not the highest state, is by implication a middle state. But, thirdly, a definite idea of a middle state subsequently grew up. Two distinguished fathers of the Eastern Church, Gregory Nazianzen, and Gregory of Nyssa, leaned to it;[2] and the Pelagians seem to have held it unchallenged till Augustine—who himself, in his earlier theological life, inclined to it—rebuked them. But this state was introduced only to meet the case of infants, not of heathens; though on the same principle in which the former were admissible into it, the latter were also; for those who have made the most of inferior opportunities are in no worse case than those who have had none. But the early Church stopped short of any large application of the doctrine of a middle state; checked by the absence of any allusion to it

---

[1] Augustine appeals to this established opinion in the case of infants in his controversy with Vincentius Victor:—' Never believe, or say, or teach that infants dying before they are baptized can attain to the remission of original sin, if you wish to be a Catholic—*si vis esse Catho-* *licus*. (De Anima, l. 3. c. ix.) This is opposed to the most fundamental Catholic faith—contra Catholicam fundatissimam fidem.'—De Anima, l. 2. c. xii. *See* Wall on 'Infant Baptism,' part 1. c. 15; part 2. c. 6.
[2] NOTE XVI.

in Scripture, and reluctant to give substance, shape, and expansion to an idea in which Christians had no practical concern, for the aim assigned to *them* was no middle one, but the highest.

But while we have before us as the view on the whole of the early Church before Augustine's time, with respect to the virtuous heathen and unbaptized infants, partly implied and partly expressed, a middle state, it is indifferent to the question before us whether this state was a distinct one or only a lower rank of one and the same heavenly state; the only point important to observe being, that the penalty of original sin was a privation, not a positive evil.

The doctrine of original sin, thus explained and modified, was not inconsistent with natural reason and justice. It did not contradict the truth of common sense, that one man is not responsible for another man's acts, because it did not attach any such judicial consequences to the sin of Adam, as required such a responsibility to justify them. The penalty of original sin was a particular state and condition of the human race, which would not have been unjustly ordained, had there been no original sin at all. The infliction of positive evil and pain as a punishment is wholly contrary, indeed, to natural justice, except on the ground of personal guilt; but every one must admit, that the Author of nature has a perfect right to allot different degrees of good to His creatures, according to His sovereign will and pleasure; and that He is not bound in justice to give either the highest moral capacities, or their accompaniment, the highest capacities for happiness to all, because He is able to bestow these when it pleases Him. We see, in the order of nature, and in the constitution of the world around us, the greatest variety on this head; and on the same principle on which God has created different kinds of beings He may also create the same kind with higher or lower faculties. A lower capacity, then, for virtue and happiness in the human race, was no injustice as a consequence of the sin of Adam; because it was no injustice had it been no consequence of anything, but been assigned to man originally at his creation, as that measure of good which it pleased God to appoint for him. For, though the fall was the occasion and cause of this measure being assigned, it is not unjust to do that for a particular reason which you have a right to do without a reason; the agreement of the act itself with justice being supposed, no great importance, at any rate, will attach to such a further question. Nor is temporary pain, again, an injustice, if it is designed to lead to ultimate happiness; but might have been justly imposed by God on mankind at the creation, and independently of the sin of Adam, for that end.

From such a limited and modified doctrine of original sin let us turn to the doctrine of a later school.

The Western Church has, as a whole, entered more deeply into the mysteries of the inner man than the Eastern has, into that mixed sense of spiritual weakness and desire, of a void which no efforts can fill, and of a struggle endless upon all natural principles. This disposition has characterised her great schools; has largely hinged her great conflicts and divisions; the portions which the Reformation separated from the main body have retained it; the Roman and Protestant churches meet in it; and the West has been the providential exponent of the doctrine of S. Paul. Tertullian first set the example of strength and copiousness in laying down the nature and effects of original sin; he was followed by Cyprian and Ambrose. But language did not as yet advance out of the metaphorical stage; and apostacy, captivity, death, in a word, the *corruption* of human nature, was all that was yet asserted. But language could not ultimately rest in a stage in which, however strong and significant, it did not state what definite thing had happened to human nature in consequence of the fall, and just stopped short of expressing what, upon a real examination, it meant. If a man is able to do a right action, and does a wrong one, he is personally guilty indeed, but it cannot be said that his nature is corrupt. The passions and affections may be inconveniently strong, and so the nature be at a disadvantage; but no mere strength of the passions and affections shows the nature corrupt so long as the will retains its power. On the contrary, the nature is proved to be fundamentally sound, by the very fact of its being equal to the performance of the right act. The test of a sound or corrupt nature, then, is an able or an impotent will; and if a corruption of nature means anything at all, it means the loss of freewill. This was the legitimate advance which was wanted to complete the expression of the doctrine; and this complement it was left to S. Augustine to give.

S. Augustine's position respecting freewill had its commencement at a date in the history of man earlier than the corruption of his nature, viz. at his creation. Philosophy raises an insuperable difficulty to the freedom of any created will; for freedom of the will implies an original source of action in the being who has it, original not relatively only, in the way in which any cause, however secondary, is original as compared with its effect, but absolutely; and to be an original cause of anything is contrary to the very essence of a being who is not original. Tertullian had a distinct philosophical conception of this difficulty, and met it by the only answer open to a believer in freewill; an assertion of the truth together with an acknowledgment of the difficulty. Originality is the highest form of being; and everything which does not move itself, whatever be its grandeur or sublimity as a spectacle, is intrinsically despicable, in comparison with that which does. The Divine Power, then, resolving upon its own highest exertion, chose originality itself as a subject of creation, and made a being which, when made, was in its turn truly creative, the author and cause of its own motions and acts. And whereas the creature would, as such, have possessed nothing of his own, God by an incomprehensible act of liberality, alienated good from Himself in order that the creature might be the true proprietor of it, and exhibit a goodness of which His own will was the sole cause.[1] And this re-

[1] 'Sola nunc bonitas deputetur, quæ tantum homini largita sit, id est arbitrii libertatem. . . . Nam bonus natura Deus solus. . . . Homo autem qui totus ex institutione est, habens initium, cum in-

dounded ultimately to God's glory, for the worthiest and noblest creature must know Him best. Tertullian, then, distinctly and philosophically recognised a created will which was yet an original cause in nature. But S. Augustine, while on the ground of Scripture he assigned freewill to man before the fall, never recognised philosophically an original source of good in the creature. As a philosopher he argued wholly upon the Divine attribute of power, or the operation of a First Cause, to which he simply referred and subordinated all motion in the universe; and laid down in his dicta on this subject the foundation of scholastic necessitarianism.[1]

Thus philosophically predisposed, the mind of S. Augustine took up the doctrine of original sin as handed down by the voice of the Church and by a succession of writers, and brought the whole mass of language which three centuries had produced, and which up to his time had advanced in copiousness and illustration, rather than in strength of meaning, to a point. He explained the corruption of human nature to mean the loss of freewill; and this statement was the fundamental barrier which divided the later from the earlier scheme and *rationale* of original sin. The will, according to the earlier school, was not substantially affected by the fall. Its circumstances, its means and appliances, were altered, not itself; and endowed with spiritual aids in Paradise; deprived of them at the fall; re-endowed with them under the Gospel, it retained throughout these alterations one and the same unchanged essential power, in that power of choice whereby it was, in every successive state of higher or lower means, able to use and avail itself of whatever means it had. But in Augustine's scheme the will itself was disabled at the fall, and not only certain impulses to it withdrawn, its

itio sortitus est formam qua esset, atque ita non natura in bonum dispositus est, sed institutione; non suum habens bonus esse sed institutione. . . . Ut ergo bonum jam suum haberet homo, emancipatum sibi a Deo, et fieret proprietas jam boni in homine et quodammodo natura, de institutione ascripta est illi quasi libripens emancipati a Deo boni, libertas et potestas arbitrii, quæ efficeret bonum ut proprium.'—Adv. Marc. l. 2. c. 6.

[1] See p. 4.

power of choice was gone, and man was unable not only to rise above a defective goodness, but to avoid positive sin. He was thenceforth, prior to the operation of grace, in a state of necessity on the side of evil, a slave to the devil and to his own inordinate lusts.

Such a difference in the explanation of original sin necessarily produced a corresponding difference in the estimation of heathen morals. Augustine and Clement both regard the heathen character as faulty; but there are two distinct types of a faulty character. It is a rule in morals, that the morality of the man must precede the morality of the action, that some general condition must be fulfilled in the agent's character before any particular act can be pronounced good in him; this morality of the man, the fulfilment of this general condition, is the foundation. One type, then, of a faulty character is that of a character good at the foundation, and only failing in degree; another is that of a character bad at the foundation. The fruits of the former are solid, as far as they go; but the apparently good fruits of a fundamentally corrupt character are hollow, and are not real virtues. Such a character may display, for example, affection to individuals, generosity upon occasions, or courage, or industry; but upon such a foundation these are not virtues. This is the distinction between the faultiness which Clement and the faultiness which Augustine attributes to heathen morality. Clement allows the foundation to exist—this general condition to be fulfilled in a degree—in the heathen, because he considers nature able in a degree to supply it; he therefore regards heathen morality as real and solid, as far as it goes, though imperfect. But Augustine does not admit the power of nature to supply such a foundation in any degree whatever; for constituting which he requires a certain state of mind, which he considers to be only possible under grace, viz. faith, so interpreting the texts, 'Without faith it is impossible to please God,' and 'whatsoever is not of faith is sin.'[1] He therefore regards heathen

[1] 'Sed absit ut sit in aliquo vera virtus, nisi fuerit justus. Absit autem ut sit justus vere, nisi vivat ex fide: " Justus enim ex fide vivit."

morality as bad at the foundation, and therefore as a hollow, false, and only seeming morality itself. Nor does he admit the existence of a good heathen, though he admits that the heathen did actions which in Christians would be good ones.[1] And though he allows that the Divine image in which man was created did not wholly disappear at the fall, a remainder (to preserve man's identity in the two states) of a rational nature is alone admitted. He extends this view to heathen philosophy. Acknowledging in some systems a greater likeness to Christian truth than in others, he speaks of heathen philosophy as a whole with coldness, distrust, and hostility, warning the Christian against it. He looks on the truth it promulgates as external to Christian truth and not mingling with it, and sees a barrier between the two where the earlier fathers only saw a gradual ascent.[2]

But, though no goodness in the heathen is admitted, he allows different degrees in evil, and that some men in a state of nature have been less sinful than others, such as

---

Quis porro eorum qui se Christianos haberi volunt, nisi soli Pelagiani, aut in ipsis etiam forte tu solus, justum dixerit infidelem, justum dixerit impium, justum dixerit diabolo mancipatum ? Sit licet ille Fabricius, sit licet Fabius, sit licet Scipio, sit licet Regulus, quorum me nominibus, tanquam in antiqua Curia Romana loqueremur, putasti esse terrendum.'—Contra Julianum, Pelag. l. 4. n. 17.; *see*, too, Contra Duas, Ep. l. 3. n. 14. 23.

[1] 'Hi qui naturaliter quæ legis sunt faciunt, nondum sunt habendi in numero eorum quos Christi justificat gratia; sed in eorum potius quorum etiam impiorum nec Deum verum veraciter justeque colentium, quædam tamen facta vel legimus vel novimus vel audimus, quæ secundum justitiæ regulam non solum vituperare non possumus, verum etiam merito recteque laudamus; quanquam si discutiantur quo fine fiant, vix inveniuntur quæ justitiæ debitam laudem defensionemve mereantur.'—De Spirit. et Lit. l. 1. n. 48.

[2] Eosque (Platonists, Pythagoreans, &c.) nobis propinquiores fatemur.—De Civit. Dei, l. 8. c. 9.

'Cavet (Christianus) eos qui secundum elementa hujus mundi philosophantur, non secundum Deum, a quo ipse factus est mundus. Admonetur enim præcepto Apostolico: "Cavete ne quis vos decipiat,"' &c. (Col. ii. 8.)—De Civit. Dei, l. 8. c. 10.

It is worthy of remark, that while Clement sees in the 'rudiments of the world' which S. Paul speaks of, the objects of intellectual apprehension, as distinct from, but subsidiary to, those of faith (Strom. l. 6. c. 8.), Augustine sees in them carnal and corrupt ideas only. The latter interpretation agrees more with the text, in which, however, S. Paul is speaking only of a certain portion of heathen philosophy, not the whole of it: but the difference in the interpretation of the Apostle shows the different feeling of the two writers on this subject.

Socrates and Fabricius; but it is difficult to say whether he allows, in this admission, any relaxation in the servitude of the natural will, any kind or degree of liberty of choice as still left in it, or whether he only means that the evil passions are less strong in some natural constitutions than in others. Indeed, if it be asked to what extent Augustine's law of *peccatum pœna peccati* operated,—whether that relation of necessary effect in which actual sin stood to original applied to all the actual sin of man in a state of nature,—whether the want of power to avoid sin involved in original sin was a want of power to avoid every excess of sin which, as a matter of fact, had been committed in the world,—and so whether the whole of that mass of depravity and crime which the history of mankind presented went back, according to his doctrine, to original sin, as the necessary development of that one seed,—it must be replied, that his language varies on this subject. He sometimes represents the whole of this mass of actual sin as the necessary effect of original, and accounts for the different degrees in it by supposing different degrees of original sin; that is to say, by supposing, the impotence of the will remaining the same in all, different degrees of strength in the evil passions and inclinations. Sometimes he only represents a part of it as such, and the rest as added by the man himself.[1] But the language in which this modification of the effect of original sin is expressed is obscure and uncertain; nor is it easy to see whether those additions are only additions, as effects or additions to a cause, or whether they are additions man himself has made in the use of a lower kind of freewill still left in his nature. Thus much is certain, however, that such a liberty of choice, if it is allowed by Augustine, is not the liberty to choose good, but only lesser evil, and therefore is not properly freewill; though whether a will which can do the one and not the other is a tenable conception, is a question into which we need not enter.

Original sin was thus represented, in its nature and effects, by Augustine, as positive sin, and not as, according

[1] Note XVII.

to the earlier interpretation, a loss of higher goodness only; and this difference was followed by a corresponding difference in the punishment attached to it. S. Augustine held a state of positive evil and pain, and not a privation of higher happiness only, as the punishment of original sin. Inclined, at an earlier stage of his theological life, to the position of a middle state for unbaptized infants, as a convenient solution of a difficulty, a stronger subsequent view of the guilt of original sin rejected it; and in the controversy with the Pelagians he not only attacked that position, but made an argumentative use of the contrary one as proved from Scripture. The Pelagians adopted the position of a middle state as fitting in with their own scheme, which they had constructed upon a mixed ground of their own peculiar doctrine, and of deference to the general belief of the Church. Denying original sin altogether, they could not admit any positive punishment as due to unbaptized infants, much less a punishment in hell; while deference to general belief prevented the assignment of heaven. A middle place, therefore, between heaven and hell, exactly served their purpose; neither punishing the innocent being nor exalting the unbaptized one. But Augustine attacked this position energetically as one which in effect abolished original sin itself; arguing forcibly, that only two places were mentioned in Scripture, heaven and hell, and that, therefore, a third place, which was neither the one nor the other, was an unauthorised invention of man. He then used the scriptural position of only two places as a positive argument in support of his doctrine of original sin. For if there were only two places, and those guilty of original sin were excluded by the general belief of the Church from heaven, hell only remained for them; and a punishment in hell necessarily implied a positive original guilt to deserve it.[1]

The position of a middle state then rejected, Augustine

[1] 'Istam nescio quam medietatem quam conantur quidam parvulis non baptizatis tribuere.'—De Pecc. Merit. et Rem. l. 28. 'An tandem aliquando extra regnum Dei infelices futuros fatemini parvulos non renatos? Dicite ergo hujus infelicitatis meritum, verbosi et contentiosi, qui negatis originale peccatum.'—Op. Imp. 2. 113. 'Qui velut defensione justitiæ Dei niteris, ut evertas quod de parvulorum non

assigned a punishment in hell to original sin, and, allowing differences in degree, still left some degree or other of that punishment necessary for that sin. The heathen who had not sinned against the light had a milder punishment in hell than those who had; but ignorance was only allowed to procure a mitigation of it, not a release from it. Those who knew our Lord's will and did it not, were beaten with many stripes; those who knew it not and did it not, with few stripes.[1] With respect to unbaptized infants, his language varies in strength. The severest consigns them to the flames of hell; the most lenient to such a punishment as left existence under it better than deprivation of being; —a limitation which might appear to leave no room for positive punishment at all, as it might be said that it would be better not to exist than to exist eternally in any degree of pain; but such refinements are hardly worth pursuing. A middle language consigns them to the mildest punishment which there is in hell. On the whole, some true punishment in hell is assigned to unbaptized infants.[2]

This whole doctrine of original sin, its effects and its punishment, we must observe, is but the legitimate drawing out, in statement and consequence, of the true and scriptural doctrine of original sin. The corruption of human nature followed deservedly, according to that

regeneratorum damnatione tota sentit ecclesia, nunquam dicturus es grave jugum super parvulos unde sit justum, si non trahant originale peccatum.'—2. 117. See NOTE XVIII.

[1] 'Sed et illa ignorantia quæ non est eorum qui scire nolunt, sed eorum qui tanquam simpliciter nesciunt, neminem sic excusat ut sempiterno igne non ardeat, si propterea non credidit, quia non audivit omnino quod crederet; sed fortasse ut mitius ardeat. Non enim sine causa dictum est "Effunde iram tuam in gentes quæ te non noverunt;" et illud quod ait Apostolus, "Cum venerit in flamma ignis dare vindictam in eos qui ignorant Deum."'—De Grat. et Lib. Arb. c. iii.

'Sicut enim non impediunt a vita eterna justum quædam peccata venialia sine quibus hæc vita non ducitur: sic ad salutem æternam nihil prosunt impio aliqua bona opera, sine quibus difficillime vita cujuslibet pessimi hominis invenitur. Veruntamen sicut in regno Dei velut stella ab stella in gloria different sancti; sic et in damnatione pœnæ sempiternæ tolerabilius erit Sodomæ quam alteri civitati: et erunt quidam duplo amplius quibusdam gehennæ filii: ita nec illud in judicio Dei vacabit, quod in ipsa impietate damnabili magis alius alio minusve peccaverit.'—De Sp. et Lit. l. 1.c. 28.

[2] NOTE XVIII.

doctrine, upon the sin of Adam. But the corruption of human nature can only be adequately defined as the loss of freewill or necessary sinfulness; and sin deserves eternal punishment, and deserving it will, according to the Divine justice, infallibly obtain it, unless it is forgiven. The consignment, therefore, of heathens and unbaptized infants to the punishment of hell, extreme result as it was, was but the result of the true doctrine; because, in the absence of the only authorised sign of Divine forgiveness, these lay under the full guilt of a sin which deserved such punishment. There was no authority, indeed, for the positive assertion of the fact of such punishment; for the *fact* implies that no forgiveness by any other means has been obtained, and nobody can know whether God may not choose to employ other means to this end besides those of which He has informed us; and if an exception to the necessity of baptism is allowed in certain cases, it can not be arbitrarily limited; nor does the doctrine of original sin itself at all restrict the means by which its guilt may be removed. In asserting the *fact*, then, Augustine plainly exceeded the premiss which the true doctrine supplied; but, so far as he left all, who lay under the guilt of original sin, under *desert* of eternal punishment, he no more than drew out the true scriptural and Catholic doctrine. But, while he interpreted the revealed doctrine on the whole legitimately and faithfully, he failed in not seeing or not allowing a place to the counter-truth of natural reason. As Scripture declares the nature of every man to be corrupt in consequence of Adam's sin, and from that corruption sinfulness necessarily follows, and from that sinfulness desert of eternal punishment,—so Scripture and reason alike declare, that one man is not responsible for another man's sins; and from that position it follows that the posterity of Adam are *not* as such sinful; and from that, that they do *not* as such deserve eternal punishment. It was wrong, then, to draw out a string of consequences from the doctrine of original sin, and state them as absolute truths, when they were contradicted at every step by a set of parallel consequences from another truth, which was equally certain, and to which Scripture itself bore equal testimony. It was quite true that the doctrine of original sin, did it stand alone, withdrew from the heathen the whole foundation of virtue, and so represented a good heathen as impossible. But this was only one aspect of his state; there was also another, in which he came before us as capable of virtue; and, under the check of a mystery, the plain and natural facts of the case might be acknowledged. And the same may be said, with respect to the heathen, on the question of future punishment. These were truths, then, to be held with a special understanding in accordance with the partial premiss from which they were derived; they were not to be stated as absolute truths, such as are drawn from ascertained data, like the truths of natural philosophy. It was incorrect to deduce conclusions of the same certainty from an incomprehensible relationship, which would be drawn from ordinary and known ones, and to argue in the same way from a mysterious Divine wrath, as if it were the same affection with which we are cognisant in ourselves and in common life. The doctrine of original sin ought not to be understated or curtailed because it leads to extreme conclusions on one side of truth; and Augustine, who is not deterred by such results from the full statement of it, is, so far, a more faithful interpreter of it than an earlier school. But those who draw out this doctrine to the full, and do not balance it by other truths, give it force at the expense of tenableness and justice.

From the Augustinian statements relating to original sin two inferences remain to be drawn. First, the doctrine of original sin itself was a sufficient premiss for a doctrine of predestination. The latter consigns a certain portion of mankind, antecedently to actual sin, to eternal punishment; but if antecedently they deserve such punishment, the consignment to it is a natural consequence of such desert, and is no injustice. But, secondly, Augustine says more than that persons under the guilt of original sin *deserve* eternal punishment; for he asserts that they *are* punished eternally. But such actual punishment is more than a premiss for, for it is itself an instance of, predestination. It evidently does not depend on a man's conduct in what part of the world he is born, whether in a Christian part or a heathen; or in what state as an infant he dies, whether with baptism or without it. These are arrangements of God's providence entirely. If such arrangements, then, involve eternal punishment, the Divine will consigns to such punishment antecedently to all action—which is the doctrine of predestination. A true predestination, then, is seen in full operation in his theology, before we come to the specific doctrine; and we have substantially at an earlier stage all that can be maintained at a later.

## CHAPTER V.

### AUGUSTINIAN DOCTRINE OF PREDESTINATION.

FROM S. Augustine's doctrine of original sin, I proceed to his statements on the subject of predestination. S. Augustine, then, held the existence of an eternal Divine decree, separating, antecedently to any difference of desert, one portion of the human race from another; and ordaining one to everlasting life and the other to everlasting misery. This doctrine occurs frequently in many of his treatises; wholly pervades some, and forms the basis of his whole teaching in the latter portion of his theological life. It will be impossible, therefore, by one or two extracts to represent duly the position which this doctrine has in his writings; but the following may be taken as samples of a general language on this subject.[1]

[1] The dates of the four following extracts are,—of the first A.D. 426, of the second, A.D. 428, of the third, A.D. 421, of the fourth, A.D. 417. But the *Liber ad Simplicianum*, written A.D. 394, contains substantially the same doctrine, though being written just as he was crossing the boundary line, and passing from one system to another, it winds about so and alternates and oscillates so long between one conclusion and another, that it is with some difficulty that we ascertain what his real conclusion is. He ends, however, in adopting the strong interpretation of S. Paul: and his argument, which is to reconcile the text, 'Many are called but few chosen,' with an effectual call—*effectrix vo-*

'Whoever, therefore, are separated by Divine grace from that original damnation, we doubt not but that there is procured for them the hearing of the Gospel, that when they hear they believe, and that in that faith which worketh by love they continue unto the end; that even if they go astray they are corrected, and, being corrected, grow better; or that if they are not corrected by man, they still return into the path they left, some being taken away from the dangers of this life by a speedy death. All these things in them He worketh whose handiwork they are, and who made them vessels of mercy; He who chose them in His Son before the foundation of the world according to the election of grace; "and if of grace, then no more of works, otherwise grace is no more grace." Of such the Apostle saith, "We know that all things work together for good to them that love God, who are called according to His purpose." Of them none perish because all are elect; and they are elect because they are called according to the purpose; and that purpose not their own, but God's; of which He elsewhere saith, "That the purpose of God according to election might stand, not of works but of Him that calleth.
. . . . . If any of these perish, God is deceived, but none doth perish, for God is not deceived. If any of these perish, God is overcome by man's corruption; but none doth perish, for God is conquered by nothing. They are chosen to reign with Christ, not as Judas was chosen, of whom our Lord said, "Have I not chosen you twelve, and one of you is a devil," but chosen in mercy as He was in judgment, chosen to obtain the kingdom as He was to spill

*catio*—runs thus: Is it that they are called and that the call is not effectual, because they do not will to obey it? This does not agree with the text, 'Not of him that willeth,' &c.; for the contrary, not of God that giveth mercy, but of him that willeth, would then be true as well. Is it, then, because God calls some in a way which He knows will be effectual, and gives this call to some and not to others. So that of the latter it might be said, *possent alio modo vocati accommodare fidei voluntatem?* He decides in favour of this interpretation, on the ground that it agrees with the text, 'Not of him that willeth,' &c.; while the contrary cannot be said of it, because the effectual call thus defined depends not on man's will but on God's, who would have given it to others besides those to whom He has given it, if He had pleased. *Quia si vellet etiam ipsorum misereri, posset ita vocare, quomodo eis aptum esset.*

his own blood . . . . . These it is who are signified to Timothy, where, after saying that Hymenæus and Philetus were subverting the faith of some, the Apostle adds, " Nevertheless, the foundation of God standeth sure, having this seal, the Lord knoweth them that are His." . . . . . Their faith, which worketh by love, either never faileth, or, if it does, is repaired before life is ended ; and, all intervening iniquity blotted out, perseverance unto the end is imputed to them. But those who are not about to persevere are not, even at the time when they live piously, to be reckoned among that number ; because they are not separated from that mass of perdition by the Divine foreknowledge and predestination ; and therefore are not called according to His purpose, and therefore not chosen.'—*De Correptione et Gratia*, c. vii.

Again: 'Such is the predestination of the saints, the foreknowledge that is, and preparation of the Divine acts of grace, by which every one is infallibly saved who is saved. But for the rest, where are they but in that mass of perdition where the Divine justice most justly leaves them ? Where the Tyrians are, and the Sidonians are, who would have been able to believe if they had seen the miracles of Christ ; but who, inasmuch as faith was not destined for them, were denied the *means* of faith as well. Whence it is evident that some have a Divine gift of intelligence implanted in their natures, designed for exciting them to faith, provided they see or hear preaching or miracles which appeal to that gift ; and yet being, according to some deeper judgment of God, not included within the predestination of grace, and separated from the mass of perdition by it, have not those Divine words and those Divine acts brought before them, and so are not enabled to believe.[1]

[1] Ex quo apparet habere quosdam in ipso ingenio divinum naturaliter munus intelligentiæ, quo moveantur ad fidem, si congrua suis mentibus vel audiant verba, vel signa conspiciant: et tamen si Dei altiore judicio, a perditionis massa non sunt gratiæ prædestinatione discreti, nec ipsa eis adhibentur vel dicta divina vel facta, per quæ possent credere, si audirent utique talia vel viderent. In eadem perditionis massa relicti sunt etiam Judæi qui non potuerunt credere factis in conspectu suo tam magnis clarisque virtutibus.

The Jews who would not believe our Lord's miracles were left in the mass of perdition, and why? The Evangelist tells us, "That the saying of Esaias the prophet might be fulfilled which he spake, Lord, who hath believed our report, and to whom hath the arm of the Lord been revealed? Therefore they could not believe, because that Esaias said again, He hath blinded their eyes and hardened their hearts, that they should not see with their eyes and understand with their hearts, and be converted, and I should heal them." But the hearts of the Tyrians and Sidonians were not thus hardened, for they would have believed if they had seen such miracles. That they were able to believe, however, was of no service to them, when they were not predestinated by Him whose judgments are unsearchable and His ways past finding out; any more than their not being able to believe would have been of disservice to them if they had been thus predestinated by God to the illumination of their blindness and the taking away of their heart of stone.[1] With respect to the Tyrians and Sidonians, indeed, there may be possibly some other interpretation of the passage; but that no one comes to Christ except it be given him, and that this is given only to those who are elected in Him before the foundation of the world, this must beyond all question be admitted by every one whose heart is not deaf to, while his ear hears, the Divine oracles.'—*De Dono Perseverantiæ*, c. xiv.

Again: 'The Lord knows those that are His. All things work together for good for those alone who are called according to His purpose; the called according to His purpose, not the called simply, not the many called, but the few chosen. For whom He did foreknow He also did predestinate to be conformed to the image of His Son, that he might be the firstborn among many brethren; and whom He did predestinate them also He called; and whom He called them also He justified; and whom He justified

---

[1] Sed nec *illis* profuit quod poterant credere, quia prædestinati non sunt ab eo cujus inscrutabilia sunt judicia, et investigabiles viæ; nec *istis* obfuisset quod non poterant credere, si ita prædestinati essent, ut eos cæcos Deus illuminaret, et induratis cor lapideum vellet auferre.

them He also glorified. All things work together for good to those who were chosen before the foundation of the world by Him who calleth those things which be not as though they were; to the elect according to the election of grace, who were chosen before the foundation of the world freely and not on account of any good works foreseen. Within that number of the elect and the predestinated, even those who have led the worst lives are by the goodness of God led to repentance . . . . Of these our Lord spoke when He said, " This is the Father's will which hath sent me, that of all He hath given I should lose nothing." But the rest of mankind who are not of this number, but who, out of the same lump of which they are, are made vessels of wrath, are brought into the world for the advantage of the elect. God does not create any of them indeed without a purpose. He knows what good to work out of them: He works good in the very fact of creating them human beings, and carrying on by means of them this visible system of things.[1] But none of them does He lead to a wholesome and spiritual repentance. All indeed do, as far as themselves are concerned, out of the same original mass of perdition treasure up unto themselves after their hardness and impenitent heart, wrath against the day of wrath; but out of that mass God leads some in mercy to repentance, and others in judgment does not lead.'—*Contra Julianum Pelag.* l. v. n. 14.

Again: 'There is a certain defined number of saints in God's foreknowledge (*Dei præscientia definitus numerus sanctorum*) who love God because God hath given them His Holy Spirit shed abroad in their hearts, and to whom all things work together for good; who are called according to His purpose . . . . . There are others, too,

[1] Cæteri autem mortales qui ex isto numero non sunt, et ex eadem quidem ex qua et isti, sed vasa iræ facta sunt, *ad utilitatem nascuntur istorum*. Non enim quenquam eorum Deus temere ac fortuito creat, aut quid de illis boni operetur ignorat; cum et hoc ipso bonum operetur, quod in eis humanam creat naturam, et ex eis ordinem præsentis sæculi exornat. Istorum neminem adducit ad pœnitentiam salubrem et spiritualem.

called, but not chosen; and, therefore, *not* called according to His purpose. The former are the children of promise, the elect, who are saved according to the election of grace, as it is written, "But if of grace, then no more of works, otherwise grace is no more grace." These are the vessels of mercy, in whom God even by means of the vessels of wrath makes known the riches of His glory . . . . . But the rest of mankind—who do not pertain to this society, but whose soul and body, nevertheless, God hath made, together with whatever also belongs to their nature apart from its corruption—are created by a foreknowing God on this account, that by them He may show how little the freewill of fallen man can do without His grace; and that by their just and due punishment the vessels of mercy, who are separated from the original mass not by their own works, but by the free grace of God, may know how great a gift has been bestowed upon them, that every mouth may be stopped, and that he that glorieth may glory in the Lord.'[1]—*Epist.* 186, c. vii.

The general conclusion to which these passages point, is that S. Augustine held the predestinarian doctrine; viz. that God by an eternal decree prior to any difference of desert, separated one portion of mankind from another, ordaining one to eternal life and the other to eternal punishment.[2] But it will be proper to enter into some distinctions which are drawn on this subject in order to separate S. Augustine's doctrine from another and a different doctrine of predestination.

A certain limited and qualified doctrine of predestination is held by some schools of divines opposed to the predestinarians, who maintain the doctrine to be a sound and scriptural one, but maintain the predestination to be first to privileges and means of grace, not to final happiness; or, secondly, if to final happiness, to be a predesti-

[1] Ut in his ostenderet liberum arbitrium sine sua gratia quid valeret; ut in eorum justis et debitis pœnis vasa misericordiæ, quæ non suorum meritis, sed gratuita Dei gratia sunt ab illa concretione discreta, quid sibi collatum esset addiscerent.

[2] See Hooker's Statements of S. Augustine's Doctrine. NOTE XIX.

nation in consequence of foreseen virtue and holiness in the individuals predestinated. A third modification, which rests upon a distinction between individuals and the body, and allowing predestination to be to final glory, applies it to the Church as a whole, and not to individuals, is evidently only the second in another form. For, as no one can mean to say that the whole of the visible Church is predestinated to eternal glory, by the Church as a body must be meant the truly virtuous and pious members of the Church whom God predestinates to glory in consequence of foreseeing this piety and virtue in them. Now, had S. Augustine only held predestination in this sense, that God determined from all eternity to admit a certain portion of mankind to certain religious privileges and to reward the pious and virtuous with eternal glory, he would only have held what no Christian, or even believer in natural religion, can deny. It is evident that God has admitted a certain portion of mankind to certain religious privileges to which He has not admitted others; and, as He has done this, it is certain that He has eternally decreed to do it. And it is certain that God will finally reward men according to their works; and, as this will be His act, and this the reason of it, it is certain He has eternally decreed the one and foreseen the other. Such a doctrine of predestination as this, then, is no more than what everybody must hold. But the passages which have been quoted contain very clearly a different doctrine of predestination from this. And this difference will appear the more decisively, the more we enter into the particulars of S. Augustine's view.

In the first place, we find S. Augustine always speaking of predestination as a mystery, a dark and perplexing doctrine, contradictory to our natural ideas of the Divine justice, and requiring the profoundest submission of human reason in order to its acceptance. For example, he says, in the text (John vi. 45): 'Every one that hath heard and hath learned of the Father cometh unto me.'

'Very far removed from our fleshly senses is that school in which God is heard and teaches—*valde remota est a sensibus carnis hæc schola in qua Pater auditur et docet.* We see many come to the Son, because we see many believe in Christ: but where and how they heard and learned this of the Father we see not. Too secret is that grace; but that it is grace who can doubt? This grace thus secretly imparted is rejected by no heart, however hard.[1] Indeed, it is given for that purpose, viz. that this hardness of heart may be removed. When the Father is heard, and teaches the man within to come to the Son, He takes away the stony heart and gives the heart of flesh, thus making sons of promise and vessels of mercy prepared for glory. But why does He not teach all to come to Christ? Because those whom He teaches He teaches in mercy, and those whom He teaches not He teaches not in judgment. "For He hath mercy on whom He will have mercy, and whom He will He hardeneth." . . . . . And to him who objects why doth He yet complain, for who hath resisted His will? the Apostle answers, not by denying the objection, but urging submission under it: O man, who art thou that repliest against God?"[2]

Again: 'Why, when both alike hear, and, supposing a miracle, both alike see, one believes and another does not believe, lies in the abyss of the riches of the wisdom and knowledge of God, whose judgments are unsearchable, and who, without iniquity, has mercy upon whom He will have mercy, and whom He will, hardeneth. For His decrees are not unjust, because they are incomprehensible.'[3]

Again: 'It displeases him (the objector in Rom. c. ix.) that God complains of sinners whom, as it appears to him, He hardens. But God does not harden sinners by obliging them to sin, but by withholding grace, such grace being withheld from those from whom it is withheld, according to an occult justice, infinitely removed from human perceptions.'[4]

[1] Nimium gratia ista secreta est, gratiam vero esse quis ambigat? Hæc itaque gratia, quæ occulte humanis cordibus divina largitate tribuitur, a nullo duro corde respuitur.

[2] De Præd. Sanct. c. viii.
[3] Epist. 194. c. iii.
[4] De Div. Quæst. ad Simplic. l. i. Q. 2. n. 16.

## Augustinian Doctrine

Again: 'Why He wills to convert some, and to punish others for being unconverted (*quare illos velit convertere, illos vero pro aversione punire*), let none presume to ask as if to blame God . . . . . for the law of His secret justice rests with Him alone (*consilium occultioris justitiæ penes ipsum est*).'[1]

S. Augustine, then, regarded predestination as a perplexing mystery,—a doctrine which disagreed with our natural ideas of God's justice, and which could only be defended by a reference to His inscrutable and sovereign will.

I will single out the term 'hidden justice—*occulta justitia*,' as expressing in a summary and convenient form this characteristic of the doctrine held by him. S. Augustine asserts, as every one who believes in the existence of a God must do, that God is just, and therefore that the decree of predestination and reprobation which He has from all eternity made is just; but he adds, that this justice is of a nature not addressed to our natural faculties and perceptions, or discernible by them. Natural justice—the rule of rewarding and punishing according to desert—is justice, and is also a justice cognisable by our natural faculties; predestinating justice is as real justice as natural, but is not thus cognisable. The one is justice and also *apparent* justice; the other is justice, but not apparent justice—*i.e.* apparent *in*justice.

But such language as this is very inapplicable to a doctrine of predestination, which is no more than the assertion that God has determined from all eternity to admit some portions of mankind and not others to certain privileges and means of grace; or, that God has determined to reward or punish those respectively who He sees will be virtuous or vicious. There is nothing mysterious in the doctrine of predestination as thus explained, nothing from which natural feeling or reason shrinks, nothing which requires any deep submission of the intellect to accept. That God should reward the virtuous and punish the wicked is the simple rule of justice, and that He should

[1] De Pecc. Merit. et Rem. l. 2. c. xviii.

give privileges to some which He does not give to others, is no injustice.

It may be said, indeed, that the admission of one portion of mankind to peculiar religious privileges and advantages not enjoyed by the rest is a mystery; that there is something inexplicable in that great inequality of God's administration in this respect which we see in the world, especially the remarkable one of one part of the world only having been admitted into the Christian Church, while far the larger part has been left in pagan darkness and ignorance: but it cannot be said, that this is a mystery in the sense of being a scandal or offence to our reason. It is a mystery, in the first place, as being a fact which we are obliged to refer simply to the Divine will and pleasure; but in this sense many of the commonest events which take place in the world are mysteries. It is one thing to be uninformed, and another to be scandalised; one thing not to have curiosity satisfied, and another to have reason perplexed. It is a mystery also in a sense somewhat stronger than this; for without imposing as obligatory, our moral nature yet favours the rule of equal dealing, and its bias is in that direction; so that exceptions to it are not in themselves acceptable to us. But neither in this sense is it a difficulty or scandal; being only the violation of a rule which is not obligatory. Indeed, this bias of our minds is one which easily submits, on the first due consideration, that there may be good reasons for the inequality we see in the Divine dispensing of religious privileges. And, on the whole, provided the great rule of justice be kept to, that men are rewarded and punished according to their use of the means given them, the general sense of mankind allows the Almighty the right to apportion the means themselves as He thinks fit, and give some higher, and some lower, without making any difficulty of the matter. Particular persons, indeed, have embraced so rigid and importunate an idea of justice, that they have not been able so to satisfy themselves, but have insisted on an absolute equality of spiritual condition for all. And truly the idea of justice, like other ideas, may be unduly nourished; and persons, by brooding narrowly upon it, may get themselves to regard many things as grievances, both in human society and the system of Providence, which they would not otherwise have done. But such an idea of justice is not supported by the general feeling of mankind, which has adopted a larger and more liberal one.

Inequality, then, in the dispensing of religious privileges, is not a difficulty to reason or contrary to justice; but S. Augustine speaks of predestination as a difficulty, and contrary to our instinctive ideas of justice; and therefore must have included something more than this kind of inequality in his idea of what predestination was.

Indeed, the very circumstances of the argument which S. Augustine is carrying on, if any one will consider them, will be found to involve something more than this as his meaning of predestination; for, had he meant no more than this, there would have been no occasion for this defence of the doctrine at all. In arguing with an infidel he might have had to answer the objection of these inequalities in the Divine dispensation; but he is defending the doctrine of predestination not against an infidel, but against a Christian objector—*i.e.* an objector who at the very outset admits such inequalities, and therefore would not object to, or call out a defence of that doctrine on that ground. Indeed, S. Augustine's opponent is not only a Christian, but sometimes even a Catholic Christian, he having to defend this doctrine not only against Pelagians but against opponents within the Church.[1] But it is absurd to suppose such an opponent taking, against a particular doctrine, a ground only suitable to an infidel arguing against revelation altogether, just as it would be absurd, on the other hand, to suppose S. Augustine not giving the ready and obvious answer to such an objection if brought. He answers his opponent by referring him to God's secret and inscrutable will; but had mere inequality

---

[1] The Church of Marseilles, which, through Prosper and Hilary, protested against the doctrine of the book *De Correptione et Gratia*, and were answered by the book *De Prædestinatione Sanctorum*.

been his opponent's ground of objection, he would have answered him much more decisively by referring him to the broad and evident fact of the inequality in the Divine dispensing of means of grace involved in the very existence of Christianity, not to say in the very order of God's natural providence.

But the general admission of mystery, darkness, and apparent contrariety to justice which S. Augustine makes with respect to predestination, is only a preliminary, however decisive an answer, to such an interpretation of his doctrine as would reduce it to the qualified doctrine of predestination above referred to. The qualified doctrine drew distinctions, according as it wanted them, between individuals and the body as the subjects of predestination, between the means of grace and final happiness as the gift in it, and between foreseen merits and arbitrary choice as the reason and ground of it. But none of these distinctions appear in the Augustinian statements of the doctrine, which quite plainly and simultaneously assign to predestination individuals as its subjects, final glory as its gift, and a sovereign and inscrutable choice on the part of God, as distinguished from foreseen merits in the predestinated person, as its reason and ground.

He applies, in the first place, predestination to individuals, speaking of the subjects of it as 'these' and 'those' (*illi, isti*), and 'many' (*multi, plurimi*). The question put by the objector to the doctrine, and met by him with the answer of God's inscrutable will, is, 'Why God liberates this man rather than that—*cur istum potius quam illum liberet.*'[1] And the predestinated are considered as amounting to a certain definite number of persons. 'I speak,' he says, 'of those who are predestinated to the kingdom of God, of whom the number is so certain that no one can be added to them or taken from them.'[2]

It is evident, in the next place, that S. Augustine is speaking of the predestination of these individuals to final glory, and not to means of grace only; asserting, as he does, that by predestination 'every one is infallibly saved

[1] Præd. Sanct. c. viii.     [2] De Corr. et Grat. c. xiii.

who is saved—*certissime liberantur quicumque liberantur,*' and that 'of the elect none perish,'[1] and everywhere speaking of predestination as predestination to eternal life.

It is equally evident that he does not mean that these individuals are predestinated to eternal life on account of foreseen goodness in them. This was the ground on which predestination was placed by some maintainers of a qualified doctrine on this subject in S. Augustine's time; but it met not with his agreement but strong condemnation; and those who held it are argued with as opponents not so far gone as the Pelagians, but still labouring under formidable error. The distinction of foreseen merits was a regular and known distinction in the controversy on this question at that day, and was thus disposed of. Thus, commenting on the text, 'Ye have not chosen Me, but I have chosen you' (John xv. 16), he says, 'This, then, is the immoveable truth of predestination. The Apostle says, "He hath elected us in Him before the foundation of the world." If this is interpreted, then, to mean that God elects men *because He foresees they will believe,* and not because He is about to make them believing, against such a foreknowledge as this the Son speaks, saying, " Ye have not chosen Me, but I have chosen you," for upon this interpretation God would rather have foreseen that they would choose Him, and so deserve to be chosen by Him. They are chosen therefore before the foundation of the world by that predestination by which God foresees his own future work; and they are chosen out of the world by that calling by which God fulfils what He predestines.'[2]

Again, on the text (Eph. i. 4) 'According as He hath chosen us in Him before the foundation of the world, that we should be holy and without blame before Him in love.' '"He foreknew," says the Pelagian, "who were about to be holy and without blame by the exercise of their free-will, and therefore chose them before the foundation of the world in His foreknowledge, because He foreknew that

---

[1] De Dono Pers. c. xiv.
[2] De Præd. Sanct. c. xvii.—Quod profecto si propterea dictum est quia *præscivit Deus credituros* esse .... Electi sunt autem ante mundi constitutionem ea prædestinatione in qua Deus sua futura facta præscivit: electi sunt autem de mundo ea vocatione, qua Deus id, quod prædestinavit, implevit.

they would be such." But the Apostle says, "Chose not because we were, but that we *might be* holy and without blame." They were to be such, then, *because* He elected them and predestinated them to be such by His grace.'[1]

The text, again (Rom. ix. 11), respecting Jacob and Esau, 'For the children being not yet born, neither having done any good or evil, that the purpose of God according to election might stand, not of works, but of Him that calleth,' is strongly insisted upon as obviously, and at first sight disproving the conditional ground attributed by some to predestination; and the explanation by which this natural inference from the passage is met, viz.—that the election of Jacob in preference to Esau, though not caused by any difference of conduct between them at the time, inasmuch as they were not yet born, *was* yet caused by the difference which was *to be* and which God *foresaw*, is rejected, as depending on a distinction wholly irrelevant; it making no difference to works as a cause of election, whether they operate thus as present or as foreseen works. 'Jacob was not loved because he was of such a character, or because he was to be; but he was made of such a character because he was loved—*non ideo quia talis erat, vel talis futurus erat dilectum, sed talem, quia dilectus est, factum*. The Apostle does not lie. Jacob was not loved on account of works, for if of works, then no more of grace; but he was loved on account of grace, which grace made him to abound in works.'[2]—'"It is not of him that willeth, or of him that runneth, but of God that showeth mercy?" God had not mercy on Jacob, therefore, because Jacob willed and ran; but Jacob willed and ran because God had mercy. For the will is prepared by the Lord.'[3]—'"Jacob have I loved, but Esau have I hated." The Apostle speaks of an election, where God does not find something done by another for Him to choose, but something to choose which He Himself does—"*ubi Deus non ab alio factum quod eligat invenit, sed quod inveniat ipse facit.*" As he says of the remnant of Israel, "There

[1] De Præd. Sanct. c. xviii.  
[2] Op. Imp., Contra Jul. l. 1. c. 133.  
[3] Ibid. c. 141.

is a remnant according to the election of grace; and if by grace, then is it no more of works, otherwise grace is no more grace."[1] Wherefore ye are foolish who, when the truth says, "Not of works, but of Him that calleth," say, on account of *future* works which God foresaw that Jacob would do, and therefore loved him; contradicting the Apostle's own words. As if the Apostle would not have said, not on account of present, but of future works, if he had meant this—"*quasi non posset dicere, non ex præsentibus sed ex futuris operibus.*"[2]

The ground of foreseen merits is thus expressly rejected by S. Augustine as the ground of predestination, which is referred, instead, to an absolute and inscrutable Divine choice. Though one distinction must be here made. The most rigid predestinarian must in one sense allow that God predestinates the elect to eternal life in consequence of goodness foreseen in them. For, however absolutely God may predestinate particular persons to eternal life in the sense of certainty, He plainly does not do it absolutely in the sense of requiring no qualifications. His predetermination, then, to give them eternal life must suppose the foresight of these qualifications for it in them, though it is the foresight of qualifications which He Himself has determined to give them by the operation of efficacious grace. 'God foresees His own future work.' He has decreed from all eternity to make, and therefore foresees that He will make, Jacob of such a character. But this is predestination in consequence of foreseen goodness, in quite a different sense from that which is intended in the modification of the doctrine above referred to. The effect of that modification is to make the *whole* of predestination conditional,—God predestinating persons to eternal life in consequence of something which by virtue of the Divine attribute of foreknowledge He certainly foresees, but which is in itself contingent, depending on the will and efforts of the persons themselves. But of the distinction now spoken of this is not the effect. For though, according to it, God predestinates the elect to their final reward

[1] Rom. xi. 5, 6.     [2] Contra Duas, Ep. Pel. l. 2. n. 15.

relatively to their qualifications for it, He predestinates them absolutely to those qualifications; so that, though one part of predestination is dependent upon another, the whole is unconditional.[1]

It is indeed observable that, when S. Augustine is charged by the Pelagians with fatalism, he does not disown the certainty and necessity, but only the popular superstitions and impieties of that system. He rejects the appeal to the stars as absurd, and distinguishes between the operation of fate which is for good and evil alike, and that of Divine grace which is for good only; sin and its punishment being referable wholly to man. But he does not disown a Divine predestination, upon which the future happiness and misery of mankind depend.[2]

Such being S. Augustine's doctrine of predestination, the ground on which the justice of such a doctrine is defended has already appeared in so many of the extracts given, that it is hardly necessary to recur to it. Had mankind continued in the state in which they were originally created, the consignment of any portion of them antecedently to all action to eternal punishment, would have been unjust. But all mankind having fallen from that state by their sin in Adam, and become one guilty mass, eternal punishment is antecedently due to all; and therefore none have any right to complain if they are consigned antecedently to it; while those who are spared should thank God's gratuitous mercy.

To this mass of perdition, this apostate root, we are referred for the defence of the justice of predestination. 'Those who are not freed by grace, whether they have not had the opportunity of hearing, or whether they have heard and refused to obey, or whether they have not lived

[1] 'Effectum prædestinationis considerare possumus dupliciter: uno modo in particulari, et sic nihil prohibet aliquem effectum prædestinationis esse causam alterius . . . . Alio modo in communi; et sic impossibile est quod totus prædestinationis effectus in communi habeat aliquam causam ex parte nostra.'—Sum. Theol. P. 1. Quæst. 23. Art. 5.

[2] 'Fatum qui affirmant de siderum positione, ad tempus quo concipitur quisque vel nascitur, actus et eventa pendere contendunt: Dei vero gratia omnia sidera progreditur . . . . Deinde fati assertores et bona et mala hominum fato tribuunt.'—Contra Duas, Ep. l. 2, n. 12.

to be old enough to hear, but died before receiving the washing of regeneration to save them, are all justly condemned; inasmuch as they are none of them without sin, original or actual. For all have sinned, either in Adam or in themselves, and come short of the glory of God. The whole mass, therefore, deserves punishment; and were this punishment inflicted upon all, it would be inflicted beyond all doubt justly.'[1]—'It is unjust, say they, that when both are in one and the same evil case, this man should be liberated and that man punished. But it were just that both should be punished. Who can deny this? Let us give thanks, then, to the Saviour, for that He does not repay to us what, by the damnation of others like us, we know to be our due. Were every man liberated, it would not be seen what sin deserved; were no man, what grace could bestow . . . . But the whole lump deserving condemnation, justice repays the due shame, grace bestows the unmerited honour.'[2]—'Forasmuch as that one man in whom all have sinned is also in each individual punished.'[3]—'Grace alone separates the redeemed from the lost, alone divides those whom a common original sin formed into one mass of perdition . . . . . The whole human mass was so justly condemned in the apostate root, that, were none rescued from that damnation, none could blame God's justice. Those who are rescued are rescued gratuitously; those who are not, only show what the whole lump deserved, even the rescued themselves, had not undeserved mercy succoured them.'[4]—'Divine Scripture calleth those inexcusable whom it convicts of sinning knowingly. But neither does the just judgment of God spare them who have not heard: "for as many as have sinned without law shall also perish without law." And however they may appear to excuse themselves, He admits not this excuse who knows that He at first made man upright, and gave him the commandment to obey; and that sin has not passed to his posterity but by his misuse of freewill. Men are not condemned without having

[1] De Nat. et Grat. c. iv.
[2] Ep. 194. c. 2.
[3] Ep. 186. c. 4.
[4] Enchiridion, c. 99.

sinned, inasmuch as sin hath passed to all from one, in whom, previous to their separate individual sins, all have sinned in common. And on this account every sinner is inexcusable, either by the guilt of his origin or the addition of his own will, whether he knows or whether he is ignorant; for ignorance itself is sin beyond question in those who are unwilling to learn, and in those who are not able is the punishment of sin. So that of both the excuse is unjust, the damnation just . . . . . What did He love in Jacob but the free gift of His own mercy, what did He hate in Esau but original sin?'[1]

One peculiar argument for predestination drawn from the Incarnation should be added to the general body of statement which we meet with in S. Augustine on this subject—an argument which is remarkable as showing how intimately the doctrine of predestination is connected with the fundamental truths of Christianity. Original sin is its main basis; but an oblique proof of it is here drawn from the assumption of the Man Jesus into unity of person with God.[2]

'The most eminent instance of predestination and grace is the Saviour Himself, the Mediator of God and man, the Man Christ Jesus; for by what preceding merits of its own, either of works or faith, did that human nature which was in Him earn this? Answer: How did the Man Jesus merit to be, as assumed into unity of person with the co-eternal Word, the only begotten Son of God? What good in him preceded? What did he do, believe, ask, antecedently, that he should attain to this ineffable dignity? Was not this Man, by virtue of his assumption by the Word, from the first moment that He was Man, the Son of God? Was it not as the only Son of God that that woman full of grace conceived him? Was he not born the only Son of God of the Holy Ghost and the Virgin Mary by a singular dispensation? Was there any fear

---

[1] Ep. 194. c. 6. 8.
[2] Edwards, in his book 'On the Freedom of the Will,' uses the same argument in the chapter on 'the acts of the will of the human soul of Jesus Christ, necessarily holy, yet truly virtuous, praiseworthy, rewardable,' &c.

then, that, on coming to mature age, that man should sin in the exercise of freewill? Or, had he not freewill on that account; nay, a will on that very account, and because He could not serve sin, all the more free? All these singular and wonderful privileges human nature in him received, without any preceding merits of its own. And will any man dare to say to God, "Why was not I so privileged? . . . . . Why, when nature is common, is grace so different? Why is there respecting of persons with God?" What, I will not say, Christian, but sane man would say this.' From the case of Him, then, who is our Head, we may understand the operation of grace; how from the Head it diffuses itself, according to the measure of each, through all the members. By what grace that Man was made from the beginning Christ, by that grace is every man who is such made from the beginning of his faith a Christian: reborn of the spirit of which he was born; forgiven his sins by the same Spirit by whom he was made to have none. This is the predestination of saints, which shone chiefly in him who is the Saint of saints. In so far as he was Man, the Lord of glory was Himself predestinated—predestinated to be the Son of God . . . . . Jesus was predestinated to be of the seed of David according to the flesh, and according to the Spirit of holiness the Son of God with power . . . . . As, then, that one Man was predestinated to be our Head, so are we many predestinated to be his members. Let human merits, which perished in Adam, be silent, and let grace reign. Whoever finds in our Head preceding merits to cause his singular generation, may find in his members the same to cause their regeneration. But as that generation was not a reward, but a free gift to Christ, so is our regeneration no reward, but a free gift to us . . . . . He makes us believe in Christ, who made him that Christ in whom we believe.[1]

Again: 'God therefore took the nature of man, *i.e.* the rational soul and flesh of the Man Christ, by a singu-

---

[1] De Præd. Sanct. c. xv. *See* De Dono Perseverantiæ, c. xxiv., Op. Imp. l. 1. c. 138.

larly wonderful and wonderfully singular adoption; so that, without any preceding merits, that Man was from the beginning of his human life the Son of God, even as he was one Person with the Word, which is without beginning. For no one is so blindly ignorant as to dare to say that, born of the Holy Spirit and the Virgin Mary, the Son of Man, he obtained, by the merit of a sinless life and the good use of freewill, the Divine Sonship;—to say this in the face of the text: "The Word was made flesh." For where did this take place but in the Virgin's womb, where the Man Christ began to be. . . . . That gratuitous nativity joined in unity of person man with God, the flesh with the Word. Good works then followed that nativity, and did not merit it. There was no risk, when human nature was thus ineffably taken into unity of Person by the Word of God, that it should sin in the exercise of freewill:—that nature being so assumed by God that it admitted of no evil motion of the will. As, therefore, this Mediator was, by reason of his assumption, never evil but always good; so those whom God redeems by his blood are made by him eternally good out of evil.'[1]

This is an argument, however, for predestination which admits of much the same answer which was given to the argument drawn from original sin. The sinless life of the Man Jesus was undoubtedly an infallible consequence of the Incarnation; for He could not be one with God and be capable of sinning. His goodness was therefore a necessary goodness; and one Man, in being predestinated from all eternity to a union with God, was predestinated to a perfect holiness. The Incarnation is thus a premiss for a doctrine of predestination. But it should be remembered what kind of premiss this is, that it is not a truth of nature or reason which we comprehend, but a mysterious and incomprehensible truth; and therefore that the inference drawn from it is alike a mystery and not an ascertained and complete truth, like a logical consequence from a known premiss.

The conclusion, then, to which S. Augustine's general

[1] De Corr. et Grat. c. xi.

statements, given at the commencement of this chapter, of the doctrine of predestination, naturally led, has only obtained confirmation and accuracy from further examination and the subsequent particulars into which we have entered. The characteristic of S. Augustine's doctrine, compared with the scriptural one is, that it is a definite and absolute doctrine. Scripture, as a whole, as has been said,[1] only informs us of a mystery on the subject; that is to say, while it informs us that there is a truth on the subject, it makes no consistent statement of it, but asserts contrary truths, counterbalancing those passages which convey the predestinarian doctrine by passages as plain the other way; but S. Augustine makes predestinarian statements and does not balance them by contrary ones. Rather he endeavours to explain away those contrary statements in Scripture. Thus he evades the natural force of the text that 'God would have all men to be saved,' by supposing that it only means that no man is saved except through the will of God;[2] or that 'all' means not all men, but some out of all classes and ranks of men: on the same rule on which we understand the phrase 'ye tithe all herb,'[3] as meaning not that the Pharisees gave literally a tenth of all the herbs in the world, but only of all kinds of herbs.[4]

---

[1] Chapter II.
[2] Enchiridion, c. ciii.; Contra Jul. Pelag. l. 4. c. viii.; Ep. 217. c. vi.
[3] Luke ii. 42.
[4] 'Neque enim Pharisæi omnia olera decimabant. . . . Ita et illic omnes homines, omne hominum genus intelligere possumus.'—Enchiridion, c. ciii.

The text that God is no respecter of persons is, in its general spirit, a counter text to the predestinarian ones. But its opposition is not exact, because it supposes a difference of rank, or other advantages, in the individuals, which is not respected; whereas predestination applies to those between whom there is *no* difference, all deserving condemnation. Upon this ground S. Augustine rejects his opponent's application of this text altogether as incorrect: 'Nec ulla est acceptio personarum, in duobus debitoribus æqualiter reis, si alteri dimittitur alteri exigitur, quod pariter ab utroque debetur.'—Contra Duas, Ep. l. 2. c. 7. 'Cur ergo in regnum cœlorum, non accepto regenerationis lavacro, parvulus nullus intrabit? Nunquidnam ipse sibi parentes infideles vel negligentes, de quibus nasceretur elegit? Quid dicam de inopinatis et repentinis innumerabilibus mortibus, quibus sæpe etiam religiosorum Christianorum præsumuntur, et baptismo præripiuntur infantes;

S. Augustine then takes that further step which Scripture avoids taking, and asserts a determinate doctrine of predestination. He erects those passages of Scripture which are suggestive of predestination into a system, explaining away the opposite ones; and converts the obscurity and inconsistency of Scripture language into that clearness and consistency by which a definite truth is stated. His was the error of those who follow without due consideration that strong first impression which the human mind entertains, that there must be some definite truth to be arrived at on the question under consideration, whatever it may be: and who therefore imagine that they cannot but be doing service, if they only add to what is defective enough to make it complete, or take away from what is ambiguous enough to make it decisive. Assuming arrival at some determinate truth necessary, he gave an exclusive development to those parts of Scripture which he had previously fixed on as containing, in distinction to any apparently opposite ones, its real meaning. But the assumption itself was gratuitous. There is no reason why Scripture should not designedly limit itself, and stop short of expressing definite truth; though whether it does so or not is a question of fact. If Revelation as a whole does not state a truth of predestination, that stopping short is as much a designed stopping short, as a statement would have been a designed statement. Nor are we to be discontented with the former issue, when the comparison of one part of God's word with another fairly leads to it; to suppose that an indeterminate conclusion must be a wrong one, and to proceed to obtain by forced interpretation what we had failed to do by natural. If Revelation as a whole does not speak explicitly, Revelation did not intend to do so: and to impose a definite truth upon it, when it designedly stops short of one, is as real an error of interpretation as to deny a truth which it expresses.

cum e contrario sacrilegorum et inimicorum Christi aliquo modo in Christianorum manus venientes, ex hac vita non sine sacramento regenerationis emigrent. . . . Ista cogitent, ista considerent, hic audeant dicere Deum vel acceptorem in sua gratiâ personarum, vel remuneratorem meritorum.'—Ep. 194. n. 32.

## CHAPTER VI.

### AUGUSTINIAN DOCTRINE OF GRACE.

THE doctrine of absolute predestination implies the doctrine of efficacious or irresistible grace, for the end implies the means; and therefore, if eternal life is ensured, the necessary qualifications for that life, which are holiness and virtue, must be earned also. But these can only be ensured by such a Divine influence as does not depend for its effect on the contingency of man's will; *i.e.* by what divines call irresistible or efficacious grace—a grace which S. Augustine accordingly maintains.

The language which the Church has always used for expressing the relation in which grace stands to the human will has been that grace *assists* the will; and such a term implies in its natural meaning an original power in ourselves, to which this assistance was given, and by which it must be used—an assistance, in short, which is no more than assistance. S. Augustine, however, in adopting the authorised expression, and speaking of grace as assistance, is obliged by his system to use the term in a meaning exceeding this natural and obvious one, viz. not as assistance, but as control; though he arrives at his definition of such a controlling grace only gradually, after long familiarity with the subject, and when controversy has strengthened and sharpened his ideas.

S. Augustine early in his theological life commits himself to an idea of the Divine Power as being a power of creating perfect goodness in the creature, and defends in his book *De Libero Arbitrio*, written against the Manicheans, the act of God in not creating man thus perfect at once, but only with the power of becoming so; arguing that God dispensed different kinds of advantages [1] accord-

[1] 'Bona quibus male uti malus potest, et quorum esse usus non potest malus;' the one being free-will or the power of being good, the other goodness itself.—De Lib. Arb. l. 2. c. 17., *et seq.*; De Pecc. Merit. et Remiss. l. 2. c. 18.

ing to His own sovereign will, and that a lesser good is not to be undervalued because it is not a higher one. The passage, however, expressing as it does the fitness of *both* kinds of goods to be Divine gifts, he appeals to in his 'Retractions' to prove how, even in an early work, and before his mind had expanded on the subject of grace, he had laid down the principles of his subsequent teaching.[1]

The first regular attempt, however, at a definition of the characteristic power of Gospel grace, occurs in the treatise '*De Gratiâ Christi*,' in which he calls it 'the assistance of will and action—*adjutorium voluntatis et actionis*.'[2] It will of course be evident at first sight that this definition does not of itself describe an irresistible grace, but would apply to a simply assisting one as well. But, considered in connection with the context, and taken in the meaning which its opposition to another definition of grace fastens upon it, it will be found to imply the former. It was asserted by the Pelagians that, inasmuch as the power of willing and acting in one way or another (*possibilitas utriusque partis*) was inseparable from human nature, human nature had of itself the power to will and act aright; but that this power needed to be assisted by grace (*ut possibilitas semper gratiæ adjuvetur auxilio*).[3] To this Augustine replied, that not only the *power* to will and act was assisted by grace, but that will and action itself were; and therefore to the Pelagian definition of grace, as the 'assistance of power' (*adjutorium possibilitatis*), he opposed his own, 'the assistance of will and action' (*adjutorium voluntatis et actionis*). Now, by assisting will and action we should naturally and ordinarily understand assisting the power to will and act, taking the words will and action loosely to signify the faculties; for acts themselves are not susceptible of assistance, being already done. Nor, therefore, should we naturally see any difference at all of meaning in these two expressions, assistance of power and assistance of action.

---

[1] Retract. l. 1. c. 9.
[2] I give the Jansenist turn to the phrase *gratia quæ adjuvat voluntatem et actionem*.
[3] De Grat. Christi, c. iii.

But if this ordinary meaning is disclaimed for the expression assistance of action, and, instead of being identified with, the latter is contrasted to, the assistance of the power to will and act, it must follow that by assistance of action a grace of a stronger kind is meant than that which assists the power to act; and what can that grace be but one which causes action itself—*i.e.* irresistible grace?

Indeed, this absolute sense is fastened on the word *adjutorium* in this, Augustine's, definition of grace, by the mode in which the same word is used in the rival and opposing definition. For the word carries to the phrase *adjutorium voluntatis et actionis* the same meaning that it bore in the phrase *adjutorium possibilitatis* (for the two sides differ not about the meaning of assistance, but about what is assisted). But in the latter phrase it bears the sense of causing as well as of assisting; for the Pelagians said this power (*possibilitas*) was given by God in the first instance as well as assisted when had. The word therefore bears the same sense in the phrase '*adjutorium voluntatis et actionis*,' and implies the gift or causation of will and action, and not only the assistance of it.

But the meaning of this definition of grace, which is evident hitherto with some difficulty, and only by a close and exact process of comparison, is abundantly clear and manifest when we come to S. Augustine's own explanation and exposition of it. He says: 'Pelagius in his first book on Freewill thus speaks: "We have," he says, "a power of taking either side—*possibilitatem utriusque partis*—implanted in us by God, as a fruitful and productive root, to produce and bring forth according to men's different wills; and either shine with the flower of virtue, or bristle with the thorns of vice, according to the choice of the cultivator." In which passage, not perceiving what he says, he establishes one and the same root of good and evil men, against evangelical truth and apostolical teaching. For our Lord says, that a good tree cannot bring forth evil fruit, nor an evil tree good fruit. And the Apostle

Paul, when he says that cupidity is the root of all evil, intimates also that love is the root of all good. If, therefore, the two trees good and evil are two men good and evil, what is the good man but the man of a good will; that is, the tree of a good root? And what is the evil man, but the man of an evil will; that is, the tree of an evil root? And the fruits of these two trees are acts, words, thoughts; which if good proceed from a good will, and if evil from an evil will . . . . . It is not true, then, as Pelagius says, that there is one and the same root of good and evil men: for there is one root of good men, viz. love; and another root of evil men, viz. cupidity: although it is true that that power is capable of both roots —*illa possibilitas utriusque radicis est capax*—because a man is able not only to have love but also to have cupidity.'[1]

He proceeds to say that love, which is the root of good actions, is a free gift of God, and not given according to our merits.

Now this passage evidently contains a different doctrine, as to the source of our actions, from the doctrine of freewill. The doctrine of freewill is that we *do* possess a power of taking both sides, and act well or ill according as we use it; that therefore good and evil acts may both arise out of one root or one and the same moral condition of the agent. But Augustine denies the residence in man of a power to act either way, on the logical or speculative ground of the absurdity of supposing, that both virtue and vice can come out of the same moral condition of the agent, as this neutral state of power would be; and maintains that human actions proceed either out of a moral condition which necessarily produces right action, or out of a moral condition which necessarily produces wrong. He denies therefore the doctrine of freewill. He admits, indeed, that man is capable of either moral condition— or, to use his own language, capable of either root; but this is not the doctrine of freewill, which is, that the same moral condition, or the same root, is capable of either

[1] De Grat. Christi, c. xviii.

fruit. The former is only the admission of the obvious fact, that man has a capacity, in the first instance, both for good and evil; an admission which is quite consistent with the subsequent necessity of either in him; just as a material is capable, in the first instance, of any one out of many different forms; but when it has once received a particular form, is necessarily of that form which it has received.

The whole of the book, however, *De Gratiâ Christi*, is one comment on the *adjutorium voluntatis et actionis*, as involving the sense of irresistible grace, as the following passage on illuminating grace will exemplify: ' Our Lord saith, " Every man that hath heard and hath learned of the Father, cometh unto Me." Whosoever therefore doth not come, of him it is not right to say, " He hath heard and learned, indeed, that he should come, but he does not will to do what he has learned." That is not rightly said, if we speak of that mode of teaching which God employs through grace. For if, as the truth saith, " Every man that hath learned, cometh," if any man hath not come, neither hath he learned. It is true, indeed, a man comes or does not come, according to the choice of his will. But this choice is alone if he does not come; it cannot but be assisted if he does come; and so assisted as that he not only knows what he should do, but also does what he knows. Wherefore, when God teaches not by the letter of the law, but by the grace of the spirit, He so teaches as that what a man learns he not only perceives by knowing it, but also pursues by willing it, and accomplishes by doing it. By that Divine mode of teaching will itself and action itself, not only the natural power of willing and acting, are assisted. For, were our *power* alone assisted by this grace, our Lord would have said, " Every man that hath heard or hath learned of the Father *is able* to come to Me." But He has not said this, but " Every man that hath heard and hath learned of the Father *cometh* unto Me." . . . . . Every man that hath learned of the Father is not only able to come, but comes; wherein not only the proficiency of the power, but the affection of the will, and the effect of action is included.'[1]

The grace, then, to which Augustine gives the name or description of '*adjutorium voluntatis et actionis*,' we find, on examining his own account and explanation of it, to be endowed with the effect of action ; to be a grace, not only given in order that such and such actions may be done, but also causing those actions to be done in fact.

But such a phrase as '*adjutorium voluntatis et actionis*' is obviously a very imperfect and awkward description of irresistible grace; being, in fact, not of itself any description of it at all, but depending entirely on the definition to which it is opposed and on the context generally, for its meaning. Indeed, hitherto, Augustine appears rather feeling his way toward some clear and exact definition of the grace for which he is arguing, than really defining it. His language as a whole has one evident meaning; but it is only as a whole that it has: it effects its object by large, varied, and diffuse statement and explanation ; but in aiming at point it altogether fails, and cannot concentrate itself in definition. As his doctrine of grace, however, obtains a more familiar hold of his mind, and perpetual controversy multiplies thought and language about it, and the subject by being turned over repeatedly is seen in every aspect, his ideas become more exact and his choice of terms greater ; and out of the accumulation of statements he is at last able to fix on one to serve as a complete definition of this grace.

In the book '*De Correptione et Gratia*' he draws a clear distinction between two different kinds of grace, which he calls respectively 'an assistance without which a thing cannot be done,' and ' an assistance by which a thing is done' (*adjutorium sine quo aliquid non fit*, and *adjutorium quo aliquid fit*). He first draws a strong distinction between the wants of man before and man after the fall, and then gives this as the corresponding distinction in the nature of the grace by which these respective wants are supplied. Man even before the fall, upright and per-

[1] De Grat. Christi, c. xiv.

fect being as he was, and possessed of freewill, stood in need of grace to enable him to act aright; nor could he do anything acceptable to God by his own natural strength. But as an upright being and possessed of freewill he only stood in need of assisting grace, he was strong enough to have the ultimate choice of good and evil thrown upon him, and only wanted grace to advance and aid the choice when made. So great a burden might be placed upon him, because he was able to bear it, and was no penalty, but the sign of strength and perfection. To man, then, before the fall 'an assistance without which a thing is not done' was given; that is to say, an assistance which he could not do without, but which did not effect anything unless he added the exercise of his own original choice to it,—that which is commonly called assisting grace. But at the fall this whole state of things ceased. The fall deprived man of freewill, and inclined his nature irresistibly to evil. In this state he was too weak to bear the ultimate choice of good and evil being thrown upon him, and must perish if it was. The grace, therefore, which is given to man after the fall is not the assistance 'without which a thing *is not* done,' but that 'with which a thing *is* done;' that is to say, an assistance, upon which being given, the effect of a renewed heart and renewed will follows certainly. A grace is now given him suited to an entirely impotent nature, wholly controlling choice and action, and leading irresistibly to good.

Augustine explains at length the difference between these two kinds of grace, and the reason for it: 'Adam was in the midst of good which he had received from the goodness of his Creator; but the saints in this life are in the midst of evil, out of which they cry aloud to God, "Deliver us from evil." He amidst that good needed not the death of Christ; them from guilt, hereditary and personal, the blood of that Lamb absolveth. He had not need of that assistance which they implore, saying, "I see another law in my members warring against the law of my mind, and bringing me into captivity to the law of sin which is in my members." In them the flesh lusteth against the spirit, and the spirit against the flesh; and in this struggle, labouring and endangered, they ask for strength through Christ's grace to fight and conquer. He, tried and harassed by no such conflict, enjoyed in that place of bliss internal peace.'[1] . . .

'The first man, therefore, had an assistance, which he could desert if he willed, and in which he would abide if he willed; not one by which he was made to will. This is the first grace which was given to the first Adam: but a stronger than this is given in the second Adam. For the first is a grace of which the effect is, that a man may have righteousness *if he wills:* the second is a more powerful one, of which the effect is, *that he wills,* and wills so strongly and loves so ardently, that the will of the flesh is conquered by the contrary will of the spirit. Nor was that a small assistance by which the power of a concurrent free-will was acknowledged; being so great, as that he could not remain in good without it, though if he willed he could desert it. But this is so much the greater, as that it is not enough to say that lost freewill is repaired by it, not enough to say that a man cannot attain to or abide in good without it, but with it can if he will; except we add also, that *it makes him to will.*'[2]

'For we must distinguish between one kind of assistance and another. There is one assistance, without which something is not done, and another by which something is done. For example, food is a thing without which we cannot live; but we have it and die. And therefore food is an assistance without which it is not effected, not an assistance by which it is effected, that we live. On the other hand, if happiness be given to a man he is forthwith happy. Happiness, therefore, is an assistance by which something is, not an assistance without which something is not, effected. The first man received the gift of being able not to sin, able not to die, able not to desert good: that assistance of perseverance was given him without which he could not be, not an assistance by which he was persevering. On the other hand, to the saints, who by

[1] De Corr. et Grat. n. 29.   [2] Ibid. n. 31.

grace are predestinated to the kingdom of God, not such an assistance of perseverance as this is given, but such an assistance as that perseverance *itself* is given—*tale ut eis perseverantia ipsa donetur;* not only a gift of perseverance, without which they cannot be, but a gift by which they cannot but be persevering—*non solum ut sine isto dono perseverantes esse non possint, verum etiam ut per hoc donum non nisi perseverantes sint.*[1] . . .

'In truth, a greater freedom, and one fortified and confirmed by the gift of perseverance, is necessary against so many and so great temptations, such as there were not in Paradise; that, with all its affections, terrors, errors, the world be conquered. This the martyrdom of the saints has shown. For Adam, yielding to no terror, but rather using his freewill against the command of a terrible God, stood not firm in so great felicity, and so great facility of avoiding sin: but they, against a world not terrible only but raging, stood firm in the faith: though he saw those present advantages which he was about to leave, and they saw not the future ones which they were about to gain. Whence this, but by His gift from whom they obtained mercy, that they might be faithful.[2] . . . .

'Perseverance, then, was not given to Adam as a Divine gift, but the choice of persevering or not was left to himself, because his will, created as it was without sin and without concupiscence, was furnished with such strength, that it was worthy of such a choice being committed to it; so great goodness and facility of living well was his. But now, after that great freedom has been lost by sin, it remains that human infirmity be assisted with greater gifts.[3] . . . . God not wishing His saints to glory in their own strength, but in Him, gives them more than that assistance which He gave to the first man; for inasmuch as they will not persevere except they both can and will, He gives them by an act of free grace the power and the will both. For if their own will were left in such a way as that if they willed they would persevere, without it

---

[1] De Corr. et Grat. n. 34.   [2] Ibid. n. 35.   [3] Ibid. n. 36.

being provided that they should will, their will must succumb amid so many infirmities, and persevere they could not. Therefore such a succour is afforded to the infirmity of their will as that by Divine grace action takes place, without it being possible to fall away or be overcome.[1] Thus, weak though it is, this will fails not and is not conquered. The feeble will of man, through the Divine strength, perseveres in a yet imperfect goodness, when the strong and sound will of the first man did not in its more perfect. The strength of freewill failed, because, through that assistance of God without which a man cannot, if he wills, persevere, was not wanting, such assistance as that by which God works in a man to will, was. God left it to the strong man to do, *if* he willed; to the weak He has reserved, as a gift from Himself, to will unconquerably what is good and unconquerably persevere in it.'[2]

Such is the distinction between the two kinds of grace by which the spiritual wants of man before the fall and after are respectively supplied,—the grace of the paradisal, and the grace of the gospel dispensation. Under the former dispensation grace was weak, because nature was strong; under the latter, grace is absolute, because nature is impotent. Human nature is too corrupt and weak now to have anything left to itself to do; and it must be treated as such, and be taken in hand with the understanding that everything must be done for it. It is past all but the strongest remedy, a self-acting one. The distinction rests upon the doctrine of the fall of man and the change it introduced into his nature. The doctrine of the fall of man asserts an essential change in the powers of his moral nature to have followed from that event, in consequence of which he cannot will or do anything aright now of his own natural strength. But if man in natural state has not the power to will aright, he has not, Augustine says, freewill. Accordingly it is assumed in this argument that this is the difference between man before, and man after the fall; that

[1] 'Ut divina gratia indeclinabiliter et insuperabiliter ageretur.' The acknowledged MS. reading, though some editions have 'inseparabiliter.'

[2] De Corr. et Grat. n. 38.

before he had a will which exerted a power of its own[1], and after has not; and Augustine comes to the question of the nature of Christian grace, with the understanding that grace has now to deal with a being who has not freewill. But what kind of grace, he then naturally argues, is to restore and reclaim such a being, to raise him to spiritual life, and make him persevere in it, but an over-mastering and controlling grace? Less power in the grace would suffice if there were some in the being; for if there is any power in nature, the complement of it only is needed from grace; but if there is none, grace must supply the whole. Had man freewill, grace, to be suited to his condition, must recognise it, leave it to act, and suspend its own effect upon its action. But when man has freewill no longer, to leave the effect of grace dependent upon his freewill is a mockery. If he is to be reclaimed at all, he must then be reclaimed by an absolute act of power, and grace must either do everything for him or do nothing.

Here there is a clear and express definition of irresistible or efficacious grace,—the assistance with which a thing is done—*adjutorium quo aliquid fit,*—as distinguished from assisting grace—*adjutorium sine quo aliquid non fit;* or, as abbreviated by the Jansenist divines, the *adjutorium quo,* as distinguished from the *adjutorium sine quo non.* According to this definition, if the grace defined is given, the effect takes place—*aliquid fit;* the renewal and conversion of the man follows in fact. By this definition, then, the *effect* is made the test, whether the grace is given or not; and a grace, of which the bestowal is thus tested, is by the very terms an irresistible and efficacious one.

But, while preceding statements are at last embodied in a definition, the definition does no more than embody and give point to them; for a grace, of the bestowal of which the effect is the test, has been described all along. 'If every man that hath learned cometh unto Christ, if any man hath not come, neither hath he learned.'[2]—'If

---

[1] Potentia liberi arbitrii.—De Corr. et Grat. c. xi.

[2] De Grat. Christi, c. xiv.

every one that hath heard and learned of the Father
cometh, whoever hath not come hath not heard or learned
of the Father. For if he had heard or learned, he would
have come. For there is no one that hath heard or learned,
and cometh not; but every one, as saith the truth, that
hath heard and learned of the Father cometh.'[1] Here the
test of grace, whether it is given or not, is the effect. If
a man is admitted to hearing and learning, *i.e.* to illuminating grace, the effect of a new life or coming to Christ
follows: if this effect does not follow, he has not been admitted to this grace. We do indeed sometimes use the
words hearing and learning in the sense of a man's own act
of attending to what is told him, and profiting by what is
taught him; and in this sense the words would express
here, not the enlightening grace of God, but a man's own
use of that grace; and therefore not the giving of a grace,
but a man's own use of it, would be the thing tested here
by the effect. But the obvious sense of this passage, and
the whole nature of the discussion, to which it belongs,
exclude such a meaning of the words hearing and learning
here, which mean the fact of being told and being taught, or
the act of another telling or teaching. A certain teaching
of God, then[2], that is to say, a *grace*, is the thing of which
the bestowal is in these passages tested by the effect; and to
this purpose Augustine criticises the common saying, that
'God's mercy to us is in vain if we do not will,' remarking,
'I do not know how this can be said, for if God has mercy
we also will—*si Deus misereretur etiam volumus:* God has
mercy on no man in vain—*nullius Deus frustra misereretur.*'[3]
This is to adopt the test of the effect. The saying '*Agis si
agaris*—thou actest if thou art acted on[4]' does the same,
its force lying in the contrast and inseparableness at the
same time of an influence *on* the man and an act *of* him.
The saying 'Grace gives merit, when it is given itself—
*gratia dat merita cum donatur*[5],' the term merit meaning

[1] De Præd. c. viii.
[2] Iste *docendi* modus quo per gratiam *docet* Deus.
[3] De Div. Quæst. ad Simp. l. 1. n. 12, 13.
[4] Serm. 128. c. 7.
[5] Ep. ad Vitalem, 217. n. 5.

in Augustine's use of it right action, does the same. Again, 'Grace is given, that the faults both of nature and will may be conquered; for that which is impossible with man is easy to God. But those to whom the grace of God is not given become sinners, unrighteous men. Though these too live for the advantage of the children of mercy, that the sight of them may subdue their pride; reminding them that what has been given to them is God's free gift, and not of their own deserving.'[1] The test of the effect is clearly adopted here: the conquest of sin and continuance in it being respectively attached to the bestowal of grace and the withholding of it.[2]

A general body of language to the same effect must be noticed, in which a holy disposition and conduct is put forward as a Divine gift and a Divine creation. It is certain from revelation, that God is the Giver of every good thing; and this truth is applied absolutely by Augustine to the subject of human action, which, when good, is described as being a Divine gift. Conversion is a Divine gift—*donum Dei etiam ipsa ad Deum nostra conversio*[3]: so is obedience—*donum obedientiæ*; a good life—*bene vivere donum divinum*; merit or deserving action—*Dei dona sunt, et Dei gratia conferuntur universa merita justorum*[4]; perseverance—*donum Dei perseverantia*[5]; faith in its beginning—'*gratuito munere nobis datur*[6];' even the very beginning, 'when men begin to have faith which they had not—*incipiunt habere fidem quam non habebant*[7];' faith in its increase—*augmentum, incrementum, supplementum fidei donum Dei.*[8]

[1] Op. Imp., Contra Jul. l. iv. c. 129.
[2] 'Nulla omnino medicinalis Christi gratia effectu suo caret; sed omnis efficit ut voluntas velit, et aliquid operetur.... Primo igitur hoc probat, quod apud Augustinum gratia et opus bonum ita reciprocentur, ut quemadmodum ex gratiâ data mox effectum operis consecutum inferre solet; ita vice versâ, ex defectu operis gratiam non esse datam. Quo ratiocinandi modo indicatur gratiam tanquam causam, et operationem voluntatis bonam velut effectum, esse, ut philosophi loquuntur, convertibiles, et a se mutuo inseparabiles.'—Jansen. De Gratiâ Christi Salvatoris, l. 2. c. 25.
[3] De Grat. et Lib. Arb. c. v.
[4] De Dono Pers. c. ii.
[5] Ibid. c. i.
[6] Ep. 194. n. 12.
[7] Ibid. 217. n. 29.
[8] De Præd. c. ii.

Again, it is certain from revelation that God is the Creator of every thing visible and invisible; and this truth is also applied absolutely by Augustine to the subject of human action; which, when good, is described as being a Divine creation. And if a reason is asked for this limitation, inasmuch as, according to the argument, God would be the Creator of all action, good as well as bad, the answer is ready, that bad action, or sin, is not a *thing*, but only a negation. Sin is 'nothing,' according to Augustine. The faculties of mind and body which are used in a sinful action, are indeed things, and are the creatures of God: but the sin itself is not a thing, and is consequently not a creature. God is indeed the Author of all that *is*, of every substance; but sin is not a substance, and *is* not. It is a declination from substance and from being, and not a part of it; true being and true substance being necessarily good, and 'is good,' and 'is' being convertible propositions. It is unnecessary to enter at large here into this distinction. It is obvious that some explanation or other is wanted in order to prevent the conclusion that God is the Author of evil; and it is enough to say that this difficulty is seen and is in some way disposed of.

This idea of human virtue and piety, as a Divine creation, is indeed, in itself, a scriptural one; a point which deserves consideration. The attribute of God as Creator, in the strict sense of the word, is a truth almost peculiar to the Bible; for though this truth may be considered a part of natural religion, it has not practically been brought out under that dispensation; the more general notion having been, that God was the Former of the world, and put it into shape, but was not the Maker of its substance. The human mind appears to have had great difficulty in reaching the idea of positive causation of existence, making substance out of nothing; such a power appearing even to those who entertained a system of religion, and admitted the existence of a Deity and our duties to Him, incredible, fictitious, and monstrous. A material was accordingly provided for the great Architect, ready at hand for Him to work upon and put into shape; and matter was made a co-eternal substance with the Deity. The timidity or fastidiousness of philosophy thus weakened essentially the great idea of God's omnipotence; but the Bible sustains it in a remarkable way upon this head. Exemplifying the rule, that 'the foolishness of God is wiser than men, and the weakness of God is stronger than men,' Scripture puts forward prominently, and as a fundamental truth, that very idea which appeared thus monstrous and untenable to the philosopher, viz. that God is the true Creator of the world, and made substance out of nothing.

This difference between the Bible and ancient philosophy is specially important as regards one division of the creation, viz. the world invisible. Philosophy did not speak of the intelligent soul as being a created substance, but rather as being an emanation of the Divine mind; thus making it part of the Deity Himself, and forestalling the peculiar subjection which it derives from creation. But the Bible teaches that the intelligent soul is a created substance, as truly as matter is. The subjection which belongs to the creature thus attaches to the soul in the system of the Bible; the susceptibility to and need of influence, the capacity for being moulded and controlled by that Being by whom it was originally made, and dependence upon this moulding and controlling Power. The Divine power in Scripture thus extends from the first act of creating the substance of the soul to the kindred one of creating it morally; of forming and fashioning the inner man, inspiring holy acts, imparting holy dispositions, and confirming and sustaining them afterwards. This absolute dominion over men and irresistible power over their hearts is illustrated by the similitude of a potter, who makes what he pleases of his clay; now forming it and then breaking it, now preserving it and then rejecting it.[1] The New Testament both interprets and sustains the language of the Old; appealing to this similitude and describing renewed hearts as a Divine creation. 'Shall the thing formed say to Him that formed it, why hast Thou made me thus?'[2] 'If any man be in Christ, he is a new creature.'[3]

[1] Isaiah, xxix. 16; xlv. 9; lxiv. 8; Jeremiah, xviii. 6.
[2] Rom. ix. 20.
[3] 2 Cor. v. 17.

'In Christ Jesus neither circumcision availeth anything, nor uncircumcision, but a new creature.'[1] 'We are His workmanship, created in Christ Jesus unto good works, which God hath before ordained, that we should walk in them.'[2]

This language, however, receives in Scripture a limitation of meaning from the general doctrine of man's freewill which Scripture inculcates. But Augustine uses this language absolutely, and adds to its strength and definiteness. Thus, 'God *makes* men good in order that they may do good acts—*ipse ergo illos bonos facit ut bona faciant.*'[3] God 'makes faith—*fidem gentium facit.*'[4] 'He makes men believers—*facit credentes.*'[5] God 'makes men to persevere in good.'[6] 'God calls whom He vouchsafes to call, and makes whom He will religious—*Deus quos dignatur vocat, et quem vult religiosum facit:*' a saying of S. Cyprian's, often quoted, on which he affixes a literal meaning. 'Man never does good things which God does not make him do—*quæ non facit Deus ut faciat homo.*'[7] 'The Holy Spirit not only assists good minds, but makes them good—*non solum mentes bonas adjuvat, verum etiam bonas eas facit.*'[8] 'There is a creation, not that by which we were made men, but that of which a man already created spoke, "create a clean heart in me;" and that of which speaks the Apostle, "If any man be in Christ, he is a new creature." We are therefore fashioned and created in good works, which we have not ourselves prepared, but God, that we should walk in them.'[9]

Nor is this language used by S. Augustine in a qualified sense, simply to express vividly the power of God's assisting grace, as if giving and creating were meant by Him to be conditional upon, and supplemental to, a certain exertion of man's own freewill, understood though not expressed; for he distinctly disclaims this qualification, making a difference in this very respect between the gift of obedience

[1] Gal. vi. 15.
[2] Eph. ii. 10.
[3] De Corr. et Grat. c. xii.
[4] De Præd. c. ii.
[5] Ibid. c. xvii.
[6] De Corr. et Grat. c. xii.
[7] Contra Duas, Ep. l. 2. c. xxi.
[8] Ibid. l. 4. c. vii.
[9] De Grat. et Lib. Arb. c. 8.

or holiness and the ultimate gift of eternal life. Eternal life is the gift of God, but it is given according to merit; that is, it is a gift upon certain conditions, viz. the conditions of obedience and holiness in the persons to whom it is awarded. But the conditions themselves of obedience and holiness are not given according to merit, but are gifts unconditional and gratuitous. The gift of eternal life is a reward, and not a gift only; but that for which it is a reward is not *itself* a reward, or given upon condition of endeavours and exercise of will by the man himself, but is a free gift —*dona sua coronat Deus, non merita tua*[1]—God crowns His gifts and not thy merits. 'Eternal life is the recompense of preceding merits; but those merits of which it is the recompence are not prepared through our own sufficiency, but are *made* in us by grace; it is given to merits, but the merits to which it is given are themselves given —*data sunt et ipsa merita quibus datur*.'[2] God at the last judgment has respect to His own gifts in those who appear before Him, not distributing eternal life to this person or that, according to His own sovereign will and pleasure only, but according to a rule; that is to say, according as persons show the possession of certain previous gifts of His own to them; but those gifts themselves are not to be divested of their proper character of gifts because a reward is based upon them,—the second gift is indeed upon the basis of the first, but the first gift is upon no basis at all but the Divine will and pleasure. Here, then, is a contrast which establishes the sense of the term gift as used of the qualifications for eternal life, as the more simple and natural one of a gift absolute, for so used it is *opposed* to the gift conditional.

Thus he handles the text 'Turn unto Me, and I will turn unto you[3];' a text of which the natural meaning is, that if a man does his part according to the power of free agency which he possesses, God will do His in the way of pardon and reward. 'They, the Pelagians, gather from this text, that the grace wherewith God turns to us is given as a reward for our own turning of ourselves to God; not

[1] See Note, p. 8.     [2] Ep. 134. n. 19.     [3] Zech. i. 3.

considering that unless this very conversion to God were the gift of God, it would not have been said, "Turn us, Thou God of Hosts,"[1] and "wilt Thou not turn again and quicken us," and "Turn us then, O God our Saviour,"[2] and the like. What else is coming to Christ but turning to Him by faith? and yet He saith, "No man can come unto Me except it were given him of my Father."[3] All that this passage asserts is, that obedience is a gift of God as well as salvation. But obedience is next made a gift of God in distinction to salvation. 'When the Pelagians say, that that grace which is given at the end—*i.e.* eternal life, is awarded according to preceding merits,—I reply, true, if they understand these merits themselves to be gifts of God.'[4] 'But how could the just Judge award the crown, if the merciful Father had not given the grace? How could there be the crown of righteousness, if the righteousness by grace had not preceded? How could this final reward be given to merit, if the merit itself had not been given as a free gift?'[5] Here the qualified sense of gift, viz. as a gift according to merit or upon the fulfilment of certain conditions, is allowed of the ultimate gift of eternal life, only on the understanding that it is denied of the preparatory gift of the righteousness which qualifies for it. The crown of righteousness is a reward, but the righteousness itself is not a reward; *i.e.* anything given in consideration of preceding endeavours of man's own will. And the gift of obedience is described as a gift residing in the individual previous to action of his own; for Augustine lays it down as the object of the institution of preaching, that those who have this gift may be instructed as to the application of it—'*ut qui haberent donum obedientiæ, quibus jussis obediendum esset audirent.*'[6]

---

[1] Ps. lxxx. 7.

[2] Ps. lxxxv. 4. 6.

[3] John, vi. 65; De Grat. et Lib. Arb. c. v.

[4] Ibid. c. vi.

[5] Again: 'Itaque, charissimi, si vita bona nostra nihil aliud est quam Dei gratia, sine dubio et vita æterna quæ bonæ vitæ redditur, Dei gratia est: et ipsa enim gratis datur, quia gratis data est illa cui datur. Sed illa cui datur tantummodo gratia est: hæc autem quæ illi datur, quoniam præmium ejus est, gratia est pro gratia, tanquam merces pro justitia.'—C. viii.

[6] De Dono Pers. c. xix.

There is another evidence of the sense in which Augustine uses the term gift, as applied to a holy life and conduct, in an argument in constant use with him, drawn from the fact of prayer. We pray, he says, not only for external good things, but for spiritual dispositions and habits; for virtue, holiness, obedience, both for ourselves and others. But a request implies that we suppose the thing asked for to be in the gift of him from whom we ask it, and that he is able to bestow it or not, according to his will and pleasure, otherwise there is no reason to account for our asking. If we ask God for holiness then, and obedience, it follows that we suppose holiness and obedience to be properly in His gift.[1] 'If God so prepared and worked a good will in a man as only to apply His law and teaching to his freewill, and did not by a deep and occult vocation so act upon his mind, that he complied with that law and teaching, beyond a doubt it would be enough to expound and preach to that man, and there would be no necessity to pray that God would convert him or give him perseverance when converted. If these things are to be prayed for then, and you cannot deny that they are to be, what remains, but that you confess that these things are gifts? for you must ask God for what He gives.'[2]

It is evident that this argument defines an absolute gift of holiness and obedience, for the force of the argument lies in pushing the act of prayer to its extreme consequences; and this is the logical consequence of prayer, as a request for holiness and obedience from God. It is undoubtedly of the very nature of prayer to suppose the subject of its request to be simply in God's gift; so far as a thing is not in God's power to give, so far it is not the

[1] 'Frequentationibus autem orationum simpliciter apparebat Dei gratia quid valeret : non enim poscerentur de Deo quæ præcipit fieri, nisi ab illo donarentur, ut fierent.'— De Præd. Sanct. c. xiv.
'Si alia documenta non essent, dominica oratio nobis ad causam gratiæ quam defendimus sola sufficeret. Siquidem ut non discedamus a Deo non ostendit dandum esse nisi a Deo, cum poscendum ostendit a Deo. Qui enim non infertur in tentationem non discedit a Deo.'
'Ecclesia orat ut increduli credant. Deus ergo convertit ad fidem. Orat ut credentes perseverent : Deus ergo dat perseverantiam in finem.'—De Dono Pers. c. vii.

[2] Ep. 217. ad Vitalem, n. 5.

subject of prayer. If the act of prayer, then, in the case of asking for goodness from God, is to be pushed to its logical consequences, it must follow from it that goodness is God's absolute gift. Upon the doctrine of freewill, when the act of prayer extends to such requests as these, it is understood in such a sense as to forestall this consequence of it; but Augustine embraces himself, and presses upon others the extreme consequences of prayer.

He adds that which is necessary to make this view a consistent one, that prayer itself also is the gift of God; for it would be evidently inconsistent to make other spiritual habits the gift of God, if that habit which was a means to those was not a gift of God too.[1]

Another convincing proof of the sense in which Augustine uses the terms gift and creation, as applied to a holy life, is his express connection of this gift with predestination, and the referring of it to God's secret and mysterious will. Had he simply meant by these terms that God crowned man's own endeavours, and gave the increase if man make a beginning, such a doctrine would have approved itself naturally to our sense of justice, and would not have needed any reference to mystery for its defence. But Augustine bases this gift of holiness and obedience upon mystery. 'Deaf as thou art, hear the apostle thanking God that they have obeyed the doctrine from the heart; not that they have heard the doctrine preached, but that they have obeyed it. For all have not obeyed the Gospel, but *those to whom it is given to obey*; just as to know the mysteries of the kingdom of God is given to some, but to others is not given.'[2] . . . . .

Again; 'As begun and as perfected, faith is alike the gift of God; and that this gift is given to some and not to others cannot be doubted without opposing the plainest declarations of Scripture. Nor should this disturb any believer who knows that from one man all went into justest condemnation; so that, were none rescued, God could not be blamed, the real deserts even of those who are rescued being the same with those of the damned. It belongs to

[1] De Dono Pers. c. xxiii.; Ep. 194. c. iv.  [2] Op. Imp. l. 2, c. 230.

God's unsearchable judgments, and His ways past finding out, why He rescues one man and not another. O man, who art thou that repliest against God? Bow to the rebuke, rather than speak as if thou knowest that which God who wills nothing unjust has yet willed to be secret.'[1] Again : ' God converts to faith. God gives perseverance. God foreknew that He would do this. This is the predestination of the saints whom He elected in Christ before the foundation of the world, that they should be holy and without blame before Him in love, having predestinated us unto the adoption of children by Christ Jesus to Himself, according to the good pleasure of His will ; in whom we have obtained an inheritance, being predestinated according to the purpose of Him who worketh all things after the counsel of His own will. . . . . . But why is not the grace of God given according to merit? I reply, because God is merciful. And why is He not merciful to all? I reply, because He is just. His justice on some shows how freely His grace is given to others. Let us not then be ungrateful, because according to the pleasure of His will, and the praise of His glory, the merciful God frees so many from a just perdition when He would not be unjust if He freed nobody. From one man have all gone, not into any unjust condemnation, but a just one. Whoever is freed then, let him love the grace ; whoever is not freed, let him acknowledge the justice. God's goodness is seen in remitting, His equity in exacting, His injustice in nothing.'[2] Again on the text ' It is He that made us and not we ourselves.' ' He therefore makes sheep—*facit oves.* . . . . . Why dost thou cast freewill in my teeth, which will not free for righteousness except thou be a sheep? He it is who makes men sheep, who frees human wills for works of piety. But why, when there is with Him no respect of persons, He makes some men sheep, and not others, is, according to the Apostle, a question more curious than becoming. O man! who art thou that repliest against God? Shall the thing formed say to Him that formed it, Why hast Thou made me thus? This ques-

[1] De Præd. c. viii.　　　　[2] De Dono Pers. c. vii. viii.

tion belongs to that abyss from which the Apostle shrank with dread, exclaiming, " O the depth of the riches both of the wisdom and knowledge of God!" . . . . . Why this man receives, and that man does not receive, when neither deserves to receive, measuring thy strength, examine not; enough that we know that there is no iniquity with God. . . . . . The vessels of mercy understand how entirely in their own case mercy is gratuitous, when those, with whom they share one common lump of perdition, receive their just punishment.'[1]

In these passages the gift of obedience, the gift of faith, the gift of perseverance, the creation of the holy and good man, or sheep as he is called, are treated as the effects of the Divine predestination, and are accounted for on a mysterious principle. It is, therefore, a proper gift and creation of which he is speaking, and not a mere crowning of human endeavours after holiness, for which such an account would be both superfluous and unsuitable. For there could be no occasion to go to mystery for the explanation of a proceeding of which so very natural and intelligible account could be given, as of God's giving the advancing and perfecting grace in proportion as man exerts his own faculties and will.

To sum up briefly, then, the evidences, as far as we have gone, of the Augustinian doctrine of grace; there is first an express definition of the nature of grace, under the Gospel dispensation, arrived at after much thought and effort, and much handling and discussing of the subject; a definition according to which the grace of the Gospel is an assistance productive of that effect upon man's life and conduct for which it is given—*adjutorium cum quo fit*. And this definition is sustained by a general body of language describing goodness and holiness as a Divine gift and a Divine creation, not in a secondary and qualified but a natural and proper sense of the terms, as shown by the caution annexed, that this gift is not given according to merit,—*i.e.* according to any conditions which man himself previously fulfils; by the argument from

[1] Contra Duas, Ep. Pel. l. 4. c. 6.

prayer, and by the express referring of this gift and this creation to the mystery of the Divine predestination. But a grace which is always productive of the effect upon life and conduct for which it is given—a grace which gives and creates goodness absolutely is an effective or irresistible grace.

This *rationale* is, then, confirmed by examples from Scripture. 'I wish,' says S. Augustine to the Pelagian who accounted for change of heart from bad to good by self-discipline and self-mortification on the part of man, which Divine grace seconded, 'I wish you would tell me whether that Assyrian king whose bed the holy Esther abhorred, when he sat on the throne of his kingdom, clad in glorious apparel, and covered with gold and precious stones, and was very dreadful, and looked at her with a countenance inflamed with indignation, so that the queen fainted with fear—whether that king had already " run to the Lord, and desired to be led by Him, and suspended his will upon His will, and by cleaving constantly to Him had been made one spirit with Him" (he quotes the Pelagian statement), "by the power of his freewill; whether he had given himself up to God, and mortified all his will, and put his heart in God's hand." It would be madness to think so; and yet God converted him, and changed his fury to mildness. But who does not see that it is a much greater thing to convert an opposite indignation into mildness, than to convert a heart pre-occupied with neither the one nor the other affection, but midway between the two? Read then, and understand, behold and confess, that not by law and teaching from without, but by a marvellous and ineffable power within, God produces in the hearts of men, not only true revelations, but also good wills.'[1]

The particular conclusion from this passage is, that, in the change from a bad to a good state of mind in the case of Ahasuerus, Divine grace could not have waited for any motive of the will; his will having been up to the very instant of that effect taking place violently opposed to such

[1] De Gratiâ Christi, n. 25.

a change; the general one is, that if grace alone turned the raging and hostile will of that monarch, it can certainly do the same with other wills in a more neutral state.

The conversion of S. Paul is appealed to as another instance of the operation of such a grace. 'I pardon you,' he says to his Pelagian opponent Julian, 'that on a very deep matter you are mistaken, as a man may be—*ignoscendum est quia in re in multum abditâ, ut homo falleris*. God forbid that the intention of the omnipotent and all-foreseeing One should be frustrated by man. Little do they think about, or small power have they of thinking out a weighty matter, who suppose that God omnipotent wills anything, and through weak man's resistance cannot do it. . . . . . If, as you say, men are not recalled by any necessity from their own evil intentions, how was the Apostle Paul, yet Saul, breathing slaughter and thirsting for blood, recalled from his most wicked intention by the stroke of blindness and the terrible voice from heaven, and from the prostrate persecutor, raised to be a preacher and the most laborious one of all? Acknowledge the work of grace. But God calls one man in this way, and another in that, whomever He prefers to call, and the wind bloweth where it listeth.'[1] That is, acknowledge the work of God, not only in this particular instance, but in all cases of conversion from a wicked to a holy life. The operation of a grace absolutely determining the will of man comes, as it were, visibly before us, as in the case of S. Paul. But God calls one man in this way, and another in that— *alium sic, alium autem sic*. Because He does not call all those whom He calls in the same striking and visible manner in which He called S. Paul, do not infer any difference of principle upon which His calls are conducted; for the laws of God's spiritual dealings are uniform, and He makes one saint in the same way fundamentally in which He makes another. In the gentlest and most gradual conversions, then, acknowledge the operation of the same power which operates in that of S. Paul.

S. Peter is brought forward as another instance of the

[1] Op. Imp. l. 1. c. 93.

operation of such a grace upon the will; or of grace alone and by itself determining it or causing the particular will of the man to be the will which it is. 'What will you oppose to the text "I have prayed for thee, Peter, that thy faith fail not?"[1] Will you dare to say that even the prayer of Christ could not have procured indefectible faith for Peter, had Peter wished that it should fail; that is, had been unwilling to persevere? As if Peter could possibly will anything else but what Christ had prayed that he should will! True, indeed, Peter's faith would have failed, if Peter's will to be faithful had failed. But the will is prepared by the Lord, and therefore Christ's prayer for him could not be ineffectual.'[2] This passage is clear. Peter's faith would have failed if Peter's will had; but Peter's will would not be anything else but what God had determined it to be, and God had determined that it should be faithful.

It remains now to inquire whether anything is said of the nature or quality of this grace in itself—itself, I mean, as distinguished from its effects, by which alone it has hitherto been described. And to this question the answer is, that Augustine identifies this grace with the disposition of love.

Christian love is a general affection toward God and man, productive of all the virtues and the whole of obedience. 'Love is the fulfilling of the law.'[3] 'If we love one another, God dwelleth in us and His love is perfected in us.'[4] But this love is, according to the doctrine of free-will, a *result*, an ultimate habit, gained by the endeavours of the man himself assisted by Divine grace. But in the system of Augustine it appears as a primary disposition imparted to the soul by an act of free grace; not the reward and effect of, but a gift preceding and producing, a good course of life. That which is the infallible root of general obedience is implanted in the man at the outset. The grace of love is infused into his heart. In consequence of the indwelling of this gift, he cannot but take pleasure in

[1] Luke, xxii. 32.
[2] De Corr. et Grat. c. viii.
[3] Rom. xiii. 10.
[4] 1 John, iv. 12.

God's law, obeying it not out of servile fear and in the spirit of bondage, but in the freedom of a renewed and converted inclination. The gift of love makes that sweet to him which before was difficult, nay impossible. Not that those who have the gift enjoy the full virtue of it all at once, and immediately find a holy life pleasant to them; but in proportion as the virtue of it comes out, they do find this result; and the gift ultimately, by means of this power inherent in it of accommodating the human will to the Divine, inclination to law, does produce a saving and acceptable obedience.

Thus, in a passage which has been quoted, Augustine lays down one root of good men, viz. love, and another root of evil men, viz. cupidity; adding, 'The virtue of love is from God, and not from ourselves, for Scripture says, "Love is God, and every one that loveth is born of God and knoweth God;" and "Whosoever is born of God doth not commit sin," and that because " he cannot sin." Nor have our preceding merits caused this love to be given us; for what good merits were we able to have at the time when we did not love God? That we might have that love, we were loved before we had it; as the Apostle John saith, "Not that we loved God, but that He loved us," and "We love Him because He first loved us." For what good could we do if we did not love, or, *how can we not do good if we do love?*'[1]

Here love, which is described as a necessary root of good action, or involving a good life in the individual who has it, is also made an original and primary gift of God to man. 'Who hath it in his power to secure, either that something delighting should come across him, or that it should delight him when it does? When a holy life delights us then, this delight is inspired and given by the grace of God, and not gained by our own will, or endeavours, or works; this very will, these very endeavours, and these very works, being His gifts.'[2]

Again: 'When we ask assistance from Him to work righteousness, what ask we but that He should open what

[1] De Grat. Christi, c. xxi. *et seq.*  [2] De Div. Quæst. ad Simpl. l. 1. n. 21.

was hid, and make sweet what was unpleasant? . . . . .
There precedes in the will of man a certain appetite for its
own power, so that it becomes disobedient through pride.
Were this appetite away, nothing would be difficult, and
man, as he now seeks his own will, would quite as easily
not have sought it. But there has come upon him, as a
just punishment, such a corruption of nature, that it is now
disagreeable to him to obey the Divine law. And unless
this corruption is overcome by assisting grace, no one is
converted to obedience ; unless healed by the operation of
grace, no one enjoys the peace of obedience. But by whose
grace is he conquered and healed, but by His to whom it
is said, " Turn us, then, O God our Saviour, and let Thine
anger cease from us "? which, if He does to any, He does
to them in mercy; while to those to whom He does it not
He does it not in judgment. And who shall say to Him
(whose mercy and judgment all pious minds celebrate),
what doest Thou? Wherefore even His saints and faithful
servants He heals slowly in some faults, so that good delights them less than is sufficient for fulfilling the whole
law ; in order that, tried by the perfect rule of His truth, no
flesh may be justified in His sight. Nor is such imperfection intended for our condemnation, but only our humbling,
and to remind us of our dependence on this same grace ;
lest, attaining facility in everything, we think that our own
which is His. . . . . Let us be wise, and understand that
God sometimes does not give even to his saints, with respect
to any work, either a certain knowledge, or a victorious
delight—*victricem delectationem*—in order that they may
know that not from themselves but from Him is that light
by which their darkness is illuminated, and that sweetness
by which their land yields her fruit.'[1]

Love, which he calls delight and sweetness, is described
in this passage as a ' conquering ' or irresistible grace; upon
the bestowal of which certain effects of life and conduct
follow naturally, though not always in a full measure, but
only in proportion to the amount imparted of the gift

[1] De Pecc. Mer. et Rem. l. 2. c. xix.

itself. And being such a gift, it is described as a free gift; not half given by God, half attained by man, or given in proportion to our natural striving after it. For why it is given to one more than another he treats as a mystery, or a question belonging to the secret counsels of God; whereas, on the latter supposition there would have been no difficulty to account for. Moreover, the gift is described throughout as preceding and producing action, and not following it.

Again: 'The appetite for good is from God; the most high, unchangeable good; which appetite is love, of which John saith, "Love is of God." Not that its beginning is of us, and its perfecting of God, but that the whole of love is from God. For God avert such madness as to make ourselves prior in His gifts and Him posterior; seeing, it is said, "Thou preventest him with the blessings of sweetness." For what can be meant here but that appetite for good of which we speak. For good begins to be desired as soon as it begins to be sweet. But when good is done through fear of punishment, and not through love, good is not done well. It is done in the act, but not in the heart, when a man would not do it if he could refuse with impunity. The blessing of sweetness is therefore given as a grace whereby that which is commanded delights us, and is desired and loved.'[1] Again: 'If grace co-operates with a previously existing good will, and does not prevent and produce that will, how is it truly said that "God worketh in us to will," and that the will is prepared by the Lord, and that "Love is of God," love which alone wills beatific good?'[2] Again: 'When the love of God is shed abroad in our hearts, not that love is meant with which He loves us, but that love by which He makes us lovers of Him; as the righteousness of God is that by which He makes us righteous of free grace, and the salvation of God that by which He saves us, and the faith of Jesus Christ that by which He makes us believers.'[3] Again: God alone gives

[1] Contra Duas, Ep. l. 2. c. viii.
[2] Op. Imp. l. 1. c. 95.
[3] De Spirit. et Lit. c. xxxii.

love; for "Love is of God." This you will not reckon among your assistances of grace, lest you should concede the truth, that the very act of obedience is of that grace.'[1] Again: 'Thou mentionest many things by which God assists us, viz. by commanding, blessing, sanctifying, coercing, exciting, illuminating; and then mentionest not, by giving love; whereas John saith "Love is of God," and adds, "Behold what manner of love the Father hath bestowed on us, that we should be called the sons of God."'[2] Again: 'If among the kinds of grace you refer to you would place love, which the Scriptures most plainly declare to be not from ourselves but from God, and to be a gift of God to His own sons, that love without which no one lives piously, and *with which a man cannot but live piously;* without which no one has a good will, and with which a man *cannot but have* a good will, you would then define a true freewill, and not inflate a false one.'[3]

Throughout these passages the gift of love is described as a disposition of mind necessarily productive of holy action, and at the same time it is described as the gift of God without any qualification of the simple and natural sense of that term. And, lastly, this gift is identified expressly with efficacious or irresistible grace, as that grace was formally defined above; it being described as a gift 'with which a man cannot but live piously—*cum qua nemo nisi pie vivit*,' which is a repetition of the language above—'*adjutorium cum quo aliquid fit; donum per quod non nisi perseverantes sunt.*'[4]

Having thus shown, what it was the object of this chapter to show, that Augustine held the doctrine of efficacious or irresistible grace, I shall conclude with two observations.

It is evident, then, in the first place, that this doctrine is no more than a supplemental one to the doctrine of predestination described in the preceding chapter. If there be a Divine decree predestinating from all eternity antecedently to any acts of their own certain individuals

[1] Op. Imp. l. 3. c. 114.
[2] Ibid. l. 3. c. 106.
[3] Op. Imp. l. 3. c. 122.
[4] Pp. 163. 165.

of the human race to everlasting life, there must be an instrument for putting this decree into effect. The grace of which the discussion has occupied this chapter is this instrument. It imparts absolutely to the predestinated persons those acts and dispositions which are the conditions of this final reward. The Divine decree, in ensuring this end to certain persons, ensures them the means to it; but piety and virtue are the necessary means for attaining this end; this decree therefore necessarily involves, as its supplement, a grace which ensures the possession of piety and virtue.

In the next place I will guard the reader against a mistake which is not unlikely to arise with respect to this doctrine. For it may be asked whether the assertion of an efficacious or irresistible grace involves more than maintaining that there is such a grace which God chooses to give to certain select and privileged persons, without maintaining that it is the *only* grace by which holiness and salvation can be obtained? Whether it cannot be held that God gives an irresistible grace to some, and also gives a sufficient grace to the rest? Whether the higher gift to a select number, which ensures holiness, is not compatible with the lower one to the rest, which gives them the power to attain it?

But, indeed, if we consider the matter, such a question as this will be seen to proceed from a confusion of thought on this subject. For upon what ground does any one hold that there is this irresistible grace, except on the ground that human nature needs it, and cannot do without it? but if human nature cannot do without it, nothing short of it is sufficient. This is the ground on which Augustine raises the doctrine, and on which all who do maintain it do maintain it. Indeed, on what other ground can it be seriously maintained? For whether or not it *might* attach as a superfluity to a nature able to do without it, its existence could not be other than a mere conjecture in such a case. For *asserting* its existence there must be an adequate reason given; and what adequate reason can be pretended, except that which is given, viz. that it is necessary? Were this grace, then, maintained as a superfluity, there might consistently be maintained together with it another grace short of it, and only sufficient; but it is maintained as remedial to a fatal disease, as supplemental to an absolute want. The first dispensation did not provide it because man could do without it; the second provides it because he cannot. If an irresistible grace then is maintained at all, it cannot be maintained as *a* grace along with the other or merely assisting one, but must be maintained as *the* grace of the Gospel dispensation,—the grace by the operation of which all the goodness and holiness there is in men arises. To endeavour, then, to combine it in one system with the other would be to treat it apart from and in opposition to the very ground on which we suppose it to exist. The doctrine of an absolute predestination cannot combine with any other account of the origin of human goodness; it must either be denied altogether, or applied to the whole. An antecedent moral inability in the whole human mass is the very occasion of that decree, which is made for no other reason than to provide a remedy for it. It follows, that while those who are affected by its remedial provisions are endowed with that certainty of attaining to holiness which they impart; those whom the decree does not affect remain in their original inability; and therefore, that, besides those who have an irresistible grace, there are none who have sufficient.[1]

---

[1] Bishop Overall appears to have fallen into the error of endeavouring to combine irresistible grace to some with sufficient grace to all: 'These two things agree very well together, that God, in the first place, proposed salvation in Christ to all, if they believed, *and common and sufficient grace* in the means divinely ordained, if men were not wanting to the Word of God and to the Holy Spirit; then, secondly, that He might help human infirmity, and that the salvation of men might be more certain, that He thought good *to add a special grace*, more efficacious and abundant, to be communicated to whom He pleased, by which they might not only be able to believe and obey, if so inclined, but also actually be inclined, believe, obey, and persevere.'—Overall on the Quinquarticular Controversy, quoted by Mr. Goode, 'Effects of Infant Baptism,' p. 129.

## CHAPTER VII.

#### AUGUSTINIAN DOCTRINE OF FINAL PERSEVERANCE.

IN the preceding chapter it has been shown that the grace of the Gospel dispensation is, according to the doctrine of S. Augustine, an efficacious and irresistible one. But the question still remains in what measure this grace is given, how much of it is required for accomplishing the object for which it is designed, viz. the individual's salvation. Must it be given to him in perfect fulness, *i.e.* every moment and act of his life without exception? Or is a less measure of it sufficient? and if so, what is that measure?

The answer to this question is, that the measure of this grace which is required for salvation is the same as the measure, whatever it may be, of goodness and holiness which is required. As this grace is the efficacious cause of goodness, exactly as much is wanted of the cause as is wanted of the effect. And to ask this question is exactly the same as to ask, how much goodness is required for salvation.

If the question, then, be asked, how much goodness is required for salvation? while it is plain that no definite amount can be fixed upon in answer, a certain indefinite one can be. Disobedience and sin for an indefinite portion of life are not incompatible with it; but a man must *on the whole* have manifested a good character. And if it be asked, further, what constitutes such a manifestation, and what is the test of goodness on the whole? the answer is, the end of life—that which the man is at the close of the state of probation in which he has been placed.

The amount of efficacious grace, then, which is required in order to salvation, is that which produces this final state of goodness, *i.e.* the grace of final perseverance. And therefore I shall endeavour, in this chapter, to explain the doctrine of final perseverance; first as a test, and secondly as a grace.

I. It will be evident, on slight consideration, that the doctrine of final perseverance, so far as that doctrine is simply the adoption of a particular test of an acceptable and saving obedience, is no predestinarian one, but simply one of morals and religion. Some test is wanted of what constitutes in the individual goodness on the whole; and this doctrine supplies a test, viz. the character of the individual at the end of life. The doctrine does not, indeed, in form adopt the end of life, but continuance *up to* the end, as this test. But it is evident that in continuance up to the end, nothing is ruled as to when that course of goodness which is to be thus continued is to begin. The literal and absolute end of life is, indeed, excluded as such a point of commencement; for there cannot be continuance up to the end if the end takes place immediately. But, interpreting the end of life liberally, it is left open in this test whether such goodness commences at the beginning of life, or at the middle, or at the end. And though an obedience which continues up to the end is doubtless more valuable if it commenced at the beginning of life than if it commenced at the middle, and if it commenced at the middle of life than if it commenced at the end, still so long as it begins in sufficient time to be a fair and substantial continuance in goodness, it fulfils the requirements of the test.

The principle, then, on which such a test goes, and on which it recommends itself to adoption, is the obvious and natural one, embodied in the old maxim τέλος ὅρα, look to the end, the principle, that the end determines the character of the whole to which it belongs. This rule applied to the case of man's moral character leads us to decide, that if he ends virtuously he is on the whole a good man; or, on the other hand, that if he ends immorally, he is on the whole a bad man. Solon, indeed, applied this rule to determine the question, not of a man's moral character, but of his happiness in life; and here it does not literally apply. For it cannot be said to be true, that the happiness of a man's life does depend on the happiness or misery of its end; because happiness being a thing of present sensation, if the sensation has been, there has been happiness. The fact has already taken place, then, before the end comes; and whatever that end may be, it cannot cause what has taken place not to have. A man therefore who has had uninterrupted happiness up to the end of his life, but has then fallen into misfortune, has undoubtedly had more happiness than one who has been miserable up to the end of his life, but has then become prosperous. Solon's assertion applies properly not to the state and condition of the persons themselves, but to their position in the minds of the survivors; for we naturally think of a man afterwards as we last knew him. However prosperous, therefore, a man has been up to the end, if at the end he falls, then, inasmuch as that is the last we saw of him, and he disappeared from that time, and was no more seen, we carry his image in our minds connected with this fall and adversity. If the melancholy association is the last in order, it cannot be corrected, but is fixed and unchanging; and the same is true of the contrary one. It was a natural law of association, then, which the philosopher observed, of which this was the result. When he said that a man's happiness in life was decided by its end, that end was *imagined* as still going on; it was not the real termination of life but an ideal continuation of it, and, as being ideal, unending, for we can always summon the idea. The two young men who, after their work of piety in drawing their sacred mother to the temple, fell asleep in the holy precincts and died, enjoy an eternal rest *in our minds*. Their sweet and blissful repose still in idea goes on. And so the other who died in victory fighting for his country enjoys an eternal transport *in our minds*. The image of repose, and the image of glory stay for ever. Such an ideal end of life, were it real, would indeed be the test of a man's happiness in life; because the eternal continuation of a life is the greater portion of it, and the happiness of the greater portion is the happiness of the life as a whole. But the literal end of life is no such test.

But a test which is deceptive as applied to the estimation of a man's happiness is true as applied to the estimation of his goodness. For there is a peculiarity in the composition or organisation of moral character which makes it apply. It might appear, indeed, at first sight, that as happiness is present sensation, so goodness is present action; and therefore, that if any portion, large or small, of a man's life has been conducted well, there has been so much goodness which cannot be reversed, whatever state of sin may succeed it. But this is not a true statement of the case. Present action is certainly present goodness, goodness for the time; but goodness for the time is not goodness absolutely. Moral character is subject to this law, that change in it affects not only the individual's present life, but his relation to his former, disconnecting him with it. The change from bad to good conduct disconnects him with the bad; the change from good to bad disconnects him with the good. Good after bad and bad after good, exert each a rejective power over the past, to his loss and to his relief respectively. For a man cannot turn from bad to good conduct sincerely and heartily without such a sense of aversion, grief, and disgust for his former life as amounts to a putting it away from him, a severance of it from his proper self; and in like manner he cannot turn from a good behaviour to a bad entirely, without such an indifference to or contempt of virtue as amounts to a disowning and rejection even of his own. Thus he loses his property in one set of actions as he turns to another. The actions, indeed, that he has performed remain for ever his in the sense that he is the person that performed them; but they cease to be his in the sense that they affect his character. From this law, then, it follows necessarily, that the character of the man is the character which he has at last, inasmuch as he has no other but that, being dispossessed, by the fact of having it, of any different one which he may have had before. The question of property in acts is the whole of the question of the goodness or badness of the man; for how can his previous actions, good or bad, affect him, except they belong to him? This law, then, determines the question of property in acts, and it determines it by the fact of what come latest. The man's previous virtue or vice for the time are not his absolutely, unless they are his then; they wait in suspense for that final appropriation. The question of property in the case of happiness or pleasure is perfectly simple; for happiness being only a present sensation, can only belong to the present possessor, but goodness is more than present action, and therefore wants another proprietor besides the present agent.

Indeed, one view which is held of change of character in persons rejects the idea of real or substantial change in them altogether, and, whatever they become at last, regards them as having been really of that character from the first. According to this view, change is interpretative simply and not actual, as regards the man's substantial temper; it only shows that his former character was superficial, and that he had at the time another underneath it, which was really his character, in spite of appearances. Thus the end interprets the whole of life from its beginning, and we wait in suspense till it arrives, in order to ascertain not what a man will on the whole turn out, but what he has been all along. This view rests for its ground upon a certain presumed necessity for a unity of the moral being. It appears to be dividing one person into two, to say that he was once a good man, and is now a bad man; and the division of his moral unity is considered to be as much a contradiction as the division of his personal. The popular aspect, then, of change of character, as an actual change or division of it, is used as a convenience, just as a metaphor might be used which expressed a truth with practical correctness and perhaps even greater vigour than a literal statement would, while another and a deeper view is really taken of such change.

And this explanation of change of character is undoubtedly a natural and true one, properly understood, and with a certain limitation. A man who changes his character cannot indeed be said to have had his later character before in the same sense in which he has it after, nor can such a meaning be intended; at the same time he must have had this character before in the sense of having its seed or root,—that out of which it grew. For it is contrary to experience and common sense to suppose that a change of character can take place all at once, without previous preparation and growth; nor can there be any doubt that men have even the sure root of alteration in them a longer or shorter time before they actually alter—*i.e.* the altered character itself, before it comes out and manifests itself; the substance having existed in the shape of secret habits of mind, of which the formation may date very far back. But if the idea of moral unity is pushed further back than this, and the root which contains the man's subsequent character be made coeval with the man, this cannot be done without entrenching upon freewill; and therefore such a supposition, though it may be entertained as an approach to some truth on this subject with which we are unacquainted, cannot be entertained absolutely. I will add, that we find in Scripture both aspects of change of character; the popular aspect of it as real change, and the esoteric as only external. The prophet Ezekiel uses the former when he says, 'If the wicked will turn from all his sins that he hath committed and keep all My statutes, and do that which is lawful and right, he shall surely live, he shall not die. All his transgressions that he hath committed they shall not be mentioned unto him; in his righteousness that he hath done he shall live. But when a righteous man turneth away from his righteousness, and committeth iniquity, and doeth according to all the abominations that the wicked doeth, shall he live? All his righteousness that he hath done shall not be mentioned: in his trespass that he hath trespassed, and in his sin that he hath sinned, in them shall he die.'[1] St. John uses the latter when he says, 'They went out from us, but they were not of us; for if they had been of us they would no doubt have continued with us; but they went out that they might be made manifest that they were not all of us.'[2]

The doctrine of final perseverance, then, so far as it is the adoption of a test of saving goodness, is only the doctrine of trial and probation explained. The doctrine of trial and probation is, that we are placed in this world in

[1] Ezekiel, xviii. 21, 22, 24.   [2] 1 John, ii. 19.

order to prove by our actions whether we are worthy of reward or punishment in an eternal world to come. The doctrine of final perseverance is, that those actions are not estimated simply with regard to quantity, but also with regard to order; that what constitutes a good or bad life is not the mere *aggregate* of them, in which case it would not signify whether they came at the beginning or end of life, for so long as there was enough of them to satisfy the Judge, it would be indifferent how the number was made up; but their *succession*, whether prior or posterior in life: in other words, not the acts themselves, but their relation to the man, whether they are appropriated by him or not; for this is what their order of prior or posterior tests.

And as the doctrine of final perseverance as a test is only the doctrine of trial and probation explained; so the objections to it on the ground of justice are only of the kind which attaches to the general doctrine of trial and probation. The doctrine indeed that the whole period of trial must be judged by its termination, prominently suggests the question, in the case of a bad termination of it, Why is this period terminated *now*? As the end makes all the difference, why could not that end have been postponed? Why could not the period have been extended to sufficient length to give room for another, and so, by a small addition to its duration, the whole of its effects have been removed? But it is evident that this objection applies to the end of all trial whatever, and upon whatever rule proceeding, whether that of the order of actions or of the aggregate simply. In either case a longer period might, as far as we see, have produced a different issue from that of a shorter one. The whole doctrine of trial and probation is indeed incomprehensible to us; for, whereas probation must in the nature of the case be limited, we cannot understand how a limitation of it can be so arranged as to be perfectly just and equitable; how it is that a person at a particular time is completely tried and proved: notwithstanding which difficulty, the doctrine of trial and probation is a doctrine both of revelation and natural religion.

The test of final perseverance does indeed, in some of

its applications, appear to be open, not only to this objection, which applies to all limited probation, that we do not see its justice, but to a positive charge of injustice. For in the case of a person who has lived uprightly and religiously up to the end of life, but has then yielded to some temptation and fallen into sin, it does appear unjust that the end should undo the whole of the life previous, and deprive him of any advantage from it; and the rule of final perseverance seems at first to impose such a result. But this will be found, upon consideration, not to be the case. The rule of final perseverance is the rule, that a man must be judged according to his final character; but what in a particular case *is* the final character it does not and cannot determine. Some rules indeed are of such a kind that they appear when laid down to decide their own application; and the rule which identifies a man's character, good or bad, with his final one, will appear, unless we are on our guard, to decide the particular fact of his final character, its goodness or badness; the change which is presented to observation in the particular case appearing to be, without any further reflection, the change which is supposed in the rule. But it is evident that we should be deceived here by an apparent connection between two things which are really separate. No rule can possibly decide its own application; it supposes the case to which it applies and does not discover or select it. On the question, whether such and such a case is one of change of character, we must take the best evidence which our own experience and observation can apply, as we would on any other question of fact. In the case of a man who at the end of a life of steady virtue falls into sin, we ought certainly to be slow to believe that such sin is a real change of character. His previous good life, though of no avail as a counterbalance, supposing a real change from it, is yet legitimate evidence on the question whether there is such change; and evidence, as far as it goes, against it. For there is a difficulty in supposing that one who had evinced such steadiness and constancy should fall away really, however he might appear to do so; and both reason and charity direct us to a favourable supposition, except something very peculiar in the case prevents it.[1]

The rule of final perseverance, then, as a test, is not itself unjust; but whether it is unjust or not in its application depends upon our discrimination and charity in applying it. This rule is not intended to over-ride our natural ideas of justice, as if because we admitted it, we allowed a self-applying power to it, to which those ideas must succumb; but those ideas of justice must be our guide in applying the rule. We must apply it then in the particular case, according to the evidence; and remember that, after all, we cannot apply it with certainty, because God only knows the final state of man's heart. There cannot in that case be any unjust application of the rule, because its application will be suspended altogether. Indeed this rule, when we go to the bottom of it, issues after all in being substantially no more than the rule that a man must be judged according to his character; for by a man's character we *mean* his final character, and no character previous to it. The rule then is certain, because it is no more than the rule, that the good are rewarded and the bad punished; but it cannot be applied to the individual with certainty, because we do not know who are the bad, and who are the good.

II. Final perseverance has thus far been treated of as a *test*, in which sense the doctrine is no predestinarian one, but only one of ordinary religion and morality. But it remains to see what produces, in the Augustinian system, this saving obedience of which final perseverance is the test, that is, to consider final perseverance as a *grace*.

Final perseverance, then, is maintained by S. Augustine to be the free gift of God; that is to say, not a gift bestowed in consideration of the man's previous acts, or as an assistance to his own efforts, but an absolute gift bestowed upon certain individuals of the human race, in accordance

---

[1] The following is not a cautious statement of S. Augustine's, though it admits of explanation: Potius hanc perseverantiam habuit unius anni fidelis *et quantum infra cogitari potest*, si donec moreretur fideliter vixit, quam multorum annorum, si exiguum temporis ante mortem a fidei stabilitate defecit.—De Dono Perseverantiæ, c. 1.

188     *Augustinian Doctrine*     CHAP. VII.

with an eternal Divine decree which has predestinated them to the privilege of it. This is quite evident from the previous chapter, and requires strictly no further proof. For there is no necessity, after it has been shown that *all* goodness under the Christian dispensation is on the Augustinian doctrine a free and absolute Divine gift, to show that a particular measure and degree of it is upon the same doctrine such a gift; and final perseverance is, as I have shown, only a particular measure and degree of goodness; such a one, viz., as avails for the man's salvation. What is said of the whole is of course said of the part. Nevertheless, the grace of final perseverance occupies so prominent a place in the Augustinian system, that it appears proper to explain the position of this grace in particular, and to show that what is said of grace in general is said of this measure of it.

In the first place, then, S. Augustine says generally that final perseverance is a gift. 'Will any one dare to assert that final perseverance is not the gift of God? . . . . We cannot deny that final perseverance is a great gift of God, coming down from Him of whom it is written, " Every good gift and every perfect gift is from above, and cometh down from the Father of lights." '[1] 'Perseverance is the gift of God, by virtue of which a man perseveres in Christ unto the end.'[2] 'We pray that the unbelieving may believe: faith, therefore, is the gift of God. We pray that the believing may persevere: final perseverance, therefore, is the gift of God.'[3] 'Why is perseverance asked of God, if it is not given by God? It is mocking Him to ask Him for what you know He does not give, for what you can give yourself. We pray " Hallowed be Thy name ;" that is to say, we pray that, having been sanctified in baptism, we may persevere in that beginning. We pray, therefore, for perseverance in sanctification. . . . . If we receive that perseverance, then, we receive it as the gift of God, that great gift by which His other gifts are preserved.'[4]—'He makes men to persevere in good who makes men good. He

[1] De Corr. et Grat. c. vi.
[2] De Dono Pers. c. i.
[3] Ibid. c. iii.
[4] Ibid. c. ii.

gives perseverance who makes men stand. The first man did not receive this gift of God, perseverance.'[1]

Final perseverance, then, is, according to S. Augustine, a Divine gift. And that he uses the word gift here in its natural sense as a free gift, not a conditional one, depending on man's own disposition and conduct, is evident from the following considerations.

First, he makes final perseverance a gift in the same sense in which the end of life is a gift: but the end of life is undoubtedly an absolute gift of God; *gift*, I say, because we are supposing a case here in which it is advantageous to the person, and not the opposite,—it is entirely an arrangement of Providence when death takes place.

S. Augustine urges strongly that in certain cases, the end of life, that is to say, the circumstance of the end of life taking place at the time it does, *makes* final perseverance. He takes the case of persons who die young, or when their characters are unformed, but die while their minds are as yet innocent and uncorrupted. Such persons, he says, attain final perseverance, because they do as a fact continue in goodness up to the end; but their final perseverance is evidently made by the occurrence of the end while they are in a good state of mind, not by their own stability and constancy. That it is not any stability of principle in the person which constitutes in such cases final perseverance is plain, he argues, because final perseverance takes place, even where no principle of stability exists, but the very reverse; because it takes place even in cases where the person, had he lived, would have lapsed: and he quotes for this assertion the text from the Book of Wisdom, ' Speedily was he taken away, lest that wickedness should alter his understanding, or deceit beguile his soul.' Here, he observes, is manifestly a case in which the person's lapse, had he lived longer, was foreseen, and yet final perseverance takes place; in which, therefore, it is manifest that final perseverance takes place not by the stability of the man, but by the act of God in putting an end to his life at the time He does, which is purposely fixed so as to prevent

[1] De Corr. et Grat. c. xii.

a lapse. And if the want of authority in the Book of Wisdom, as not being part of the sacred book, is alleged, he replies that he can do without the text; because even were the certainty of a lapse lost to his argument, all that his argument really wants is the danger of one [1]; for that, if there is the danger of a lapse, it cannot be the man's stability which constitutes his final perseverance, but the act of God in forestalling his trial. What *makes* final perseverance in such cases then, is, he concludes, the Divine location of the end of life. And thence he argues immediately that in such cases final perseverance *itself* is a Divine gift. 'Consider how contradictory it is to deny that perseverance up to the end of this life is the gift of God, when He undoubtedly gives the end of life whenever He pleases; and the giving of the end of life before an impending lapse *makes* final perseverance.'[2] 'How is not perseverance unto the end of God's grace, when the end itself of life is in God's power, and God can confer this benefit even on one who is not about to persevere?'[3]

Having proved one kind of final perseverance by this argument to be a Divine gift, he then infers that all final perseverance whatever is the same. There may be a wide interval between the final perseverance of one who is snatched from impending trial by some sudden illness or accident, and that of one who has been reserved for trial and has sustained it without falling; but if the one kind is the gift of God, the other is too. 'He who took away the righteous man by an early death, lest wickedness *should* alter his understanding, preserves the righteous man for the length of a long life, that wickedness *does not* alter his understanding.'[4] 'Perseverance amid hindrances and persecutions is the more difficult; the other is the easier: but He to whom nothing is difficult can easily give both.'[5]

The substance of this argument is, that the power of resisting temptation is as much a gift of God as the removal from temptation. Death can only be effective of

[1] De Præd. c. xiv.
[2] De Dono Pers. c. xvii.
[3] Ep. 217. c. vi.
[4] De Præd. c. xiv. (980.)
[5] De Dono Pers. c. 2.

final perseverance as being a removal for ever from temptation. And therefore to say that perseverance, which consists in sustaining temptation, is as much a gift of God as that which is caused by the occurrence of death, is only to say, that the power of sustaining temptation is as much a gift of God as the removal from temptation. And so the argument is sometimes put by S. Augustine, the substance being given apart from this particular form of it, which alludes to the end of life. 'God is able to convert the averse and adverse wills of men to His faith, and work in their hearts a sustaining of all adversities and an overcoming of all temptation; inasmuch as He is able *not to permit them to be tempted* at all above that they are able;' the resistance to temptation is pronounced to be in the power of God to give, because the protection from temptation is in His power.[1]

Such an argument is, indeed, more ingenious than sound; for it does not follow that because God spares some persons on particular occasions the exercise of a certain power of choice and original agency inherent in their nature, that therefore such a power does not exist, and would not have been called into action by another arrangement of Providence. But the argument itself, which is all that we are concerned with here, certainly shows the sense in which S. Augustine uses the term 'gift' of final perseverance. For there can be no doubt that removal from temptation is an absolute and free gift of God; it being entirely an arrangement of His providence what temptations we encounter in the course of our life, and what we do not. If perseverance, therefore, in spite of temptation, is as much a gift of God as the removal from temptation, it is a gift simple and absolute. And there can be no doubt that the occurrence of the end of life at a particular time is an arrangement solely of God's providence. If all perseverance, then, is alike the gift of God, while one kind of it is said to be constituted by the occurrence of the end of life at a particular time, all perseverance is a gift of God simple and absolute.

[1] De Dono Pers. c. ix.

Again, he places the gift of perseverance on the same ground as the gift of baptism, with respect to the principle or law upon which it is bestowed. Some persons, he observes, have baptism given to them, and others have not; and in like manner some have the gift of perseverance given to them, and others have not.[1] Now, it is obvious that the gift of baptism is a free gift, the bestowal of which depends solely on God's will and pleasure, who gives it to whom He pleases and from whom He pleases withholds it. Thus the population of Europe is baptized, the population of Asia is not; evidently not because the inhabitants of Europe have done anything to deserve it which the inhabitants of Asia have not done, but simply owing to an arrangement of Providence. We see with our eyes that a man's baptism results from causes wholly irrespective of his own conduct, such as the part of the world he was born in, in what communion, from what parents. There can be no more genuine instance, then, of a free gift than baptism; and, therefore, if final perseverance is a gift in the same way in which baptism is, final perseverance is a free gift.

It remains to add, that the notes of genuineness which were observed in the last chapter to attach to the word 'gift,' as used by S. Augustine, of grace in general, attach to the word equally as used by him of this particular measure of grace, final perseverance. These notes were contained in the caution that grace was not given according to merit; in the argument from prayer; and in the entire reference of the matter to a ground of mystery, the bestowal or withholding of grace being attributed wholly to God's secret counsels and sovereign will. All this is applied in particular by S. Augustine to the grace of final perseverance. It is not given according to merit; it is given in the same sense in which other gifts which the act of prayer assigns to God's absolute bounty are given; and the reason why it is given to one man and not to another is altogether a mysterious and incomprehensible one, belonging to the secret counsels of God. A considerable part of

[1] De Dono Pers. cc. ix. x.; De Corr. et Grat. c. viii.

the books '*De Dono Perseverantiæ*[1]' and '*De Correptione et Gratiâ*'[2] is devoted to proving that the gift of final perseverance is not given according to merit; that is to say, in consideration of any previous acts or efforts of the man himself. And the whole of the beginning of the former book is occupied with proving that final perseverance must be God's gift, inasmuch as we ask God for it, both in our own behalf and that of others, and what we ask God for we necessarily confess to be in His power to give or to withhold.

With respect to the law upon which the gift of perseverance is given to one man and not to another, he says, 'If any one asks me why God does not give perseverance to those who by His grace lead a Christian life and have love, I reply, that I do not know, I recognise my measure in that text, "O man, who art thou that repliest against God? O the depth of the riches both of the wisdom and knowledge of God! How unsearchable are His judgments, and His ways past finding out." So far as He deigns to reveal His judgments, let us be thankful; so far as He hides them, let us not murmur. Say you, who oppose yourself to Divine grace, you are a Christian, a Catholic, and boast of being one, do you admit or deny that final perseverance is the gift of God? If you allow it to be, then you and I are alike ignorant why one receives it, and another does not; then you and I are alike unable to penetrate the unsearchable judgments of God.'[3] Again: 'Of two children, why one is taken and the other left (*i.e.* baptized and not baptized), of two adults, why one is so called, that he follows the caller, and the other either not called at all or not *so* called, belongs to the inscrutable judgments of God. Of two pious men, why final perseverance is given to one and not to the other, belongs to His still more inscrutable judgments.'[4] Again: 'It is evident that both the grace of the beginning and the grace of persevering to the end is not given according to our merits, but according to a most secret, most just, most wise, most

[1] De Dono Pers. c. viii. *et seq.*
[2] De Corr. et Grat. c. xii.
[3] Ibid. c. viii.
[4] De Dono Pers. c. ix.

beneficent will; inasmuch as whom He hath predestinated those He hath also called with that call of which it is said, "The gifts and calling of God are without repentance."'[1] Again: 'Wonderful indeed, very wonderful, that to some of His own sons, whom He has regenerated and to whom He has given faith, hope, and charity, God does not give perseverance! that He who oftentimes pardons and adopts the stranger's (unbeliever's) son, should withhold such a gift from His own! Who but must wonder, be astonished, and amazed at this!'[2] Again: 'I am speaking of those who have not the gift of perseverance, but have turned from good to evil, and die in that declination; let them (his opponents) tell me why God did not take such persons out of this world while they were yet unchanged? Was it because He could not? or was it because He foresaw not their future wickedness? They cannot assert either of these without perversity and madness. Then why did He do so? Let them answer this question before they deride me, when I exclaim, "How unsearchable are His judgments, and His ways past finding out!" Either God gives that gift to whom He will, or Scripture lies. . . . . Let them confess this truth at once, and why God gives that gift to one and not to another,—condescend without a murmur to be ignorant with me.'[3]

Final perseverance, then, is, upon the Augustinian doctrine, the true and absolute gift of God to certain members of the human race; to whom, according to an eternal decree, He has determined to give it: and it has that prominent place which it has in the predestinarian scheme, because it is that measure of Divine grace which is sufficient for salvation. The predestinarian doctrine is that certain persons are predestined by God from all eternity to be saved; but God only saves the righteous, and not the wicked. It must therefore be provided, in accordance with this doctrine, that those persons shall exhibit as much goodness of life as is necessary for the end to which they are ordained; and final perseverance is this measure of goodness. The gift of final perseverance, then,

[1] De Dono Pers. c. xiii.   [2] De Corr. et Grat. c. viii.   [3] Ibid. c. viii.

is the great gift which puts into execution God's eternal decree with respect to the whole body of the elect. He may predestine some to a higher and others to a lower place, but He predestines all the elect to a place in the kingdom of heaven; and therefore, while He provides that some shall exhibit higher and others lower degrees of sanctity and goodness, He provides that all shall exhibit enough for admission; which sufficiency is final.perseverance.

## CHAPTER VIII.

#### AUGUSTINIAN DOCTRINE OF FREEWILL.

THE preceding chapters have exhibited a full and systematic scheme of predestinarian doctrine, as held by S. Augustine, who asserts in the first place an eternal Divine decree, whereby one part of mankind has been, antecedently to any moral difference between the two, separated from the other, and the one ordained to eternal life, and the other to eternal punishment;[1] and next supplies a grace for putting it into effect.[2] But while he lays down this doctrine of predestination and irresistible grace, S. Augustine at the same time acknowledges the existence of freewill in man—*liberum arbitrium*; an admission, which, understood in its popular sense, would have been a counterbalance to all the rest of his scheme. The question, however, immediately arises, what he means by freewill; whether he uses the word in the sense which the ordinary doctrine of freewill requires, or in another and a different sense. Persons are apt indeed to suppose, as soon as ever they hear the word freewill, that the word must involve all that those who hold the regular doctrine of freewill mean by it. It remains, however, to see whether this is the case in S. Augustine's use of the word.

The doctrine of freewill consists of two parts; one of

[1] Chap. V. [2] Chaps. VI. and VII.

which has respect to the existence of the will, and the
other to the mode in which it is moved and determined.
That part which respects the existence of the will, the
doctrine of freewill, and the contrary doctrine, hold in
common. No person in his senses can deny the *fact* of the
will, that we will to do this, that, and the other thing, that
we act with intention, design, deliberation. We are directly
conscious of all this. No predestinarian, therefore, however rigid, denies it; and the whole set of sensations which
are connected with willing, or the whole fact of the will, in
its minutest and most subtle particulars, is the common
ground both of him and his opponent. But the fact of the
will admitted, the further question remains, how this will
is determined; that is, caused to decide on one side or
another, and choose this or that act. The doctrine of
freewill is that the cause of this decision is the will itself,
and that the will has a power of self-determination inherent in it. This appears to the maintainers of this doctrine the natural inference from that whole fact of willing,
of which they are conscious, so that they could not draw
any other without seeming to themselves to contradict
plain reason. Nobody can assert indeed that he is conscious distinctly, and after the mode of clear perception,
of a power of determining his own will, for all that he is
distinctly conscious of is his will itself. Nevertheless, the
will as we feel and experience it, acting with struggle,
effort, resolution, summoning up of force, and deliberate
choice of alternatives, has so much the appearance of being
self-determining and original, that when the notion is suggested that it is not, such a notion is felt to be contrary
to an idea which we naturally and instinctively have respecting our will, its originality appearing to be implied
in this kind of motion and operation. Nor is this self-
determining power of the will interfered with by the doctrine of assisting grace, which is so formed as to admit the
human will as an original agent, co-operating with grace.
The doctrine of freewill, then, is that the will is determined by itself, or is an original agent, as distinguished
from the assertion simply of a will in man, which latter it

holds in common with the rival and opposite doctrine respecting the will.

The validity indeed of this whole distinction between the will itself and the will as self-determining, *i.e.* the existence of this self-determining power in the will over and above the fact of willing, is denied by the school of metaphysicians, who take against the common doctrine of freewill and favour that of necessity. They maintain freewill to consist in the simple fact of will; that we act willingly and without constraint; and they deny that we can go any further than this, or see anything whatever more than this fact, however far we may try to look. They say that in this consists the whole of freewill, that this is all we mean or can mean by it; and that if we try to go any deeper, we involve ourselves in confusion and absurdity. This position is among others maintained by Locke, whose great fairness of mind and anxiety to represent faithfully and exactly the truth respecting the human mind and its constitution entitle his opinions on this subject to much consideration, because he does not appear to have started with any bias one way or another on the examination of the question, but to have decided according to what he thought the plain facts of the case. I cannot but think, however, that his love of exact truth and the test of actual perception and apprehension which his philosophy applies, have been carried too far in this instance, and led him into a mistake. For this test cannot be applied with absolute strictness in all cases, as I have often said; there being truths of reason, which do not admit of it, truths in their very nature indeterminate and indistinct; to which class belongs the truth now in question, that of the self-determining power of the will.

Locke's elaborate argument on this subject divides itself into two questions; one whether *the will is free,* the other whether the man or the agent *is free to will.*

The first question is not really the question at issue between the two sides; for what those who maintain the self-determining power of the will mean by the *will* being free, is, that the agent is *free to will*: nor does their position at all necessarily involve the particular expression,—freedom of the will, which Locke first impugns in his argument, though they use it as a convenient mode of stating the real truth for which they contend. Locke, however, first examines this expression, and starts the question in this particular form, whether *the will is free*; and he decides against its freedom on the ground that freedom is a power and the will a power, and that a power cannot be predicated *of* a power, power being the attribute of an *agent*. Freedom, he says, is the *power* to act as we will. 'So far as a man has power to think or not to think, to move or not to move, according to the preference or direction of his own mind, so far is a man free. . . . . . The idea of liberty is the idea of a power in any agent to do or forbear any particular action, according to the determination or thought of his mind.'[1] Freedom, then, being the power to act as we will, assert this power of the will, he says, and what does it become?—the power of the will to act as it wills; *i.e.* for this is the only act the will can do, the power of the will to will as it wills. But this is a power which is contained in the very act of willing, and does not go at all beyond the mere fact of will. So that, he argues, when we would attribute this power—*i.e.* freedom—to the will, we find immediately that we are making no assertion beyond that of the will itself, not advancing a step farther, but going on like a rocking horse upon the same ground. Though in a certain incorrect way he allows this freedom to be asserted of the will, because its exertion *is* thus *ipso facto* freedom. 'If freedom can with any propriety of speech be applied to power, it may be attributed to the power that is in man to produce or forbear producing, by choice or preference, which is that which denominates him free, and *is freedom itself*. But if any one should ask whether freedom were free, he would be suspected not to understand well what he said; and he should be thought to deserve Midas' ears, who, knowing that rich was a denomination for the possession of riches, should demand whether riches themselves were rich.'[2]

[1] Essay, book 2. c. 21.  [2] Essay, book 2. c. 21.

But the question whether the will is free being thus decided, the next follows, whether the man is free to will; which is, as has been just said, the real question at issue between the two sides. On this question, then, he first decides—and no one will oppose him—that the man is not free in the case of any proposed action, generally and altogether in respect of willing; but that he must will one thing or another, either doing the act or abstaining from it. 'Willing or volition being an action, and freedom consisting in a power of acting or not acting, a man in respect of willing or the act of volition, when an action in his power is once proposed to his thoughts as presently to be done, cannot be free. The reason whereof is very manifest; for it being unavoidable that the action depending on his will should exist or not exist, and its existence or not existence following perfectly the determination and preference of his will, he cannot avoid willing the existence or not existence of that action; it is absolutely necessary that he will the one or the other. . . . . . This, then, is evident, that in all proposals of present action, a man is not at liberty to will or not to will, because he cannot forbear willing.'

It being decided, then, that the man must will one way or another—*i.e.* is not free to will neither way—Locke comes at last to the question, which is the only real one between the two sides, and upon which the whole controversy turns—Is he free to will *either* way? And he settles it thus summarily. 'Since, then, it is plain that in most cases a man is not at liberty, whether he will or no, the next thing demanded is, *Whether a man be at liberty to will which of the two he pleases?* This question carries the absurdity of it so manifestly in itself, that one might thereby be sufficiently convinced that liberty concerns not the will. For to ask whether a man be at liberty to will either motion or rest, speaking or silence, *which he pleases*, is to ask whether a man can will what he wills, or be pleased with what he is pleased with. A question which, I think, needs no answer; and they who can make a question of it, must suppose one will to determine the acts of another, and another to determine that, and so on *in infinitum.*'

Upon this ground it is decided that the man or agent does not determine his own will. But is not this an argument which simply takes advantage of the difficulties of language, with which questions like these are beset? The position that the man determines his own will is stated in a *form* in which it becomes absurd, and then the charge of absurdity is brought against the position itself. It is described as the assertion, that '*the man is at liberty to will which of the two he pleases*,' or wills. And certainly in this form the position is absurd; for it assumes the previous existence of a particular decision of the will, as the condition of the power or liberty of the man to make it. But though in loose speech the self-determining power of the will may sometimes be expressed in this way, the truth really intended and meant does not depend on such an expression of it. The truth which is meant, is not the man's power to will *as he wills* or pleases, but simply his power to will; that his will rises ultimately and originally from himself as the agent or possessor of the will: in other words, that that whole affair of the man willing is an original event.

The question of such a self-determining power in the will may be called 'an unreasonable, because unintelligible question;'[1] and the other ground be preferred, as simpler and more common sense and straightforward, that will is will, and that that is all that can be said about it. But if truths are to be rejected because they are indistinct, indefinite, and incapable of consistent statement, we must reject a large class of most important truths belonging to our rational nature.[2] This self-determining power in the will cannot be stated accurately, nor can it be apprehended accurately; but have we not a perception in this direction? Is there not a rational instinct which speaks to our originality as agents, as there is a rational instinct which tells us of substance, of cause, of infinity? And does not this instinct or perception see a certain way, so that we have

[1] Essay, book 2. c. 21. s. 14.     [2] *See* Chap. II.

some sort of idea of the thing in our minds? Locke's rejection of this power in the will on such a ground appears to be inconsistent with his admission of the class of indistinct ideas?[1] For if we admit such a kind and order of truths, we are arbitrarily to exclude such a truth as this from the benefit of it—a truth which is felt and asserted by the great mass of mankind? But this is the line which Locke takes on this question. He sees there is no *distinct* idea of originality or self-determination in the human mind; and he does not allow such an idea a place as an indistinct one. He thus rests ultimately in the simple fact of will, as the whole of the truth of the freedom of the will. 'For how can we think any one freer, than to have the power to do what he will? . . . . We can scarce tell how to imagine any being freer than to be able to do what he wills.'[2]

It must be added, that important results in theology follow the decision of this question respecting the will, one way or another. On the supposition of a self-determining power in the will, and so far as it is a true one, the Divine justice is freed from all substantial difficulty; for moral evil is brought instantly home to the individual, who is made responsible for it, and so justly subject to punishment. But deny this power, and suppose the will to be moved from without, and the Divine justice is immediately challenged, and we are involved in whatever difficulty accompanies the depravation of moral beings from a source external to themselves, and their punishment when their depravation has proceeded from such a source. I am speaking of the latter doctrine as held definitely or exclusively. It may be said, indeed, that the will which is thus moved from without is still will, the will of the individual, —that it has all the properties which we can distinctly conceive of will; but these characteristics of will will not prevent the difficulties which arise from this theory of its motion or determination. And this perhaps is worth the consideration of those who not so much deny the self-determining power of the will, as set the question aside as

[1] Note IV.   [2] Essay, book 2. c. 21. s. 21.

unimportant; as if the acknowledgment of will as a fact were the only thing of real importance. Of course, if this is so, it is impossible to be in the wrong on this subject; for nobody in his senses can deny the fact of the will. But the further question of its determination cannot be said to be unimportant, both in itself, and as involving these theological results. It makes a difference in what way we decide it.

A distinguished writer of the present day, Archbishop Whately, adopts this line: 'Let, then, necessitarians of all descriptions but step forth into light, and explain their own meaning; and we shall find that their positions are either obviously untenable, or else perfectly harmless and nearly insignificant. If in saying that all things are fixed and necessary, they mean that there is no such thing as voluntary action, we may appeal from the verbal quibbles which alone afford a seeming support to such a doctrine to universal consciousness; which will authorise even those who have never entered into such speculations as the foregoing, to decide on the falsity of the conclusion, though they are perplexed with the subtle fallacies of the argument. But if nothing more be meant than that every event depends on causes adequate to produce it, that *nothing is in itself contingent, accidental or uncertain*, but is called so only with reference to a person who does not know all the circumstances on which it depends,—and that it is absurd to say anything could have happened otherwise than it did, *supposing all the circumstances connected with it to remain the same*,—then the doctrine is undeniably true, but perfectly harmless, not at all encroaching on free agency and responsibility, and amounting in fact to little more than an expansion of the axiom, that it is impossible for the same thing to be and not to be.'[1]

Archbishop Whately in this passage more than *tolerates* necessitarianism, because he adopts it. He asserts that 'nothing is in itself contingent, accidental, uncertain,' and that, supposing all the circumstances connected with it to remain the same, '*it is absurd to say anything could have*

[1] Appendix to Archbp. King, On Predestination, p. 99.

*happened otherwise than as it did.*' This is the doctrine of necessity. Suppose two men under exactly the same circumstances as regards a particular temptation to which they are subjected—the same even to the minutest particulars. Let the circumstances which are thus identical be not external only, but internal ones. Let them have the same amount of inward bias or inclination, and let this inclination be acted upon from without by a whole, complex, manifold and intricate machinery of invitations and allurements, precisely the same in both cases. Let every thing, in short, which is properly *circumstantial—i.e.* is not the very act of the will itself—be by supposition the same in both cases. Now, the doctrine of freewill is, that these two agents may, under this entire and absolute identity of circumstances, act differently; the doctrine of necessity is that they must act the same. According to the doctrine of freewill there is an ultimate power of choice in the human will, which, however strongly it may be drawn, or tempted, or attracted to decide one way or another by external appeals or motives, is not *ruled* and *decided* by such motives, but by the will itself only. This is the self-determining power of the will, the assertion of which is the characteristic of that doctrine. Under this identity of circumstances, an original act or motion of the will is said to take place, which may be different in the two persons, and be the one single difference in the whole of the two cases. On the other hand, the necessitarian maintains that where the circumstances, external and internal, are really and completely alike, there is not room for this further difference; but that the issue will be the same in both cases, and both will act alike. Archbishop Whately's position, that 'supposing all the circumstances connected with it to remain the same, it is absurd to say anything could have happened otherwise than as it did,' is identical with this necessitarian one. He adds, that this assertion that the event must always be the same under the same circumstances, is 'little more than an expansion of the position that it is impossible for the same thing to be and not to be.' Of course, supposing it true that the whole of the circumstances of an act or event amount to and really are and constitute that act or event itself, it immediately follows, that to say that under the same circumstances the same event will take place, is an identical assertion. But that the assertion should be thus identical supposes that circumstances *do* constitute the act or event; *i.e.* it sets aside and ignores an original motion of the will under the circumstances, as if it had no place in the question, and there were no such thing : which is the necessitarian assumption. The Archbishop slightly qualifies his remark indeed, and only calls the two assertions *nearly* identical : the assertion that the same event must take place under the same circumstances 'amounts to *little more than* an expansion of the axiom that it is impossible for the same thing to be and not to be.' But surely the two assertions must be either absolutely and completely identical, or not at all. For if it is not true, wholly and *entirely*, that identity of circumstances is the identity of the act, what is the reason of this defect of truth ? It is—for there can be no other,—that there is an original motion of the will, which may be different in spite of the circumstances being the same. But if there *is* an original motion of the will in the case, then the whole position that the same circumstances will produce the same event or act falls at once to the ground ; another principle comes in, which altogether upsets the necessary force of circumstances, and produces the widest possible differences of acts under circumstances exactly the same.[1]

---

[1] A position maintained in another passage in Archbp. Whately's Essay, is in tendency and language, necessitarian, though it admits of an explanation. 'But some may say, have I the power of choosing among several motives at once present to my mind? or must I obey the strongest ? for if so, how can I enjoy freewill ? Here, again, is an entanglement in ambiguous words : "must" and "obey" and "strongest" suggest the idea (which belongs to them in their primary sense) of *compulsion*, and of *one person* submitting to *another* ; whereas here they are only used figuratively, the terms "weak" and "strong," when applied to motives, denoting nothing but their greater or less tendency to prevail (that is, to *operate* and *take effect*) in practice, so that to say "the stronger motive prevails" is only another form of saying that "that which prevails prevails!"'—P. 95. Now,

## of Freewill.

The writer, indeed, appears to think that the admission of the fact of the will, or 'voluntary action,' is itself a safeguard against necessitarianism; and that necessitarians have to be driven by argument into the acknowledgment of this fact; the admission of which, when they are forced to see and confess it, makes them virtually cease to be such. But all necessitarians acknowledge *in limine*, and without any difficulty, the fact of the will; indeed, every one of sound mind must.

I will not, however, understand Archbishop Whately in this passage as more than neutral; tolerating the necessitarian, and treating the question between him and his opponent, provided the fact of the will is admitted, as one of no importance. But perhaps even this assertion should be modified. It is true, indeed, that, so long as men acknowledge a will, responsibility, and moral obligations, there is nothing in necessitarianism to interfere with practical religion. But still the theory has important consequences in theology, and largely affects our idea of the Divine dealings, which it represents under an aspect repulsive to our natural feeling and sense of justice. And though a mystery must be acknowledged on this subject, it is a different thing to hold the predestinarian doctrine, as the

---

when persons talk of the stronger motive prevailing, they sometimes make the assertion in a sense involving an original act of the will itself. A man is drawn by some strong temptation towards a bad act, while conscience dissuades: the bad motive is at the first much the stronger of the two; he feels the former as almost overwhelming, while the latter is but feebly felt; but his will now comes in and deliberately increases and strengthens the conscientious motive, calling up every consideration of present or future interest to outweigh the other, and putting the advantages of the right side as vividly before the mind as possible. Thus in time what was the more feebly felt becomes the more strongly felt motive; and the man acts on the right side. In this sense, then, there is no doctrine of necessity involved in the position that a man must act upon the strongest motive. For in every act of choice between good and evil, the will either does or does not create this good stronger motive; in either case it is the man's will acting well or ill, and not the power of *externally* caused motives, which produces the result. But understanding by the term motive something simply acting from without upon the mind, to say that the stronger motive must prevail, is to say that the individual's act is decided by causes outside of himself.

Church at large does, as a mystery and with a reserve, and to hold it as a definite and complete doctrine.

The language of S. Augustine respecting the will may be put under two heads; under the first of which it does not come up to the received doctrine of freewill, and under the second is opposed to it.

I. First, freewill, as maintained by S. Augustine, does not mean *so much as* the freewill above described, or a self-determining will; but only *a will;* his language not advancing beyond that point up to which the doctrine of freewill and the opposite doctrine agree.

In examining the language of Augustine on this subject we must take care to distinguish between what he says of the freewill of man in his former perfect, and that of man in his present corrupt state. In the book *De Libero Arbitrio*, a freewill is indeed described which comes up to the above definition of it as original and self-determining. The Manichean there, not content with the fact of the human will as accounting for moral evil in the world, demands the cause of that will; and Augustine replies: 'The will being the cause of sin, you ask the cause of the will: should I discover it, will you not ask then the cause of that cause; and what limit of inquiry can there be, if you will go deeper than the very root? . . . . What cause of will can there be before will? For either this cause is will, and we are no nearer the root than we were before; or it is not will, and in that case there is no sin.'[1] Here a will is described which is truly an original agent in nature, having no cause but itself. But the will thus described is the will of man in his created, not in his fallen state.'[2] In some passages, again, quoted in a former chapter, a will was described which was self-determining and original; for it was said that the first man 'had such an assistance given him as he could use if he willed, and neglect if he willed; not one by which it was caused that he did will.'[3] His will, therefore, had no cause beyond itself, or was self-caused,

[1] L. 3. c. xvii.
[2] Cum autem de libera voluntate faciendi loquimur, de illa scilicet in qua homo factus est loquimur.— L. 3. c. 18.
[3] De Corr. et Grat. c. xi.

that is to say, self-determined and original: but this, he expressly says, was the will of the first man in his state of integrity, and not of man as now existing.

When Augustine comes to describe the will of man as now existing, he describes it simply by the fact of will or willing. There are various passages in his works, especially a passage in the book *De Libero Arbitrio*, another in the book *De Spiritu et Literâ*, and another in his Retractations explanatory of a passage in the book *De Diversis Quæstionibus ad Simplicianum*, in which it is defined with much minuteness and labour what the freedom of the will is, and in what it consists; and this definition terminates in the fact of a will. First, *freedom* itself is defined; and it is said to consist in power. We are free when it is in our power to do a thing. But what is power? for it becomes necessary now to say what power is, if there is anything to be said about it. He proceeds accordingly to define next what is meant by its being in our *power* to do a thing; and this he defines by saying that it is our having the power to do it *if we will*. 'What need for further question? we call that power where to the will is joined the ability to do. That is in a man's power which he does *if he wills*, does not do if he does not will—*quod si vult facit, si non vult non facit.*[1] Freedom being thus defined, it only remains to apply this definition of freedom to the will, which is a simple and easy process. Freedom is a power to do a thing *if we will*. Freedom of the will, therefore, is the power to *will* if we will—a power, he adds, which unquestionably every man possesses; for *if* we will, we are necessarily not only able to will, but do will: there is the act itself of willing, and therefore certainly the power for it.'[2] 'It must be that when we will, we will with freewill —*necesse est ut cum volumus, libero velimus arbitrio.*'[3]

[1] 'Quid igitur ultra quærimus: quandoquidem hanc dicimus potestatem, ubi voluntati adjacet facultas faciendi? Unde hoc quisque in potestate habere dicitur, quod si vult facit, si non vult, non facit.'—De Spir. et Lit. c. xxxi.

[2] Nihil tam in nostra potestate quam ipsa voluntas est. Ea enim prorsus nullo intervallo mox ut volumus præsto est.—De Lib. Arb. l. 3. c. 3.

[3] De Civit. Dei, l. 5. c. 10.

The definition of freewill thus stops at the fact of will as the ultimate truth beyond which nothing can be said; the basis of this definition of will being a particular definition of *power*. The question of freedom is first correctly stated as being a question of power—what it is which constitutes the power to act in this or that way; and the constitution of power is decided by making the will a necessary element in it. A distinction is acknowledged, indeed, between power and will; but a man is still not allowed to have the whole power to do a thing unless he has the will also—*ut potestate aliquid fiat voluntas aderit;* 'in order that anything may be done by power, there must be the will;' and will is a condition of power and a true ingredient in its composition. Freedom is thus first defined by power, and power is then conditionated upon will, and there the definition stops,[1] leaving the ultimate test of freewill, and, as all that is meant by it, simple will. We have freewill or the power to will *if we will*.

It will be seen that this definition of freewill exactly coincides with Locke's, quoted above. Both writers define freedom to be the power of doing *what we will*; Augustine's *ubi voluntati adjacet facultas faciendi* just tallying with Locke's 'How can we think any one freer than to have the power to do what he will?' Both writers, applying this freedom to the will, immediately discover the freedom of the will to consist in willing as it wills: Augustine saying, '*Nihil tam in nostra potestate quam ipsa voluntas est; ea enim prorsus nullo intervallo mox ut volumus præsto est:*' Locke stating freewill as 'the man's liberty to will which of the two things *he pleases*,' and challenging any one to ask 'whether freedom itself were free.'

Augustine meets the difficulty raised against the freedom of the will from the Divine foreknowledge with the same answer; viz. that as a matter of fact we have will, and that will is as such free. 'Whatever may be the tortuous

---

[1] A dictum of S. Anselm's, expresses the principle of it scientifically—*In libero arbitrio posse non præcedit sed sequitur voluntatem.* The will is the original supposition, on which the definition of power is raised.

wranglings and disputes of philosophers, we, as we acknowledge one supreme and true God, so acknowledge His supreme will, power, and foreknowledge. Nor do we fear on that account that we do not do with our will what we do with our will—*nec timemus ne ideo non voluntate faciamus, quod voluntate facimus*. . . . . . We say both that God knows all things before they take place, and that we act with our will, inasmuch as we feel and know we do not act except with our will.'[1]

This, however, being S. Augustine's definition of freewill, it must be admitted that a considerable body of language, especially his language at the commencement of the book *De Gratiâ et Libero Arbitrio*, and in the two Epistles [2] relating to the occasion on which that book was written, appears at first sight to advance upon this definition, and to imply an original and self-determining power in the will. He argues for freewill as a doctrine of Scripture, and uses the common arguments which the maintainers of the ordinary doctrine of freewill use; viz. that Scripture employs commands, promises, and threats, and speaks to men as if they had freewill. Such an argument proves that he—*i.e.* Scripture as interpreted by him—acknowledges a will in man which is truly and properly the subject of commands, promises, and threats; and can such a will, it may be asked, be anything but a self-determining one? Does not such a mode of addressing man suppose an original power of choice in him? But though this would be sound and correct as a popular inference from such language, it is not as a logical one. Logically all that can be inferred from the use of commands and threats in the Divine dealings with man is, that man has a capacity for choosing, obeying, and acting upon motives[3]; but these are opera-

[1] De Civ. Dei, l. 5. c. 9.
[2] Ep. 214, 215.
[3] Non eodem modo se habent Deus et homo ad reddendum præmium. Homo namque sicut Rex publico edicto promulgat, monètque ipse indifferens et *indeterminatus* in voluntate sua circa sibi subjectos.
. . . Non sic autem Deus. Semper æque *determinate* vult. Per meritum *innotescit* hominibus, dæmonibus, et forsitan Angelis, quale præmium quis habebit. . . . Cum dicitur, Deus vult istum propter merita præmiare, hoc est, Deus vult istum præmiare propter merita finaliter

tions of the will, and are wholly performed, if there is only a will to perform them, without going into the question what decides that will. If man has a will, which will is intended to act in the particular way of choice and obedience, he must be addressed in a manner suitable to such a design; he must be commanded, in order that he may obey, and he must have the alternative placed before him in order that He choose. But such a mode of addressing him does not necessarily prove any more than that he is possessed of a will to which those operations belong. While, therefore, in the case of Scripture we are justified in taking such language to imply an original and self-determining will in man, because Scripture is addressed to the popular understanding, and this is the popular inference to draw from such language; in the case of a philosophical writer like Augustine,—who treats of the human will and the questions belonging to it in a scientific and subtle way, and from whose language therefore we are not justified in inferring more than it logically contains,—we cannot take it as implying more than the existence of a will in a man.

Indeed, the fact of a will is all the conclusion which he himself arrives at by this argument, and all that he presses upon his readers.[1] 'These commands would not be given unless man had a will truly belonging to him with which to obey them—*nisi homo haberet propriam voluntatem, qua divinis præceptis obediret.*'—' To the man who says I cannot do what is commanded, because he is conquered by concupiscence, the Apostle says, " Will not to be overcome of evil, but overcome evil with good;" will not to be overcome—*noli vinci* implying certainly a choice of his will; for to will and not to will is of the individual's will —*arbitrium voluntatis ejus sine dubio convenitur, velle enim et nolle propriæ voluntatis est.*'—' Freewill is suffi-

ordinanda, *i.e.* vult quod talis sit finis talium meritorum secundum ordinem ab ipso talibus præstitutum, ita quod merita nullo modo antecedenter, causaliter, a priori, monent, determinant, vel actuant voluntatem divinam ad præmia reddenda. . . . Deus primo vult homini præmium et gloriam tanquam finem, et ideo vult sibi et facit merita congrua.'—Bradwardine, p. 150. *et seq.*

[1] De Grat. et Lib. Arb. c. ii. *et seq.*

ciently proved by Scripture saying, will not this, and will not that, and demanding an act of the will in doing or not doing anything. Let no one then blame God in his heart, but impute it to himself when he sins. Nor, when he does anything according to God's will, let him alienate it from his own. For when he does it willingly, then it is a good work, then a reward attaches to it—*quando volens facit tunc dicendum est opus bonum*.' Again on the text 'All men cannot receive this saying, save they to whom it is given;' he says, 'Those to whom it is not given either will not or do not what they will: those to whom it is given so will that they do what they will. That which is not received by all, but is received by some, is both the gift of God and also is freewill—*et Dei donum est, et liberum arbitrium*.' That is to say, it is freewill in him, because, from whatever source it comes, when he has it, it is his own will. These explanations all appeal to the fact of a will in man, as being sufficient to constitute a free agent, and a proper subject of promises or threats, of reward or punishment. Indeed, what these arguments are designed to remove is not any part of the predestinarian doctrine, but only a false practical inference from it; for the occasion on which this treatise was written was, that certain persons had begun to argue, that if that doctrine was true, it did not signify what kind of lives men led, because they were not responsible for them. Augustine corrects this inference by reminding them, that the predestinarian doctrine did not exclude a will in man; and that if he had a will, that made him responsible.

Augustine's doctrine of freewill, then, does not come up to that which is ordinarily understood as that doctrine; not advancing beyond that point up to which the doctrine of freewill and the opposite doctrine agree. He acknowledges a will in man, that which makes him act willingly, as distinguished from acting by compulsion and constraint; but this is saying nothing as to how that will is determined.

II. But, in the second place, we come to the question

of the determination of this will, and under this head Augustine's language is not only less than, but is opposed to, the common doctrine of freewill.

The doctrine of freewill is, as has been stated, that the will has a self-determining power, which produces right acts or wrong, according as it is exercised. On the other hand, the opponents of the doctrine of freewill object that this is an absurd and self-contradictory cause to assign to human actions; for that, if the power of acting one way or another be the cause of the distinction in human actions, —*i.e.* of the good or bad act which really ensues,—the same cause can produce opposite effects. The objection proceeds on the assumption that human actions must *have* a cause; which granted, it follows of course that such a cause cannot be a neutral or flexible thing, as this freewill or power of choice is described to be.

Now, there is a passage, which I have already quoted,[1] in which the doctrine of freewill, as thus stated, comes under the notice of Augustine. The doctrine is stated in this passage thus: that 'We have a power of taking either side—*possibilitas utriusque partis*,—implanted in us by God, as a fruitful and productive root, to produce and bring forth according to men's different wills, and either shine with the flower of virtue, or bristle with the thorns of vice, according to the choice of the cultivator.' This is a plain statement of the ordinary doctrine of freewill. There is a power of taking either side inherent in our nature; that power determines our wills, and according as our wills are determined we do good or bad actions. To this doctrine, then, thus stated, Augustine objects on the same ground as that which has been just mentioned, viz., that it gives an absurd and self-contradictory cause to human actions. Such a doctrine he says, 'establishes one and the same root of the good and the bad,—*unam eandemque radicem constituit bonorum et malorum*.' That is, he says, it maintains one and the same ultimate or original condition of the man, out of which the opposite lives and actions of the two issue; to maintain which is to

[1] De Gratiâ Christi, c. 18.

give the same cause to opposite effects. Augustine's argument proceeds on the supposition of the necessity of a cause for human actions, and is substantially the same argument with that used by Edwards, that 'an act of the will cannot directly and immediately arise out of a state of indifference;' because the act implies 'an antecedent choice,' which choice cannot be simultaneous with indifference;'[1]—the assumption in this latter argument being that actions must have a cause out of which they spring; which cause can only be calculated to produce *one* effect, and not either one or the other of two effects. The advocates of freewill, on the other hand, do not admit this assumption, and so answer the argument which is raised upon it. They allow that this power of choice is no *cause* of the determination of the will, nor do they profess it to be such; but they maintain that for a determination of the will one way or another, it is not necessary to assign a cause, such determination being an original motion of the will. It must be added, however, that in using such an argument as this, Augustine is inconsistent, for he admits in the case of the first man this power, this freewill in the complete sense, this power of either side; appealing to it, as throwing the responsibility of sin upon him, and removing it from God; after which admission, he is properly precluded from arguing upon abstract grounds against such a power.

The power of choice, as the account of the evil and good actions and lives of men, being thus set aside, S. Augustine proceeds to lay down a *rationale* of two different roots or causes for the two. 'Our Lord says, that a good tree cannot bring forth evil fruit, nor an evil tree

---

[1] 'If the act springs immediately out of a state of indifference, then it does not arise from antecedent choice or preference. But if the act arises directly out of a state of indifference, without any intervening choice to determine it, then the act not being determined by choice is not determined by the will.' . . . An antecedent choice, then, he says, must be granted. But if it is, 'if the soul, while it yet remains in a state of perfect indifference, chooses to put itself out of that state and to turn itself one way, then the soul is already come to a choice, and chooses that way. And so the soul is in a state of choice, and in a state of equilibrium, both at the same time.'—On the Freedom of the Will, part ii. sect. 7.

good fruit. And the Apostle Paul, when he says that cupidity is the root of all evil, intimates also that love is the root of all good. If therefore the two trees good and evil are two men good and evil, what is the good man but the man of good will; that is, the tree of good fruit? And what is the evil man but the man of an evil will; that is, the tree of an evil root? And the fruits of these two trees are acts, words, thoughts, which if good proceed from a good will, and if evil from an evil will. And man makes a good tree when he receives the grace of God. For he does not make himself good out of evil by himself; but of Him, and through Him, and in Him who is good. . . . . And he makes an evil tree, when he makes himself evil, when he departs from immutable good; for the origin of an evil will is that departure.'[1] In this passage the lives and actions of the good and evil man are referred in the first place to two immediate or proximate roots, and then to two ultimate or original ones. The proximate roots of the two respectively are a good and evil will, which he calls also love and cupidity. The original roots, or those from which this good and evil will themselves spring, are grace and sin. 'Man makes a good tree or root, [tree and root being synonymous here] *when he receives the grace of God*; for he does not make himself good by himself, but of

---

[1] Habemus autem, inquit, possibilitatem utriusque partis a Deo insitam, velut quandam, ut ita dicam, radicem fructiferam atque fecundam quæ ex voluntate hominis diversa gignat et pariat, et quæ possit ad proprii cultoris arbitrium, vel nitere flore virtutum, vel sentibus horrere vitiorum. Ubi non intuens quod loquatur, unam eandemque radicem constituit bonorum et malorum, contra evangelicam veritatem doctrinamque apostolicam. Nam et Dominus nec arborem bonam dicit posse facere fructus malos, nec malam bonos; et Apostolus Paulus cum dicit radicem malorum omnium esse cupiditatem, admonet utique intelligi radicem bonorum omnium charitatem. Unde si duæ arbores bona et mala sunt, duo homines, bonus et malus, quid est bonus homo, nisi voluntatis bonæ, hoc est arbor radicis bonæ? et quid est homo malus, nisi voluntatis malæ, hæc est arbor radicis malæ? Fructus autem harum radicum atque arborum facta sunt, dicta sunt, cogitata sunt, quæ bona de bona voluntate procedunt, et mala de mala. Facit autem homo arborem bonam, quando Dei accipit gratiam. Non autem se ex malo bonum per seipsum facit, sed in illo et per illum, et in illo qui semper est bonus. . . Malam vero arborem facit quando seipsum malum facit, quando a bono immutabili deficit.—De Gratiâ Christi, c. 18, 19.

Him:' that is, his own preparation of his will, by which he makes it a good will, is itself derived from grace ; man is the immediate, but grace the original agent. On the other hand, 'Man makes an evil tree or root when he makes himself evil, and departs from immutable good,' as he did by his transgression in Paradise, for so the general doctrine of Augustine interprets this allusion. A *rationale* of two different roots or causes of the lives of good and evil men is thus laid down, in the place of one and the same moral condition out of which they are supposed to arise on the doctrine of freewill.

The same argument is repeated in a passage from the book *De Peccatorum Meritis et Remissione*: 'It is strange if the will can stand at a certain point midway, so as to be neither good nor bad—*voluntas mirum si potest in medio quodam ita consistere, ut nec bona nec mala sit*. For either we love righteousness, and it is good, or we do not love righteousness, and it is bad; the bad will not coming from God, the good one coming from God, and being the gift whereby we are justified . . . a gift which to whomsoever God gives it, He gives in His mercy, and from whomsoever He withholds it, He withholds it in His judgment . . . for the law of His secret justice rests with Him alone.'[1] The writer here refuses to comprehend a neutral, and simply determinable will, and, setting aside such a *rationale* of human conduct, lays down two separate wills, good and bad, which have each possession of the agent prior to all action.

These two distinct wills, or roots or causes of human action, then, are, as has already appeared, and as the whole doctrine of Augustine shows, original sin and grace.

I. The will of fallen man is determined to evil by a cause out of and beyond the personal will or the will of the individual; *i.e.* by the transgression of the first man, or original sin; which captive will, however, is, notwithstanding, freewill, for the following reasons.

In the first place, Augustine defends its freedom upon the simple ground which has been maintained. In reply

[1] De Pecc. Merit. et Rem. l. 2. c. 18.

to the Pelagian, who presses him continually with the consequences of his doctrine, and asks how a being, who is literally unable to turn to good from the moment of his birth, can be treated as a free agent and responsible for his acts, he answers simply that he is so, inasmuch as he has a will. He does what he does with his will, and not against it. No force has compelled him to act contrary to his inclination, but he has acted according to his inclination. He has therefore acted as a free agent, and he is responsible for his acts. What more is wanted for responsibility than that a man has acted willingly, and without constraint? 'Why perplex a very plain subject. He is free for evil (*i.e.* a free agent in doing evil) who acts with an evil will. He is free for good (*i.e.* a free agent in doing good) who acts with a good will.'[1]—'Men are not *forced* by the necessity of the flesh into sin, as if they were *unwilling* (*quasi inviti*); but if they are of an age to use their own choice, they are both retained in sin by their will, and precipitated from one sin to another by their will. For he who persuades and deceives them does not work anything in them, but that they sin with their will.'[2]—'The will is that with which we sin, and with which we live well—*voluntas est qua et peccatur et recte vivitur.*'[3] It is enough for freedom, according to these statements, if we sin by or with the consent of our will.

Another answer to this difficulty is more subtle and intricate. The sin of our nature is voluntary, and men are responsible for it, because this sin proceeds from a self-determining human will in the first instance; the sin of the first man or the original sin having been committed

[1] Quid aperta implicas loquacitate perplexa? Ad malum liber est, qui voluntate agit mala: ad bonum autem liber est qui voluntate agit bona.—Op. Imp. l. 3. c. 120.

[2] 'Non itaque, sicut dicunt nos quidem dicere, et iste audet insuper scribere, "omnes in peccatum, velut inviti, carnis suæ necessitate coguntur:" sed, si jam in ea ætate suut ut propriæ mentis utantur arbitrio, et 'in peccato *sua voluntate* retinentur, et a peccato in peccatum *sua voluntate* præcipitantur. Neque enim agit in eis qui suadet et decipit, nisi ut peccatum *voluntate* committant.'—Contra Duas, Ep. l. 1. c. 3.

'Liberum arbitrium usque adeo in peccatore non periit, ut per illud peccent, maxime omnes qui cum delectatione peccant.'—Ibid. l. 1. c. 2.

[3] Retract. l. 1. c. 9.

when man had a self-determining will. The root or origin, therefore, of sin is entirely free, and it must be judged by its root or origin. Subsequently, indeed, to its origin, sin becomes not free in this sense, but necessary, and our nature is captive to it: but this does not undo the freedom of its origin. 'Sin cannot be without the will, in the same way in which we say that the fruit cannot be without the root. . . . Without the will of him (Adam) from whom is the origin of all that live, the original sin was not committed. But the contagion of it could pass to others without the will. It must exist with the will, in order that it might pass to others without the will, as a tree must have a root below, in order that it may be above without a root. . . . Sin is both with the will and without the will: it is with the will in so far as it must *begin* to be with it; it is without the will in so far as it *remains* without it.'[1] When it is said in this passage that sin remains without the will, it is not of course meant that it remains apart from all will whatever, for some kind of will must go along with a sinful act to make it the man's act; but will is here used in the highest sense as a self-determining will, such a will as the first man in his perfect state had. The meaning of this passage, then, is this: that sin began in a self-determining will; and that, therefore, though when once existing, it remains in the human race without *such* a will, it ever carries about with it the freedom and responsibility of its commencement. The human will is viewed as one stream of will, so to call it, flowing first from a fountain head in the will of the first man, as he came from the hands of his Creator, undergoing a change of its powers and condition at the fall, and with that internal change passing into all the individual members of the human race, as they are succes-

---

[1] Ego sic dixi peccatum sine voluntate esse non posse, quomodo dicimus poma vel frumenta sine radicibus esse non posse. . . . Sine voluntate esse non posset, ut esset quod in alios sine voluntate transiret; sicut frumenta sine radicibus esse non possent, ut essent quæ in alia loca transire sine radicibus possent. . . . Sine voluntate non potest esse, nam sine voluntate non potest existere ut sit; sine autem voluntate potest esse, quia sine voluntate potest manere quod existit. —Op. Imp. l. 4. cc. 97. 99.

sively born. At its fountain head this will is self-determining and free in the complete sense; but at the fall it loses this freedom, and receives into itself an inclination to evil, which operates necessarily. Thus biassed, it passes into the successive generations of individual men, as they are born, constituting them sinful beings, and issuing in sinful desires and acts. If mankind complain, then, of this captive condition, and ask why, when their will acts under a necessity they are treated as free and responsible beings subject to punishment for their acts, they are told that their will was originally free and self-determining; that it only lost that power by its own fault; and that a loss which it has brought upon itself does not give it immunity. An analogy is instituted between the effect of original sin upon the will, and the effect of habit or custom. The will of the man who is born under the influence of original sin is treated as identical with the will which committed that sin; just as the will of an individual who is under the force of a bad habit is identical with the will which contracted that habit. And this view accounts for an apparent contradiction which we meet with in Augustine, in speaking of the will. He talks of will as being essentially original and the cause of itself, or self-determining; being this, as being will [1]; and he also speaks of will as if the fact of a will, whatever were its cause, made a true and genuine will. He is first speaking of will as a whole, and secondly of will in a particular stage. Will as a whole must be original and self-determining; that is, there must have been a time in the history of the will when it was so: otherwise we make sin simply necessary in the world, and fasten its authorship on the Deity. But will in a particular stage or condition may be the conscious fact of willing, and no more, acting really under a necessity. Such an explanation, however, is wholly mystical.

II. The will of man is determined to good by grace, and yet it is freewill; just as his will, when so determined by original sin to evil, was free: because it is true will;

[1] P. 206.

because the man acts willingly and without constraint. 'The human will is not taken away, but is changed from evil to good by grace—*voluntas humana non tollitur, sed ex mala mutatur in bonam.*'[1]—'Freewill is one of the gifts of God; not only itself but the goodness of it—*non tantum ut sit sed etiam ut bonum sit.*'[2]—'It is certain that when we will, we will; but it is He who makes us to will—*certum est nos velle cum volumus, sed ille facit ut velimus bonum.* It is certain that when we do we do; but He makes us to do, by giving the most effective strength to the will—*certum est nos facere cum facimus, sed ille facit ut faciamus, præbendo vires efficacissimas voluntati.*'[3]—'Some will to believe, others do not; because the will of some is prepared by God, the will of others is not —*aliis præparatur aliis non præparatur voluntas a Domino.* . . . . Mercy and justice have been respectively exerted in the very wills of men—*misericordia et judicium in ipsis voluntatibus facta sunt.*'[4] That is to say, the will is moved and determined by Divine grace, but it is still will, and freewill.

A higher sense, however, than that of freedom from constraint and force, or simple willingness, though at the same time including this latter sense, is sometimes given to the term freewill; viz., that of freedom from the yoke and bondage of sin, the dominion of evil inclinations and passions. The term freedom is raised from its neutrality and appropriated to a good condition of the will; such condition being still, however, not freedom in the sense of power of choice, but a state of servitude to good,—the contradictory of servitude to evil.

S. Paul speaks of two bondages, a bondage to righteousness and a bondage to sin; and of two freedoms, a freedom from righteousness and a freedom from sin. And S. Augustine, following him, says: 'The will is always free in us, but not always good; for either it is free from righteousness, and under bondage to sin, or it is free from

---

[1] De Gratiâ et Lib. Arb. n. 41.
[2] De Pecc. Merit. et Rem. l. 2. c. 6.
[3] De Gratiâ et Lib. Arb. n. 32.
[4] De Præd. Sanct. c. 6.

sin, and under bondage to righteousness.'[1] Here the term free is evidently used not in the sense of free *for* evil or good, *i.e.* with the power of doing either; but as meaning free *from* evil, and free *from* good. There is a state of mind in which the good principle is dominant and supreme, and the man in entire subjection to it or under its yoke; a state of mind in which the will has reached such a point of strength on the good side, as that the man could not act against it, without such a violence as it would be absurd to suppose him committing toward himself. There is a state of mind also in which evil has this dominance and supremacy. Freewill is here understood as will, which is either free from this yoke of good, or free from this yoke of evil. In this sense of the word free, then, the freedom of the will is inconsistent with a power of choice; for, according to this use of the term, a freewill, so far from having ability to do evil or good, has its very name, because it is either not able to do evil on the one hand, or not able to do good on the other. It is not a will which has yet to make its choice, but which is already determined, and is an acting will on one side or the other. Nor has such a freewill arisen in the first instance by a power of choice, because such a freewill there has *always been* on the evil side or the good; 'the will is always free in us,' *i.e.* is always in one of these states of freedom or the other. Were the change from the bondage of evil, of which Augustine speaks, a change from this bondage to evil to a *power* of choosing evil or good (and this is what on the common doctrine of freewill is understood by the freedom of grace as distinguished from the bondage of nature), a power of choice in the will would then come in. But this change is simply an exchange of one bondage for another,—a

---

[1] 'Semper est in nobis voluntas libera, sed non semper est bona. Aut enim a justitia libera est, quando servit peccato, et tunc est mala: aut a peccato libera est, quando servit justitiæ, et tunc est bona. Gratia vero Dei semper est bona, et per hanc fit ut sit homo bonæ voluntatis, qui prius fuit voluntatis malæ.'—De Grat. et Lib. Arb. n. 31.

'Liberum arbitrium et ad malum et ad bonum faciendum confitendum est nos habere: sed in malo faciendo liber est quisque justitiæ servusque peccati; in bono autem liber est nullus, nisi fuerit liberatus ab illo.'—De Corr. et Grat. n. 2.

bondage to good for a bondage to evil; and, therefore, there is no room for the introduction of this power.

A state of bondage to righteousness, then, or a state in which the will is necessarily good, is, according to this scheme, a state of freewill; only as yet it has that name in common with the corresponding state on the side of evil. S. Paul uses the terms bondage and freedom, instead of in a respectively favourable and unfavourable sense, in a neutral one; and S. Augustine follows him. But the application of the term is afterwards restricted and appropriated to the good side; and the good state of the will is called the freedom, in contrast with the other, which is called the slavery of the will.[1]

It appears, then, upon a general examination of the language of Augustine respecting freewill, first, that it does not come up to that which we call the doctrine of freewill, not going beyond that simple acknowledgment of a will in which that doctrine and its opposite agree; and, secondly, that it is opposed to that doctrine, his language being that the will has, notwithstanding its freedom, no self-determining power, but is determined to evil and to good respectively by original sin and by grace.

It is true, indeed, that language of an apparently opposite kind to this is to be found occasionally in S. Augustine; but when such language is examined, it will be found to be only verbally opposite to, and really in harmony with, the doctrine which has been exhibited. S. Augustine uniformly indeed holds a *co-operation* of the human will with Divine grace, and co-operation seems to imply two original agencies meeting and uniting in the same work; but on examination we find that the term, in S. Augustine's use of it, does not imply this. The co-operation of the human will with Divine grace only commences, according to S. Augustine, after the human will has undergone that whole process which has been just described; that is to say, after it has been moved by the sole action of Divine grace into a state of efficiency.

[1] 'In tantum libera est (voluntas) in quantum liberata est (a dominante cupiditate).'—Retract. l. 1. c. 15.

'He works in us that we will, and that is the beginning, He co-operates with us when we will, and that is the perfecting, of the work. Being confident of this very thing, says the Apostle, that He which hath begun a good work in you will perfect it until the day of Jesus Christ. That we will, therefore He works in us without us; and when we will, and so will that we do, He co-operates with us— *ut ergo velimus sine nobis operatur, cum autem volumus et sic volumus ut faciamus, nobiscum operatur*. And we can do no good works of piety without Him first operating that we will, and then co-operating with us when we will. Of God operating that we will it is said, "It is God that worketh in us to will." Of God co-operating with us when we will, and so will that we do, it is said, "We know that all things work together for good to them that love God."'[1] The condition of the human will is here divided into two stages, in the former of which God simply operates upon it, in the latter co-operates with it. The former stage lasts till the will is effective, till we will and so will that we do; that point attained the latter stage commences, and God co-operates with this will, and this will co-operates with Him. It is evident from the very terms of this division what the nature of this co-operating human will is; that it is not an original agent, but a will that has been made to be what it is by grace wholly. That such a will co-operates with grace is no more than to say, that grace co-operates with grace; for that which the pure effect does, the cause does really and properly. Grace is the original, the will is only an instrumental co-operator. The dictum '*Gratia ipsa meretur augeri, ut aucta mereatur perfici,*' expresses the same doctrine, making the simple bestowal of grace the reason of its further bestowal, so that grace is its own augmenter, and increases upon an internal law of growth.

It is such a mode of co-operation as this which the following passage describes: 'It is plain that human righteousness, although it is not done without the human will, is to be attributed to the operation of the Divine,

[1] De Grat. et Lib. Arb. c. xvii.

which is the reason we cannot deny that the perfection of that righteousness is possible even in this life; because all things are possible to God, both what He does when His own will solely operates, and what He does when the wills of His creatures operate with Him—*sive quæ facit sola sua voluntate, sive quæ co-operantibus creaturæ suæ voluntatibus, a se fieri posse constituit.*'[1] Here is a co-operation mentioned of the human will with the Divine, but it is a co-operation subordinated to an absolute power in the Divine will. Whatever therefore such co-operation in the human will involves, it does not involve any dependence of the *issue* upon it, inasmuch as such issue is secured by the absolute power of the Divine will to produce it. The power is on one side, the co-operation on another; co-operation abstracted from power is instrumental co-operation.

The same mode of co-operation is described in the following extract: 'When God wills the salvation of a man, no will of man resists Him. For to will or not to will is in the power of the willing or unwilling man in such sense only that it does not impede the Divine will or frustrate the Divine power—*sic enim velle seu nolle in volentis aut nolentis est potestate, ut Divinam voluntatem non impediat, nec super et potestatem.*'[2] Here it is said that in a particular sense a man's will is in his own power, and were the sense in which this were allowed a free and natural one, nothing more would be wanted for a testimony on the side of freewill. But we see at once that it is anything but a free and natural sense in which this power is conceded; for it is conceded under the salvo, that this power does not interfere with the natural operation of another power, which other power is absolute. But what is power which is itself the subject of absolute power? Had S. Augustine wished to admit a real power in the human will, there are many plain and simple modes in which he might have done it, as a common language in theology, both ancient and modern, on this subject shows. But he only admits a power which is negatived by an entire

[1] De Lit. et Spirit. c. 5  [2] De Corr. et Grat. c. xiv.

subordination to another power; and a will with such a negatived power over itself is not an original but an instrumental co-operator with the Divine will.

One passage, however, has attracted remarkable attention, in consequence of one particular phrase, contained in it, appearing at first to involve very decidedly the position of a self-determining will: 'If it be said that we must beware of interpreting the text, "What hast thou which thou hast not received?" of the *believing* will, and asserting, because this proceeds from a freewill which was a Divine gift at our creation, that therefore it is *itself* a Divine gift, lest we attribute to God the authorship of sin as well;—I say, that a believing will is not to be attributed to God solely because it proceeds from freewill, but because it depends upon the Divine persuasion, either external or internal; though it belongs to the individual's will *to agree with or dissent from this persuasion*. God's mercy always anticipates us, and He works in man the will to believe; but to assent to or dissent from the Divine will belongs to the individual will. Nor does this at all contradict the text, "What hast thou which thou hast not received?" but rather confirms it. The soul cannot receive these gifts without consenting; because, what it has and what it receives is from God: to have and receive belongs to a possessor and receiver.' He then decides why this Divine persuasion, to which this assent of the will is necessary, is effectual with some, and not with others, and decides it by a reference to the inscrutable will of God.[1]

[1] 'Si autem respondetur, cavendum esse ne quisquam Deo tribuendum putet peccatum, quod admittitur per liberum arbitrium, si in eo quod dicitur, " *Quid habes quod non accepisti?* " propterea etiam voluntas qua credimus dono Dei tribuitur, quia de libero existit arbitrio, quod cum crearemur accepimus; attendat et videat, non ideo, quia ex libero arbitrio est, quod nobis naturaliter concreatum est; verum etiam quod visorum suasionibus agit Deus, ut velimus et ut credamus, sive extrinsecus, per evangelicas exhortationes . . sive intresecus, ubi nemo habet in potestate quid ei veniat, in mentem, *sed consentire vel dissentire propriæ voluntati sest.* His ergo modis quando Deus agit cum anima rationali, ut ei credat (neque enim credere potest quodlibet libero arbitrio si nulla sit suasio vel vocatio cui credat) profecto et ipsum velle credere Deus operatur in homine, et in omnibus misericordia ejus prævenit nos: *consentire autem vocationi Dei, vel ab ea dissentire, sicut dixi, propriæ volun-*

We have, then, in this passage the expression, '*assentire vel dissentire propriæ voluntatis est*;' and this expression seems at first sight to involve a self-determining will. But it will be seen, that in the course of the statement it receives a different explanation. In this passage S. Augustine is discussing the question, whether the will to believe is given by God; and he answers, first, that it is given by God because it arises out of that freewill which was given to man at his creation. But then he remarks, that this answer is not enough, because sin also arises out of freewill, and sin is not the gift of God. What is the difference, then, he asks, in the mode in which they respectively arise, which makes one the gift of God, and the other not? He decides that this difference lies in a certain calling or persuading on the part of God, which is necessary in order to produce the believing will—*neque enim credere potest quodlibet libero arbitrio, si nulla sit suasio vel vocatio cui credat.* And to this calling and persuasion the natural will has to consent, in order for it to be effectual; for that 'assenting or dissenting belongs to the natural will— *consentire vocationi Dei vel ab ea dissentire propriæ voluntatis est.*' The believing will, then, is a Divine gift, inasmuch as it is the result of a Divine calling with which the human will agrees. But then the question immediately arises, whether this is not a compromise which really gives up the whole point, and makes the believing will not a gift which man receives simply, but something which he acquires by an act of his own. And to that he replies, that it is not, because consent is only the necessary mode in which the will receives a gift: consent being, in fact, nothing but the act itself of receiving; so that to say that the will must consent in order to receive, is

*tatis est.* Quæ res non solum non infirmat quod dictum est, "Quid habes quod non accepisti?" verum etiam confirmat. Accipere quidem et habere anima non potest dona, de quibus hoc audit, nisi consentiendo: ac per hoc quid habeat et quid accipiat, Dei est; accipere autem et habere, accipientis et habentis est. Jam si ad illam profunditatem scrutandam quisquam nos coarctet, cur illi ita suadeatur ut persuadeatur illi autem non ita: duo sola occurrunt interim quæ respondere mihi placeat " O altitudo divitiarum " et " Numquid iniquitas apud Deum?"'—De Spiritu et Literâ, l. 1. n. 60.

nothing more than to say that the will must receive when it receives—*accipere et habere utique accipientis et habentis est.* The believing will thus comes out, after due explanation, a simple gift, to which the only consent is one which is involved in the mere fact of it being given; viz. reception and possession. And, lastly, why one man has this gift, and another not, is explained by a simple appeal to mystery.

Any one who carefully examines this passage will see that the explanation here given of it is the only one by which a consistent meaning is secured for it throughout. A phrase apparently owning an original power in the human will to accept or reject the Divine operation upon it, is admitted; but as soon as it has been admitted it is explained in a particular way, and reduced into entire harmony with a theory of omnipotent grace, resting upon a basis of mystery.[1]

To sum up in one distinction the general argument of this chapter, the Augustinian doctrine of freewill may be said in a word to describe the nature of freewill as being a mode of action, not a source of action—taking source in its proper sense as an original source. The *mode* of human

[1] Jansen (De Gratiâ Christi, pp. 220, 225, 908, 936, 955, 980, 989) properly explains various passages of Augustine from which the Jesuits Bellarmine, Suarez, Molina, Lessius, and others had extracted a freewill meaning, as applying to the will of man as created, or simply to will as such. But while such explanation is sometimes required on his own side, nothing can be more far-fetched and artificial than the Jesuit interpretations of the great pervading dicta and fundamental positions of Augustine; if interpretations deserve that name which are obvious and barefaced contradictions to, rather than explanations of, S. Augustine's meaning, as Lessius' interpretation of the Augustinian predestination as *conditional* and incomplete (pp. 955, 981) his view of Augustinian election as *ex prævisis operibus* (p. 989): and his and Molini's explanation of *gratia efficax,* as efficacious *si voluntas cum ea co-operari velit* (p. 936), omitting the whole consideration that this consent of the will is itself, according to Augustine the *effect* of grace. Having excluded Augustinianism from the pale of tolerated opinion, the Church of Rome is obliged to prove that S. Augustine was not Augustinian. But the plain language of S. Augustine refutes such interpreters, and forces one of two alternatives upon them, either that they tolerate his doctrines, and so keep him in communion with their Church, or anathematise his doctrines, and confess that S. Augustine does not belong to their communion.

action is free. We act willingly and without compulsion whenever we truly act at all ; for action forced upon us is not our own, but another's, and to act willingly is to act freely. We act with deliberation, choice, preference, on certain principles, and to certain ends. But it does not follow, it is argued, that our mode of action decides anything as to the source of action : we act *as we will*; but the question still remains how we come to will. Underneath all our sensations of original agency, it is maintained, a deeper cause operates, and that which is not the will produces the movements and acts of the will. 'Men are acted upon, that they may act, not that they may not act —*aguntur ut agant non ut ipsi nihil agant.*' A translation cannot give the point of the original, which is literally that 'men are *acted* that they may act;' the passive and the active of the same verb being used to express the more pointedly the entire sequency of an effect from a cause. Men act—*agunt*, that is the effect; they are *acted upon* —*aguntur*, that is the cause which accounts for the whole of the effect. The whole cause then, of human acts is beyond the agent himself. But the agent is not nevertheless inert, because he is not a cause; on the contrary, he is an *agent*, he acts. He is not caused to do nothing ; caused to be idle, passive, motionless; an actor is the very thing he is caused to be. That is to say, his mode of acting, which is wholly free, coexists with a source of action which is external.—' When we will we will, but He makes us to will—*certum est nos velle cum volumus, sed ille facit ut velimus bonum.*' An objector is supposed to say that he must be the cause of his own acts because he wills them. But he is told that his mode of action, which is free, decides nothing as to its source. That a man should be 'forced to will—*cogatur velle*,' would be a contradiction; for, ' if he is forced he does not will, he cannot will unwillingly—*cum enim cogitur non vult, et quid absurdius quam ut dicatur nolens velle.*'[1] But there is no contradiction in his being *made* to will, because the will cannot resist before it exists, and therefore cannot be opposed to

[1] Op. Imp. l. 1. c. 134.

its own formation. It is the same distinction of mode and source. "You do not understand," Augustine tells the Pelagian who brings against him the text 2 Tim. ii. 21: "If a man, therefore, *purge himself*,' &c., as proving man to be the proper source of his own acts, 'you do not understand that both assertions are true, that the vessels of glory prepare themselves, and that God prepares them. For God makes that man does—*ut faciat homo facit Deus.*'— 'What can be more absurd than your idea that because the motives of the will are unforced, we are not to inquire *whence* they are, as if a cause were contradictory to their freedom, as forcing them *to be*? Is a man *forced* to exist, because he has an origin? Before he existed, was there anything to be forced? The will has an origin, and yet is not forced to be; and if this origin is not to be sought for, the reason is not that it should not be, but that it need not,—that it is too manifest. The will is from him whose the will is; the angel's will from the angel, the man's from the man, God's from God. God, in working a good will in man, causes a good will to arise in him whose the will is—*agit ut oriatur ab illo bona voluntas cujus est voluntas*; just as He causes man to spring from man.'[1] No language could indicate more fully the nature of the will, as an active, living, willing will, internal and truly our own, than this which goes even the length of claiming an originality of the will within, and making it arise out of ourselves. But, on the other hand, this very originality

[1] Op. Imp. l. 1. c. 101.

Quid autem vanius definiti ... tuis, qui propterea putas n... quærendum unde sit volunt... motus est animi cogente nu ... enim dicatur, ut putas, u... non erit verum quod dic... *cogente nullo*: quia illud ... eum cogit esse; et ideo ... alicunde, ne cogatur esse ... titiam singularem! Non ... alicunde ipse homo, qui ... coactus esse, quia non era... geretur antequam esset. P... alicunde est voluntas, et ... cogitur; et si ejus origo quærenda non est, non ideo quærenda non est quod voluntas alicunde non sit, sed quia manifestum est unde sit. Ab illo est enim voluntas cujus est voluntas; ab angelo scilicet voluntas angeli, ab homine hominis, a Deo Dei, et si operatur Deus in homine voluntatem bonam, id utique agit, *ut oriatur ab illo bona voluntas, cujus est voluntas*; sicut agit ut homo oriatur ab homine; non enim quia Deus creat hominem, ideo non homo ex homine nascitur.—Op. Imp. l. 5. c. 42.

of the will is not original; this very source within us is derived from a source without us. This rise of the will out of ourselves is no more opposed to its true causation by Divine grace, than the birth of man from man is opposed to man's creation by Divine power. The will is a middle cause between God and the act, as man is a middle cause between God and the human birth. It is a cause, but that very cause is caused; *i.e.* the will is an absolutely free mode of action, but not a true original source of action. Such a doctrine is not fairly open to the charge commonly brought against it, that it converts man into a machine, and degrades him to the level of matter; for it does not do so. A machine has no will; but this doctrine expressly admits in man a will. But it allows a will as a mediate, and not a first cause, of action.

The Augustinian doctrine of freewill having been thus stated, it only remains to point out wherein lies its peculiarity, in what the true difference between it and the ordinary doctrine of freewill consists.

The first characteristic, then, that we observe in the doctrine which we have been considering, is, that it combines freewill with necessity. The terms themselves necessity and necessary are not indeed in constant use in Augustine though he does use them; maintaining man in a state of nature to be under 'a necessity to sin—*peccati necessitas*,'[1] and under grace to be recalled by necessity to a spiritual life—*necessitate revocari*.[2] Not selecting them for his own use—conveying as they do to ordinary minds the idea of force—when challenged by his Pelagian opponent to admit them, he does not refuse; only securing a distinction between a co-active and a creative necessity. But though the word itself is not in constant use, other words which signify the same thing are; and therefore

---

[1] Op. Imp. l. 5. c. 61.
[2] Op. Imp. l. 1. c. 93. 'Necessitatis inerat plenitudo.'—L. 5. c. 59. 'Attende eum qui dicit, *Quod nolo malum hoc ago*, et responde utrum necessitatem non habeat.'—L. 5. c. 50. 'Quia vero peccavit voluntas secuta est peccantem peccavit habendi dura necessitas, donec tota sanetur infirmitas . . . ita ut sit etiam bene vivendi, et nunquam peccandi voluntaria felixque necessitas."—De Perfectione Justitiæ, c. 4.

this doctrine may be called, in the first place, a combination of freewill with necessity.

The peculiarity, however, of the Augustinian doctrine does not lie in this combination; for the combination itself is not, when we examine the matter, open to any substantial objection. We are apt, indeed, at first to think that no will can be in any sense free that acts necessarily; but a little reflection will show us that this is a first thought resulting from not properly knowing our own admissions on this subject. We attribute to the Supreme Being, the angels, and saints in their state of reward, a necessity on the side of goodness; but we attribute to God, the angels, and the saints the operation of a genuine will. We attribute to the evil spirits and the wicked, in their state of punishment, a necessity on the side of evil, and together with it the same genuine will. Necessity indeed only operates in matter in this lower world; inevitable growth, inevitable decay, organisation, and disorganisation, are only seen in the animal, vegetable and mineral bodies; but in the eternal world, the intelligent substance acts necessarily, and that which moves with certainty in the direction of good or evil is *will*. The Supreme Will, being essentially good, cannot contradict itself; the will of the wicked cannot agree with, the will of the righteous cannot recede from, the Will Supreme. Indeed, we are conversant with certain approaches to necessity in human conduct in this life. It is the essential characteristic of habit, that it makes acts to be performed by us as a matter of course, implants a kind of law in our minds, by which we act in this or that way; and therefore habit is called a second nature. But we do not consider that men who have formed habits, virtuous or the contrary, do not act with freewill.

Nor, again, does the peculiarity of S. Augustine's doctrine, as it does not lie in the combination of freewill with necessity, lie either in the source which he assigns to such necessity, which is one external to the agent. The doctrine of an eternal state of reward and punishment, which all Christians admit, asserts the transference of human wills into a state of necessity, both for evil and good, by an act of Almighty Power; that the wills of wicked men are, on their departure from this life, put by this act into a state in which they are beyond recovery; those of the good into a state in which they are beyond lapse. The power of choice being, according to the doctrine of freewill, retained by man so long as he remains in this world, its determination, on his departure to another, is caused not by an act of his own, but by a Divine act of judgment or of reward, as it may be. Thus all God's moral creatures pass, at a particular stage of their being, by an act of Divine Power, from a state in which their wills are indeterminate and may choose either good or evil, to a state in which they necessarily choose one or the other. While there is life there is hope, and there is fear. The most inveterate habits of vice still leave a power of self-recovery in the man if he will but exert it; the most confirmed habits of virtue still leave the liability to a fall. The resources for a struggle between good and evil remain up to the time of departure from life, when a change takes place which no thought can reach, and by a Divine act the will, remaining the same in substance, is changed fundamentally in condition, and put out of a state of suspense and, in ordinary language, *freedom,* into one of necessity.

But the combination of necessity, and that a necessity communicated to the will from without, with freewill, being admitted on both sides, the peculiarity of Augustine's doctrine lies in the *application* of this principle; in the reason, the time, and the manner he assigns to its operation. That state of the will to which an original power of choice attaches is upon the doctrine of freewill identical with a state of trial; and this consideration gives us the reason and time of the introduction of necessity, as well as the manner of its operation according to the doctrine of freewill. The ground of its introduction is final reward and punishment; the time of its introduction is after a state of trial; and the manner of its operation consists in the absence of struggle, effort, or interruption; in the entire, continuous, and natural yielding of the will to the impulses of good or evil. The strife is over in the mind of man; and the will, finally rooted, goes on producing good or evil acts and motions with the ease and uniformity of physical law. But in S. Augustine's application of the principle, the reason, and time of its introduction, and mode of operation, are all different. Necessity is not the reward or punishment of a previous exercise of liberty of choice, but the effect of original sin on the one hand, and an eternal Divine decree of mercy on the other. And with the difference of reason for, the *time* of its introduction is also different. It does not succeed and come after a state of trial, but is simultaneous with it, and is in full operation in this life, instead of being reserved for the next. And the manner of its operation is for the same reason different, exhibiting the struggle, the variableness, and interruption incident to this present state of existence. The difference between the trial, effort, and alternation of the present, and the peace and serenity of the future life, which is upon the doctrine of freewill a difference between a state of liberty and a state of necessity, is, according to the predestinarian, only a difference between two modes of operation on the part of the same necessity. That grace from which good action necessarily follows is not given with uniformity in this life, sometimes being given and sometimes not, to the same individual; whereas, in the eternal world it is either given wholly or taken away wholly, always given or never; so that there the determination of the will is constant for good or for evil. Its mode of operation, then, in this life is variable, in the next uniform; here, with pain and effort to the man, with trouble and anxiety, the feeling of uncertainty, and other feelings exactly like what we should have, supposing our wills were free and our acts contingent; there with ease, security, and bliss; here preparatory, there final; here after the mode of trial, there after the mode of reward.

Such a difference between two doctrines of necessity, it will be seen, involves all the difference between a doctrine of necessity and a doctrine of freewill. The former gives to freewill that period which is the turning part of man's existence, this life; to necessity only that future state which is here decided. The latter gives to necessity both the future state itself and the decision of it.

## CHAPTER IX.

### SCHOLASTIC THEORY OF NECESSITY.

THE teaching of S. Augustine had that result which naturally follows from the keen perception and mastery of a particular truth by a vigorous, powerful, and fertile mind; endowed with an inexhaustible command and perfect management of language, which seconded and acted as the simple instrument of the highest religious ardour and enthusiasm. Copious and exuberant, and concise and pointed, at the same time; bold, ingenious, and brilliant, yet always earnest and natural, he did not write so much in vain. As the production of a single mind, the quantity of the writing had a unity, force, and wholeness which told with surprising effect upon the Church. The large aggregate of thought and statement came in one effective mass and body. One such writer is in himself a whole age, and more than an age of authorship; a complete school, and more than a school of divinity. He had, moreover, the advantage of an undoubted and solid ground of Scripture; an advantage which his deep and full knowledge of the sacred text, and wonderful skill and readiness in the application of it, enabled him to use with the greatest effect. He erected on this ground, indeed, more than it could legitimately bear, and was a one-sided interpreter. Still he brought out a side of Scripture which had as yet been much in the shade, and called attention to deep truths which had comparatively escaped notice in the Church. He brought to light the full meaning of S. Paul, and did that which the true interpreter does for his teacher and master,—fastened the great doctrine of the Apostle, in its full and complete sense, upon the Church.

Such an exposition had as great and as permanent success as could have been anticipated. The doctrine of S. Augustine reigned in the mediæval Church, and moulded its authoritative teaching, till the Reformation produced a reaction ; and the Roman Church, apprehensive of the countenance which it gave to some prominent doctrines of the Reformers, and repelled by the use—sometimes unfair and fanatical—made of it, fell back upon a strong doctrine of freewill. The Thomists took an important part, indeed, in the Council of Trent, and had sufficient influence to guard its decrees from any turn unfavourable to themselves. But they ceased after the Reformation to be a prominent and ruling school, and gave place to the Jesuits, who, as the antagonists by position and calling of the Reformation, formed their theology in express opposition to it, and abandoned the Augustinian ground. The Jansenists attempted a revival of it, to which their enthusiasm and devotion gave a temporary success, sufficient to alarm the dominant school: but authority finally suppressed it, and ejected them, and practically with them the Augustinian doctrine, from the Roman Church.

The mediæval Augustinian school presents us with the names of Peter Lombard, S. Bernard, S. Anselm, Thomas Aquinas, Bradwardine,[1] and others.[2] Among these Lombard and Aquinas occupy the first place as formal and systematic theologians. The former of these, however, is more of a compiler and collector of extracts and references, than an exponent and a constructor. His collection of statements, indeed, arranged on a plan, and extending over a large ground, is in itself an exposition, and an able one ; and it

---

[1] I cannot wholly understand, except as unfavourably characteristic of that age, the great mediæval reputation of Bradwardine, called the 'profound doctor.' A dull monotony characterises his speculations, which are all spun out of the idea of the Divine Power, or of God as the Universal Cause ; but spun into airy subtleties, which want the substance of solid thought and argument, and are more like the shadows and ghosts of reasonings than the realities.

[2] The predestinarian controversy in the Gallican Church, which arose out of the statements of Gotteschalcus, in the ninth century, does not offer much valuable material to the theological student. I give the principal points of it in NOTE XX.

formed the great text book of the Church for centuries. But it is not an argumentative exposition; it does not expand and develop by statement and reasoning theological ideas. Aquinas, however, supplies the deficiencies of Lombard, and, taking up the scheme and ground-plan which the older commentator furnishes, applies the argumentative and philosophical talent to it, and fills it out with thought; enriching it at the same time with large additions from the stores of heathen philosophy. Aquinas is accordingly the great representative of mediæval Augustinianism—I might say, of mediæval theology. He reflects the mind—he embodies the ideas and sentiments of the mediæval Church. In him, as in a mirror, we see the great assumptions, the ruling arguments of the theological world; the mode of inference which was considered legitimate; the way of solving difficulties which was thought satisfactory. In his large and capacious mind we see the collective theological thought and philosophy of the middle ages. He fails, indeed, in a power which it was reserved for a modern age to call forth from the human mind—the analytical one. He does not turn his mind inward upon itself to examine its own thoughts and ideas, and compare received and current truths with the original type from which they are copied. In this sense he does not apprehend and realise truths: because he does not put his mind into that attitude in which it has alone the power of seeing its own processes, ideas, and modes of entertaining truth—the attitude of reflection and turning inward of the mind upon itself. No one can see a thing but by looking at it; the mediæval mind did not look within, or examine itself; it could not, therefore, see itself—*i.e.* get such knowledge as has been since proved to be attainable of its own operations and ideas. It was left for a later age to call attention to this world of internal discovery, and force the human mind back upon itself; changing that progressive habit, in which it had so long exclusively indulged, of following up and arguing interminably upon truths, into the stationary one of examining the truths themselves. Aquinas accepts the received statements and positions, and expands them with argumentative subtlety and power. And the vast amount of statements and positions which his mind includes and thus expands and treats argumentatively is surprising; showing a truly enormous grasp and capacity, somewhat analogous to that of a great statesman, who, without penetrating far below or aiming at a deeper understanding of the particular subjects and questions presented to his consideration than he practically wants, embraces an immense quantity of such particulars; all of which he treats argumentatively and is ready to discuss, and come to a conclusion and decision upon them. The argumentative edifice, however, of Aquinas, for want of this later and inward attitude of mind, shows deep deficiencies; and especially that great vice of the scholastic intellect—distinguishing without a difference; a fault which arises from accepting the superficial meaning of statements, or the words themselves, without going into their real meaning, which would often show that different words really meant the same thing.

Taking Aquinas, therefore, as the representative of mediæval Augustinianism, I shall endeavour in this and the following chapter to give an account of his system so far as it touches on the particular subject of the present treatise. The examination will disclose some forms of thought and modes of arguing with which a modern mind will not sympathise, but to which it will rather appeal as showing how differently the intellect of man reasons in different ages, and how the received thought of one period becomes quaint and obsolete in another. The system, however, will be found as a whole to rest upon some broad and common assumptions, which have always formed, and always will form, an important portion of the basis of human opinion.

The doctrine of predestination, then, in the system of Aquinas, rests mainly on philosophy, and rises upon the idea of the Divine Power. This fundamental position was laid down, this religious axiom stated with jealous exactness and the most scientific strength of language, and the rest was deduced by way of logical consequence from it. God was the First Great Cause: His will the source of all things, the spring of all motions, all events: it could not be frustrated, it must always be fulfilled : 'God hath done whatsoever He would—*omnia quæcunque voluit fecit, in cœlo et in terra.*' This was contained in the very idea of Omnipotence; for no agency can be impeded but by stronger agency, and none can be stronger than Omnipotence: it was contained in the very idea of the Divine Felicity ; for no one can be perfectly happy whose will is not fulfilled, and the Supreme Being is perfectly happy.[1] Though the Divine Will, then, acted by mediate and secondary causes, both in the physical and moral world, these causes were no more than mediate ones, and fell back upon the First Great Cause, from which they derived all their efficacy. Nor, because a secondary cause failed of its effect, was there, therefore, any failure of the power of the First Cause. One particular cause was impeded in its operation by another; the action of fire by that of water, the digestive functions of the stomach by the coarseness of the food: but the qualities of the water and the food were also particular causes, acting under the Universal Cause as much as those which they impeded. Thus what seemed to recede from the Divine Will according to one order, returned to it under another; and the failure of the particular cause was the success of the universal.[2]

[1] 'Voluntas Dei causa est omnium quæ naturaliter fiunt, vel facta sive futura sunt. . . . prima et summa causa omnium specierum et motionum.'—Lombard. l. 1. Distinct. 45. 'Cassari non potest, quia illa voluntate fecit quæcunque voluit, in cœlo et in terrâ, cui, teste Apostolo, nihil resistit.'—Distinct. 46. 'Nulla causa impeditur nisi ab aliquo fortiori agente, sed nihil est fortius Divina voluntate. . . . Præterea, diminutio gaudii si voluntas non impleatur, sed Deus felicissimus.'—Aquinas in Lombard. Distinct. 47. 'Causalitas autem Dei qui est primum agens, se extendit usque ad omnia entia, non solum quantum ad principia speciei, sed etiam quantum ad individua principia.'—Summa Theologica, P. 1. Quæst. 22. Art. 2.

'In hujusmodi autem causis non est infinitus processus, est ergo aliqua omnium una prima quæ est Deus.'—Bradwardine, p. 190. 'Omne movens posterius est instrumentum primi moventis, alias enim non est posterius naturaliter eo, sed prius vel etiam coæquum.'—p. 173.

[2] 'Quod si aliqua causa particularis deficiat a suo effectu, hoc est propter aliquam aliam causam particularem immediantem, quæ continetur sub ordine causæ universalis. Unde effectus ordinem causæ universalis nullo modo potest exire.'

To the position that the Divine Will was the cause of things that were, succeeded the further one, that it *could* have caused everything that was, without a contradiction in terms, *possible*.[1] And stated thus indefinitely, this position also was only a legitimate expansion of the idea of the Divine Power. We evidently cannot restrict the Divine Power to the simple causation of the existing world, without reducing it to a cause acting itself under a necessity, or to a kind of fate. If we liberate the First Cause, however, from this tie, and suppose it to act freely, causing some effects and not others, according to its own sovereign will and pleasure, we cannot state its Power less narrowly than as a Power of causing anything which is, in the nature of things, possible. But while the scholastic position was in itself legitimate, it was carried out unsoundly and hastily. Its maintainers advanced beyond the indefinite ground that God could cause every thing that was possible, to state what was possible; and they determined that the Supreme Being could, had it pleased Him, have made the whole universe more perfect than it was, both by adding to its parts and species, and by making the existing ones better, and not only better but faultless. The universe was finite, and what was finite could be added to; and the scale which ascended from this created world to infinity had numberless places unoccupied, which the Creator could have filled up, and successive types of being which He could have embodied and expressed, had He so willed, and so increased the ranks and orders of the existing universe. The existing species, too, could have been

—Sum. Theol. P. 1. Q. 19, Art. 6. 'Sicut lignum impeditur a combustione per actionem aquæ.'—Q. 22. Art. 2. 'Sicut indigestio contingit præter ordinem virtutis nutritivæ ex aliquo impedimento, puta ex grossitie cibi, quam necesse est reducere in aliam causam, et sic usque ad causam primam] universalem. Cum igitur Deus sit prima causa universalis non unius generis tantum, sed universaliter totius entis, impossibile est quod aliquid contingat præter ordinem divinæ gubernationis; sed ex hoc ipso quod aliquid ex una parte videtur exire ab ordine Divinæ providentiæ, quo consideratur secundum aliquam particularem causam, necesse est quod in eundem ordinem relabatur secundum aliam causam.' —Sum. Theol. P. 1. Q. 103. Art. 7.

[1] Cum Deus omnia posse dicitur, nihil rectius intelligitur quam quod possit omnia possibilia. — Sum. Theol. P. 1. Q. 25. Art. 3.

made better, and even without fault, for God could, had it pleased Him, have created a universe in which there was no evil; and man himself could have been made so that he neither could nor would even wish to sin.[1]

The fundamental idea of the Divine power thus laid down was applied strictly to the motions of the human will, or to human actions. God was the cause of all the motions of the human will, but He caused them by means of the will itself, as a mediate and secondary cause. The great scheme of Divine Providence contained two great classes of secondary causes,[2] one necessary, the other contingent. The course of nature was conducted by means of necessary causes, or causes acting necessarily; which class, again, had two different operations and effects, according to the difference of the natures to which it was applied. In fixed and permanent natures, the operation of necessary causes was unfailing, and they could not by possibility fall short of their effects; such was the operation of fixed and unalterable law in the motions of the heavenly bodies, presenting to us an instance of a world which was without change, and of which it was said, that above the sphere of the moon was no evil. In generable

[1] 'Potest Deus meliorem rem facere, sive etiam rerum universitatem, quam fecit.'—Lombard, L. 1. Dist. 44. 'Secundum philosophum albius est quod est nigro impermistius: ergo etiam melius est quod est impermistius malo: sed Deus potuit facere universum in quo nihil mali esset. . . . Quantum ad partes ipsas potest intelligi universum fieri melius. Sive per additionem plurium partium, ut scilicet crearentur multae aliae species, et implerentur multi gradus bonitatis qui possunt esse, cum etiam inter summam creaturam et Deum infinita distantia sit; et sic Deus melius universum facere potuisset. . . Vel potest intelligi fieri melius quasi intensive, quasi mutatis omnibus partibus ejus in melius . . . et sic etiam esset (melioratio) Deo possibilis.'—Aquinas, in Lomb. L. 1. Dist. 44.

'Utrum Deus potuerit facere humanitatem Christi meliorem quam fit.'—'Quamvis humana natura sit Divinitati unita in persona, tamen naturae remanent distantes infinitum, et ex hoc potest esse aliquid melius humana natura in Christo.'—Aquinas, in Lomb. Dist. 44. Art. 3.

'Talem potuit Deus hominem fecisse qui nec peccare posset nec vellet; et si talem fecisset quis dubitet eum meliorem fecisse.'—Aug. sup. Gen. ad Lit. xi. 7. Quoted by Lomb. l. 1. Dist. 44.

[2] Causae mediae — proximae—secundae.—'Omnium quae sunt causa est Dei voluntas . . . mediantibus aliis causis, ut sic etiam causandi dignitas creaturis communicaretur.'—Aquinas, in Lomb. Dist. 45.

and corruptible natures they had a failing operation, and alternately attained and fell short of their effects: the Universal Cause, however, being alike effective in either case, and good alike the result; for the corruption of one thing was the generation of another.[1] The second class of causes was contingent or voluntary, operating in those creatures which had in addition to nature the principle of will. The effects, then, which took place in the world took place necessarily, or contingently, according to the character of those mediate and secondary causes which were respectively in operation; but in either case these causes were but mediate, and fell back upon the First Great Cause, from which they derived all their virtue as secondary ones. The Supreme Being fitted like causes to like effects, necessary to necessary, contingent to contingent;[2] but His will it was which gave to these causes their respective natures, and made one necessary and the other contingent.[3] He moved matter, and He moved will by

---

[1] 'In his autem qui consequuntur finem per principium quod est natura invenitur quidam gradus, eo quod quarundam rerum natura impediri non potest a consecutione effectus sui, et iste est gradus altior sicut est in corporibus cœlestibus. Unde in his nihil contingit non intentum a Deo ex defectu ipsorum; et propter hoc Avicenna dicit quod supra orbem lunæ non est malum. Alius autem gradus naturæ est quæ impediri potest et deficere, sicut natura generabilium et corruptibilium; et quamvis ista natura sit inferior in bonitate, tamen bona est.' —Aquinas, in Lomb. l. 1. Dist. 39.

[2] 'Quibusdam effectibus præparavit causas necessarias ut necessario evenirent; quibusdam vero causas contingentes, ut evenirent cont n-genter, secundum conditionem proximarum causarum.'—Sum. Theol. P. 1. Q. 23. Art. 4.
'Ita omnia movet secundum eorum conditionem; ita quod ex causis necessariis per motionem divinam sequuntur effectus ex necessitate; ex causis autem contingentibus sequuntur effectus contingentes.'— 1ma 2dae Q. 49. Art. 4.
'Effectus consequitur conditionem causæ suæ proximæ.'—Aquinas, in Lomb. l. 1. Dist. 39.

[3] Dicendum est quod hoc contingit propter efficaciam Divinæ voluntatis . . . Vult enim quædam Deus necessario, quædam contingenter, ut sit ordo in rebus ad complementum universi. Et ideo quibusdam effectibus aptavit causas necessarias, ex quibus effectus ex necessitate proveniant; quibusdam autem causas defectibiles, ex quibus effectus contingenter proveniant. Non igitur propterea effectus voliti a Deo eveniunt contingenter, quia causæ proximæ sunt contingentes; sed propterea quia Deus voluit eos contingenter evenire, contingentes causas ad eos præparavit.'—Sum. Theol. 1ma Q. 19. Art. 8.

causes alike of His own arbitrary and sovereign creation. He produced the motions of the physical world by necessary, the motions of the human will by voluntary causes; but these voluntary causes were set in motion by Himself; God was the cause of the will.[1] The aims, the designs, the deliberations, and the acts of man were subjected to the Divine Will, as being derived ultimately from it; and man's providence was contained under the Divine, as the particular cause under the universal.[2]

Such was the logical consequence of the idea of the Divine power, as regards the human will. Under the notion of the will, as a mediate cause, the Augustinian schoolmen left out no function, action, or characteristic of will of which the human soul is conscious. They acknowledged every internal act and sensation which belongs to us as having and exercising will; that which every reasonable man who does not deny the plainest facts must admit. They brought all these characteristics to a point, and expressed them in one term—self-motion. The will moved itself, was the cause of its own motion, the mistress of its own acts; it was in its power to will or not to will. Man moved himself to action by his freewill. But this self-motion was only admitted as an internal impression, and was not allowed to counteract or modify the dominant position of one absolute causality. The will was a principle of motion to itself; but it was not, therefore, the *first* principle of such motion,—it did not follow that this principle of motion was not itself set in motion by something else. The will was the *internal* principle of its own motion; but this self-determining power moved the will as *causa proxima*, not as *causa prima*; the internal principle was only a secondary one, succeeding to a first principle, which was external to the will. The will, though it moved itself, was moved *ab alio* to this motion. Nor

---

[1] 'Voluntatis causa nihil aliud esse potest quam Deus.' — Sum. Theol. 1$^{ma}$ 2$^{dae}$ Q. 10. Art. 6. 'Deus est causa prima movens et naturales causas et voluntarias.'—1$^{ma}$ Q. 83. Art. 1.

[2] 'Providentia hominis continetur sub providentia Dei sicut particularis causa sub causa universali.'—Sum. Theol. 1$^{ma}$ Q. 23. Art. 2.

was the true and genuine voluntariness of its motions at all effected by their source being external. For the Supreme Mover did not, by setting natural causes in motion, hinder the acts in which such causes issued from being natural; no more, when He set in motion the voluntary causes, did He hinder the acts in which they issued from being voluntary. Rather He Himself caused in these acts their voluntariness, and their naturalness respectively, working in each nature according to its peculiarity—*in unoquoque operans secundum ejus proprietatem.*[1]

And this consideration supplied the answer to the question how our wills could be moved from without, and yet feel no force, no constraint, but all its motions go on exactly as if they originated in ourselves. There were two kinds of necessity, the necessity of force, and the necessity of nature or inclination. The necessity of force was *vi termini* opposed to inclination, and if it prevailed, prevailed in spite of it. and was attended with the sensation to the man of being forced or obliged to do a thing. But the necessity of inclination, or that which made the inclination to be what it was, could only be felt as inclination, not as force. For the inclination itself was to begin with that which such necessity had made it to be; it could have felt nothing contrary to it, nothing violating it, in

---

[1] 'Voluntas domina est sui actus, et in ipsa est velle et non velle; quod non esset si non haberet in potestate movere seipsam ad volendum.'—1ᵐᵃ 2ᵈᵃᵉ Q. 9. Art. 3.

'Liberum arbitrium est causa sui motus : quia homo per liberum arbitrium seipsum movet ad agendum. Non tamen hoc est necessitate libertatis *quod sit prima causa sui id quod liberum est*; sicut nec ad hoc quod aliquid sit causa alterius, requiritur quod sit prima causa ejus. Deus igitur est prima causa movens et naturales causas et voluntarias. Et sicut naturalibus causis, movendo eas, non aufert quin actus earum sint naturales, ita movendo causas voluntarias, non aufert quin actiones earum sint voluntariæ, sed potius hoc in eis facit ; operatur enim in unoquoque secundum ejus proprietatem.'—Sum. Theol. 1ᵐᵃ Q. 83. Art. 1.

'De ratione voluntarii est quod principium ejus sit intra ; sed non oportet quod hoc principium intrinsecum sit primum principium non motum ab alio. Unde motus voluntarius, *etsi habeat principium proximum intrinsecum, tamen principium primum est ab extra ;* sicut et primum principium motus naturalis est ab extra, quod scilicet movet naturam.'—1ᵐᵃ 2ᵃᵉ Q. 9. Art. 3.

'Ipse actus liberi arbitrii reducitur in Deum sicut in causam.'—1ᵐᵃ Q. 23. Art. 2.

that which was not its combatant, or its coercer, but its cause.[1]

Now it is evident that such a scheme as this is necessitarian, and is inconsistent with the ordinary doctrine of freewill; because freewill is here not truly self-moving, and an original spring of action. It is not a first cause, but a second cause, subordinated to another above it, which sets it in motion. But the will, as a link in a chain of causes and effects, is not freewill, in the common and true understanding of that term, according to which it means an original source of action. Freewill is here *reconciled* and made *consistent* with the Divine Power; brought into the same scheme and theory. But it is of itself a sufficient test that a system is necessitarian, that it maintains the Divine Power in *harmony* with freewill. The will as an original spring of action is irreconcilable with the Divine Power, a second first cause in nature being inconsistent with there being only one First Cause. To reconcile freewill, then, with the Divine Power is to destroy it; because such a reconciliation can only be effected by subordinating one to the other, in the way just described, as second cause to first cause, and so depriving the will of that which constitutes its freedom, in the common acceptation of the word, viz. its originality. Freewill to be true freewill must be inconsistent with the other great truth; it must be held as something existing side by side with the Divine Attribute, but never uniting to our understanding with it. This inconsistency, this absence of relation, is the only security for its genuineness; the removal of which is, therefore, fatal to it. When, in the place of philosophical disagreement, we have philosophical unity, one consistent scheme and theory, one connection of part with part, one

[1] 'Hæc igitur coactionis necessitas omnino repugnat voluntati. Nam hoc dicimus esse violentum quod est contra inclinationem rei. Ipse autem motus voluntatis est inclinatio quædam in aliquid: et ideo, sicut dicitur aliquid naturale, quia est secundum inclinationem naturæ; ita dicitur aliquid voluntarium, quia est secundum inclinationem voluntatis. Sicut ergo impossibile est quod aliquid simul sit violentum et naturale; ita impossibile est quod aliquid simpliciter sit coactum, sive violentum, et voluntarium. Necessitas autem naturalis non repugnat voluntati.'— 1ᵐᵃ Q. 82. A. 4.

harmony of cause with cause, we have, in the place of two truths, one truth, and the Divine Power is maintained, but freewill is abandoned.

Such a compact and harmonious theory, however, encountered *in limine* one great difficulty. Upon the idea of the Divine Power, thus singly and determinately carried out, and made the exclusive *rationale* of all the facts in the universe, how were we to account for the origin of evil? The existence of evil was a plain fact. Was God the cause of it? That could not be; for God could not possibly will evil. Did it exist in spite of Him, and against His will? That could not be; for God could not possibly be deficient in power. Then how was its existence to be accounted for?

Now, evil is sometimes understood in a negative rather than in a positive sense,—in the sense of a defect and falling short, of lesser as contrasted with greater good; and in this sense it was not difficult to account for the existence of evil in the universe. For if we considered it inconsistent with the justice and benevolence of God, that He should not make everything the very best, where were we to stop in our demand? We could not pause till we reached in our wishes the very highest point of all, and arrived at the Uncreated Perfection itself. Wherever we stopped below this culminating point, the same charge could be urged as now, that things were not made so good as they could be made. But a desire that tended straight to the confusion of the distinction between the creature and God, and could not be satisfied but by a contradiction, was absurd; and a charge which would always be made, whatever the Creator might do, was untenable. The possibility, then, of things being made better argued no envy in God who made them worse, and the existence of evil, in the sense of lesser good, was no real difficulty at all.[1]

---

[1] 'Cuilibet finito possibilis est additio; sed cujuslibet creaturæ bonitas finita est. Ergo potest sibi fieri additio, sed creatura nunquam potest attingere ad æqualitatem Dei. Nec alia mensura divinæ bonitatis sibi debetur quam secundum determinationem divinæ voluntatis, et ideo nulla invidia in Deo resultat, si rem meliorem facere potuit quam fecerit.'—Aquinas, in Lomb. Dist. 43. Q. 1. A. 1.

But evil existed in the world, not only in the sense of lesser good, but in that of positive evil; and this was a more difficult fact to account for. The explanations of this fundamental difficulty, then, by the Augustinian schoolmen may be placed under two heads: under the first of which the explanation is almost purely verbal, and can hardly be said to come into *contact* even with the real difficulty; while under the second the difficulty is really confronted, and an effort of a philosophical kind made to solve it.

I. The first of these verbal explanations which I will instance, and which is a rather extreme specimen of its class, is an attempt to pare down by simple artifices of language the opposition of the Divine Will to evil, till it reaches a point at which it substantially ceases, and becomes a manageable truth to the metaphysician. It is evident that, so long as the opposition of the Divine Will to evil remains decided and absolute, there being this evil as a plain fact in the world, such opposition affects the attribute of the Divine Power; because if God does not will evil, it would appear that evil takes place only because He has not the power to prevent it. The aim, therefore, was to reduce by niceties of expression this opposition of the Divine Will, until that will ceased to disagree with evil, and, as a consequence, its frustration ceased; and with it the danger to the attribute of Power. A distinction was accordingly drawn between 'God not willing evil —*mala velle*' and God not willing that evil should *take place*—*velle mala non fieri*; and, allowing that God did not will evil, it was determined that He *did* will that evil should *take place*. Again, those who objected to this position as being opposed to the goodness of the Divine Will, made a distinction between 'God *not willing* that evil should take place' and 'God willing that evil should *not take place*;' accepting the former, but rejecting the latter formula, the difference being in the situation of the negative adverb in the two statements; which in the one is next to 'willing,' in the other to 'taking place;' and these denied accordingly that 'God willed that evil should *not* take place.'[1] Here, then, are two modifications of the opposition of the Divine will to evil, one professing to be an improvement on the other. But it is obvious that such modifications are no more than plays on words, and can lead to no result; because in proportion as these statements reduce the opposition of the Divine Will to evil, they cease to be, in their natural meaning, true; while in proportion as an artificial interpretation relieves them of falsehood, it divests them also of use for the purpose for which they are wanted. They either deny a characteristic of the Divine Will, and in that case they are false; or they admit it, and in that case they fail of their object of relieving the attribute of the Divine Power.

Again, a distinction was made between the Divine Will and the signs of it,—*voluntas* and *signa voluntatis*; between the will itself of God, and those outward expressions of it which were given in accommodation to our understandings and for the practical purposes of life and

---

[1] 'Alii dicunt *quod Deus vult mala esse vel fieri, non tamen vult mala.* Alii vero quod *nec vult mala esse nec fieri.* In hoc tamen conveniunt et hi et illi quod utrique *fatentur Deum mala non velle.* Utrique vero rationibus et auctoritatibus utuntur ad muniendam suam assertionem. Qui enim dicunt Deum mala velle esse vel fieri suam his modis muniunt intentionem. Si enim, inquiunt, mala non esse vel non fieri vellet, nullo modo essent vel fierent, quia si vult ea non esse vel non fieri, et non potest id efficere, scilicet ut non sint vel non fiant, voluntati ejus et potentiæ aliquid resistit, et non est omnipotens, quia non potest quod vult, sed impotens est sicut et nos sumus, qui quod volumus quandoque non possumus. Sed quia omnipotens est et in nullo impotens, certum est non posse fieri mala vel esse nisi eo volente. Quomodo enim invito eo et nolente posset ab aliquo malum fieri, cum scriptum est, Rom. 9., *voluntati ejus quis resistit?* Supra etiam dixit Augustinus quia necesse est fieri si voluerit. Sed vult mala fieri aut non fieri. Si vult non fieri non fiunt; fiunt autem, vult ergo fieri.

'Illi vero qui dicunt Dei voluntate mala non fieri vel non esse, inductionibus præmissis ita respondent, dicentes Deum *nec velle mala fieri, nec velle non fieri, vel nolle fieri, sed tantum non velle fieri.* Si enim vellet ea fieri vel esse, faceret utique ea fieri vel esse, et ita. esset auctor malorum. . . . Item si nollet mala fieri, vel vellet non fieri, et tamen fierent, omnipotens non esset. . . . Ideoque non concedunt Deum velle mala fieri ne malorum auctor intelligatur, nec concedunt eum velle mala non fieri, ne impotens esse videatur, sed tantum dicunt eum *non velle mala fieri.*'—Lombard, l. 1. Dist. 46.

conduct,—precept, prohibition, permission, and the like—*præceptio, prohibitio, permissio*; between a real and a metaphorical will of God,—the one being called *voluntas beneplaciti*, the other *voluntas signi*.[1] And the object of this distinction is the same with that of the preceding ones; viz. to enable the theologian to refer to a Divine Will, which was in some way not opposed to evil, and with which, therefore, evil could co-exist without risk to the attribute of the Divine Power. That will of God which came into contact with our understandings, which commanded and which prohibited, was opposed to evil; and this will could be violated, neglected, and trodden under foot by the passion and the pride of man. But that secret and ulterior will which lay behind this external and ex-

[1] 'Aliquando vero *secundum quandam figuram* dicendi voluntas Dei vocatur, quod secundum proprietatem non est voluntas ejus: ut præceptio, prohibitio, consilium, ideoque pluraliter aliquando Scriptura voluntates Dei pronuntiat. Unde Propheta psalm 110. *Magna opera Domini, exquisita in omnes voluntates ejus*, cum non sit nisi una voluntas Dei quæ ipse est. . . . Ideo autem præceptio et prohibitio atque consilium, cum sint tria, dicitur tamen unumquodque eorum Dei voluntas, quia ista sunt *signa* divinæ voluntatis: quemadmodum et signa iræ dicuntur ira, et dilectionis signa dilectio appellantur; et dicitur iratus Deus, et tamen non est ira in eo aliqua, sed signa tantum quæ foris fiunt, quibus iratus ostenditur, ira ipsius nominantur. Et est figura dicendi, secundum quam non est falsum quod dicitur, sed verum quod dicitur *sub tropi nubilo obumbratur*. Et secundum hos tropos diversæ voluntates Dei dicuntur, quia diversa sunt illa quæ per tropum voluntas Dei dicuntur.

'Magna est adhibenda discretio in cognitione Divinæ voluntatis, quia et *beneplacitum Dei* est voluntas ejus, et *signum* beneplaciti ejus dicitur voluntas ejus. Sed beneplacitum ejus æternum est, signum vero beneplaciti ejus non.'—Lombard, l. 1. Dist. 45.

'Voluntas Dei distinguitur in voluntatem beneplaciti et voluntatem signi. . . De Deo quædam dicuntur proprie, quædam metaphorice. Ea quæ proprie de ipso dicuntur, vere in eo sunt; sed ea, quæ metaphorice dicuntur de eo, per similitudinem proportionabilitatis ad effectum aliquem, sicut dicitur ignis Deutero. 4., eo quod sicut ignis se habet ad consumptionem contrarii, ita Deus ad consumendam nequitiam. . . . *Deus potest dici aliquid velle dupliciter; vel proprie, et sic dicitur velle illud, cujus voluntas vere in eo est, et hæc est voluntas beneplaciti. Dicitur etiam aliquid velle metaphorice, eo quod ad modum volentis se habet, in quantum præcipit, vel consulit, vel aliquid hujusmodi facit. Unde ea, in quibus attenditur similitudo istius rei ad voluntatem Dei, voluntates ejus metaphorice dicuntur, et quia talia sunt effectus, dicuntur signa.*'—Aquinas, in Lomb. l. 1, Dist. 45. A. 4.

pressed one, was not opposed to any, but harmonised with all facts; and evil was no rebel against it, but its subject; nothing impeded, then, but everything in heaven and earth fulfilled this eternal, incomprehensible Will, which was of the essence of God, and which was God.

Now, this distinction is drawn with greater breadth, boldness, and strength than the preceding ones; but it is open to the same answer, viz. that so far as it denies the disagreement of the Divine Will with evil it is false, so far as it admits it it is useless for its purpose. This position of a real will of God which is different from His expressed will may be interpreted in two ways. It may be understood as meaning that the real will of God is in true and actual harmony with evil, the expressed being only an outside show, which is useful in some way for the Divine government of mankind in this present state, and the maintenance of this existing system. And a theory like this has been put forward in modern times, representing the Divine Will, as expressed in the distinction of good and evil, as a mere mask, concealing a deeper truth behind it; a truth of pure fact, in which good and evil meet and are united, and each is good. The commands and prohibitions, the promises and the terrors of the moral law, are according to such a theory but a display, which deludes the mass, but is penetrated by the philosopher. And understood in such a way this position does indeed get rid most effectually of the difficulty of the existence of evil as being against the will of God, and so a sign against His Power. But then, understood in such a way, this position is false and impious. We cannot suppose any difference between the real and the expressed will of God,[1] without destroying the basis of all morals and religion.

---

[1] 'Et si illa dicantur Dei voluntas, ideo quia signa sunt Divinæ voluntatis, non est tamen intelligendum Deum omne illud fieri velle quod cuicunque præcipit, vel non fieri quod prohibuit. Præcepit enim Abrahæ immolare filium, nec tamen voluit; nec ideo præcepit ut id fieret, sed ut Abrahæ probaretur fides; et in evangelio præcepit sanato ne cui diceret; ille autem prædicavit ubique, intelligens Deum non ideo prohibuisse, quin vellet opus suum prædicari, sed ut daret formam homini, laudem humanam declinandi.'—Lomb. l. 1. Dist. 45.

But if this position does not mean this, as in the minds of those who maintained it it did not, it is not available for the object for which it is designed. For all it means to assert in that case is the incomprehensibility of the Divine Will, and that there is some mysterious sense in which everything which takes place agrees with this will; but this is not to explain the difficulty of the co-existence of evil with that will, but only to state it.

A distinction, again, was drawn between an antecedent will of God—*voluntas antecedens*, and a posterior will—*voluntas consequens*; the former of which willed a thing absolutely—*simpliciter*, the latter conditionally—*secundum quid*[1]; and the former of which was opposed to evil, the latter not. Thus God willed the salvation of all men on the one hand absolutely; and that will, which was opposed to all evil, to sin and punishment alike, could be frustrated—*imperfectio antecedentis voluntatis*. But, on the other hand, He willed this salvation conditionally—*i.e.* on the supposition that men were good; and this will, which was not opposed to the evil of punishment if men were bad, could not be frustrated, being as much fulfilled in the damnation of men as in their salvation. This distinction, then, had the same aim as the former; viz., to establish a Divine Will which was not opposed to evil, and which therefore the existence of evil did not frustrate, and so interfere with the Divine Power. But while the difficulty which this distinction professes to meet is in the case of the will antecedent simply confessed instead of solved, it is only evaded instead of solved in the case of the will consequent. God wills the salvation of men on the condition that they are good; which will, if they are bad, is

---

[1] 'Voluntas Dei duplex, antecedens et consequens . . . propter diversas conditiones ipsius voliti. Si in homine tantum natura ipsius consideretur, æqualiter bonum est omnem hominem salvari, et hoc Deus vult, et hæc est voluntas antecedens. . . . Consideratis autem circumstantiis, non vult omnem . . . non volentem et resistentem.' —Aquinas, in Lomb. l. 1. Dist. 46. Q. 1. A. 1.

'Quicquid vult Deus voluntate consequenti totum fit, non autem quicquid vult voluntate antecedenti; quia hoc non simpliciter vult, sed secundum quid tantum; nec ista imperfectio est ex parte voluntatis, sed ex conditione voliti.'—In Lomb. Dist. 47. Q. 1. A. 1.

not opposed to the evil of their punishment. The evil of *punishment*, then, is here accounted for and made to agree with the Divine Power, because made to agree with the Divine Will: but what account is given of the evil of that sin which is the reason of punishment? This evil is passed over altogether. Yet it is a plain evil which takes place in the universe, and we must either say that the will of God is opposed to it or not; the former alternative being apparently inconsistent with the Divine Power, the latter with the Divine Goodness. The difficulty put off at one stage thus meets us at another; and an evil remains which we cannot without impiety assert not to be opposed to the Divine Will, and the existence of which therefore is inconsistent apparently with the Divine Power.

II. To these verbal explanations, however, there succeeded two which were attempts at real explanation. One of these was the argument of variety, which was put in two forms; under the first of which, however, it did not satisfy its own employers, who used it with evident misgivings, though they would not deprive themselves of its aid altogether. Should there not be evil in the world, that the contrast may heighten the good and set it off to better advantage? Would the good be appreciated as it should be, and its real nature come to light, but for this evil? And in this way is not evil of the perfection of the universe—*de perfectione universi*? The solution was a tempting one; but it was resisted, on the ground that the loss which evil caused was greater than the compensation it gave for it; inasmuch as it took away absolute good, and only gave comparative.[1] The solid justice of this

---

[1] 'Illud sine quo universum melius esset non confert ad perfectionem universi: sed si malum non esset universum melius esset, quia malum plus tollit uni quam addit alteri, quia ei cujus est tollit bonitatem absolutam, alteri autem addit bonitatem comparationis.'—In Lomb. l. 1. Dist. 46. Q. 1. A. 3.

Yet Aquinas reverts to this *ra-tionale* of the existence of evil with approval: 'Dicendum quod ex ipsa bonitate Divina ratio sumi potest prædestinationis aliquorum et reprobationis aliquorum. . . . Ad completionem enim universi requiruntur diversi gradus rerum, quarum quædam altum et quædam infimum locum teneant in universo.'—Sum. Theol. $1^{ma}$ Q. 23. A. 5.

reply embraces within a short compass all the points of
the case. Variety is a sound explanation indeed of a certain
class of evil. The decay and corruption of the vegetable
world set off by contrast the birth and growth;
summer is all the more agreeable for winter ; the decay of
autumn heightens the freshness of the spring. And on
the same law rest is all the more pleasant after fatigue,
food after hunger; and much even of the higher and more
intellectual kind of pleasure is relished the more for the
void and dulness alternating with it. But this is only by
a law of our nature in present operation, in consequence
of which change is necessary for us, though at the cost of
pain. Such a law is acknowledged to be a sign of great
imperfection. And, what is more to the purpose, all these
are cases in which ourselves alone and our own enjoyment
are concerned. To inanimate nature it is all the same
whether it decays or endures, lives or dies; and therefore
we need not take *its* part in the matter into account.
But when we come to moral evil the case is very different.
It is true the law of comparison or contrast operates even
here, and we are pleased with the virtue which meets us
in the world, all the more for the evil which we see in it.
Indeed, the nature or quality of goodness—the light that
issues from a good character, is so completely seen in the
sense and degree in which we do see it, by means of this
assistance—*i.e.* by the contrast between this goodness and
a background of average and indifferent character, formed
as an image in our mind from the experience of human
life—that it is difficult to contemplate without some surprise
and awe the signal and noble use which the wickedness
of the world answers ; inasmuch as for anything we
see to the contrary, in the present state of our capacities,
in which contrast seems to be so essential to true perception,
virtue could not be appreciated as it is without this
contrast, or be the bright light which it is without this
dark background. The light shineth in darkness. But
though moral evil answers this high purpose in the world,
is it a sufficient account of its existence that it does so ?
Is it just that one man should be wicked in order that the

virtue of another may be set off? The spectator may derive benefit from the contrast, but there is another whose interests are quite as important as his.

And the same may be said of the use of which the moral evil in the world is, for the trial, purification, and confirmation of the good. The wickedness of the bad portion of mankind is indeed one of the principal means by which the good portion is educated and disciplined; the pride and tyranny of one man serve to produce the virtue of patience in another; the wrongs of the world subdue and temper, its corruptions and temptations fortify, those minds that are disposed to make this use of them. But though the schoolman appeals to this effect of moral evil as a justification of its existence,[1] such an argument admits of the obvious answer, that it is not just that one man should be wicked in order that another should be good.

The argument of variety, however, was put in another form, and another explanation extracted from it. The principle of variety demanded that there should be different natures in the universe; and that, besides such natures as were subject to necessary laws, there should be other nobler ones possessing will. But this conceded, moral evil, it was said, followed. For such natures as the latter must, as the very condition of this higher good, have the power of going wrong and receding from the end designed for them; and, with the power to do so, the fact would in some instances take place.[2] Now, this is a substantially

---

[1] 'Si enim omnia mala impedirentur, multa bona deessent universo; non enim esset vita leonis, si non esset occisio animalium; nec esset patientia martyrum si non esset persecutio tyrannorum.' —Sum. Theol. 1ᵐᵃ Q. 22. A. 2.

'Multa bona tollerentur, si Deus nullum malum permitteret esse; non enim generaretur ignis nisi corrumperetur aer; neque conservaretur vita leonis, nisi occideretur asinus.'—Q. 48. A. 2.

[2] 'Sed in nobilioribus creaturis invenitur aliud principium præter naturam, quod est voluntas, quod quanto vicinius est Deo, tanto a necessitate naturalium causarum magis est liberum. . . . Et ideo taliter a Deo instituta est ut deficere posset. . . . Si autem inevitabiliter in finem tenderet per divinam providentiam tolleretur sibi conditio suæ naturæ.'—In Lomb. 1. 1. Dist. 39. Q. 2. A. 2.

'Perfectio Universi requirit ut sint quædam quæ a bonitate deficere possint: *ad quod sequitur ea interdum deficere.*'—Sum. Theol. 1ᵐᵃ Q. 48. A. 2.

different argument from the former, and is perhaps the nearest approach we can make to an account of the existence of moral evil in the world. But it is in truth no explanation; for is this will of the creature to which evil is referred an original cause or only a secondary one? If the former, this argument only explains one difficulty by another as great, the existence of evil by the existence of an original cause in nature besides God. If the latter, the existence of moral evil falls back, as before, upon the First Cause; the human will in that case being no such barrier intervening between moral evil and God, as is wanted for the present purpose.

But the principal explanation which was given of this difficulty, and that in which Aquinas appears finally to repose, was borrowed from his master. Every reader of S. Augustine is familiar with a certain view of the nature of evil, to which he constantly recurs, and which he seems to cherish in his mind as a great moral discovery, a fundamental set-off and answer to the great difficulty of the existence of evil, and the true and perfect mode of extricating the Divine attribute of Power from the responsibility of permitting it,—the position, viz. that evil is nothing—*nihil*. God was the source; and as being the source of, included and comprised, all existence. Evil was a departure from God. Evil, therefore, was a departure from existence. External to God, it was outside of all being and substance; *i.e.* was no-being or nothing.

Aquinas adopts this position, and improves upon it in his usual way. Evil was nothing in another sense besides that of pure negation, which is the common meaning of nothing, viz., that of *privation*. Every nature aimed at good as its perfection or true existence; evil was a deprivation of this good or true existence. In the case of evil, then, there was something in our idea antecedent to it, of which it was a loss or absence. That which every nature truly and properly was, was in scholastic language its form, whence the formal cause of a thing is that which makes a thing to be what it is. Evil was a privation of *form*. There was an end, and there was an *action* proper to every thing in the universe; evil was inordination to the end, a defect of action.[1] The evil proper to the nature of fire was cold; the evil proper to the nature of water was drought. Thus while, in the collision of different natures in the universe, the defect of one was the growth of another, the evil to each nature was the defect of that nature.[2] Everything, so far as it *was*, was good—*omne ens in quantum hujusmodi bonum*; and evil was no-thing—*non-ens*, and no part of the universe.[3]

And that which was true of evil in general, was true in particular of moral evil. The act of sin was defined as an act contrary to the end for which the moral creature is designed, or, as is expressed in modern language, to the constitution of man—*actus inordinatus*; which consisted, however, of two separate and distinct parts. The *act*—*actus peccati*—was simply the material, bodily or mental, employed in the sin, whether outward motion, or inward passion, feeling, desire; and this was real substance and part of the universe of God. A man who committed, for example, an act of intemperance or anger, sinned *with* and *by* the natural sensation of hunger or thirst, or the natural passion or resentment, as the internal material of his sin; he sinned with the motion of his mouth by which he eat or drank, or with a motion of his arm by which he struck a blow, as its external material. All these motions, then, considered simply as such, whether within or without, were

---

[1] 'Causam formalem nullam habet, sed est magis *privatio formæ*: et similiter nec causam finalem, sed magis est *privatio ordinis ad finem*.'—Sum. Theol. 1ᵐᵃ Q. 49. A. 1.

'Malum quod in defectu actionis consistit, semper causatur ex defectu agentis.'—A. 2.

Cum omnis natura appetat suum esse et suam profectionem, necesse est dicere quod et perfectio cujuscunque naturæ rationem habeat bonitatis. Unde non potest esse quod malum significet quoddam esse, aut quandam formam, seu naturam. Relinquitur ergo quod nomine mali significetur quædam absentia boni.—1ᵐᵃ Q. 48. A. 1.

[2] 'Corruptio aeris et aquæ est ex perfectione ignis. . . . Si sit defectus in effectu proprio ignis, puta quod deficiat a calefaciendo, hoc est propter defectum actionis, sed hoc ipsum quod est esse deficiens accidit bono cui per se competit agere.'—1ᵐᵃ Q. 49. A. 1.

[3] Nihil potest esse per suam essentiam malum.—1ᵐᵃ Q. 49. A. 3. Malum non est pars universi quia neque habet naturam substantiæ neque accidentis, sed privationis tantum.'— In Lom. l. 1. Dist. 46. Q. 1. A. 3.

substantial; and the act of sin, as such, *existed*. But the inordinateness of the act, or the *sin* of it—the error in the use and application of these natural passions, these bodily organs, was no *thing*.[1] As evil in the case of fire was a defect of the natural action of fire, so evil in the case of the will was a defect of the natural action of the will.

This position, then, was applied as the key to the solution of the great difficulty of the existence of evil. The difficulty of the existence of evil respected its cause, how evil had an existence at all, when the Universal Cause, or cause of everything, could not have given it. It was a direct answer, then, to this difficulty, to say that it was a mistake to begin with, to suppose that evil *had* existence. This original mistake removed, all was clear; for that which had no existence needed no cause,[2] and that which needed no cause could dispense with the Universal Cause. A universal cause was necessary; but this inconvenience attended it, viz. that it *was* universal, and thus contracted responsibilities from which it had rather be relieved. This *rationale* exactly relieved it of its inconvenient charge. Evil was regarded in an aspect in which it ceased to belong to the domain even of a universal cause. The fact or phenomenon of evil, emptied of true or logical essence, had no place in the nature of things; seen everywhere, it existed nowhere, a universal nothing attending on substance as a shadow, but no occupant of room, and without insertion in the system. This unsubstantial presence, this *inane* in the midst of things, escaped as such the action of the First Cause; unsusceptible, as a pure negative, of connection or relation, it was in its very nature a breaking off from the chain of causes and effects in nature, and not a link of it.[3] Had evil a cause, indeed, it could have but

---

[1] 'Peccatum est actus inordinatus. Ex parte igitur actus potest habere causam, ex parte autem inordinationis habet causam eo modo quo negatio vel privatio potest habere causam.'—1$^{ma}$ 2$^{dae}$ Q. 75. A. 1.

[2] Malum causam formalem nullam habet.—1$^{ma}$ Q. 49. A. 1.

[3] 'Effectus causæ mediæ secundum quod exit ordinem causæ primæ non reducitur in causam primam. . . . Defectus a libero arbitrio non reducitur in Deum sicut in causam.'—1$^{ma}$ 2$^{dae}$ Q. 79. A. 1.

one, viz. God; but nothing had no cause, and was, therefore, wholly independent of the Universal Cause.

Such an explanation as this, however, it is hardly necessary to say, is no real explanation of the difficulty. It is undoubtedly the first truth of religion that true being and good are identical. The same argument, which proves a First Cause at all, proves His goodness; and if Being in the Cause must be good, being in the effect must be good too; for the effect must follow the nature of the cause. Nor can we avoid this conclusion but by a scheme of dualism, which allows an evil first cause of being; and, therefore, evil being as its effect. So far the above *rationale* is true, and is the proper contrary to dualism. But this first truth of sound religion is, when examined, no explanation of the mystery of the existence of evil, but only another mode of stating it. We rightly say that true being is identical with good; but how comes there to be being which is not true being? On the religious ground, and as believers in a God, we say, that evil cannot be an existing thing; because God is the Author of everything, and yet not the Author of evil. But plain common sense tells us clearly enough that evil exists, and exists just as really as good. A man commits some act of violence under the influence of strong passion, malignant hatred, revenge, cupidity; his state of mind is as intense as possible; there is the fullest determination and absorption in the act. Is not this something—something going on and taking place in his mind? We may distinguish, indeed, between the animus and the material of the act, or, in the scholastic language, between the act and the sin; but this distinction applies as much to good acts as to bad. The virtue of a good act is something quite distinct from the feelings and faculties of mind and body employed in it, of which it is the direction. If virtue, then, is something, is not vice something too?

The real source of these argumentative struggles and vain solutions was the original position respecting the Divine Power, which, however true, was laid down without that reserve which is necessary for this kind of truth. It is evident that the Divine Power is incomprehensible to us, and that therefore we cannot proceed upon it, as if it were a known premiss, and argue upon the vague abstract idea of omnipotence in our minds as if it were the real truth on this subject. Aquinas himself defines the Divine Power at the outset with a reserve: it was the power of doing any thing which was possible—*omnia possibilia*; and the principle he lays down with respect to the sense in which the Divine attributes are to be understood is philosophical; viz. that they are to be understood neither as wholly the same with (*univoce*), or wholly different from, the corresponding attributes in man (*æquivoce*), but as *analogous* to them—*analogice*.[1] The univocal sense confounded God with the creature; the equivocal hid God from the creature, removing and alienating Him altogether as an object of human thought; the analogical allowed an idea of God, which was true as far as it went, but imperfect. But though the human mind, under scholasticism, saw, as it always must do whenever sane, its own ignorance, it did not see it so clearly or scientifically as it has done subsequently, when a later philosophy has thrown it back upon itself, and forced it to examine its own ideas, how far they go, and where they stop short. The mediæval mind forgot, then, in the conduct of the argument, the principle it had laid down at its commencement; and, just as a boy in learning a problem of Euclid sees some critical point of the demonstration, but does not see it sufficiently clearly, or master it enough to carry it with him throughout the proof, the schoolman first saw that he was ignorant, and then argued as if he knew. Thus, notwithstanding the preliminary reserve in the definition of the Divine

---

[1] 'Tribus modis contingit aliquid aliquibus commune esse, vel univoce, vel æquivoce, vel analogice. Univoce non potest aliquid de Deo et de creatura dici . . . et ideo quidam dicunt quod quicquid de Deo et creatura dicitur, per puram æquivocationem dicitur. Sed hoc etiam non potest esse quia in his quæ sunt pure æquivoca ex uno non agnoscitur alterum, ut quando idem nomen duobus hominibus convenit. Cum igitur per scientiam nostram deveniatur in cognitionem Divinæ scientiæ, non potest esse quod sit omnino æquivocum. Et ideo dicendum quod scientia analogice dicitur de Deo et creatura; et similiter omnia hujusmodi.' — Aquinas, in Lomb. l. 1. Dist. 35. Q. 1. A. 4.

Power, the vague abstract idea of omnipotence prevailed as if it were a known premiss in the argument, entailing these struggles with the fact of evil as the consequences of it; for with absolute power in God to prevent it, how could evil exist? Hence these vain efforts of reason, these blind explanations; for it was necessary to reconcile a *known* premiss with facts. As an unknown premiss, the Divine Power is in no contradiction to the fact of evil, for we must know what a truth is before we see a contradiction in it to another truth; and with no contradiction, no solution would have been wanted. But the schoolman vaguely fancied that he knew his premiss, and therefore involved himself in these elaborate and futile explanations. We may admire indeed an obstinate intellectual energy, which struggles against insuperable difficulties, and tries to beat down by force what it cannot disentangle, and lay down a path which must be stopped at last. We admire his resolution, as we would that of some strong animal caught in a net, the thin meshes of which it would burst any moment with the least part of that blind force which it exerts, were it not that their multiplicity and intricacy baffle it. But the resignation of the philosopher is to be admired more, who has one great difficulty at starting, and a tranquil path after it, who sees to begin with the inexplicableness of things, and is saved by the admission from the trouble of subsequent solution. The clear perception by the mind of its own ignorance is the secret of all true success in philosophy; while explanations which assume that the constitution of things can really be explained, can only be a fruitless waste of strength. The fault of the schoolman throughout this whole argument is, that he vaguely imagines, that he really can explain the origin of evil; that he sets out with that aim; that he really fancies himself in a line of discovery while he argues, and thinks that he has in his conclusion something of the nature of a true solution. He does not actually profess so much, but his general argument betrays the latent assumption in his mind. His fault then was a want of a clear and acute perception of his own ignorance;

such a perception as the mind acquires by the long-sustained stationary attitude of reflexion upon itself. There must be a pause, a cessation from active speculation and inference, from argument, from words, while the reason looks within, and observes itself. The passive attitude required for this simple act of sight, more difficult really than all active arguing, requires a lull and a calm, an interruption of the busy operations of the mind, a voluntary suspension of the motion of that whole machinery of active thought, which is generally going on in intellectual minds, and constitutes their normal state. But the schoolman was always busy, always arguing, always in the thick of words, always constructing *upon* assumption, and pushing on to conclusion after conclusion. He could not afford the time to stop to examine fairly a single assumption on which he went. He had not the patience to pause, and look within. He had other work always to do, as he thought more important. A passive attitude was intolerable to a mind accustomed exclusively to busy construction; and thought internal and without words to one, to whom words were the great machinery by which he thought. Put him to such a task, and he would feel like a workman without his accustomed tools, or like a man of practical talent and energy shut up in a dark room and told to think. The consequence was, that it was a chance whether his assumptions were true or false. When he thought as a man and with mankind at large, they were right; when he thought as a philosopher they were too often mistaken, extreme and unqualified when they should have been limited, and absolute when they should have been with a condition and reserve.

## CHAPTER X.

### SCHOLASTIC DOCTRINE OF PREDESTINATION.

THE last chapter explained the scholastic theory of the physical predetermination of the will, or the subordination of the will to the universal cause—a philosophical doctrine of necessity. To this theory succeeded the proper or Augustinian doctrine of predestination, which went upon the basis of original sin. All mankind being previously in a state of ruin owing to original sin, God chose to exercise His mercy upon some of this whole mass, His judgment upon others; to bring some to glory, and others to punishment. Nor was this Divine determination in favour of one, and against the other portion of the human race, to be attributed to any foreseen difference of character between the two: this difference of character being the effect of that determination, instead of the determination the effect of that difference. On the principle that the end includes the means, the predestination of the individual to eternal life included in it the bestowal of all those qualifications of virtue and piety which were necessary for his admission to that final state. These qualifications were therefore the effect, and not the cause of predestination, for which no cause was to be assigned but God's sovereign will and pleasure.[1] Nor had the creature any ground of complaint against this Divine arrangement. For all deserved eternal punishment; and therefore those upon whom the punishment was inflicted only got their deserts, while those who were spared received a favour to which they had in justice no right, and were indebted to a gratuitous act of mercy, and an excess of the Divine goodness.[2]

[1] Præscientia meritorum non est causa vel ratio prædestinationis. . . . Manifestum est quod id quod est gratiæ est prædestinationis effectus; et hoc non potest poni ut ratio prædestinationis, cum hoc sub prædestinatione concludatur. Si igitur aliquid aliud ex parte nostra sit ratio prædestinationis, hoc est præter effectum prædestinationis. Non est autem distinctum quod est ex libero arbitrio et ex prædestinatione, sicut nec est distinctum quod est ex causa secunda et causa prima.—1ᵐᵃ Q. 23. A. 5.

Electio Dei qua unum eligit et alium reprobat rationabilis est, nec tamen oportet quod ratio electionis sit meritum; sed in ipsa electione ratio est divina bonitas: ratio autem reprobationis est originale peccatum.—Aquinas, vol. 8. p. 330.

[2] Voluit Deus in hominibus, quantum ad aliquos quos prædestinat, suam repræsentare bonitatem per modum misericordiæ parcendo, et quantum ad aliquos quos reprobat, per modum justitiæ puniendo. . . . Neque tamen propter hoc est iniquitas apud Deum, si inæqualia non inæqualibus præparat. Hoc enim esset contra justitiæ rationem, si prædestinationis effectus ex debito redderetur, et non daretur ex gratia.

The doctrine of necessity, however, explained in the last chapter, and the doctrine of predestination, are in substance the same doctrine, and only differ in their ground, which is in one a ground of philosophy, in the other one of Scripture. The schoolmen attached indeed to these two doctrines different functions and operations of the Divine Power. Under the one, God acted as universal mover; under the other as special mover; under the one He exerted a natural power, under the other a spiritual or grace; under the one He moved men to a good proportionate to their nature, under the other to a good exceeding the proportions of nature;[1] under the one He supported the natural goodness of man unfallen, under the other He healed man fallen. And in all acts in which the special power operated, the general power operated too: so that God acted in both capacities, in the case of the same act.[2] But thus described as two separate and distinct actions, the universal and special action were really only the same action, in a higher and lower degree, of the Divine motive Power over the human will.

Thus clearly and strongly laid down, however, the doctrine of Aquinas and the Augustinian schoolmen on the subject of predestination has been mistaken in a well-

In his enim quæ ex gratia dantur, potest aliquis pro libitu suo dare cui vult plus vel minus, dummodo nulli subtrahat debitum, absque præjudicio justitiæ. Et hoc est quod dicit paterfamilias. Matt. 20. 15. 'Tolle quod tuum est et vade; an non licet mihi quod volo facere?'—1ma Q. 23. A. 5.

[1] Deus movet voluntatem hominis sicut Universalis motor ad universale objectum voluntatis, quod est bonum; et sine hac universali motione homo non potest aliquid velle. . . . Sed tamen interdum specialiter Deus movet aliquos ad aliquid determinate volendum, quod est bonum, sicut in his quos movet per gratiam.'—S. T. 1ma 2dae Q. 10. A. 6.

Est duplex hominis beatitudo; una quidem proportionata humanæ naturæ, ad quam scilicet homo pervenire potest per principia suæ naturæ: alia autem est beatitudo naturam hominis excedens, ad quam homo sola divina virtute pervenire potest secundum quandam Divinitatis participationem."—1ma 2dae Q. 62. A. 1.

[2] Homo in statu naturæ integræ potest operari virtute suæ naturæ bonum quod est sibi connaturale, absque superadditione gratuiti doni, licet non absque auxilio Dei moventis.—1ma 2dae Q. 109. A. 3.

Secundum utrumque statum natura humana indiget Divino auxilio, ad faciendum et volendum quodcunque bonum, sicut primo movente. Virtute gratuita superaddita indiget ad bonum supernaturale.—Ibid. A. 2.

known treatise, which professes to give a *résumé* of the opinions of the schools on this subject. Archbishop Laurence asserts the predestination maintained by the schoolmen to be, a predestination in consequence of foreseen good works in the individual. 'Almighty God before the foundations of the world were laid, surveying in His comprehensive idea, or, as they phrased it, in His prescience of simple intelligence, the possibilities of all things, before He determined their actual existence, foresaw, if mankind were created, although He willed the salvation of all, and was inclined to all indifferently, yet *that some would deserve eternal happiness, and others eternal misery*; and that, therefore, He approved and elected the former, but disapproved or reprobated the latter. Thus grounding election upon foreknowledge, they contemplated it not as an arbitrary principle, separating one individual from another, under the influence of a blind chance, or an irrational caprice; but on the contrary, as a wise and just one, which presupposes a diversity of nature between those who are accepted, and those who are rejected. Persuaded that God is the fountain of all good, that from His Divine preordination freely flows the stream of grace, which refreshes and invigorates the soul, they believed that He has regulated His predetermination by the quality of the soil through which His grace passes, and the effects which in any case it produces, not restricting His favours, but distributing them with an impartial hand; equally disposed toward all men, but, because all are not equally disposed toward Him, distinguishing only such as prove deserving of His bounty. . . . . . They considered the *dignity of the individual as the meritorious basis of predestination*.'[1]

The first remark that this passage suggests, is that the writer confuses all the schoolmen together, and attributes one common opinion to them on this subject; whereas there were different schools amongst them, as among modern thinkers, some taking the predestinarian side, and others that of freewill; though the great names are chiefly on the former side. The writer, however, treats them all

[1] Laurence's Bampton Lectures, pp. 148. 152.

as one school, and considers the predestination taught by the Augustinian Aquinas to be of the kind which he here describes; *i.e.* a predestination on the ground of foreseen good life. Of course if this is so, this is all the difference between predestinarianism and the doctrine of freewill. But I cannot understand how he can put this interpretation upon the doctrine of Aquinas, when the latter plainly and expressly asserts the contrary; viz., that foreseen merits are *not* the cause of predestination,—*præscientia meritorum non est causa vel ratio predestinationis*, but predestination the cause of these foreseen merits; these merits being the effect of grace, and grace the effect of predestination;—*id quod est gratiæ est prædestinationis effectus*. Archbishop Laurence appears to have been misled by two classes of expressions in Aquinas, one relating to contingency, the other, to human blame and responsibility.

He refers in support of this interpretation of the doctrine of Aquinas, to the latter's assertion of contingency. 'The mistakes upon this subject of those who have but partially consulted the speculations of the schools (he is speaking of those who have interpreted these speculations in a predestinarian sense) seem to have arisen from the want of properly comprehending what was meant by the *effect* of predestination, *an effect always supposed to be contingent*; the operations of freewill, whether with or without grace, being considered only as foreknown, and not necessarily predetermined.'[1] And he quotes a passage relating to *contingent* causes, as distinguished from necessary ones—'Although all things are subject matter of Providence, all things do not take place *necessarily*, but according to the condition of their proximate causes,— *secundum conditionem causarum proximarum*,'[2] which are in some cases not necessary but contingent causes. Archbishop Laurence understands this assertion of contingency as a denial of the doctrine of necessity, and an assertion of the received doctrine of freewill. But the system of Aquinas, as explained in the last chapter, does not verify

[1] Bampton Lectures, p. 152.
[2] Aquinas in Lomb. l. 1. Dist. 40.
Q. 3. A. 1.; Bampton Lectures, p. 354.

such an inference from his use of the term contingent. Aquinas divides proximate or mediate or secondary causes into two classes, necessary and contingent; but the contingent causes are still mediate causes only, not original ones. They are as in complete subordination to the first cause, as necessary causes are; only differing from the latter in their manner of operation, which is variable and irregular, instead of fixed and uniform. And the human will, as a contingent cause, is no more than a mediate one. God is cause of the will—*ipse actus liberi arbitrii reducitur in Deum sicut in causam*. Contingency then in acts is not, according to the doctrine of Aquinas, opposed to their ultimate causation from without; which is the doctrine of necessity: contingency is a certain mode in which things take place; and volition is such a mode in the case of actions; but volition is a mode, and not the cause, in the sense of original cause, of them.

There is another set of expressions in the Augustinian schoolmen relating to human blame and responsibility, to which Archbishop Laurence refers. 'To the inquiry why some are unendowed with grace, their answer was, because some are not willing to receive it, and not because God is unwilling to give it; He, they said, offers His light to all: He is absent from none, but man absents himself from the present Deity, like one who shuts his eyes against the noonday blaze.'[1] The language he refers to is that of Aquinas, whom again he quotes as saying that there are two reasons why grace, where it is withheld, is withheld; one because the man is not willing to receive it, the other because God does not will to give it; of which two the latter is posterior in order to the former—*talis est ordo ut secundum non sit nisi ex suppositione primi.*[2] Understanding the want of desire for grace, referred to here, to be the opposition of the individual's free and self-determining will, he takes these expressions as involving the common doctrine of freewill, that God offers His grace to all, while man rejects or accepts it according to his own choice. But the fault

[1] Bampton Lectures, p. 151.
[2] Aquinas in Lomb. l. 1. Dist. 40. Q. 4. A. 2.

in the human agent here referred to is not one to be confounded with the fault of individual choice: it is the original fault of the whole race. All mankind are to begin with, according to the doctrine of original sin, disinclined to grace, and, so far as themselves are concerned, reject it. Aquinas then can assert that the reason why grace is withheld is man's own fault, without committing himself in saying so to the common doctrine of freewill. It is the old position which meets us in S. Augustine. The will of man is naturally a corrupt and faulty will, but it is so at the same time necessarily, and as the effect of original sin. Responsibility attaches to it as being will; the voluntary agent is as such susceptible of praise or blame—*ut ei imputetur aliquid ad culpam vel ad meritum*;[1]—and legitimately comes under a dispensation of rewards and punishments. Such is the sense in which man's fault is said by Aquinas to be the first cause why grace, where it is withheld, is withheld. It is the faulty will of the race, not the mere choice of the person, which is this cause; which faultiness is therefore consistent with necessity, and not opposed to it. It is a further test of such a sense, that the will thus represented as the original barrier *against* grace, is next represented as wholly able to be changed and made a different will, *by* grace. 'God is able when, where, and in whomever He pleases, to convert men's evil wills from evil to good.'[2] It follows that when man's will *is* changed from evil to good, it is by His irresistible power; and therefore that the admission into a state of grace takes place, according to this system, on a ground quite different from that on which Archbishop Laurence considers it to do, upon his too hasty and superficial interpretation of the scholastic language. Indeed, if none are to be considered necessitarians who make man a responsible being, and lay his sins and their consequences at his own door, there cannot be a Christian necessitarian; for we must either do

[1] S. T. 1ᵐᵃ Q. 22. A. 2.

[2] 'Quis tam impie desipiat, ut dicat Deum malas hominum voluntates quas voluerit, et quando voluerit et ubi voluerit in bonum non posse convertere.'—Augustine, quoted by Lombard, l. 1. Dist. 47. 'Neque ideo præcepit omnibus bona, quia vellet ab omnibus bona fieri, *si enim vellet utique fierent.*'—Ibid.

this, or charge God with them—which latter no Christian can do. The most rigid predestinarian writers impose this responsibility upon man.[1]

[1] Archbp. Laurence's use of the following statement in Aquinas (B. L. p. 151.) shows the same want of insight into his system, and the same contented resting on the apparent meaning of particular language, without any consciousness of a different interpretation, which in a vast and intricate theological fabric might be reflected from other quarters upon it. 'Dicendum quod electio divina non præexigit diversitatem gratiæ, quia hæc electionem consequitur; sed præexigit diversitatem naturæ in divina cognitione, et facit diversitatem gratiæ, sicut dispositio diversitatem naturæ facit.'—In Lomb. l. 1. Dist. 41. Q. 1. A. 2. He infers from this that election is asserted by Aquinas to be on the ground of foreseen merits in the individual,—a *diversitas naturæ* in the good man from that of the bad man. But this very statement says that this *diversitas naturæ* is the effect of a divine arrangement or disposing—*dispositio diversitatem naturæ facit*. And when we turn to the part of Aquinas' system which relates to grace, we find that a certain Divine preparation of the man, while in a state of *nature* and previous to a state of grace, is necessary as a preparation *for* grace — *præparatio voluntatis humanæ ad consequendum ipsum gratiæ habitualis donum—auxilium gratuitum Dei interius animam moventis.*—1ᵐᵃ 2ᵈᵃᵉ Q. 109. A. 6. Gratiæ causa non potest esse actus humanus per modum meriti, sed *dispositio naturalis* quædam in quantum per actus præparamur ad gratiæ susceptionem. —Aquinas, vol. viii. De Præd. This is, then, the *dispositio naturæ* here referred to, which is a Divine moulding of the natural man to fit him for grace. The statement, again, on which Archbp. Laurence relies— Dicendum quod quamvis Deus, quantum in se est, æqualiter se habeat ad omnes, non tamen æqualiter se habeant omnes ad ipsum, et ideo non æqualiter omnibus gratia præparatur (in Lomb. l. i. Dist. 40. Q. 2. A. 2.)—cannot be reposed in against a whole interpretative force of the system explaining it the other way. In the first stage of original sin all men do *æqualiter se habent ad Deum:* but God lifts some out of this state, and others not, previously, as we have just seen, to conferring actual grace upon them. In this intermediate stage, then, all men do *not æqualiter se habent ad Deum*, but some are and some are not in a preparatory state for grace: but this difference is the result of the Divine will.

Archbp. Laurence relies on Calvin's dissatisfaction with Aquinas, but the instance to which he refers is no case of substantial disagreement between the two, but only of a difference between a more subtle and a broader mode of statement. Calvin censures the refinement or quibble—*argutia*, of Aquinas in saying that foreseen human merit, though not the cause of predestination on God's part, may be called the cause of it in a certain way—*quodammodo* —on man's part; because God, having predestinated men to goodness, predestinates them to glory because they are good. Such a statement makes no difference in the doctrine of predestination as a whole; because though one part of it is regarded as dependent on another, the whole is made to depend on the Divine will solely. But Calvin dislikes the subtlety as interfering with the breadth of the doctrine:

To the doctrine of predestination thus laid down by Aquinas succeeded a corresponding doctrine of grace. If eternal happiness is ensured to the individual by a Divine decree, the means to it, *i.e.* a good life, must be ensured also; and this can only be ensured by the operation of a Divine grace or influence upon him, the effect of which is not dependent on his own will, but is necessary. Aquinas accordingly proceeds to lay down the doctrine of effective or irresistible grace.

And first it must be observed that, without appending the *term* efficacious, the use of which was introduced by the later Thomists, grace of itself bears in Aquinas the *sense* of efficacious, *i.e.* means something, which simply by the fact of its being given us by God, and of the man himself having it, has the effect of making the man good and acceptable to God. The leaning to the side of free-will which has marked church authority for the last three centuries, has impressed for the most part upon the term grace the sense of assisting grace; *i.e.* a Divine influence which excites, prompts, suggests, and encourages, but which depends on the human will for its proper and intended effect, and does not issue in any good act or good and acceptable state of mind, unless the will has by an original movement of its own converted it to use. And this is perhaps the sense in which grace is more generally and popularly understood at the present day. But the Augustinian schoolmen, following their master, do not mean by grace such an influence as this, but a different one; one which, when received, produces of itself its designed effect —an acceptable and justifying state of the soul. They divide grace into two great kinds, one which is designed for the good of the individual, and makes him acceptable

'Ac ne illam quidem Thomæ argutiam moramur, præscientiam meritorum non ex parte quidem actus prædestinatis esse prædestinationis causam; ex parte autem nostra, quodammodo sic vocari posse, nempe secundum particularem prædestinationis æstimationem; ut quum dicitur Deus prædestinare homini gloriam ex meritis, quia gratiam ei largiri decrevit qua gloriam mereatur.'—Instit. 1. 3. c. 22. s. 9.

Between the Augustinian and Thomist doctrine of predestination, and that of Calvin, I can see no substantial difference. Note XXI.

to God,—*gratia gratum faciens*; the other, which is not the grace of acceptableness, but only some gift or power with which the individual is endowed for the benefit of the church,—*gratia gratis data*.[1] The former grace becomes when imparted a quality of the soul, a certain graciousness and goodness belonging to it, as beauty belongs to the body —*nitor animæ*.[2]

The question then is how this grace is obtained in the first place, and how in the next place it is sustained and preserved. Is it obtained by any merit of the individual in the first place, *i.e.* is it the reward of any original exertion of the will? Or, if not obtained in this way, is it *preserved* in this way, *i.e.* by the freewill of the individual sustaining and guarding it? In either of these cases such a grace as this involves no doctrine of efficacious and irresistible grace; because in the former case it is a state of the mind which the will has in part earned; in the latter it is one, which, though the individual is endowed with it, by an act of God, as Adam according to the authorized doctrine was with a certain good disposition at his creation; the individual has to maintain, as Adam had, by his own freewill. But if this grace is neither obtained nor preserved by the freewill of the individual, but is given in the first instance as a free gift of God, and sustained afterwards by the supporting power of God, exerted gratuitously and

---

[1] Duplex est gratia, una quidam per quam ipse homo Deo conjungitur, quæ vocatur *gratia gratum faciens*; alia vero per quam unus homo cooperatur alteri ad hoc, quod ad Deum reducatur : hujusmodi autem donum vocatur *gratia gratis data*; quia supra facultatem naturæ, et supra meritum personæ homini conceditur. Sed quia non datur ad hoc ut homo ipse per eam justificetur, sed potius ut ad justificationem alterius cooperetur, ideo non vocatur gratum faciens. Et de hac dicit Apostolus 1. ad Cor. 12. 7. Unicuique datur manifestatio spiritus ad utilitatem, scilicet, aliorum.

Gratia autem gratum faciens ordinat hominem immediate ad conjunctionem ultimi finis; gratiæ autem gratis datæ ordinant hominem ad quædam præparatoria finis ultimi, sicut per prophetiam et miracula. Et ideo gratia gratum faciens est multo excellentior quam gratia gratis data.—1$^{ma}$ 2$^{dae}$ Q. iii. A. 1. 5.

Gratia habitus gratus a Deo— causa efficiens meriti . . . Virtutes theologicæ et supernaturales, non sunt minus efficaces similium actuum quam virtutes morales.—Bradwardine, p. 364. *et seq.*

[2] Gratia est nitor animæ sanctum concilians amorem.—1$^{ma}$ 2$^{dae}$ Q. 110. A. 2.

arbitrarily; it then involves the doctrine of efficacious grace; for there is no room at either end for any original motion of the will, upon which the possession of such grace depends.

But the latter is, according to the Thomist doctrine, the mode in which this grace is obtained and preserved. First, the primary possession of this grace is not owing, in whole or in part, to any merit or original act of will in the individual. It was laid down that to a man who prepared himself as much as possible for grace, grace was still not necessarily given;—*non necessario data se præparanti ad gratiam et facienti quod in se est.*[1] But if a man's best possible preparation of himself for it was no claim in the eye of God to it, the bestowal of it evidently did not depend upon any thing in a man himself, but proceeded upon a different law. And when we are let into the real meaning of this position, the same conclusion is still more clear. For when this position comes to be explained, as it is further on in the argument, it turns out to be only another form of the position that nobody *can* prepare himself, either in whole or in part, for grace, *i.e.* have any original share in this work. The preparation of the human heart for the reception of grace was a Divine work, in which God was the mover, and the human will the thing moved.

The distinction indeed of operating and co-operating grace, *gratia operans et cooperans*, appears at first sight to imply an original act of the will, with which Divine grace co-operates, and which is co-ordinate with that grace. But as explained, it carries no such meaning with it, and issues in a verbal subtlety. Two acts are attributed to the will, one interior, the other exterior, the one being the substance of the act, the other its manifestation; the one the real moral act itself, the other that act as expressed in outward form. Of these two acts then, the former is attri-

[1] Homo comparatur ad Deum sicut lutum ad figulum, secundum illud Jer. 18. 6. *Sicut lutum in manu figuli sic vos in manu mea.* Sed lutum non ex necessitate accipit formam a figulo, quantumcunque sit præparatum. Ergo neque homo recipit ex necessitate gratiam a Deo, quantumcunque se præparet.—1$^{ma}$ 2$^{dae}$ Q. 112. A. 3.

buted to Divine grace alone,—*gratia operans*, the human will not co-operating with it, but being simply moved by it. The latter is allowed to co-operate with Divine grace. But this is no independent but a wholly moved and dictated co-operation. The will having being wholly moved to action by grace, that action is then called a co-operation with grace.[1]

The bestowal of justifying grace, then, does not, in the system of Aquinas, depend in the first instance upon any act of man's will; nor does its continuance depend on it either. The continuance of this grace depends on the gift of perseverance, which is a gratuitous gift of God, given to whom, and withheld from whom He will;[2] and to which no life and conduct of man can afford any claim. Suppose a person in a good present state of mind, leading a good life, and therefore, for the time being, in a state of acceptance; the question is, upon what law does this state of things *last*? Does its permanence depend on the individual's own original will, which performing its part in the guard and maintenance of this state, God performs His,

---

[1] 'In illo effectu in quo mens nostra et movet et movetur, operatio non solum attribuitur Deo sed etiam animæ; et secundum hoc dicitur gratia cooperans. Est autem in nobis duplex actus; *primus quidem interior voluntatis; et quantum ad istum actum voluntas se habet ut mota;* Deus autem ut movens; et præsertim cum voluntas incipit bonum velle, quæ prius malum volebat; et ideo secundum quod Deus movet humanam mentem ad hunc actum, dicitur gratia operans. *Alius autem est actus exterior, qui cum a voluntate imperetur, consequens est quod ad hunc actum operatio attribuatur voluntati.* Et. . . . respectu hujusmodi actus dicitur gratia cooperans.'—1ᵐᵃ 2ᵈᵃᵉ Q. iii. A. 2.

[2] 'Homo etiam in gratia constitutus indiget ut ei perseverantia a Deo detur. . . . Postquam aliquis est justificatus per gratiam, necesse habet a Deo petere perseverantiæ donum; ut scilicet custodiatur a malo usque ad finem vitæ. Multis enim datur gratia quibus non datur perseverare in gratia.'—1ᵐᵃ 2ᵈᵃᵉ Q. 110. A. 10.

'Omne quod quis meretur a Deo consequitur, nisi impediatur per peccatum. Sed multi habent opera meritoria, qui non consequuntur perseverantiam; nec potest dici quod hoc fiat propter impedimentum peccati, quia hoc ipsum quod est peccare, opponitur perseverantiæ; ita quod si aliquis perseverantiam mereretur, Deus non permitteret illum cadere in peccatum. Non igitur perseverantia viæ non cadit sub merito. . . . Perseverantia viæ non cadit sub merito, quia dependet solum ex motione divina, quæ est principium omnis meriti. *Sed Deus gratis perseverantiæ bonum largitur cuicunque illud largitur.*'—1ᵐᵃ 2ᵈᵃᵉ Q. 114. A. 9.

and supplies the complement? Not, according to Aquinas. The continuance of this state of things is, from moment to moment, a gratuitous act of God's sustaining power, who keeps up this moral and spiritual fabric, as He does that of the material world, so long as it suits His sovereign pleasure, and no longer. The creature cannot conditionate this Will Supreme, or impose any obligation in justice upon it, in this matter. Thus, guarded at both ends from dependence on the human will, given as the free gift of God in the first instance, and sustained by His absolute power afterwards, justifying grace—*gratia gratum faciens*, was effective or irresistible grace.

So far, however, the Thomist doctrine of grace was only the Augustinian doctrine, which was a perfectly simple one, regarding the operation of grace as the action on each successive occasion of Divine power; upon which action the effect of goodness in the soul followed, and upon its cessation or interruption ceased. But the schoolmen added to this doctrine a distinction, which, though founded in reason and nature, ended, in their hands, in greatly burdening and perplexing it. Aristotle had laid down the very natural position, that what constituted a man good, was not the good act on the particular occasion, but a *habit* of mind: this habit was productive, indeed, of acts, and defined as such; but still it was from having this source of acts in his mind, that a man was good, rather than from the acts considered in themselves. As grace was concerned, then, with the production of goodness, the schoolmen, incorporating the Aristotelian doctrine of habits with the doctrine of grace, maintained that God imparted goodness in the shape of *habit*; and the result was, the distinction between habitual and actual grace—*gratia habitualis et actualis*[1];—a distinction which, in their

---

[1] 'Homo ad recte vivendum dupliciter auxilio Dei indiget: uno quidem modo quantum ad aliquod *habituale donum*, per quod natura humana corrupta sanetur, et etiam sanata elevetur ad operanda opera meritoria vitæ æternæ, quæ excedunt proportionem naturæ: alio modo indiget homo auxilio gratiæ, *ut a Deo moveatur ad agendum.* . . . et hoc propter duo; primo quidem ratione generali, propter hoc quod nulla res creata potest in quemcunque actum prodire, nisi virtute motionis

mode of carrying it out, produced such a labyrinth of compartments and network of verbal subtleties, that it requires some patience in a reader to extricate any meaning at all from such confusion, or arrive at the substance and kernel of the system, amidst such obstructions.

Aquinas then commences with laying down, in general terms, the doctrine of *infused habits*,—a doctrine which, as I have explained in a preceding chapter, is in itself a natural one, and agreeable to our experience. He asserts, in the first place, that there are such things as natural habits[1], or dispositions, moral and intellectual, which are born with men; though he artificially limits the former to such as are evidently connected with the bodily temperament, such as temperance. And upon this foundation of natural truth, he proceeds to erect another, and a more important class of infused habits, connected with grace.

Besides habits infused by nature, then, there were habits 'infused by God;' which differed from the natural virtues in this, that they were designed for the spiritual good of man, as the former were for his temporal and worldly. These were certain imparted holy dispositions, or spiritual virtues, produced in the soul without any efforts of its own—*quas Deus in nobis sine nobis operatur*.[2]

divinæ: secundo ratione speciali propter conditionem status humanæ naturæ; quæ quidem licet per gratiam sanetur quantum ad mentem, remanet tamen in eo corruptio et infectio quantum ad carnem . . . et ideo necesse est nobis ut a Deo dirigamur et protegamur, quia omnia movet et omnia potest. . . . *Donum habitualis gratiæ non ad hoc datur nobis ut per ipsum non indigeamus ulterius divino auxilio.*'—1$^{ma}$ 2$^{dae}$ Q. 110. A. 9.

[1] 'Sunt in hominibus aliqui habitus naturales. . . . In appetitivis autem potentiis non est aliquis habitus naturalis secundum inchoationem ex parte ipsius animæ. . . Sed ex parte corporis . . . sunt enim quidam dispositi ex propria corporis complexione ad castitatem vel mansuetudinem, vel ad aliquid hujusmodi.'—1$^{ma}$ 2$^{dae}$ Q. 51. A. 1.

[2] 'Habitus homini a Deo infunduntur. . . . Ratio est quia aliqui habitus sunt quibus homo bene disponitur ad finem excedentem facultatem humanæ naturæ, . . . et quia habitus oportet esse proportionatos ei ad quod homo disponitur secundum ipsos, ideo necesse est quod etiam habitus ad hujusmodi finem disponentes, excedant facultatem humanæ naturæ. Unde tales habitus nunquam possunt homini inesse, nisi ex infusione divina.'—Though God is also able to infuse common habits, such as are ordinarily acquired by acts.—'Deus potest producere effectus causarum secundarum

First in order, came the Theological virtues,—Faith, Hope, and Charity. Then came the gifts—*Dona*; which were seven in number,—Wisdom, Understanding, Knowledge, Counsel, Piety, Fortitude, and Fear. But, besides these, were also infused moral virtues—*virtutes morales infusæ*; which were the same in matter with natural or acquired virtues, but differed in the end or motive, which was a spiritual one, while that of the former was natural. The acquired, and the infused, virtue of temperance, for example, were both expressed by the same acts; but the one aimed at bodily health, or an undisturbed exertion of the intellectual faculties, the other at spiritual discipline.

Now, so far as the schoolman in this scheme simply asserts that God can, and often does, implant holy dispositions and habits in human souls, without previous discipline and training on their part; or maintains the principle of infused habits, as distinguished from habits acquired by acts, his position is a natural one, and agrees with our experience, as well as with the doctrine of the early Church. We mean by a habit, a certain bias or proneness to act in a particular direction; and this bias or proneness is obtained in one way by successive acts. But it would be untrue, and contrary to the plainest facts of nature, to suppose that this is the only way in which such a bias of the mind is ever obtained. God evidently imparts it to men, at birth, in different moral directions; for we see them born with particular dispositions and characters. And as He imparts it at birth, He appears also sometimes to impart it on subsequent occasions, by powerful impulses, communicated to the souls of man, either internally, or by the machinery of his outward providence; by sudden junctures, emergencies, in private or public life. We see great changes produced in men's characters by these exciting causes, and their minds put, by the force of events, into particular states and tempers, which they retain afterwards.

absque ipsis causis secundis. . . . Sicut igitur quandoque ad ostensionem suæ virtutis producit sanitatem absque causa naturali; quæ tamen per naturam posset causari; ita etiam quandoque infundit homini illos habitus qui naturali virtute possunt causari.'—1$^{ma}$ 2$^{dae}$ Q. 52. A. 4$^a$.

That is to say, habits are sometimes imparted to men at once, and from without, in distinction to being the result of successive acts. The doctrine of *Conversion,* is the application of this truth to the department of religion : what this doctrine asserts being, that God, by particular impulses, either wholly internal or connected with outward events, imparts at once a religious disposition or habit to the mind; so that, from being careless and indifferent, it immediately becomes serious ; which is undoubtedly sometimes the case. So far, then, as the schoolman simply maintains in this scheme the position of infused habits, or that habits need not necessarily be obtained by acts, he maintains a true and natural doctrine. And this was an important modification of the Aristotelian doctrine, which rested too exclusively upon acts as the cause of habits. So acute an observer, indeed, of facts, as that great philosopher was, could not but see himself that this cause did not apply in all cases ;—and the observation extracted from him a partial modification of his own system, in the shape of the admission of *natural virtue*—φυσικὴ ἀρετή. But the addition of *infusion,* as a formal and regular cause, in the case of habits, was a substantial modification of the Aristotelian doctrine. It was, however, a modification, which naturally followed from Christianity. The idea of the Divine power, which was not fully embraced by the Pagan philosopher, was brought out by the true religion, and applied to the moral, as well as to the physical world, to the department of will, as well as that of matter. In other words, it taught a doctrine, which the pagan philosopher did not hold, that of Divine Grace ; which immediately became a fresh element in the argument, and supplied a new cause for the formation of the habit.

But, while the scheme thus rested upon a basis of nature and truth, two great causes of confusion were at work in it. One was an unreal or artificial distinction in the subject matter of acquired and infused habits. It will be evident to any one, on reflection, that the distinction between these two kinds of habits, is a distinction simply in the mode in which they are formed, and not at all in the nature or matter of the habits themselves; the same state and disposition of mind being formed in the one case by time, custom, successive acts, and in the other by Divine power producing it, without the aid of these previous steps. All habits, as such, then, whatever be their subject matter, or rank, come alike under both these modes of formation: an ordinary moral habit, such as honesty or temperance, is as much a subject of infusion as a spiritual one, such as faith or charity; and a spiritual habit, such as faith or charity, is as much a subject of acquisition, as a common moral one of temperance or honesty. Infusion and acquisition apply alike to both. A habit of faith is acquired by acts of faith, and a habit of love by acts of love; and the natural or Aristotelian law of the formation of habits, is as true of spiritual as of common moral habits. Again, the commonest moral dispositions are as capable, as spiritual ones, of being imparted in the other way, *i.e.* without previous acts; and we see them so imparted often at birth. But Aquinas artificially appropriates infusion to spiritual virtues, acquisition to moral ones;[1] as if the former were never acquired by acts, and the latter never but by them. It depends on the dispensation under which a person is individually placed, in what way he obtains either spiritual or moral habits; whether both are the simple growth of time and acts in him, or whether he obtains both in the more immediate way: though we must not so divide the two modes of formation of character as to forget that both may go on together in the same person, and that mankind are all more or less under both systems.

Another cause of confusion was the technical and quaint division of these habits, followed by the artificial subordination of one division to another, the attempt being to construct them into one harmonious machinery for the building up of the human soul,—one set, at the point where its power failed, being taken up, and its action carried on by another. The Theological virtues, Faith, Hope, and Charity, were infused habits. But though, their

[1] He admits natural moral virtue in a limited way, p. 291.

infusion into a particular soul being supposed, these were true habits or dispositions of that soul; they were passive and inert, not producing acts until they were removed from another quarter to do so. They were habits indeed, but elementary ones, imperfectly possessed, and rather of the nature of *principles* or faculties—*principia supernaturalia,* corresponding to the natural faculties of man— *principia naturalia.*[1] While the natural will of man, then, could put the natural principles into action, because these were possessed perfectly, it could not, of itself, put into action the supernatural principles. To put these into action another spiritual force was necessary.[2] To the theological virtues, therefore, succeeded the *Dona.* Now it is true that a habit does not move itself to action, but requires to be put in motion by a particular act of freewill, on one theory, by a particular act of grace, on another. But the *Dona* were themselves only imparted habits. Here, then, was one set of habits, which was necessary to put in motion another. And as the *Dona* succeeded the theological virtues, the 'infused moral virtues' succeeded the *Dona;* being those final and settled spiritual habits to which the supernatural principles in man, *i.e.* the theological virtues, tended; as the acquired habits were the completion of his natural principles.[3] Yet this accumula-

[1] Et quia hujusmodi beatitudo proportionem humanæ naturæ excedit, principia naturalia hominis non sufficiunt ad ordinandum hominem in beatitudinem prædictam; unde oportet quod superaddantur homini divinitus aliqua principia, per quæ ita ordinetur ad beatitudinem supernaturalem, sicut per principia naturalia ordinatur ad finem connaturalem: *et hujusmodi principia dicuntur virtutes theologicæ:* tum quia habent Deum pro objecto, tum quia a solo Deo nobis infunduntur.—1$^{ma}$ 2$^{dae}$ Q. 62. A. 1.

[2] Manifestum est quod virtutes humanæ proficiunt hominem, secundum quod homo natus est moveri per rationem. Oportet igitur inesse homini altiores perfectiones, secundum quas sit dispositus ad hoc quod divinitus moveatur; *et istæ perfectiones vocantur dona.*—1$^{ma}$ 2$^{dae}$ Q. 68. A. 1. The Theological virtues are imperfect agents and cannot move without the Dona.—Prima (naturalis) virtus habetur ab homine quasi plena possessio: secunda autem (theologica) habetur quasi imperfecta. Sed id quod imperfecte habet naturam aliquam non habet per se operari, nisi ab altero moveatur. . . . Ad finem ultimum naturalem ad quam ratio movet, secundum quod est imperfecte formata per theologicas virtutes, non sufficit ipsa motio rationis, nisi desuper adsit instinctus Spiritus Sancti.—A. 2.

[3] Loco naturalium principiorum conferuntur nobis a Deo virtutes

tion of habits, rising one above another in formal scale' this whole complex machinery, did not complete the moral being, who seemed always approaching the terminus of action, and never attaining it.

For, secondly, habitual grace, with all this multiplicity of internal construction, could still not put itself in action. It was still no more than a habit of the mind, imparted by God: and no habit, as has been just said, can put itself in action; for a man does not necessarily do a thing, in fact, because he has a certain disposition to do it. It became then a vital question, what it was which put habitual grace into action. Was it the freewill of man? If it was, then the human will had an original and independent act assigned to it; a position which was contrary to this whole scholastic doctrine of grace. It was not freewill, then, but another and a further grace, which set in motion habitual, viz. grace actual—*gratia actualis*.[1] This was the completion of the system, the key-stone of the arch. Habitual grace could be admitted without any serious drawback from the power of the natural will; for God might impart a certain disposition, or continuous impulse; while it depended wholly on the independent motion of the will, whether the man acted upon it or not. The turning and distinctive assertion in the system, then, was the assertion of actual grace, as that which moved habitual: and to this cardinal position the Thomists, and their successors the Jansenists, directed their most zealous and anxious attention, repelling all interference with it as a subversion of the whole Gospel doctrine of grace. The admission of habitual grace set aside as one which the Semi-Pelagian or even the Pelagian could make, without danger in principle to his theory; grace actual was defended as the central fort of Christian truth in this department.[2]

theologicæ. . . . Unde oportet quod his etiam virtutibus theologicis proportionaliter respondeant alii habitus divinitus causati in nobis, qui sic se habent ad virtutes theologicas, sicut se habent virtutes morales ad principia naturalia virtutum.—1$^{ma}$ 2$^{dae}$ Q. 63. A. 3.

[1] See p. 290.
[2] *Non est habitus qui facit facere*, says Jansen. No habit, he urges, is the cause of action, but *liberum arbitrium* at the time.—De Gratiâ Christi, pp. 186, 996. Nec est lux vel habitus quæ velle vel non velle, videre vel non videre faciunt, sed

As then in the simpler and Augustinian, so in the complex and Aristotelian statement of the doctrine of grace, in which the distinction of habitual and actual is introduced, Aquinas maintains, we see, an irresistible or effective grace. Habitual grace is guarded carefully at both ends from dependence on the human will. It was alike imparted and applied by an act of Divine Power. Had the spiritual habit been either obtained in the first instance by an act of the will, or, when imparted as a free gift, depended for its use on the will, a place for freewill would have been allowed. But if freewill comes in neither at the beginning nor at the end, neither as obtaining the habit in the first instance nor as using it in the next, or causing it to terminate in act, one operation of an irresistible Divine influence is maintained throughout.

The *Summa Theologica* thus lays down a doctrine of absolute predestination, with its complemental doctrine of irresistible grace—that the whole world, being by original sin one mass of perdition, it pleased God of His sovereign mercy to rescue some and to leave others where they were; to raise some to glory, giving them such grace as neces-

tantummodo *sine quibus* actus volendi vel videndi *non fit.* — p. 935. And this motion of *liberum arbitrium* at the time, is produced by grace at the time—*gratia specialis, actualis* — adjutorium gratiæ actualis quod tunc datur, quando *actu* volumus et operamur. . . . inspirans etiam habitualiter justis velle et operari.—pp. 151. 153. He adds: Tota disputatio cum Pelagio de justorum, hoc est, habitualem gratiam jam habentium fervuit. . . Non ita deliravit Pelagius, ut existimaret justitiam habitualem, ad opera justa suo modo non adjuvare. —p. 153. 'Actualis gratia' thus gives the 'completum posse,' which is 'per liberum arbitrium remotior, per fidem propinquior, per charitatem multo propinquior, per actualem gratiam,' really had.—p. 338. This position is maintained as the only one which cuts off the ground of merit from man. Did he use habitual grace by his own power of choice, he would have the merit of his own use of this grace (p. 186.); but if this grace is put in action by another grace, no ground of merit in the man himself remains. And a distinction is drawn in this respect between fallen man and the angels.—Hinc nascebatur ut neque volitiones neque actiones angelorum essent specialia Dei dona, hoc est, non eis Deus speciali donatione seu gratia largiretur. Tantummodo enim donabat ea in radice, quatenus eis adjutorium quoddam gratiæ tribuebat, sine quo . . . non poterant: sed ipsum velle, agere, et perseverare, non eis dabat adjutorium gratiæ, sed propria voluntas . . . Tunc igitur velle et agere bonum non erat speciale Dei donum, sed tantum generale.—pp. 935, 936.

sarily qualified them for it, and abandon the rest, from whom He withheld such grace, to eternal punishment. But this formal scheme laid down, the attentive reader of Aquinas will next observe a certain general leaning and bias towards a modifying interpretation of it. Having constructed a system on the strict Augustinian basis, the mind of the great schoolman appears to have shrunk from the extreme results which it involved; and without committing himself to any substantial difference from his master, he yet uses modes of speaking suggestive of another view of the question than that which he had borrowed from him; and a phraseology, which is not casual, but set and constant, insinuates a relaxation of the Augustinian doctrine.

And first I will make the preliminary remark, that a difference is to be observed in the general tone of these two great theological minds, tending more or less to affect their respective views on this subject. Aquinas is more of a philosopher than his master, and has greater sympathies with the human mind as such, with the natural intellect, reason, and moral ideas of mankind. His vast acquaintance with heathen philosophy opens his mind to the valuable gifts even of unenlightened man, his deep reflections upon himself, his knowledge of God,—true as far as it goes,—and his advancement in virtue, under the guidance of reason and conscience. Nor is the deference which he shows to heathen authority, in philosophical and moral questions, altogether consistent with the position which his formal theology, as an Augustinian, assigned to unconverted human nature, which it represented as in the depths of sin, and unable to do or to think anything good. The perplexity, again, with respect to the existence of evil, appears in a deeper and more sensitive form in the mind of Aquinas than it does in that of his master. Augustine sees as a theologian an inexplicable mystery; but Aquinas shows more of that human sentiment, with respect to the great fact of evil in the world,[1] which has rested

[1] Bradwardine has less scruple.—Ecce triplex bonum ex reprobis: utilitas electorum, bonum naturæ, seculique ornatus. Ponatur quoque

upon so many of the deep and philosophical minds of different ages, and especially of modern times, disquieting some, and sobering and subduing others. His perception not dulled by the commonness and constancy of the fact, as inferior ones are, but ever retaining something of a first surprise, acknowledges, as the eye of a naturalist would some remarkable law in his department, the prevalence of moral evil in this lower world—*bonum videtur esse ut in paucioribus*;—a fact which, as he cannot explain, he endeavours to outweigh, conjecturing some compensation for it in other parts of the universe, and isolating this sublunary world as one exception to a universal law. This sphere of natural evil, of generation and corruption, was small in comparison with the world of heavenly bodies, whose existence was eternal and fixed. This sphere of moral evil in the majority was small, again, in comparison with the angelic world, where a different law was in operation; and the angels who stood were much more in number than those who fell, and, *perhaps*, even than the whole number of the condemned, both men and demons—*et forte etiam multo plures quam omnes damnandi dæmones et homines*.[1] Such a line of thought had a bearing upon the present question, and tended to affect his view upon it; because an attempt to reduce the amount of evil in the universe at large disposed to reducing, as far as might be, the alarming estimate of it in this world.

The distinction, then, involved in Augustinian predestination and reprobation, being a distinction between posi-

secundum pium zelum multorum, licet non secundum scientiam, quod totus infernus cum omnibus suis domesticis reprobatis tolleretur de medio, essetque cœlum tantummodo cum civibus suis sanctis; tunc seculum esset multum perfectum, et si Deus sic fecisset multum bene fecisset. Nunc autem tanto perfectius et tanto melius fecit Deus, quantum *perfectionis et bonitatis continent in se illæ nobiles creaturæ damnatæ*, quantum etiam resplendentiæ et apparentiæ purioris illa *comparatio* veluti contrarietatis extremæ confert justis, tanquam scintillæ fulgentibus, et ut stellæ. *Quis enim vel cujus ratio prohibuisset Dominum ab initio, si fuisset placitum coram eo, creasse cœlum plenum electis in gloria, et infernum plenum reprobis in pœna,* ut hoc illi comparate apparuisset gloriosius et fuisset? Non deerunt tamen qui hos humano misererentur affectu, et pia compassione contenderent sic facere non debere.—p. 355.

[1] In Lomb. l. 1. Dist. 39. Q. 2. A. 2.

tive good and positive evil, goodness and wickedness, and
their consequences, eternal happiness and eternal misery,
to two portions of the world respectively; there is a tendency in the language of Aquinas to reduce this distinction to a distinction between higher and lower good. Two
kinds of happiness are laid down in his system, 'one of
which is proportioned to human nature, and to which a
man can arrive by this principle of his own nature; the
other exceeding human nature, and to which a man can
arrive only by Divine virtue and by a participation of the
Divinity, according to the text in S. Peter, that we are by
Christ made partakers of the Divine Nature.'[1]  Here,
then, are two kinds of happiness, and two kinds of virtues,
which respectively qualify for them. There is one class
of virtues, which fits a man for his place in the order of
nature, and makes him a worthy member of the world of
God's natural providence—*secundum quas homo se bene
habet in ordine ad res humanas*; another class, which
fits a man for a place in a supernatural order of things
and a heavenly citizenship—*ad hoc quod sint cives sanctorum et domestici Dei*.[2] Expressed with scholastic formality, here is a very obvious distinction, and one which
we cannot avoid observing in the world around us,—one
which is recognised in the common language and writings
of Christians. We see as a plain fact, that there is a kind
of goodness, which, as distinguished from another kind,
must be pronounced to belong to this world,—that men
may be honest, conscientious, and high-principled in their
worldly callings, still having their view confined to this
world. It is a virtuous mould and character of mind,—
that of a man who recognises the world as a true sphere
of moral action, desires to be on the right side, and culti-
vates with that view various moral qualities; who, there-

[1] Est autem duplex hominis beatitudo; una quidem proportionata
humanæ naturæ, ad quam scilicet
homo pervenire potest per principia
suæ naturæ. Alia autem beatitudo
naturam hominis excedens, ad quam
homo sola divina virtute pervenire
potest secundum quandam Divinitatis participationem; secundum
quod dicitur (2 Pet. i.) quod per
Christum facti sumus *consortes di
vinæ naturæ*.—1<sup>ma</sup> 2<sup>dae</sup> Q. 62. A. 1.
[2] 1<sup>ma</sup> 2<sup>dae</sup> Q. 63. A. 4.

fore, so far as the spiritual principle is involved in any *bonâ fide* and honest distinction of good and evil, acknowledges a spiritual law in his own nature and the constitution of things, to which he defers, and on which he frames his life and conduct; but who lowers this law by his narrow and confined application of it to present things and visible relations. This, then, is what Christian moralists call the virtue of the natural man; and its defect is in the principle of faith, which, by opening another world for them, and so enlarging their scope and field, would have given a spring and impulse to these moral perceptions, quickening and strengthening them; whereas they are now kept down to a particular level. On the other hand, it is an essential part of Christian doctrine, that there is a temper of mind so far in advance of this natural morality, as to seem to differ from it in kind; in the sense in which everything seems at its perfection and final point, to be a different thing from what it was before, as a lens burns at its centre only. This is the supernatural temper of charity.[1]

From morals the distinction of natural and supernatural is then extended by Aquinas to religion. It was obvious that the natural man had not only moral virtue of some kind, but religion as well. For, independent of the religious men which Paganism had produced, what is the obedience which the natural man, in his moral course of life, pays to his own conscience, but an obedience to God, whom he virtually recognises as speaking to him by that internal voice? And as he will obey that conscience, even at the cost of his worldly interests, suffering the greatest inconveniences rather than offend against probity and

---

[1] La distance infinie des corps aux esprits figure la distance infiniment plus infinie des esprits à la charité; car elle est surnaturelle.

Tous les corps, le firmament, les étoiles, la terre et les royaumes ne valent pas le moindre des esprits; car il connait tout cela, et soi-même; et le corps, rien. Et tous les corps, et tous les esprits ensemble, et toutes leurs productions, ne valent pas le moindre mouvement de charité; car elle est d'un ordre infiniment plus élevé.

De tous les corps ensemble on ne saurait tirer la moindre pensée : cela est impossible, et d'un autre ordre. Tous les corps et les esprits ensemble ne sauraient produire un mouvement de vraie charité : cela est impossible, et d'un autre ordre tout surnaturel.—Pascal.

honesty, it is plain that in some sense he prefers the Divine approbation to everything else. It was accordingly laid down that the natural man was able to love God above all things—*homo potest diligere Deum super omnia ex solis naturalibus sine gratia.* But the distinction was then applied that he loved God naturally, not supernaturally, 'as the source and end of natural good; whereas charity loved Him as the centre of spiritual good or happiness. Charity had, moreover, a positive communion with God, which nature had not; of which communion a certain promptitude and delight were the results, which did not belong to the natural love of God.'[1]

These two kinds of goodness, then, natural and supernatural, had their respective sources assigned to them, and the cause or motive power was pronounced, by an abbreviation, in the one case to be reason, in the other God—*Ratio et Deus*:[2] the Divine Power, however, operating alike in both cases as true and original Cause. The Divine Power, acting simply as the First or Universal Cause in nature, moved the freewill of man to natural virtue; acting in a special way or by grace, it moved the same freewill to supernatural virtue.[3] 'All things,' says Aquinas, 'are subject to Providence, and it pertains to Providence to ordain all things to their end. But the end to which created things are ordained by God is twofold. One is the end which exceeds the proportion and faculty of created nature; that is to say, the life eternal, which consists in the Divine vision,—which vision is above the nature of every creature. Another is the end proportioned to created nature, and which that nature can attain by the virtue of that nature. Now, that which cannot arrive at a point by its own virtue must be transmitted thither by another, as an arrow is sent by an archer at a mark. Wherefore, pro-

---

[1] 'Charitas diligit Deum super omnia eminentius quam natura. Natura enim diligit Deum super omnia, prout est principium et finis naturalis boni; charitas autem, secundum quod est objectum beatitudinis, et secundum quod homo habet quandam societatem spiritualem cum Deo. Addit etiam charitas super naturalem dilectionem Dei, promptitudinem quandam et delectationem.' —1$^{ma}$ 2$^{dae}$ Q. 109. A. 3.

[2] 1$^{ma}$ 2$^{dae}$ Q. 68. A. 1.

[3] 1$^{ma}$ 2$^{dae}$ Q. 10. A. 6.

perly speaking, the rational creature, which is capable of life eternal, is conducted up to it, or transmitted to it by God. Of which transmission the reason pre-exists in the mind of God, even as there exists generally the reason of the ordination of all things whatever to the end. But the reason of anything being done is a certain pre-existence in the mind of the doer of the thing itself to be done; whence the reason of the transmission of the rational creature to life eternal is called predestination—*nam destinare est mittere.*[1] While the cause, then, of natural virtue is the Divine Power acting in its ordinary function, as predetermining universally the created wills of men, the cause of supernatural virtue in man is the Divine Power acting in predestination, or in the execution of a certain special decree. 'The virtue which qualifies man for good as defined by the Divine Law, in distinction to reason, cannot be caused by human acts of which the principle is reason, but is caused in us by the Divine operation alone.'[2] And this Divine operation is carried on by means of that machinery of infused supernatural virtues above described. For 'as God provides for His natural creatures in such wise, that He not only moves them to natural acts, but even endows them with certain forms and virtues to act as principles of action and to be in themselves dispositions to such action; so into those whom He moves to attain eternal and supernatural good He infuses certain supernatural forms or qualities, by which they are sweetly and promptly disposed to attain that good.'[3] Supernatural virtue is

[1] 'Ad illud autem, ad quod non potest aliquid virtute suæ naturæ pervenire, oportet quod ab alio transmittatur, sicut sagitta a sagittante mittitur ad signum. Unde proprie loquendo, rationalis creatura, quæ est capax vitæ æternæ perducitur in ipsam quasi a Deo transmissa. Cujus quidem transmissionis ratio in Deo præexistit, sicut et in eo est ratio ordinis omnium in finem. Ratio autem alicujus fiendi existens est quædam præexistentia rei fiendæ in eo. Unde ratio prædictæ transmissionis creaturæ rationalis in finem vitæ æternæ prædestinatio nominatur; nam destinare est mittere.'— 1$^{ma}$ 2$^{dae}$ Q. 23. A. 1.

[2] 'Virtus vero ordinans hominem ad bonum secundum quod modificatur per legem divinam, et non per rationem humanam, non potest causari per actus humanos quorum principium est ratio; sed causatur solum in nobis per operationem divinam.'—1$^{ma}$ 2$^{dae}$ Q. 63. A. 2.

[3] 'Creaturis autem naturalibus sic providet ut non solum moveat eas

thus an extraordinary, natural an ordinary, gift; the one an inspiration, the other a providential endowment.

But while these two kinds of virtue, and the ends to which they respectively tend, differ in the quality of good which belongs to them, both have, according to this language, some; and the difference between these two states is one of higher and lower good, and not one of good and evil. As a disciple of S. Augustine, indeed, Aquinas is obliged formally to preserve the distinction between the natural and spiritual man as one of positive good and positive evil, and to use the terms predestination and reprobation as involving this difference; to represent inclusion within the Divine decree as salvation, exclusion from it as damnation. The pure Augustinian doctrine admitted of no medium between these two results; which it defends on the ground of an original guilt in the human race, which meets with its due punishment in one of these, with a gratuitous pardon in the other. Aquinas, then, formally adopts the Augustinian scheme, with the established defences. But a careful observation of his language will detect a contest between two different *rationales* in his mind; the Clementine view of human nature struggling with the Augustinian. Reprobation, maintained on one side in full severity, is softened down on another, and identified with a lower step in the scale of being; and the rigid Augustinian line of defence for the doctrine mixes with another, which implies a reduced doctrine to be defended. We are referred, together with an original guilt in human nature, to a principle of variety in the constitution of things, which requires that there should be higher and lower places in the universe, down even to some lowest place of all, which must be occupied. 'As created things,' he says, 'cannot attain to the Divine simplicity, it is necessary that the Divine goodness, which is in itself one and simple, should be represented multiformly in them;

ad actus naturales, sed etiam largitur eis formas et virtutes quasdam quæ sunt principia actuum. . . . Multo igitur magis illos quos movet ad consequendum bonum supernaturale æternum infundit *aliquas formas, seu qualitates supernaturales,* secundum quas suaviter et prompte ab ipso moveantur ad bonum æternum consequendum.'—$1^{m\text{æ}}$ $2^{\text{dæ}}$ Q. 110. A. 2.

and the completeness of the universe requires a difference of grades, some high and others low in it. And on this account God permits evils to take place, lest good should be obstructed by its own abundance, and to preserve this multiformity of grades in the universe. And He deals with the human race as He does with the universe,—He represents His goodness with that variety which is necessary to such representation, in the shape of mercy to those whom He spares, of punishment to those whom He reprobates. . . . . . "God willing to show His wrath, and to make His power known, endured (*i.e.* permitted) with much long-suffering the vessels of wrath fitted to destruction, that He might make known the riches of His glory on the vessels of mercy, which He had afore prepared for glory;" and "in a great house there are not only vessels of gold and silver, but also of wood and earth, and some to honour and some to dishonour." But why He has elected these, and reprobated those, there is no reason but the Divine Will, as Augustine saith, "Why He draws this man, and not that, do not inquire, if thou wouldest not err." Just as in natural things, a reason can be assigned, why out of uniform elemental matter one part is put under the form of fire, and another under the form of earth, and so on ; but why this or that part of matter is chosen for this or that form none can be, except the arbitrary will of the Creator: and as in the case of a building there is a reason why some stones or other should be put in particular places, but why these or those stones are selected to be put in the places, none—except the arbitrary will of the builder.'[1] Two interpretations evidently divide this explanation and defence of reprobation, one a severer, the other a milder one. It is spoken of as positive evil, punishment on sin—

[1] 'Sicut in rebus naturalibus potest assignari ratio, cum prima materia tota sit in se uniformis, quare una pars ejus est sub forma ignis, et alia sub forma terræ a Deo in principio condita, ut sic sit diversitas specierum in rebus naturalibus; sed quare hæc pars materiæ est sub ista forma, et illa sub alia, dependet ex simplici divina voluntate; sicut ex simplici voluntate artificis dependet quod ille lapis est in ista parte parietis, et ille in alia, quamvis ratio artis habeat quod aliqui sint in hac, et aliqui sint in illa.'—1$^{ma}$ Q. 23. A. 5.

*vindicta justitiæ*; and it is spoken of as lower good, for it is represented as a lower grade in the scale of being—*infimus locus in universo*. But, according to Aquinas, evil is no part of the universe, of which, however varied and graduated that good may be, the whole is good; so that a lower, or the lowest place in it is a place of good and not of evil. And according as reprobation is regarded in one light or the other, the appeal in defence of it is made either to original sin or the principle of variety in nature.

The religious philosophy of Aquinas, then, of which these are the hints, tends simply to two different moral creations, a higher and a lower one. The natural man is created and has the advantages of his creation; the spiritual man is created and has the advantages of his: and predestination marks for a special glory, and a higher place in the universe; but exclusion from it does not involve positive evil or misery. But it is remarkable that, while he systematically hints at such a conclusion as this, in one peculiar remote and isolated case alone does he apply it— a case outside of the general mass of moral beings which it so deeply affects, and to which the substantial interest of any application of it attaches—the case of infants dying unbaptized or in original sin. Yet the elaborate and minute care with which he examines this particular case, with a view to relieving it of the pressure which the Augustinian doctrine, in its natural meaning, left upon it, is deserving of attention; as showing the strength and firmness of the basis, which, however little built upon, was formed in the mind of the writer for a general decision on this subject.

Infants dying, then, in original sin, necessarily came, according to the pure Augustinian doctrine, under the Divine wrath which was due to that sin. Being by nature reprobates, and not being included within the remedial decree of predestination, they were, in common with all the rest of mankind who were born under this curse and were not relieved by this decree, subject to the sentence of eternal punishment; which sentence was executed upon them. However repugnant, then, to natural reason and natural feeling, the Augustinian schoolman could not expressly contradict this position; but what he could not contradict he could explain. Augustine had laid down that the punishment of such children was the mildest of all punishments in hell—*omnium esse mitissimam*. Taking this as the authorised definition of the punishment of unbaptized infants, he proceeded to raise a structure of explanation upon it. First, was the punishment of such infants *sensible punishment*—*sensibilis pœna*? No; because then it would not be *mitissima*, the mildest of all. Moreover, sensible pain is a personal thing—*personæ proprium*, and therefore inappropriate to a kind of sin which is not personal. Nor could any argument be drawn from the fact, that children suffered pain in this world; because this world was not under the strict law of justice, as the next was. Nor did this immunity from pain imply in their case any invasion of the special privilege of the saints; for they enjoyed no internal impassibility, but only a freedom from external causes of suffering. Did the punishment of such infants, again, involve affliction of *soul*—*animæ afflictionem spiritualem*? No; for such affliction must arise either on account of their sin, or of their punishment—*de culpa* or *de pœna*. But if it arose on account of their sin, it would involve despair and the worm of conscience; in which case their punishment would not be the mildest one, and would therefore be opposed to the original supposition. If it arose on account of their punishment, it would involve an opposition in their will to the will of God; in which case, their will would actually be deformed —*actualiter deformis*; which would imply actual sin, and so be contrary to the original supposition.

The punishment of such children, then, not being pain either of body or mind, what is it? Aquinas answers, it is the want of the Divine Vision, or exclusion from the sight of God—*carentia Divinæ visionis, quæ est propria et sola pœna originalis peccati post mortem*; which he proves by the following argument.

Original sin, he says, is not the corruption of natural good, but the subtraction of supernatural; its final punishment therefore must correspond, and be the exclusion, not from that end to which the natural, but from that end only to which the supernatural faculties tend. But the end of the supernatural faculties is the Divine Vision. It is the want, then, of this vision which is the punishment of original sin; not the want of any good which properly belongs to nature. 'In the other perfections and goods to which nature tends upon her own principles, those condemned for original sin will sustain no detriment.'[1]

The want of the Divine Vision, however, being thus laid down as the punishment of unbaptized infants, an argumental obstacle arose from the quarter of the original definition. For, according to Chrysostom, the exclusion from the sight of God is the severest part of the punishment of the damned; at any rate the want of that which we wish to have cannot be without affliction, and unbaptized infants wish to have the sight of God—*pueri vellent Divinam visionem habere*; otherwise their wills would be actually perverse. It would therefore appear, that this want or loss would be *affliction* to them; and therefore, that, if this were their punishment, their punishment would not be the mildest of all—*mitissima*. Nor, adds Aquinas, is it any answer to this objection to say, that this exclusion does not arise from their own personal fault; for immunity from blame does not diminish, but increase the pain of punishment: or, again, correct to say, that they are happy because they do not know what they have lost; for the soul freed from the burden of the body must know whatever reason can discover—*et etiam multo plura*.

The general solution, then, of this difficulty, is, that it is no pain to any one of well-ordered mind not to have that to which his nature is in no way proportioned, provided the want is not owing to any personal fault of his own. A man regrets the disappointment of some natural want, even though he is not to blame for it; and the

---

[1] 'In aliis autem perfectionibus et bonitatibus quæ naturam humanam consequuntur ex suis principiis, nullum detrimentum sustinebunt propeccato originali damnati.'— In Lomb. l. 2. Dist. 33. Q. 2. A. 1.

exclusion from a good exceeding nature, if he is. But the combination of blamelessness in himself and excess in the good protects him. Such a case comes under the rule of Seneca, that perturbation does not fall on the wise man for that which is unavoidable; and children dying under original sin alone are wise—*sed in pueris recta est ratio nullo actuali peccato obliquata.* They will therefore feel no more pain under the want which attaches to their condition, than a reasonable man does because he cannot fly like a bird, or because he is not a king or an emperor. Rather they will rejoice in their share of the Divine bounty, and in the natural perfections they will have attained.[1]

It will be seen that the whole of this elaborate position rests upon a particular interpretation of original sin; viz., as a privation or loss of perfection, and not a positive evil. Having constructed his system on the strict Augustinian sense of original sin, Aquinas falls back on the Clementine when he comes to an individual case; and avails himself of the milder theology of the early fathers. Such a position, however, when once laid down in the case of infants dying under original sin, evidently cannot stop short of a much wider application. Man is the same, as regards his nature, whether he dies as an infant or grows up to maturity; and therefore the whole condition of the natural man, whether

[1] Sicut nullus sapiens homo affligitur de hoc quod non potest volare sicut avis, vel quia non est rex vel imperator; cum sibi non sit debitum. . . . Si ab hoc deficiant (qui liberum arbitrium habent), maximus erit dolor eis quia amittunt illud quod suum esse possibile fuit. Pueri autem nunquam fuerunt proportionati ad hoc, quod vitam æternam haberent, quæ nec eis debebatur ex principiis naturæ, nec actus proprios habere potuerunt: et ideo nihil omnino dolebunt de carentia divinæ visionis: immo magis gaudebunt de hoc quod participabunt multum de divina bonitate, et perfectionibus naturalibus.—In Lomb. A. 2.

The question came up in the disputes at the Council of Trent, in which the majority appear to have favoured the position of Aquinas; but not without distinctions; 'For the Dominicans said that the children dead without baptism before the use of reason remain after the resurrection in a limbo and darkness under the earth, but without fire; the Franciscans say they are to remain upon the earth, and in light. Some affirmed also, that they should be philosophers, busying themselves in natural things, not without that greatest pleasure which happeneth when curiosity is satisfied by invention.'—Paul's History of the Council of Trent.

heathen or professedly Christian, is involved in this conclusion, and may demand admission to the benefit of that explanation which the particular case of infants has evoked. The life which is conducted upon principles of honesty, justice, and reason, though it be not upon that of Christian faith,—the morality of the conscientious man of the world, —in a word, the well ordered natural life, though below the spiritual, may claim not to be condemned. And while the formal theology of the Augustinian allows no interval between the child of God and the child of the devil, the faithful and the unbelieving, the spiritual and the carnal man, and their respective ends, eternal happiness and eternal misery; a modification of the meaning of a term, in one particular case, undermines in principle this whole division; punishment reduced from its positive to a merely negative and privative sense, becomes another word for a lower reward, and admits to a valuable and a substantial, though not the highest, happiness, both in this life and the next, that not inconsiderable portion of mankind who are moral without being spiritual, well disposed without faith, and reasonable without illumination.

It may be added, that the difficulty involved in these considerations is one which meets us on either theory, that of necessity or of freewill. The necessitarianism indeed of Aquinas marks the natural and the spiritual life alike as creations of God; but however we may account for them, the natural life and the spiritual life, in the sense in which they have been spoken of, exist as facts in the world; and we see these two moral classes and types around us. Scripture speaks indeed, speaks only of a way which leadeth to life, and a way which leadeth to salvation; and separates the few who attain to eternal glory from a wicked world. But it must be confessed that, when we look at the world around us, the application of the truth of Scripture is not free from difficulty, and that it depends much on the frame of mind which we assume, and the point of view which we adopt, whether society at large most aptly confirms the scriptural position, or apparently contradicts it. In one aspect all is mixture and balance in the world of moral life around us,—a nicely graduated scale of human character, division gliding into division, and shade deepening or softening into shade. Men are such combinations of good and evil, that we hardly know where to place them ; and a large portion of the world seems to occupy a middle place, in opposition to the twofold destination of mankind in Scripture to glory on the one hand, and misery on the other. The idea of a middle state has thus always recommended itself more or less as a conjecture to human thought ; and a tendency to this doctrine, even where not formally expressed, is observable in all ages of the Church ; nor, so long as the facts of the world around us remain the same, will it be otherwise. In another aspect the world presents itself to our minds in harmony with the scriptural division, as consisting of the good few and the wicked and depraved mass ; vice, selfishness, and corruption appearing the general rule, to which the disinterestedness or genuine goodness of a select number is the exception. The wickedness of the world is thus a recognised maxim in the world itself; and is one of the deepest sentiments of the human mind, whose universal judgment one wise man of even heathen times expressed in the great proverb.

In this state of the case it is needless to add, that the plain statements of Scripture on this subject are to be implicitly received, as containing certain and important truth. One great division of mankind is seen there, that of good and bad ; one great distinction of eternal lot, that of heaven and hell. It remains that those who have received this revelation should act accordingly, and, instead of forming conjectures about a middle state, live as for the highest. Those who accept a revelation generally are bound in consistency to accept its plain assertions in particulars ; nor does this obligation cease because difficulties may follow. Those who accept a revelation accept in doing so a limitation to the rights of human reason. There are great and important differences in the Christian world as to the point at which such limitation comes in ; but whether traditional interpretation of Scripture, or a present infallible one, or the letter of the Bible itself is the check, a check to private judgment is implied in the very fact of a revelation, and is the common admission of all who accept that revelation; who *so far*—and a very important and vital measure of agreement it is—agree with each other. But when men have accepted the check in general, they must submit to it in the particular case. There is no obligation indeed on any one to think any individual either better or worse than his observation or knowledge of his character warrants; rather he is bound not to do so: nor, because general statements are made in Scripture are we bound to apply them, and bring particular persons under one head or another. An impenetrable veil hides the heart of one man from another, and we see the manifestation, but not the substance, of the moral creature. In the application, then, of the scriptural assertion all is mystery and uncertainty; but the statement itself is clear and distinct; and while that dispensation of ignorance under which we are placed, in mercy as well as discipline, relieves us from the difficulties of the individual case, the general truth is calculated to produce the most salutary effect upon us.

## CHAPTER XI.

### CONCLUSION.

IT were to be wished that that active penetration and close and acute attention which mankind have applied to so many subjects of knowledge, and so successfully, had been applied, in somewhat greater proportion than it has been, to the due apprehension of that very important article of knowledge, their own ignorance. Not that all men have not acknowledged, and in some sense perceived, this truth. How, indeed, could they avoid doing so? But over and above this general and vague confession of ignorance, it might have been expected, perhaps, that more would have attained, than appear to have done, to something like an accurate or philosophical perception of it; such as arises from the mind's contemplation and examination of itself, and its own perceptions; a scrutiny into its own insight into truth, and a comparison of the different modes in which it perceives and entertains truth; which modes or kinds of perception widely differ, and being with respect to some truths, distinct, complete, and absolute, are with respect to others dim, confused, and imperfect. To judge from the way in which people in general express themselves on this subject of human ignorance, they have no very accurate perception of it; seldom going out of certain commonplace phrases and forms of speech,— forms of speech, indeed, which mean much when used by those who see their true meaning, but mean much less, though still perhaps something, when used vaguely and without attention, and because the whole thing is taken for granted immediately, and then dismissed from the mind. This general admission and confession of the fact, is all that the mass of men appear to attain to on this important question; and doubtless it is, as far as it goes, a useful and serviceable conclusion of the mind—especially in the case of devout persons, whose piety compensates for the want of clearness in their ideas, and sustains in them a perpetual practical perception of this truth, together with its natural fruits of humility, sobriety, and resignation.

But though it is undoubtedly a matter of regret that more should not have attained, than appear to have done, to something like an accurate and philosophical perception of their own ignorance; the explanation of this fact is contained in the very statement of it, as just given. For this deeper perception cannot be gained, but by those minds that have gone through something of that process of thought, which has been just referred to. Men must have reflected upon themselves, and examined to a certain extent the constitution of their own minds, their perceptions, or modes of entertaining truth, in order to have gained it. But this internal department is not one in which any large proportion of men take much interest; and a taste for this kind of inspection is perhaps rarer than any other,—I mean as a taste seriously and regularly adopted, and made a work of. Many indeed start with something like a general taste or a fancy for metaphysics, which they indulge so long as it gives them little trouble, and merely ministers to pleasing vague sensations of depth, and love of the unknown and indefinite; affording a domain for dreamy and vaporous evolutions of thought, cloudy connections, and fictitious ascents of the intellect,—reasonings somewhat akin to what people carry on in sleep, and pursued as a mere diversion and vent to, rather than an exercise of, the mind. But the taste is given up as soon as they have to examine facts, to fasten their ideas upon real things,—real truths within the actual mind,—for the purpose of apprehension and knowledge. This internal field of examination, I say, is not to the taste of any large proportion of minds; because it requires a more patient sort of attention, a more enduring and passive attitude of the whole mind, than is ordinarily congenial to the human temper. The act necessary here is an act of simple internal observation, which, while it is a very difficult one in this particular department, owing to the obscurity and subtlety of its subject matter, is at the same time a quiet one; for quiet is essential to secure correctness of observation in metaphysics as in nature. But this combination is a distasteful one to most minds. In life, practical or intellectual, the general compensation for difficulty is the pleasure of action; for passiveness, that of repose. The energetic man delights in obstacles which summon forth all his powers and put them into active operation; the labour is forgotten in the satisfaction of exertion, and the legitimate play and excitement of the whole system carry off the task, and convert it into a pleasure. The natural activity of the human mind, again, so opposed to the passive attitude ordinarily, puts up with it at certain intervals, for the sake of rest, and enjoys it. But difficulty with passiveness, is uncongenial. We want always, when we are at work, to feel ourselves in progress, in action, advancing step after step; and the attitude of standing still in thought, though it be for an important result, though it be consciously only a waiting in readiness to catch some idea when it may turn up, is, for the time that it *is* such a waiting, and previous to its reward, a painful void and hollowness of the mind. But such is the attitude which is required for true analytical thought, or the mind's examination of itself. For the ideas which are the contents of that inward world, wandering in and out of darkness, emerging for an instant and then lost again, and carried about to and fro in the vast obscure, are too subtle and elusive to be subject matter of regular and active pursuit; but must be waited and watched for, with strength suspended and sustained in readiness to catch and fasten on them when they come within reach; but the exertion being that of suspended and sustained, rather than of active and employed, strength. And if this line of thought in general is opposed to the tastes of the mass, so that even a moderate degree of application to it is too much for them, and even that lower insight into this department of truth, which minds of average ability may gain, is a part of knowledge into which they are not admitted,—by what a wide and immeasurable interval are they separated from the great analytical minds which have appeared in the world, who, with unwearied patience and keen exertion of the intellectual eye, have caught sharp glimpses of the great ideas and processes of the human reason,—quick and momentary sights, which, impressed by their vividness upon the memory, and thence transferred to paper, have enabled them in a certain sense to bring the human mind to light, to mark its main outlines, and distinguish its different perceptions or ideas; by which genuine and authentic originals they have then tested current popular and second-hand truths.

This, then, is the reason why more have not attained than have to an accurate perception of their own ignorance as human creatures. For this correcter and truer perception of ignorance is the correlative of a correcter and truer knowledge. Of the human mind there is a luminous and there is a dark side. The luminous side is that on which it clearly perceives and apprehends truths, either by simple apprehension, or by demonstrative reasoning: the dark side is that on which it does not perceive in either of these two ways; but either does not see at all, and has a blank before it, or has only an incipient and indistinct sight, not amounting to perception or apprehension.[1] In proportion, then, to the acuteness with which the mind perceives truth, either by apprehension or by demonstration, on its luminous side, in that proportion it sees the defect of perception on its dark side. The clearness of knowledge, where it is had, reveals and exposes by the contrast its absence, where it is not had; and the transition from light heightens the obscurity. Each successive step of demonstrative reasoning, by which a problem in mathematics is proved, from the first up to the conclusion, is accomplished by means of a certain light contained within it—an overpowering light, to which the mind succumbs, unable to resist its penetrating force, but pierced through by it, as by lightning. Even that elementary and primary piece of demonstrative reasoning which is called an axiom,—that first inference or extraction of one truth from another, which, in the department of demonstration, we are called upon to make,—is accomplished by means of such a vivid and penetrating light contained within it; so that the perception of the simplest axiom, where such perception is a true and not a formal one, is, by reason of this perfection of light in it, an illumination for the time of the whole intellect, and may be regarded as a kind of natural inspiration, answering to passion or emotion in moral life. In proportion, then, to the keenness with which this process goes on, is the reaction from it; after the clearness of sight the change is all the greater to its dimness and indistinctness; and the reason turning, while full of penetrating light from one side, upon the darkness of the other, receives, as it were, a shock, by the violence of the contrast. The difference between seeing truth and not seeing it, between knowledge and ignorance, is felt in a degree and manner in which those who have not attained such sight or knowledge, cannot feel it. The analytical

[1] See Chapter II.

class of intellects that, not satisfied with the vague first-sight impressions and notions of things, follow them up to that ultimate point at which they are plainly seen to be either true or false,—that draw the contents of the mind from their obscurity to the test of an actual examination, —that see clearly the truth they do see, whether as simply apprehended, or as extracted from other truth;—these minds, in proportion to the keenness with which they are conscious of perceiving truth, when they do perceive it, know that they have got hold of it, and that no power can wrest it from them,—in proportion, *i.e.*, to the measure in which, in the department of knowledge, they are filled with the light of clear apprehension or demonstrative reasoning,—see the distinction between this mode of perception and that which awaits them when they leave the scientific ground, and turn from the truths of knowledge to those of faith and of religion. They see, in consequence of their appreciation of final truth, so much the more clearly the defect of that which is not final; and that which has come to a point contrasts the more strongly, with that which comes to none, but which vanishes and is gone before it reaches a conclusion ; ever beginning, ever tending to some goal, but never attaining it; stopping short, as it does, at its very starting, and, in the very act of progress, absorbed in the atmosphere of obscurity, which limits our mental view. Then, under the influence of such a contrast, it is, that, the reason pauses, stops to consider, to reflect, and then says to itself—this is ignorance.

And these considerations, while they serve to explain why more have not attained to an accurate knowledge of their own ignorance, as human creatures, than appear to have done, serve, also, to temper our regret at such a deficiency ; for it must be seen, on the bare description of such a deep and peculiar perception of ignorance as I am now referring to, that it is a state of mind not unattended by danger. No perception of ignorance, indeed, however strong, can be charged with any *legitimate* tendency to produce unbelief ; for it does not follow that, because we see some truths clearly and others obscurely, some finally and others incompletely and but in commencement, that therefore we may not hold these latter truths so far, however little way that may be, as we do perceive them, and accept and use them in that sense and manner in which we find our minds able to entertain them. And thus the truths of natural and revealed religion, incomprehensible as they are, are proper subject matter of belief. Our minds are constituted in such a way, as that we can entertain this class of truths, which are not subject matter of knowledge, and yet fall under some indistinct sort of perception, which we feel properly to belong to us. To reject them, then, because they are seen imperfectly and obscurely, and because we have the light of clear apprehension and demonstration in one department, to claim it, and be content with nothing else in another, would be simply unreasonable. The deeper sense of ignorance, then, has no legitimate tendency to lessen belief in the truths of natural and revealed religion: more than this, it has legitimately even a direct tendency to strengthen it; because the sense of ignorance tends properly to produce humility, to subdue, chasten, and temper the mind. The natural result of seeing how poor and imperfect creatures we are, and how small and limited our capacities, is to lower our idea of ourselves, and so to put us into a frame, in which we are the more ready to accept and use whatever measure and kind of truth we may possess in this department. But it must also, on the other side, be admitted, that there is a natural tendency, in such a strong contrast as that which has been described, to overwhelm that class of truths which has the disadvantage in it; and that minds which turn, full of the clear light of apprehension and reasoning, upon the obscurity of the truths of faith, will be apt to suppose that they see nothing because they do not see clearly, and that they have a simple blank before them. And the natural impatience of the human temper will much aid such a conclusion; for men are apt to see everything in extremes, and when they have less than what they want, are instantly inclined to think that they have nothing. In this temper, then, men set down the ideas belonging to religion, as not only indistinct, but as no ideas at all, but mere void ; and urge that persons are under a mistake in supposing that they have anything really in their minds when they profess to entertain these truths,—not having, as it is asserted, any *idea* of them. In this way, then, the deeper perception of ignorance tends to lessen belief in the truths of religion ; inclining persons to set them aside altogether as truths from which our understandings are entirely separated by an impassable barrier, and with which, therefore, as lying wholly outside of us, we have no concern.[1]

Such being, then, the two arguments from human ignorance, the two modes of using and applying the fact, the question is, supposing the mass of men had that distinct and clear perception of their ignorance which analytical minds acquire, how would they use it ? Would they use it for the purpose of deepening their humility, chastising their curiosity, subduing their impatience ? Would they frame themselves upon a pattern of intellectual submission and be grateful for such a measure of insight into religious truths as God had given them? or would they use and apply it in the other way, and, struck simply by the force of the contrast between their knowledge in one department and their ignorance in another, draw from it the impatient inference, that because they did not see these truths clearly, they did not see them at all, and were rationally disconnected with them? It is to be feared that the natural impatience of the human mind would, in the majority of instances, lean to the latter inference. It is indeed true, and it is a cheering and consolatory fact, that we see a broad division among the great analytical minds on this head ; and that while some have drawn the argument for unbelief from the fact of human ignorance, others have drawn from it the argument for faith ; that to Hume and Hobbes on the one side we may oppose Butler and Pascal on the other. But could we expect that the generality of men would exert that intellectual self-discipline which

[1] This appears to have been Hume's state of mind with respect to religious truths.

these devout and reverential minds did? Would not natural impatience rather prevail, and the more immediate and obvious effect of a contrast be yielded to. And if so, are not the generality of men spared a severe trial, with probably an unfavourable issue, in not having in the first instance this deeper sense of ignorance at all? Is not their ignorance veiled in mercy from them by a kind Providence; so that, with respect to these truths, they go on for their whole lives, thinking they know a great deal more than they do? Nor does this apply to the uninstructed and uncultivated part of mankind only, but perhaps even more strongly to the learned and controversial class. For, certainly, to hear the way in which some of this class argue, and draw inferences from the incomprehensible truths of revelation, carrying them, as they say, into their *consequences* and logical results, upon which, however remote and far-fetched, they yet insist, as if they were of the very substance of the primary truth itself;—to judge, I say, from the long and fine trains of inferences drawn by some theologians from mysterious doctrines,—endless distinctions spun one out of the other in succession, and issuing in subtleties which baffle all comprehension, and are, in short, mere words and nothing more, but for which, so long as at each successive step there has been an *inference* (or something which to the controversially wound-up intellect or fancy at the time appeared such),—these persons claim the most absolute deference; as if some subtlest conception of the argumentative brain, some needle's point so inconceivably minute, that not one man in ten thousand could even see it once if he tried for his whole life, were of the very foundation of the faith;—to judge, I say, from such a mode of arguing from religious truths, one cannot avoid two reflections; one, that such persons do not know their own ignorance; the other, that it is probably a mercy to them that they do not. They do not know their own ignorance with respect to these truths; for if they did, they would see that such incomprehensible truths were not known premises, and could not be argued upon as such, or made foundation of unlimited inference: and that they do not know it is probably a mercy to them; for the very same hasty and audacious temper of the intellect which leads them to build so much upon assumptions, the nature of which they have never examined, would, had they examined it, and so arrived at a real perception of their unknown nature, have inclined them to reject such truths. Thus, in compassion to the infirmity of man, a merciful Providence hides his ignorance from him; and by a kind deceit, such as parents use to their children, allows him to suppose that he knows what he does not know. He is thus saved from unbelief, and only falls into a well-meaning, though foolish and presumptuous, dogmatism.

And now, to bring these remarks to bear on the subject of this treatise, the question of Divine grace is a question of Divine Power. Grace is power. That power whereby God works in nature is called power. That power whereby He works in the wills of His reasonable creatures is called grace.

With respect, then, to the attribute of the Divine Power, S. Augustine and his school took up, in the first instance, a hasty and ill-considered position, which, once adopted, committed them to extreme and repulsive results. And the reason of their adopting such a position was, that they were insufficiently acquainted with the limits of human reason. For it must be evident to any person of reflection, that a want of discernment on this subject is not only an error in itself, but can hardly fail to be the source of other errors; because persons who entertain a certain idea with respect to their knowledge, naturally proceed to act upon it and to make assertions; and it must be a chance whether assertions made under such circumstances are correct. I would not be understood, however, to cast any blame upon these writers. The limits of human reason are not easy to discern. It is not easy, as I have said, to judge our own pretensions, and distinguish between one part and another of that whole body of ideas and assumptions which we find within our minds. Some philosophers have settled the question summarily, by saying that we know nothing; others have extended the range of human knowledge indefinitely, and given it a right to decide upon the possibilities of things, and to judge the scheme of Providence. To draw the mean between these two extremes is the work of an acute and original judgment, and requires a peculiar constitution of mind. The tendency of even deep and able minds generally is so immediately to fasten on any assumption, especially any one relating to divine things, which appears at first sight a natural one to them, that their very power becomes a snare, and before they have reflected upon an idea they are committed to it; so that to return to the preliminary question of its truth would be in the highest degree difficult to them, as being so offensive to an already formed bias. Indeed, some minds of great pretensions appear to labour under a moral inability in this respect; their intellect, strong in pursuing an idea, is so utterly unable to stop itself for the purpose of judgment, that in reference to that particular function it may be said to have almost the imperfection of a mere instinct, rather than to operate as the true faculty of reason. This mixture of singular weakness with singular power it is which makes the task of estimating authorities so difficult; opinions of the greatest value on details and collateral points being sometimes of the very least on fundamental questions, or those concerned with the soundness or unsoundness of original assumptions. Yet assumptions and particular *dicta*, laid down in the first instance by minds of this latter class, have had great weight and a long reign in the world; one writer taking them up after another; till some person of original powers of judgment has risen up who, on comparing an assertion carefully with his own knowledge, has discovered a want of connection between the two. He has not seen such truth included within that field of apprehended truth, set out and divided from that of conjecture, in his mind; and this negative discovery once made, has, like other discoveries, approved itself to the world, people seeing it when it was pointed out to them. Such a judgment passed upon any important set of assumptions is a discovery in philosophy; and in this respect modern philosophy has improved much upon the ancient.

It has given us an acquaintance with the limits of human reason which we had not before, and has enabled us to distinguish more accurately what we know from what we do not know, what we can say from what we cannot, on some important questions; it has tested the correctness of many important assumptions: but it does not follow that those are particularly to blame who wrote before such improvement in the acquaintance with the limits of human reason took place.

On this definite basis, then, and with the great disadvantage of a less accurate knowledge of the limits of human reason than has been attained in more recent times, S. Augustine and his school proceeded to the general question of the Divine Omnipotence. And they commenced with an assumption, which no modern philosopher would allow, that the Divine Power must be an absolutely unlimited thing. That the Divine Power is not liable to any *foreign* control is a principle which every one must admit who believes properly in a Deity; but that there is no intrinsic limit to it in the possibilities of things would not be admitted, in the present state of philosophy, in which this whole subject is properly understood to be out of the range of human reason. The Divine Omnipotence must be admitted *practically* and in every sense which can be wanted for the purpose of religion; but we have not faculties for speculation upon its real nature. These writers, however, insisted on an unlimited omnipotence, arguing logically upon the simple word or abstract idea, that if omnipotence was limited, it was not omnipotence. And upon this assumption they went on to assert that God could, had He pleased, have created a better universe than He has; a universe without evil and without sin; and that, sin existing in the world, He could by His simple power have removed it, and have changed the wills of all wicked men from evil to good. Upon such an idea of the Divine Power, these writers were indeed somewhat perplexed for an answer to the objection which naturally arose to the Divine Goodness. A limit supposed to the possibilities of things is indeed an impregnable defence to the theologian on this question; for no one can be blamed for not doing that which is impossible. But if this limit is not allowed, and if God could have created a universe with all the advantages of the present one and none of its evils, and if, when moral evil had begun, He could have removed it; it is certainly very difficult to answer the question why He did not; for we necessarily attribute consummate benevolence to the Deity. The explanation of such a difficulty on the principle of variety, that evil and good together, with their respective reward and punishment, redound to the glory of God more than good alone of itself would do, is futile and puerile. Variety is, *cæteris paribus,* an advantage; and we praise God's natural creation, not only because it is good, but because that good is various. Nor would it be reasonable to object to different degrees of good in the created universe; to complain because the earth was not as beautiful all over as it is at its most beautiful part, or because all the birds of the air have not the colours of the tropical birds; or even, in moral life, because all have not the same moral capabilities or power of attaining the same goodness. But when it comes to a comparison, not of like good with varied, or of higher good with lower, but of good with evil, the case is very different.

Upon this abstract idea, then, of the Divine Power, as an unlimited power, rose up the Augustinian doctrine of Predestination and grace; while upon the abstract idea of free-will, as an unlimited faculty, rose up the Pelagian theory. Had men perceived, indeed, more clearly and really than they have done, their ignorance as human creatures, and the relation in which the human reason stands to the great truths involved in this question, they might have saved themselves the trouble of this whole controversy. They would have seen that this question cannot be determined absolutely, one way or another; that it lies between two great contradictory truths, neither of which can be set aside, or made to give way to the other; two opposing tendencies of thought, inherent in the human mind, which go on side by side, and are able to be held and maintained together, although thus opposite to each other, because they are only incipient, and not final and complete truths ;—the great truths, I mean, of the Divine Power on the one side, and man's freewill, or his originality, as an agent, on the other. And this is, in fact, the mode in which this question is settled by the practical common sense of mankind. For what do the common phrases employed in ordinary conversation and writing upon this question—the popular and received modes of deciding it, whenever it incidentally turns up—amount to but this solution? Such phrases, I mean, as that we must hold man's freewill together with God's foreknowledge and predestination, although we do not see *how* they agree; and other like formulæ. Such forms of language for deciding the question evidently proceed upon the acknowledgment of two contradictory truths on this subject, which can not be reconciled, but must be held together in inconsistency. They imply that the doctrine of predestination and the doctrine of freewill are both true, and that one who would hold the truth must hold both. The plain natural reason of mankind is thus always large and comprehensive; not afraid of inconsistency, but admitting all truth which presents itself to its notice. It is only when minds begin to philosophise that they grow narrow,—that there begins to be felt the appeal to consistency, and with it the temptation to exclude truths. Then begins the pride of argument, the ingenuity of construction, the 'carrying out' of ideas and principles into successive consequences; which, as they become more and more remote, and leave the original truth at a distance, also carry the mind of the reasoner himself away from the first and natural aspect of that truth, as imperfect and partial, to an artificial aspect of it as whole and exclusive. While the judgment, however, of man's plain and natural reason on this question is a comprehensive one, men have, on this as on other subjects, left the ground of plain and simple reason for argument and philosophy; and in this stage of things they have adopted man's freewill or the Divine Power as favourite and exclusive truths, and have erected systems upon them. The Pelagian

CHAP. XI. *Conclusion.* 307

and Augustinian systems are thus both at fault, as arising upon narrow, partial, and exclusive bases. But while both systems are at fault, they are at fault in very different degrees and manners; and while the Augustinian is only guilty of an excess in carrying out certain religious ideas, the Pelagian offends against the first principles of religion, and places itself outside of the great religious ideas and instincts of the human race.

I. The predestinarian is at fault in assuming either the Divine Power, or original sin, as singly and of itself a legitimate basis of a system,—in not allowing side by side with these premisses a counter premiss of freewill and original power of choice. While he properly regards the created will as an effect, he is wrong in not also regarding it as a first cause in nature. But while this is a decided error, and an error which has dangerous moral tendencies when adopted by undisciplined minds, it is not in itself an offence against morals or piety. The predestinarian, while he insists on the will's determination from without, still allows a will; he does not regard man as an inanimate machine, but as a living, willing, and choosing creature. And as he admits a will, he assigns in every respect the same moral nature to man that his opponent does; he imposes the same moral obligations, the same duty to God and our neighbours; he inculcates the same affections, he maintains exactly the same standard in morals and religion that his opponent maintains. It is true his theory, as taken up by the careless unthinking mass, tends to immorality; for the mass will not see distinctions, and confound the predestination of the individual, as holy and virtuous, with the predestination of the individual *as such*, to eternal life; and because the end is assured, suppose it to be assured without the necessary means and qualifications for it. And such a practical tendency in the doctrine, however justly it may be charged to a misapprehension and mistake in some who adopt it, is still a reflection upon the doctrine itself; showing how truth cannot be tampered with without bad practical effects; and that exclusive and one-sided theories are a stumbling block to ordinary minds, tending to confuse their reason and moral perceptions. Still, regarding the error of the predestinarian apart from those consequences which it tends practically to produce in the minds of the vulgar, but which are not legitimately deducible from it, it cannot perhaps be called much more than a metaphysical mistake,—an overlooking of a truth in human nature ; a truth indistinctly perceived indeed, but still perceived in that sense and mode in which many other recognised truths are perceived. The predestinarian passes over the incomplete perception we have of our originality as agents, because his mind is preoccupied with a rival truth. But this cannot in itself be called an offence against piety : rather it is occasioned by a well-intended though excessive regard to a great maxim of piety. He is unreasonably jealous for the Divine Attribute, and afraid that any original power assigned to man will endanger the Divine. He thus allows the will of man no original part in good action, but throws all goodness back upon the Deity, as the sole Source and Creator of it, forming and fashioning the human soul as the potter moulds the clay. It may be said, indeed, that his doctrine, in attributing injustice to the Deity, is inconsistent with piety : but he does not attribute injustice to the Deity; but only a mode of acting, which, as conceived and understood by us, is unjust ; or which we cannot *explain* in consistency with justice.

II. Pelagianism, on the other hand, offends against the first principles of piety, and opposes the great religious instincts and ideas of mankind. It first tampers with the sense of sin. The sense of sin as actually entertained by the human mind ; that sense of it which we perceive, observe, and are conscious of, as a great religious fact—a part of our moral nature whenever sufficiently enlightened—is not a simple, but a mysterious and a complex sense ; not confined to positive action, as the occasion of it, but going further back and attaching itself to *desire*; nor attaching itself to desire only as the effect of free choice, but to desire as in some sense necessary in us, belonging to our present condition as human beings, and such as we cannot imagine ourselves, in our present state, in some degree or other not having. Mankind know and feel that sin is necessary in this world, and cannot be avoided; yet simultaneously with this sense of its necessity they mourn over it, and feel themselves blameworthy. A sense of such a peculiar kind as this, of moral evil, is indeed mysterious and incomprehensible, but it is a fact; it is a part of a whole nature which cannot be explained, made up as it is of apparent inconsistencies and contradictions. But the Pelagian would only allow so much of this whole sense of sin in human nature as he could rationally and intelligibly account for : he could understand voluntary but not necessary sin, how man's acts, but not how his nature should humble him. He therefore rejected the doctrine of original sin. And as he tampered with the sense of moral evil, so he rejected the sense of moral weakness. He could not understand that discord and opposition in the will which the Apostle expresses in the text, 'To will is present with me, but how to perform that which is good I know not; for the good that I would I do not, but the evil which I would not that I do;' and he therefore thrust it aside for a mere abstract conception of freewill, pronounced man to have a power of doing anything to which there was no physical hindrance, and placed an absolute origin and source of good in human nature. The principle of humility in human nature which leads it to eject the source of good from itself, and place it wholly in God, was thus disowned; and with it the earnest craving of human nature for an atonement for sin; for if mankind had the power to avoid sin, and if some, as he maintained, had actually lived without it, mankind did not in their corporate capacity want a Saviour; and the sense of this vital need did not belong to human nature.

And in disowning these doctrines the Pelagian at the same time opposed himself to facts. The doctrine of the Fall, the doctrine of Grace, and the doctrine of the Atonement are grounded in the instincts of mankind. It is true we receive these truths by revelation, and should not otherwise have possessed them in anything like the fulness in which we do. But when revealed they are seen to lie deep in the human conscience. The doctrine of original sin lies deep in the human heart, which has never truly and earnestly perceived its guilt at all, without coupling with it the idea of a mysterious alloy and taint antecedent to action, and coeval with its own life. And in like manner man has in all ages craved an atonement for sin; he has always ejected the source of good from himself, and referred it to God. These are religious feelings and instincts belonging to human nature, and which can never be eradicated so long as that nature remains itself. The Pelagian, then, in rejecting these doctrines, opposed himself to facts, he separated himself from that whole actual body of sentiment, instinct, and feeling which constitutes the religious life of mankind, and placed himself outside of human nature. A true system of religion must represent these facts; these large, these deep, these powerful, these penetrating, and marvellous instincts: and it is the glory of Catholic Christianity that it does this, that it expounds faithfully the creed of the human heart, that nothing in human nature is left unrepresented in it; but that in its vast and intricate fabric of doctrine is reflected, as in a mirror, every vague perception of our nature, every inexplicable fear and desire, grief and joy; every internal discord, unfinished thought, beginning of unknown truth; all that in the religious conscience, will, and affections can or cannot be understood. But the Pelagian discarded the religion of human nature and of fact, for an idea of his own mind; because his own idea was simple and intelligible, and the religion of human nature was mysterious and complex; as if, when facts were mysterious, it were anything in favour of the truth of a religion that *it* was not. Rather as if such an absence of mystery did not prove that the system was a fiction and a fancy; the artificial production of human thought, instead of a true revelation from the Author of nature, who makes all things double one of another, and who adapts His revelations to that human nature which He has made. Nature and revelation, as having the same source, are both expressions of the same truth, and must correspond with each other. If a religion is true, then, it must harmonise with that whole complex and intricate body of feelings and ideas, of which human nature is really and actually composed. The Pelagian, then, or—to take the stronger instance—the Socinian, may appeal to the simplicity and plainness of his system, that it contains no obscure and incomplete, no discordant and irreconcilable ideas; but if he does, he boasts of a religion which is self-convicted of falsehood and delusion, and is proved on its own showing to be a dream. Such a religion may satisfy a mind that has thought out a belief for itself, and has allowed a particular line of thought to lead it out of the great circle of human feelings and instincts, but it cannot satisfy the natural wants of the human heart; it may please and amuse in comfort and tranquillity, but it will not support in distress; it may be argued for, but it cannot be loved; and it may be the creed of a philosopher, but it is not the religion of man.

In this state of the case the Church has made a wise and just distinction, in its treatment of the respective errors of the Pelagian and the predestinarian; and while it has cast Pelagianism out of its communion, as a system fundamentally opposed to Christian belief, it has tolerated predestinarianism; regarding it as a system which only carries some religious ideas to an excess, and does not err in principle, or offend against piety or morals. The seventeenth article of our Church has accordingly allowed a place for a predestinarian school among ourselves; and such a school has long existed, and still exists among us. This article indeed admits of two interpretations, and may be held and subscribed to in two ways, one suiting the believer in freewill, the other the predestinarian. It may be held as containing *one side* of the whole truth respecting grace and freewill—the side, viz., of grace or the Divine Power; but not at all as interfering with any one's belief in a counter truth of man's freewill and originality as an agent. And in this sense it only excludes a Pelagian, and not such as are content to hold a mystery on this subject, and maintain the Divine Power in conjunction with man's freewill. Or, again, this article may be held as containing a complete and whole truth; *i.e.* in a definitely predestinarian sense. But as it would be unfair in the predestinarian to prohibit the qualified, so it would be unfair in the advocate of freewill not to allow the extreme mode of holding this article, or to disallow it as permitting and giving room for a pure predestinarian school within our Church. This wise and just liberty has indeed at times offended those whom the excesses of this school have roused to hostility, or whom insufficient reflection and the philosophical bias of the day have made too exclusive and dogmatic in their opinions concerning freewill; and at the close of the last century a proposal was made by a Divine who became afterwards a distinguished prelate of our Church, to ecclesiastical authority, that the terms of the seventeenth article should be altered and so framed as to give no further license to predestinarianism.[1] But a wise caution, if not a profound theology,

[1] About this time a circumstance occurred, which then excited considerable interest, and in which the part that Dr. Porteous took has been much misinterpreted and misunderstood. The following statement in his own words will place the fact in its true point of view: 'At the close of the year 1772, and the beginning of the next, an attempt was made by myself, and a few other clergymen, among whom were Mr. Francis Wollaston, Dr. Percy, now Bishop of Dromore, and Dr. Yorke, now Bishop of Ely, to induce the bishops to promote a review of the Liturgy and Articles; in order to amend in both, but particularly in the latter, those parts which all reasonable persons agreed stood in need of amendment. This plan was meant to strengthen and confirm the ecclesiastical establishment; to repel the attacks which were at that time continually made upon it by its avowed enemies; to render the 17th Article on Predestination and Election more clear and perspicuous, and less liable to be wrested by our adversaries to a Calvinistic sense, which has been so unjustly affixed to it. . . . . . On these grounds we applied in a private and respectful manner to Archbishop Cornwallis, requesting him to signify our wishes (which we conceived to be the wishes of a very large proportion, both of the clergy and laity) to the rest of the bishops, that everything might be done which could be prudently and safely done, to promote these important and salutary purposes.'

'The answer given by the Archbishop, February 11, 1773, was in these words: "I have consulted severally my brethren the bishops, and it is the opinion of the Bench in general, that nothing can in prudence be done in the matter which has been submitted to our consideration." '—Works of Bishop Porteous, vol. i. p. 38.

in the rulers of the Church at that time rejected it. And this liberty still remains a great advantage to the Church, and a signal proof at once of judgment and discretion, and of a correct and enlarged theology. It would indeed have been a fatal mistake to have excluded from our pale an aspect of Christian truth, which simply erred in a pardonable obliquity, such as is incident to minds of the highest order, to the strongest intellect, to the deepest devotion. Such an exclusion would have shown also great ignorance of antiquity and the history of Christian doctrine : for without attaching more than undue importance to a single name, it will be allowed perhaps that what S. Augustine held is at any rate a tolerable opinion, and no sufficient ground for separation either from the communion or the ministry of the Church. He is, however, only the first of a succession of authorities that from his own age to the present have maintained and taught predestinarianism within the Church. Such a proposal with respect to the seventeenth article, from the person who made it, only shows how apt minds are to be confined to the prevailing notions of their day, and to suppose that there is no room for any other truth than what happens to have been familiar to themselves. And it should operate as a warning against similar attempts, showing, as it does, what great mistakes may be made when we trust too confidently one apparent truth ; forgetting how much it might be modified, were we in possession of the whole system to which it belongs; and how easily we may be ignorant and uninformed upon those further points upon which this modification would follow.

The formularies of our own Church, following Catholic precedent, accordingly allow predestinarianism; and this is the decision of common sense and common reason on this subject. For, so long as a man thinks nothing which is inconsistent with piety, what great difference can it make, provided his actions are good, on what particular *rationale* of causation he supposes them to be done? whether he thinks them done wholly by Divine grace, or partly by an original motion of his own will coinciding with grace?

The latter is the more large and reasonable view; but whichever of the two opinions he adopts, if he only *does* his duty, that is the great thing. The object for which this present life is given us, is not philosophy and reasoning, and the arrival at speculative truth respecting even our own wills, and how they are moved; but it is self-discipline and moral action, growth in piety and virtue. So long as this practical object is attained, mistakes of mere speculation may well be passed over. Those who give these mistakes a practical direction, indeed, and from thinking erroneously proceed to act viciously, are responsible for such an application of a speculative tenet; but those who do not so apply it, are not so responsible. Numbers of pious and earnest Christians who have laboured for the welfare and salvation of their brethren, enduring thankfully fatigue and pain, and despising the riches and honours of the world, have thought that they did all this by an irresistible Divine influence in consequence of which they could not act otherwise than they did. And what if they did think so? They took a one-sided view; but if we wait till men are perfectly fair, clear, and large in their judgment before we acknowledge them as brethren, in the case of the great majority of mankind we may wait for ever.

Such is the imperfection even of the human mind, that, under Providence, a certain narrowness of judgment often works for good, and seems to favour practical energy and zeal. How universal is that disposition in men of religious ardour, enthusiasm, and activity, to over-value some one or two particular tenets, which are either true, or which they suppose to be true; appearing to think almost more about them than they do about the whole of the rest of their religious creed, containing all the broad and fundamental truths of the religion they profess! How do they cherish and foster this tendency in their minds, as if it were the most sacred and highest characteristic of their religious life! How do they idolise these special tenets, as if to part with them were to bid farewell altogether to piety and religion! And doubtless in their particular case this even might be the result. For if minds have accustomed themselves to cling with this exclusive force to particular points, and identify religion as a whole with them, who can tell the effect of the revulsion which would take place, could they be brought to doubt the truth of these? For men go from one extreme to another, and from reposing the most absolute faith upon articles resting on small evidence, rush into disbelief of those which rest upon the strongest. And if so, who would in all cases wish to try the experiment of a change? Who but a philosopher without knowledge of mankind would, for the chance of a possible advantage, endeavour in all cases to disturb even a cherished error of the minor and pardonable class? As if minor errors were not sometimes even a safeguard against greater ones; and as if an obstinate propensity of the human mind, checked in one direction, would not run out in another; like a stream which, if you dam it up in one part, breaks its bank elsewhere, and perhaps floods a whole district. Nor is this propensity to over-estimate particular truths or supposed truths confined to any one communion; the Roman Catholic and the Protestant shows it alike; most sects and divisions of the Christian world have their favourite tenets, which individuals identify with religion as a whole, and associate intimately and fundamentally with their whole Christian prospects, as if their spiritual life and sanctification were essentially bound up with them. They seem to see in such special tenets the source of all their strength, their stay, encouragement, and consolation.

The history of the human mind, I say, shows this great imperfection in it, that it is so much more able to appreciate smaller and particular truths, real or supposed, than larger and fundamental ones. There is in the first place an advantage in this respect, belonging to the former, in the very circumstance that they are smaller; they are more easily grasped, and the whole heart embraces them, and winds itself about them more completely. There is in the next place the stimulus of rivalry and contradiction, which surrounds a peculiar and distinctive, and as such, an *opposed* tenet, with a halo of its own, and invests it with an interest which does not attach to undisputed truths. The broad doctrines of revelation are defective in this appeal to our interest, because they are so broad ; and truths which all hold are thought little of comparatively, because all hold them. What merit is there in believing what everybody else believes ? We are thrown in the case of such truths upon the intrinsic gravity and importance of the truths themselves, to the exclusion of that adventitious interest which accrues from the really irrelevant and impertinent consideration of who *hold* them—that *we* maintain and accept them in distinction to *others* who do not. Men thus glory in a privilege while they pass over coldly and slightingly a common benefit. In the case of the distinctive tenet they feel themselves champions; the befrienders of truth, and not its disciples only ; its patrons, rather than its sons. Stripped of this foreign, and thrown back on its own intrinsic interest, truth is apt to be a somewhat cold and insipid thing to the majority of men—at least in their average state of mind ; though sickness or adversity will sometimes reveal to them this truth, this solid, this really sublime and native interest belonging to it. Ordinarily, they are too apt to be little interested in it, unless supported by some external aid of this kind. There is again another and a better reason than either of those which have been given for the disproportionate estimate of particular tenets ; viz. that they really suit, assist, and support particular mental, as strong medicines do particular bodily, constitutions. But whatever be the reasons for this disposition, all sects and communions more or less exhibit it ; and men, and serious and earnest men, come forward and tell us, that they could not conduct their spiritual progress without the aid of one or other special tenet, which they assert, and really imagine to be, the spring of their energies, and the mainstay of their hopes. And among the rest, the predestinarian comes forward and says this. He says that he could not, as a spiritual being, go on without this doctrine ; that he finds it essential to him ; that without it the universe would be a chaos, and the Divine dispensations a delusion ; that he reposes in it as the only true mode of asserting the Divine Love and Power; and, therefore, his only support in this life, his only security for a better life to come. He says all this, he says it from his heart; he feels it; he believes it. Then what are we to say? What, but that, however such a result may be owing to an imperfection in his mind, this doctrine is certainly to him, under this imperfection, a strength and a consolation; and that an error and an obliquity is overruled by Providence for good?[1]

Whether the time, indeed, will ever come when men in general will see that on this and some other questions truth is twofold, and is not confined to either side singly— that our perceptions are indistinct and contradictory, and therefore, do not justify any one definite position—remains to be seen. Philosophers have from time to time prophesied a day when a better understanding would commence of man with himself, and of man with man. They have risen up from the survey of the past with the idea that it is impossible that mankind can go on for ever repeating

---

[1] 'As the workings of the heart of man, and of the Spirit of God, are in general the same in all who are the subjects of grace, I hope most of these hymns, being the fruit and expression of my own experience, will coincide with the views of real Christians of all denominations. But I cannot expect that every sentiment I have advanced will be universally approved. However, I am not conscious of having written a single line with an intention either to flatter or offend any party or person upon earth. I have simply declared my own views and feelings. . . . . I am a friend of peace; and being deeply convinced that no one can profitably understand the great truths and doctrines of the Gospel any further than he is taught by God, I have not a wish to obtrude my own tenets upon others in a way of controversy; yet I do not think myself bound to conceal them. Many gracious persons (for many such I am persuaded there are) who differ from me more or less in those points which are called Calvinistic, appear desirous that the Calvinists should, for their sakes, studiously avoid every expression which they cannot approve. Yet few of them, I believe, impose a like restraint upon themselves, but think the importance of what they deem to be truth justifies them in speaking their sentiments plainly and strongly. May I not plead for an equal liberty? The views I have received of the doctrines of grace are essential to my peace: I could not live comfortably a day or an hour without them. I likewise believe, yea, as far as my poor attainments warrant me to speak, I know them to be friendly to holiness, and to have a direct influence in producing and maintaining a Gospel conversation; and therefore I must not be ashamed of them.'—Newton's Preface to the Olney Hymns.

the same mistakes ; that they must one day see the limits of human reason, distinguish what they know from what they do not know, and draw the necessary conclusion, that on some questions they cannot insist on any one absolute truth, and condemn each other accordingly. But the vision does not approach at present any very clear fulfilment. The limits of human reason are perhaps better understood in the world now than they ever were before; and such a knowledge has evidently an effect upon controversy, to a certain extent modifying and chastening it. Those who remind men of their ignorance use an argument which, however it may fall short of striking with its full philosophical strength, and producing its due effect, appeals to an undeniable truth, before which all human souls must bow. And the most ardent minds, in the very heat of controversy, have an indistinct suspicion that a strong ground has been established in this quarter. On the other hand, this knowledge of the limits of human reason is not, and perhaps never will be, for reasons which I have given, very acute or accurate in the minds of the mass; while the tendency to one-sided views and to hasty assumption is strong, and is aided by passion and self-love, as well as by better feeling misapplied. On the whole, therefore, while improved philosophy has perhaps entirely destroyed some great false assumptions which have reigned in the world, so that these will never rise up again, it cannot subdue the temper and spirit which make such assumptions. It is able occasionally to check and qualify, but it cannot be expected that it will ever habitually regulate, theological thought and controversy. It will from time to time step in as a monitor, and take advantage of a pause and quiet interval to impress its lesson upon mankind, to bring them back to reflection when they have been carried too far, and convert for the time a sense of error into a more cautious view of truth; but it will never perhaps do more than this. Unable to balance and settle, it will give a useful oscillation to the human mind, an alternation of enthusiasm and judgment, of excitement and repose.

In the meantime it only remains that those who differ

from each other on points which can never be settled absolutely, in the present state of our capacities, should remember that they may differ, not in holding truth and error, but only in holding different sides of the same truth. And with this reflection I will conclude the present treatise. After long consideration of the subject, I must profess myself unable to see on what strictly argumentative ground the two great parties in the English Church can, on the question which has occupied this treatise—viz. the operation of Divine grace, and on other questions connected with it—imagine themselves to be so fundamentally opposed to each other. All differences of opinion, indeed, even those which are obviously of a secondary and not a fundamental kind, tend to create division and separation; for all difference in its degree is apt to be a sign of some general difference of mental mould and religious temper, and men naturally consort together according to their general sympathies and turn of mind; and for men to consort with some as distinct from others, is in itself a sort of division in the body; a division, too, which, when once begun, is apt to deepen. Such an existence of preference is suggestive of positive controversy; and men once brought together upon such an understanding, and formed into groups by special sympathies, are liable to become by this very position antagonistic parties, schools, and sides. Yet the differences of opinion in our Church, on the question of grace, and on some further questions connected with it, do not appear to be sufficient to justify either party in supposing that it differs from the other fundamentally, or so as to interfere with Christian fellowship. If the question of grace is one which, depending on irreconcilable but equally true tendencies of thought in man, cannot be settled absolutely either way, it seems to follow that a difference upon it should not occasion a distance or separation. And this remark will apply to such further and more particular questions as are connected with this general question, and are necessarily affected by the view we take upon, and the mode in which we decide the general question. Such, for example, is the doctrine of baptismal regeneration. A slight consideration will be enough to show how intimately this doctrine is connected with the general doctrine of grace; and that one who holds an extreme, and one who holds a modified doctrine of grace in general, cannot hold the doctrine of baptismal regeneration in the same sense. If a latitude of opinion, then, may be allowed on the general question, it seems to follow that an equal latitude may be allowed on this further and more particular one; and that if an extreme predestinarian, and a maintainer of freewill can maintain and teach their respective doctrines within the same communion, they need not exclude each other when they come to give to their respective doctrines their necessary and legitimate application in a particular case. I cannot, therefore, but think, that further reflection will, on this and other questions, modify the opposition of the two parties in our Church to each other, and show that their disagreement is not so great as in the heat of controversy they supposed it to be. Differences of opinion there will always be in every religious communion, so long as the human mind is as variously constituted as it is, and so long as proper liberty is allowed it to express and unfold this variety. But it depends on the discretion and temper of religious men to what extent they will allow these differences to carry them; whether they will retain them upon a common basis of Christian communion and fellowship, or raise them into an occasion of separation and mutual exclusion.

# NOTES.

## NOTE I. p. 4.

TOPLADY says, 'If God had not willed the fall, He could and no doubt would have prevented it; but He did not prevent it, *ergo* He willed it; and if He willed it, He certainly decreed it.'—Vol. v. p. 242. This is a philosophical argument proceeding upon the attribute of the Divine Power; as is the following appeal to our intellectual consistency as believers in a God: 'He alone is entitled to the name of true God who governs all things, and without whose will (either efficient or permissive) nothing is or can be done. And such is the God of the Scriptures, against whose will not a sparrow can die, nor a hair fall from our heads. Now, what is predestination but the determining will of God? I defy the subtlest Semi-Pelagian in the world to form or convey a just and worthy notion of the Supreme Being without admitting Him to be the Great Cause of all causes; also Himself dependent on none; who willed from eternity how He should act in time, and settled a regular, determinate scheme of what He would do and permit to be done, from the beginning to the consummation of the world. A contrary view of the Deity is as inconsistent with reason itself, and with the very religion of nature, as it is with the decisions of revelation. . . . . Without predestination to plan, and without Providence to put that plan in execution, what becomes of God's omnipotence? It vanishes into air; it becomes a mere nonentity. For what sort of Omnipotence is that which is baffled or defeated by the very creatures it has made.'—*Toplady*, vol. v. p. 293.

## NOTE II. p. 7.

JACKSON quotes a predestinarian statement, 'That God's irresistible decree for the absolute election of some, and the absolute reprobation of others, is immediately terminated to the individual natures, substances, or entities of men, without any logical respect or reference to their qualifications;' a position to which he attaches the following consequences: 'This principle being once granted, what breach of God's moral law is there whereon men will not boldly adventure, either through desperation or presumption, either openly or secretly? For seeing God's will, which in their divinity is the only cause why the one sort are destinated to death, the other to life, is most immutable and most irresistible,—and seeing the individual entities or natures of men, unto which this irresistible decree is respectively terminated, are immutable,— let the one sort do what they can, pray for themselves, and beseech others to pray for them, they shall be damned because their entities or individual substances are unalterable: let the other sort live as they list, they shall be saved, because no corruption of manners, no change of morality finds any mutability or change in their individual natures or entities, unto which God's immutable decree is immediately terminated. Whatsoever becomes of good life or good manners, so the individual nature or entity fail not, or be not annihilated, salvation is tied unto it by a necessity more indissoluble than any chains of adamant.' —Vol. ix. p. 370.

This is perhaps a misinterpretation of the predestinarian statement quoted. The Divine decree, it is true, is, according to that statement, 'terminated to the entities of men,' and has 'no respect to their qualifications,' as the *cause or reason* of such decree; but it may still have respect to such qualifications as the *effects* of such decree. But, whatever may be said of this particular statement, such an interpretation of it, if meant for a representation of the doctrine of predestination, is very incorrect.

## NOTE III. p. 10.

AQUINAS argues for the righteousness of Adam before the fall as supernatural, or the effect of grace, on this ground: 'Manifestum est quod illa subjectio corporis ad animam, et inferiorum virium ad rationem, non erat naturalis; alioquin post peccatum mansisset, cum etiam in dæmonibus data naturalia post peccatum permanserint.'—*Sum. Theol.* 1$^{ma}$ Q. 95. Art. 1.

This necessity of grace, however, before the fall is explained by Aquinas with various distinctions, the substance of which is, that grace is wanted for supernatural virtue only by man in his upright state, but for natural as well in his corrupt; while the assistance of God as *Prime Mover*, which he distinguishes from grace, is necessary for all acts in both states. 'Homo in statu naturæ integræ potest operari virtute suæ naturæ bonum quod est sibi connaturale absque superadditione gratuiti doni, licet non absque auxilio Dei moventis.'—1$^{ma}$ 2$^{dae}$ Q. 109. Art. 3.

'Secundum utrumque statum (corruptum et integrum) natura humana indiget Divino auxilio ad faciendum vel volendum quodcunque bonum, sicut primo movente. Sed in statu naturæ integræ poterat homo per sua naturalia velle et operari bonum suæ naturæ proportionatum, quale est bonum virtutis acquisitæ; non autem bonum superexcedens, quale est bonum virtutis infusæ. Sed in statu naturæ corruptæ etiam deficit homo ab hoc quod secundum suam naturam potest, ut non possit totum hujusmodi bonum implere per sua naturalia. Quia tamen natura humana per peccatum non est totaliter corruptum, potest quidem etiam in statu naturæ corruptæ per virtutem suæ naturæ aliquod bonum particulare agere, sicut ædificare domos,' &c.

'Virtute gratuita superaddita virtuti naturæ indiget homo in statu naturæ integræ quantum ad unum, scilicet ad operandum et volendum bonum supernaturale; sed in statu naturæ corruptæ quantum ad duo scil. ut sanetur, et ulterius ut bonum supernaturale virtutis operetur.'—1$^{ma}$ 2$^{dae}$ Q. 109. Art. 2.

## NOTE IV. p. 21.

LOCKE's theory that facts, of sense or reflexion, are the sole source of our ideas, places him in a difficulty with respect to this indistinct class of ideas. He is committed to the necessity of deriving them from this source, and tries in a roundabout way to extract them from it. 'They are ultimately grounded on and derived from ideas which come in by sensation or reflexion, and so may be said to come in by sensation or reflexion.'—*First Letter to Bishop of Worcester.* But though he is in a difficulty as to their origin, and cannot combine them with his theory, he acknowledges as a fact this class of indistinct ideas. Thus the idea of substance 'is the obscure and indistinct vague idea of something which has the relation of support or substratum to modes or accidents.'—*Ibid.* 'The idea of substance is but a supposed I know not what to support those ideas we call accidents. We talk like children who, being questioned what such a thing is which they know not, readily give this satisfactory answer, that it is something.'—*Essay*, b. ii. c. 23. 'The being of substance would not be at all shaken by my saying we had but an obscure imperfect idea of it; or indeed if I should say we had no idea of substance at all. For a great many things may be, and are granted to have being, and to be in nature, of which we have no ideas. For example, it cannot be doubted but there are distinct species of separate spirits of which yet we have no distinct ideas at all.' And as he acknowledges an idea of substance which is yet no true or adequate idea, so he does of infinity. 'The addition of finite things suggests the idea of infinite by a power we find of still increasing the same. But in endeavouring to make it infinite, it being always enlarging, always advancing, the idea is still imperfect and incomplete.'—*Essay*, b. ii. c. 17.

Though Stillingfleet then presses him hard upon the origin of such ideas, it is evident that with respect to the nature of the ideas themselves Locke has greatly the advantage in the argument; that his opponent claims a distinctness for them which mental analysis rejects, and in his alarm, as if the foundations of truth were shaken when these great ideas were discovered to be incomplete and obscure, shows a radical misapprehension as to the nature of the fundamental truths, on which much of philosophy and the whole of religion rests. No error can be greater than that of supposing that, when ideas are obscure, they are not rational ones, and then to add, as Stillingfleet does, 'if we cannot come at the rational idea' of a thing, 'we can have no principle of certainty to go upon.' Religion rests upon a set of truths which exactly miss the condition of rational truth here laid down. To disprove this condition, then, to lay down the consistency of a rational character with an obscure and indistinct one in ideas, is not to overthrow religion, but support it on the most essential head. So surely do we find that no discoveries in philosophy, metaphysical or natural, really turns out to the injury of the faith.

Hume, as Locke, acknowledges virtually this class of indistinct ideas, though not definitely and as a class. Thus, while showing with such extreme acuteness that we have no *idea* of a cause, he allows the *thing*; asserting strongly the necessity of attributing the existence of the world to a cause. 'When our contemplation is so far enlarged as to contemplate the first rise of this visible system, we must adopt with the strongest conviction the idea of some intelligent cause.'—*Natural History of Religion*, sect. xv. But we could not lay it down that a cause was necessary unless we had some idea of one. What is this then but to say, that we have some idea, but not a true one, of a cause,—an obscure, incipient idea. The very acuteness with which the philosopher has proved that we have 'no idea' of a cause thus turns to the establishment of this kind of truth that I am speaking of, obscure, incipient, or mysterious truth. Hume acknowledges too the existence of 'a vulgar, inaccurate idea of power.'—*Enquiry concerning the Human Understanding*, sect. vii. But what is this vulgar, inaccurate idea, but an idea which all mankind have, an instinct, or indistinct perception?

## NOTE V. p. 25.

MR. MILL's argument in favour of the doctrine of necessity consists of two parts: one the proof of the doctrine; the other an answer to an objection to it.

His proof of the doctrine is an inductive one. What do we mean by necessity, he asks, but causation; that, the antecedents supposed, a certain consequent will follow? Now, we observe, he says, this law of causation in every *other* department: we must therefore suppose it to exist in the department of the human will. For the proof of the existence of this law in other departments he refers us to facts, and simply appeals to observation. 'Between the phenomena which exist at any instant, and the phenomena which exist at the succeeding instant, there is an invariable order of succession .... To certain facts certain facts always do, and, as we believe, will continue to, succeed. The invariable antecedent is termed the cause; the invariable consequent the effect. And the universality of the law consists in this, that every consequent is connected in this manner with some particular antecedent or set of antecedents. Let the fact be what it may, if it has begun to exist it was preceded by some fact or facts with which it is invariably connected. For every event there exists some combination of object or events, some given concurrence of circumstances, positive and negative, the occurrence of which is always followed by the phenomenon. We may not have found out what this concurrence of circumstances may be; but we never doubt that there is such a one, and that it never occurs without having the phenomenon in question as its effect or consequence. On the universality of this truth depends the possibility of reducing the inductive process to rules.' —Vol. i. p. 338.

Here is an appeal to our observation for a proof of the law of causation. Mr. Mill does not go to any *à priori* ground on this question, or avail himself of the maxim that every event *must* have a cause. He does not appeal to any instinct of reason antecedently demanding a cause for every event; nor does he attach to the term cause any sense of necessary and inherent efficiency and productiveness in relation to its effect —' any such mysterious compulsion now supposed, by the best philosophical authorities, to be exercised by the cause over its effect.'—Vol. ii. p. 407. By cause and effect he simply means antecedent and consequent; and he appeals to our simple observation for the proof of the existence of this order and succession in things around us.

Now, it would be obviously begging the question to assert that we *observe* this uniform order and succession in the events in which the human will takes part; this would be asserting to begin with what has to be proved—viz. that this law of causation exists in the department of the human will; besides, that it would be asserting our observation of something which we evidently do not observe. For whatever uniformity we may observe in the conduct of mankind as a mass, however like one generation of men may be to another, and a preceding age of the world to a succeeding one, in general moral features and the principles on which the race is governed and acts, we evidently do not observe this uniformity in the case of individuals. And it is the case of the individual which tries the theory of necessity or causation as applying to the human will. Upon the ordinary doctrine of chances there will be much the same amount of virtue and vice in one generation that there is in others, and the same general exhibition of character will take place. The doctrine of necessity requires that the *individual* will act in the same way under the same circumstances. And this latter fact we certainly do not *observe*. Mr. Mill, then, in appealing to our observation for a proof of the law of causation, must mean to exclude from the events in which this is *observed* those in which the human will takes part; *i.e.* to appeal to our observation of material nature only. And therefore his argument, when he comes to assert this law as prevailing in the department of will, is one of induction,—the common argument from the known to the unknown. We know, he says, that this is the law upon which one large class of events takes place; we must therefore suppose it to be the law upon which another class of events, with respect to which we have not this knowledge, takes place; we observe this law in the physical world, we must therefore presume that it prevails in the moral as well.

Of such an argument as this, then, it will, perhaps, be enough to remark, that it appears to be nothing more than a presumption at the best. One class of events takes place according to a certain law; therefore another does. Is this a proof to satisfy any reasonable mind ? Such an induction is, on the first showing, in the highest degree weak and conjectural. But when we compare matter and will, and distinguish the entirely different impressions which we have with respect to our actions, and events in nature, the induction breaks down still more. Why should we suppose that events so totally different in all their characteristics, as those which take place in matter and will, should take place on the same law; and presume that, because causation or necessity rules in the physical world, it therefore does in the moral?

But while I interpret Mr. Mill's argument as an inductive one—which indeed appears to be the only kind of argument which *observation* enables him to use,—I must at the same time allow that Mr. Mill in other passages does not appear altogether to interpret his own argument in this way; and that he seems to imagine that he has more than an inductive, *i.e.* presumptive, argument—viz. one of actual consciousness and experience in his favour, on this question. 'Correctly conceived,' he says, 'the doctrine called Philosophical Necessity is simply this: that, given the motives which are present to an individual mind, and given likewise the character and disposition of the individual, *the manner in which he will act may be unerringly inferred*; that if we know the person thoroughly, and know all the inducements which are acting upon him, we could foretell his conduct with as much certainty as we

## Note V.

can predict any physical event. *This proposition I take to be a mere interpretation of universal experience, a statement in words of what every one is internally convinced of.* No one who believed that he knew thoroughly the circumstances of any case, and the characters of the different persons concerned, would hesitate to foretell how all of them would act. Whatever degree of doubt he may feel arises from the uncertainty whether he really knows the circumstances or the character of some one or other of the persons with the degreee of accuracy required; but by no means from thinking, that if he did know these things, there would be any uncertainty what the conduct would be. Nor does this *full assurance* conflict in the smallest degree with what is called our feeling of freedom.'—Vol. ii. p. 406.

I quote this passage not for the statement it contains of the doctrine of necessity so much as to call attention to the *ground* of that statement,—the nature of the argument or evidence on which the writer appears to suppose that doctrine of necessity rests. ' This proposition,' he says, ' I take to be a mere interpretation of universal experience, a statement in words of what every one is internally convinced of;' the proposition, viz. that the inducements internal and external to action supposed, the action of an individual may be predicted with as much certainty as we can predict any physical event. Mr. Mill then appeals to actual *experience*, and to *internal conviction* or consciousness, as the evidence of the doctrine of necessity. Now, if Mr. Mill were content to mean by this experience and internal conviction of necessity to which he appeals, such an indistinct or half-perception of a truth in this direction as is consistent with the same kind of perception of the contrary truth of our originality as agents, I would agree with him; and I have in this chapter accepted the necessitarian maxim, that every event must have a cause, as supplying one side of the truth on this question. But it is evident that Mr. Mill means something more than this; his argument, as an advocate of necessity *against* originality, requires a full and distinct experience and conviction on the side of necessity, not a divided one. Moreover, the ground on which he has placed the whole doctrine of necessity or causation is a ground of *observation*—that we see things, as a matter of fact, taking place in a certain order and succession. When he appeals, then, to an internal experience and conviction on the side of necessity, his argument requires him to appeal to such a full internal conviction as is grounded on observation. But can Mr. Mill really mean to assert that we *observe* a law of causation in operation in our actions, as we do in the events of the physical world? Such an assertion would be plainly untrue, and he himself would be the first to disown it; for he explains how it is that we *cannot* observe such a law in the case of human actions, as we do in nature; viz. that we have not the full antecedents before us in the former case as we have in the latter; that we do not know all the inducements, internal and external, operating in a man, and, therefore, cannot predict with accuracy what his action will be. But then what becomes of that experience and internal conviction to which he appeals on this question? If we are not able to make the *observation* that we act by a law of causation, how can we have the *experience* and the *internal conviction* that we do? What sort of conviction, on his own showing, must that be, which has positively no observation to rest upon?

The state of the case, then, appears to be this: Mr. Mill begins with an inductive or presumptive argument on this question, which, as he proceeds and advances in his explanation of it, becomes insensibly from an inductive argument, an appeal to 'internal conviction,' or consciousness. And instead of saying, the law of causation exists in the case of physical events, therefore we may *presume* it does in the case of moral ones or actions—he says at once we see, we know, we are internally convinced, we have actual experience, that our actions take place upon this law.

Having established, however, whether by induction or experience or internal conviction, necessity or the law of causation, as the law upon which the acts of the human will proceed, Mr. Mill has to meet an objection to such a position which naturally and immediately arises from our consciousness of freedom as agents. 'To the universality which mankind are agreed in ascribing to the law of causation there is one claim of exception, one disputed case, that of the human will; the determinations of which a large class of metaphysicians are not willing to regard as following the causes called motives, according to as strict laws as those which they suppose to exist in the world of mere matter. This controverted point will undergo a special examination when we come to treat particularly of the logic of the moral sciences. In the meantime I may remark that metaphysicians, who, it must be observed, ground the main part of their objection on the supposed repugnance of the doctrine in question to our consciousness, seem to me to mistake the fact which consciousness testifies against. What is really in contradiction to consciousness, they would, I think, on strict self-examination, find to be the application to human actions and volitions of the ideas involved in the common use of the term necessity, which I agree with them in objecting to. But if they would consider that by saying that a person's actions necessarily follow from his character, all that is really meant (for no more is meant in any case whatever of causation) is that he invariably *does* act in conformity to his character, and that any one who thoroughly knew his character could certainly predict how he would act in any supposable case, they probably would not find this doctrine either contrary to their experience or revolting to their feelings.'—Vol. i. p. 358.

I will stop, in the first place, to ask, what is meant by the word 'character,' in the assertion that 'a person's actions necessarily follow from his " character " ?' If the term *character* here *includes* a man's whole conduct and action, this assertion amounts to nothing. If the term means simply a certain general disposition and bias of mind, then the assertion is without proof; the assertion, I mean, that from this general disposition a particular act will follow. The main object of this passage, however, is to meet the objection to the doctrine of necessity proceeding from our consciousness of freedom as agents; an objection which Mr. Mill meets with a distinction between necessity in the sense of causation, and necessity in the '*common* use of the term,' viz. as coaction or force; necessity in the former sense not being opposed to our consciousness. The same answer is contained in the following passage: 'The metaphysical theory of freewill as held by philosophers (for the practical feeling of it, common in a greater or less degree to all mankind, is in no way inconsistent with the contrary theory) was invented because the supposed alternative of admitting human actions to be *necessary* was deemed inconsistent with every one's instinctive consciousness, as well as humiliating to the pride and degrading to the moral nature of man. Nor do I deny that the doctrine, as sometimes held, is open to these imputations; for the misapprehension in which I shall be able to show that they originate, unfortunately is not confined to the opponents of the doctrine, but participated in by many, perhaps we might say by most, of its supporters.'—Vol. ii. p. 405.

Now, it must be admitted that the doctrine of necessity is not opposed to any express and distinct consciousness on our part, for all that we are distinctly anxious of is our willing itself; we have no positive apprehension or perception of anything beyond that fact, *i.e.* of the *source* of such willing, whether this is in ourselves, or beyond and outside of us. But though we have no distinct apprehension of our own originality as agents, is there not an instinctive perception in that *direction*? Does not the whole manner in which we find ourselves, willing and choosing, debating between conflicting lines of action, and then deciding on one or other of them, lead us towards an idea of our own originality as agents, and produce that impression upon us? Would not any person, holding to his natural impression on this head, be disappointed by any explanation of these characteristics of human action, which accounted for them on any *rationale* short of originality? Would he not feel that there was something passed over, not duly acknowledged, and recognised, in any *rationale* which stopped short of this? You might explain to him that his will being caused from without did not imply any force or coaction, but that he might have all the sensations of voluntary agency while he was still really acting from causes ultimately beyond his own control; but such an explanation would not satisfy him. The feeling he has that he can decide either way in the case of any proposed action, and the regret or pleasure that he feels afterwards, according to the use which he has made of this apparent power, will make him think himself an original agent, and he will be dissatisfied with any *rationale* of his action which stops short of this.

Mr. Mill is indeed sufficiently aware of the strength of this natural conviction of originality in the human mind, to be induced to meet and satisfy its demands as far as he can in consistency with his theory; but he cannot, because his theory prevents him, really satisfy them. He admits, however, for the purpose of satisfying this claim, that a man can in a certain sense form his own character, and is an agent acting upon himself, and he draws a distinction on this head between the necessarian and the fatalist; the former of whom, according to him, allows, in keeping with true philosophy, this agency upon self, while the latter, carried away by the fallacy that the certainty of the end supersedes the necessity of the means or subordinate agencies, denies it. " A fatalist believes, or half believes (for nobody is a consistent fatalist), not only that whatever is about to happen will be an infallible result of the causes which produce it (which is the true necessarian doctrine), but, moreover, that there is no use struggling against it; that it will happen however we may strive to prevent it. Now, a necessarian believing that our actions follow from our characters, and that our characters follow from our organisation, our education, and our circumstances, is apt to be, with more or less of consciousness on his part, a fatalist as to his actions, and to believe that his nature is such, or that his education and circumstances have so moulded his character, that nothing can now prevent him from feeling and acting in a particular way, or at least that no effort of his own can hinder it. In the words of the sect (Owenite) which in our own day has most perniciously inculcated and most perversely misunderstood this great doctrine, his character is formed *for* him, and not *by* him; therefore his wishing that it had been formed differently is of no use, he has no power to alter it. But this is a grand error. *He has to a certain extent a power to alter his character. Its being in the ultimate resort formed for him is not inconsistent with its being in part formed by him as one of the intermediate agents.* His character is formed by his circumstances (including among these his particular organisation); but his own desire to mould it in a particular way is one of those circumstances, and by no means one of the least influential. We cannot, indeed, directly will to be different from what we are; but neither did those who are supposed to have formed our characters directly will that we should be what we are. . . . We are exactly as capable of making our own character, *if we will*, as others are of making it for us.'—Vol. ii. p. 410.

Here is an attempt, then, to represent the necessarian system in such an aspect as to reconcile it with all those sensations of power over ourselves and over our conduct, which are part of our internal experience. But the attempt fails, because it will not go the proper length of acknowledging such power as an original one. A man 'has, to a certain extent, a power to alter his own character.' To what extent, or in what sense? While it is 'in *the ultimate resort* formed *for* him, it is formed by him *as one of the intermediate agents*.' But does this concession of an intermediate agency satisfy the demands of natural feeling and instinct on this head? Would any person naturally regard that power of choice, of which he is conscious, as a power which he exerts in obedience and subordination to some deeper cause working underneath it, and obliging it to be exerted in a particular way? Would not a certain instinctive view he takes of this agency in him be contradicted by this view of it as *intermediate*

## Note V. 335

agency, only apparently original, and really produced by a cause beyond itself? Would not his internal sensations appear upon such a view to him a spurious outside, a kind of semblance and sham, pretending something which was not really true, and deluding him into thinking that he was an original agent when he really was not?

While, then, I fully admit, in addition to these ideas and sensations of originality and free agency, other ideas counter to them—another side of the human mind to which philosophy and theology have alike legitimately appealed, and without which neither necessarianism nor the doctrine of original sin would have arisen—I cannot think that Mr. Mill does justice to these ideas—these true perceptions, it appears to me, as far as they go—of our originality as agents.

Hume's argument on Liberty and Necessity is a very summary one. He does not, as Mr. Mill, in the first instance, appears to do, from the observed fact of causation or necessity in the physical world, *presume* the same thing in the moral; he boldly appeals at once to what he considers to be an obvious and plain fact of observation. He considers necessity, or the law of antecedent and consequent, to be as plain and obvious in the case of human actions as it is in the events of material nature. 'Our idea,' he says, 'of necessity or causation arises entirely from the uniformity observable in the operations of nature. Where similar objects are constantly conjoined together, and the mind is determined by custom to infer the one from the appearance of the other, these two circumstances form the whole of that necessity which we ascribe to matter. Beyond the constant conjunction of similar objects, and the consequent inference from one to the other, we have no idea of any necessity of connexion. If it appear, therefore, that all mankind have ever allowed, without any doubt or hesitation, that these two circumstances take place in the voluntary actions of men, and in the operations of mind, it must follow that all mankind have ever agreed in the doctrine of necessity, and that they have hitherto disputed merely from not understanding one another.'

'As to the first circumstance, the constant and regular conjunction of similar events, we may perfectly satisfy ourselves by the following considerations. It is universally acknowledged that there is a great uniformity among the actions of men, in all nations and ages, and that human nature remains still the same in its principles and operations. The same motives always produce the same actions; the same events follow the same causes. Ambition, avarice, self-love, vanity, friendship, generosity, public spirit; these passions, mixed in various degrees, and distributed throughout society, have been from the beginning of the world, and still are, the sources of all the actions and enterprises which have ever been observed among mankind. Would you know the sentiments, inclinations, and course of life of the Greeks and Romans, study well the temper and actions of the French and English. You cannot be much mistaken in transferring to the former *most* of the observations you have made with regard to the latter. Mankind are so much the same, in all times and places, that history informs us of nothing new or strange in this particular. Its chief use is only to discover the constant and universal principles of human nature, by showing man in all varieties of circumstances and situations, and furnishing us with materials from which we may form our observations, and become acquainted with the regular springs of human action and behaviour. These records of war, intrigues, factions, and revolutions are so many collections of experiments by which the politician or moral philosopher fixes the principles of his science, in the same manner as the physician or natural philosopher becomes acquainted with the nature of plants, minerals, and other external objects by the experiments which he forms concerning them. Nor are the earth, water, and other elements examined by Aristotle and Hippocrates more like to those which at present lie under our observation, than the men described by Polybius or Tacitus are to those who now govern the world.'—Section viii. *On Liberty and Necessity*, v. iv. p. 98.

No argument on the side of necessity in human actions can be simpler than this; and if there is any weight in it, the question is decided beyond controversy; for it is simply an appeal to our *observation* that such is the case, an assertion that necessity is as *visible* in human actions as it is in the events of nature. But any reader of common intelligence must see at once a fundamental error underlying this whole argument, which entirely deprives it of force. The uniformity which the writer observes in human life and conduct applies to mankind as a whole; while the principle of necessity can only be properly tested by the conduct of men as individuals. On the common doctrine of chances, mankind as a whole will be much the same in one generation and age of the world that it is in another; *i.e.* there will be the same proportion of good to bad men, the same relative amount of selfish and disinterested, generous and mean, courageous and cowardly, independent and servile characters. But the doctrine of necessity is concerned with the individual cases which compose this general average of human character; and the question upon which that doctrine turns is, whether individuals with the same antecedents—*i.e.* the same inducements, external and internal, to particular conduct—have uniformly acted in the same way. The sum total may be the same, but the question of necessity is concerned with the units which compose that sum. Have the individuals who have been bad and good, selfish and disinterested, been so in conjunction with different respective sets of antecedents; *i.e.* different circumstances, education and natural temperament? Or, have not persons under apparently the same circumstances, education, and natural temperament, turned out very differently? The latter is certainly the more natural observation of the two. But if we are forbidden to make it, and reminded that we do not know all the antecedents, circumstances, and motives, internal and external, to conduct, in the case of individuals; then at any rate nobody can pretend to have made the contrary observation, or profess to have noted a uniform conjunction of antecedents and consequents in the case of human action. And with the absence of this observation the whole of this argument falls to the ground.

## NOTE VI. p. 32.

FUIT Adam et in illo fuimus omnes.—Ambrose, Lib. 7. *in Luc.* c. 15, 24. n. 234. In lumbis Adam fuimus.—Aug. *Op. Imp.* l. 1. c. 48. Unusquisque homo cum primo nascitur.—*De Gen. Contr. Man.* l. 1. c. 23. Sic autem aliena sunt originalia peccata propter nullum in eis nostræ voluntatis arbitrium, ut tamen propter originis contagium esse inveniantur ut nostra.— *Op. Imp.* l. 1. c. 57.

Inobedientia quidem unius hominis non absurde utique delictum dicitur alienum, quia nondum nati nondum egeramus aliquid proprium, sive bonum sive malum: sed quia in illo qui hoc fecit, quando id agit, omnes eramus . . . . hoc delictum alienum obnoxia successione fit nostrum.—*Op. Imp.* l. 2. c. 163.

Ipsos quoque hoc in parente fecisse, quoniam quando ipse fecit, in illo fuerunt, ac sic ipsi atque ille adhuc unus fuerunt.—*Op. Imp.* l. 2. c. 177.

Disce, si potes, quemadmodum peccata originalia, et aliena intelligantur et nostra; non eadem causa aliena qua nostra: aliena enim, quia non ea in sua vita quisque commisit, nostra vero quia fecit Adam, et in illo fuimus omnes. —*Op. Imp.* l. 3. c. 25.

Malum est de peccato veniens originis vitium, cum quo nascitur homo . . . cujus mali reatus non innocentibus, ut dicis, sed reis imputatur. . . . Sic enim fuerunt omnes ratione seminis in lumbis Adam, quando damnatus est, et ideo sine illis damnatus non est; quemadmodum fuerunt Israelitæ in lumbis Abrahæ quando decimatus est, et ideo sine illis decimatus non est.—*Op. Imp.* l. 5. c. 12.

Per unius illius voluntatem malam omnes in eo peccaverunt, quando omnes ille unus fuerunt.—*De Nupt. et Conc.* l. 2. n. 15.

S. Anselm regards that corruption of nature which is *in* the infant at its birth as sin then and at the time *in* the infant—*cum debito satisfaciendi*; so that it is his own sin and not another's for which he is responsible in his responsibility for original sin (*De Pec. Orig.* c. 2.) ; a position to which he proceeds to give further, and very strong and exact expression : 'Originale peccatum esse injustitiam dubitari non debet. Nam si omne peccatum injustitia, et originale peccatum utique est et injustitia. Sed si dicit aliquis : non est omne peccatum injustitia, dicat posse simul in aliquo et esse peccatum, et nullam esse injustitiam : quod videtur incredibile. Si vero dicitur originale peccatum non esse absolute dicendum peccatum, sed cum additamento, originale peccatum, sicut pictus homo non vere homo est, sed vere est pictus homo, profecto sequitur quia infans qui nullum habet peccatum nisi originale mundus est a peccato. . . . . Quare omne peccatum est injustitia, et originale peccatum est absolute peccatum.' —C. 3.

Aquinas is against the imputation of another's act for the purpose of guilt, though he allows it for that of satisfaction : 'Dicendum quod si loquamur de pœna satisfactoria, quæ voluntarie assumitur, contingit quod cum unus portet pœnam alterius, in quantum sunt quodammodo unum. Si autem loquimur de pœna pro peccato inflicta, in quantum habet rationem pœnæ, sic solum unusquisque pro peccato suo punitur, quia actus peccati aliquid personale est.'—*Sum. Theol.* 1$^{ma}$ 2$^{dae}$ Q. 87. Art. 8.

The disputes at the Council of Trent on the subject of original sin touched more on the extent of the effects of it than on the *rationale* of its transmission. But the view of imputation was maintained by Catarinus against the Dominicans, who followed the Augustinian idea of original sin as real sin in the individual. 'He oppugned the transmission of sin by means of the seed and generation ; saying that, as, if Adam had not sinned, righteousness would have been infused not by virtue of the generation, but only by the will of God, so it is fit to find another means to transfuse sin. . . . . The action of Adam is actual sin in him, and *imputed* to others is original; because when he sinned all men did (*i.e.* by imputation) sin with him. Catarinus grounded himself principally, for that a true and proper sin must be a voluntary act, and no other thing can be voluntary but the transgression of Adam imputed unto all. . . . The opinion of Catarinus was expressed by a political conceit of a bargain made by one for his posterity, which, being transgressed, they are all undoubtedly bound.'—*Paul's History of Council of Trent* (Brent), pp. 165. 168.

## NOTE VII. p. 33.

JEREMY TAYLOR'S argument on original sin is directed throughout against the received and Catholic interpretation of that sin, as involving desert of eternal punishment, which he rejects as being opposed to our natural idea of justice. 'Was it just in God to damn all mankind to the eternal pains of hell for Adam's sin committed before they had any being, or could consent to it or know of it? If it could be just, then anything in the world can be just; and it is no matter who is innocent, or who is criminal, directly or by choice, since they may turn devils in their mother's bellies; and it matters not whether there be any laws or no, since it is all one that there be no laws, and that we do not know whether there be or no; and it matters not whether there be any judicial proofs, for we may as well be damned without judgment, as be guilty without action.'—Vol. ix. p. 332. 'And truly, my Lord, to say that for Adam's sin it is just in God to condemn infants to the eternal flames of hell, and to say that concupiscence or natural inclinations before they pass into any act would bring eternal condemnation from God's presence into the eternal portion of devils, are two such horrid propositions, that if any church in the world should expressly affirm them, I, for my part, should think it unlawful to communicate with her in the defence or profession of either, and to think it would be the greatest temptation in the world to make men not to love God, of whom men so easily speak such horrid things.'—p. 373. 'Is hell so easy a pain, or are the souls of children of so cheap, so contemptible a price, that God should so easily throw them into hell? God's goodness, which pardons many sins that we could avoid, will not so easily throw them into hell for what they could not avoid.'—p. 14.  'To condemn infants to hell for the fault of another, is to deal worse with them than God did to the very devils, who did not perish but by an act of their own most perfect choice. This, besides the formality of injustice or cruelty, does add and suppose a circumstance of a strange, ungentle contrivance. For, because it cannot be supposed that God should damn infants or innocents without cause, it finds out this way, that God, to bring His purposes to pass, should create a guilt for them, or bring them into an inevitable condition of being guilty by a way of His own inventing. For, if He did not make such an agreement with Adam, He beforehand knew that Adam would forfeit all, and therefore that unavoidably all his posterity would be surprised. This is to make pretences, and to invent justifications and reasons of His proceedings, which are indeed all one as if they were not.'—p. 16. 'Abraham was confident with God, "Wilt Thou slay the righteous with the wicked? shall not the Judge of all the earth do right?" And if it be unrighteous to slay the righteous with the wicked, it is also unjust to slay the righteous for the wicked. "*Ferretne ulla civitas laborem istiusmodi legis, ut condemnetur filius aut nepos, si pater aut avus deliquissent*;—It were an intolerable law, and no community would be governed by it, that the father or grandfather should sin, and the son or nephew should be punished."'—p. 39.

No one can, of course, deny the force of these arguments, resting, as they do, upon the simple maxim of common sense and common justice, that no man is responsible for another's sins. The mistake in Jeremy Taylor's mind lies in his conception of the doctrine which he is attacking. He supposes the doctrine of original sin to assert mankind's desert of eternal punishment for Adam's sin, in an ordinary and matter-of-fact sense; and he treats all the consequences of this doctrine—the Divine anger with infants and the like—as if they took place in the literal sense in which they would take place, supposing a present visible execution of this sentence, in this present and visible state of things. But the doctrine of original sin professes to be concerned with a mystery, not with a matter of fact, and to be an incomprehensible, and not an intelligible truth. For all this vivid picture, then, of injustice, and monstrous cruelty which Jeremy Taylor raises as a representation of this doctrine, there is no warrant; because the doctrine does not profess to assert anything whatever that we can understand. He argues as if human analogies gave us a sufficient and true idea of the truth asserted in this doctrine, whereas the doctrine takes us out of all human analogies. His whole argument thus beats the air, and he refutes what no sound-minded and reasonable person asserts.

His argument against the assertion of the impotence and slavery of the will, involved in the doctrine of original sin, is open to the same remark; *i.e.* that he takes it as an *absolute* assertion, whereas it is only maintained in this doctrine as *one side* of a whole truth on this subject, which is beyond our knowledge. 'To deny to the will of man powers of choice and election, or the use of it in the actions of our life, destroys the immortality of the soul. Human nature is in danger to be lost if it diverts to that which is against nature! For if it be immortal it can never die in its noblest faculty. But if the will be destroyed, that is, disabled from choosing (which is all the work the will hath to do), then it is dead. For to live and to be able to operate in philosophy are all one. If the will, therefore, cannot operate, how is it immortal? And we may as well suppose an understanding that can never understand, and passions that can never desire or refuse, and a memory that can never remember, as a will that cannot choose.'— Vol. ix. p. 47. 'When it is affirmed in the writings of some doctors that the will of man is depraved, men presently suppose that depravation is a natural or physical effect, and means a diminution of power, whereas it signifies nothing but a being in love with, or having chosen an evil object, and not an impossibility or weakness to the contrary, but only because it will not; for the power of the will cannot be lessened by any act of the same faculty, for the act is not contrary to the faculty, and therefore can do nothing towards its destruction. As a consequent of this I infer that there is no natural necessity of sinning,—that there is no sinful action to which naturally we are determined; but it is our own choice that we sin.'—p. 88.

This is the Pelagian argument for freewill which we meet with in S. Augustine; and it has the one-sidedness of that argument. Nobody, of course, can deny what is asserted here, if considered as one side of the truth; it is true that the will must have the power of choosing; that we are conscious of this power; that there is 'no natural necessity for sinning;' that 'there is no sinful action to which we are naturally determined.' All this enters into our meaning of the term will, and our consciousness of its operations. But there is another side of the whole truth respecting the will to which S. Augustine appeals: 'To will is present with me, but how to perform that which is good I know not. For the good that I would I do not, but the evil that I would not that I do. Jeremy Taylor appeals, as the Pelagians did, to a certain sense of *bare ability* to do right which we retain under all circumstances and states of mind, as if it were the whole truth on this subject; he relies absolutely upon it. He goes even to the length to which the Pelagians went, of saying 'that the power of the will cannot be lessened by any act of the same faculty,' so that however long a man may continue in a course of sin, and however inveterate the habit he may contract, he has still as much freewill as ever, and on the very next occasion of acting is as *able* to act aright as ever. But this is evidently, and on principles of common sense, untrue. Jeremy Taylor sees only that side of the human will which favours his own argument; he sees in it a simple unity, a pure undivided faculty, a power of doing anything to which there is no physical hindrance; but the will is a mixed and complex thing, exhibiting oppositions and incongruities. He proceeds upon an abstract idea of freewill —'there cannot be a will that cannot choose;' but the question is, what is the actual and real will of which we find ourselves possessed?

Taylor sees in the doctrine of original sin, according to the received strict interpretation of it, a basis of the doctrine of predestination (p. 319), and argues against them as virtually one and the same doctrine; in doing which he is right. But if the ground is only true in a mysterious sense, that which is raised upon it is only true in the same sense, and is so deprived of its definiteness, and consequently of its harshness; for a doctrine to be harsh must positively state something. As a mystery it disowns such a charge.

The received interpretation of original sin being thus rejected, Jeremy Taylor substitutes for it the more lenient interpretation put forward by the early fathers of this sin, as a deprivation, viz. of certain higher and supernatural gifts conferred upon man at his creation; an absence of perfection, as distinguished from a positive state of sin. 'This sin brought upon Adam all that God threatened— but no more. A certainty of dying, together with the proper effects and affections of mortality, were inflicted on him, and he was reduced to the condition of his own nature, and then begat sons and daughters in his own likeness, that is, in the proper temper and constitution of mortal men. For as God was not bound to give what He never promised—viz., an immortal duration and abode in this life,—so neither does it appear, in that angry intercourse that God had with Adam, that he took from him or us any of our natural perfections, but his graces only. Man being left in this state of pure naturals, could not by his own strength arrive to a supernatural end, which was typified in his being cast out of Paradise, and the guarding of it with the flaming sword of a cherub. For eternal life being an end above our natural proportions, cannot be acquired by any natural means.'—Vol. ix. p. 1. 'God gives his gifts as He pleases, and is unjust to no man by giving or not giving any certain proportion of good things; and supposing this loss was brought first upon Adam, and so descended upon us, yet we have no cause to complain, for we lost nothing that was ours.'—p. 56.

When he comes, however, to reconcile this modification

of the doctrine of original sin with Scripture, and to prove
'that in Scripture there is no signification of any corruption or deprivation of our souls by Adam's sin,' he has to
explain away texts. The text Rom. v. 18. ' By the offence
of one judgment came upon all men to condemnation,'
asserts the condemnation, κατάκριμα, of all mankind as the
consequence of the sin of Adam. Taylor explains ' damnation ' first as *pœna damni*, a loss of a higher state; and,
secondly, of temporal death—which was ' the *whole* event,
for it names no other—according to that saying of S. Paul,
" In Adam we all die."' But this is an artificial explanation of Scripture. It is true, as he observes, that ' the
κατάκριμα passed upon all men, ἐφ' ᾧ πάντες ἥμαρτον'
(p. 380); but this can only show that the natural truth is
maintained in Scripture together with the mysterious one,
not that the mysterious one is not maintained. So of the
text ' Death passed upon all men; for that all have sinned,'
he says, ' all men, that is, the generality of mankind, all that
lived till they could sin; the others that died before, died
in their nature, not in their sin.'—p. 381. He owns,
however, at last, that the language of Scripture is against
him, by falling back upon the ground of justice as overruling the natural meaning of such language. ' How can
it be *just* that the " condemnation " should pass upon us
for Adam's sin?'—p. 380.

So upon the text, ' Behold I was shapen in wickedness,
and in sin hath my mother conceived me,' he says, ' I
answer, that the words are a Hebraism, and signify nothing
but an aggrandation of his sinfulness, and are intended for
a high expression, meaning that " I am wholly and entirely
wicked." For the verification of which exposition there
are divers parallel places in the Holy Scriptures: " Thou
wast my hope, when I hanged yet upon my mother's
breast;" and " The ungodly as soon as they be born, they go
astray and speak lies," which, because it cannot be true in
the letter, must be an idiotism or propriety of phrase, apt
to explicate the other, and signify only a ready, a prompt,
a great, and universal wickedness. The like to this is that
saying of the Pharisees, " Thou wert altogether born in sin,

and dost thou teach us?" which phrase and manner of speaking being plainly a reproach of the poor blind man and a disparagement of him, did mean only to call him a very wicked person, not that he had derived his sin originally and from his birth.'—p. 27. But even were the text, 'In sin hath my mother conceived me,' only a phrase to express the depth and strength of sin in the character of the person using it, why should that depth and strength of sin be expressed in that form? Why does David, on the first deep perception of his own guilt, and the hold which sin has had over him, go back to his birth? Is it not because he cannot see how he can stop short of it? The more he considers the sinfulness of his character the more rooted it seems, and the further it appears to go back, till at last he cannot but say, that it is actually coeval with his existence. The phrase, then, though it may not be a dogmatic assertion of original sin, is an assertion of a certain depth and radical position of sin in the human soul; upon which, when realised, the doctrine of original sin naturally arises. Such phrases as this, and the others in Scripture referred to by Taylor, show that there was a truth felt respecting sin, which was expressed in this form as the most appropriate one for it, and that whenever men perceived the strength of the hold which sin had had upon them, they went to the idea of its originality, as an idea nothing short of which would do justice to that truth which they felt respecting sin, and which the fuller consciousness of their own sins had revealed to them.

So on the text, 'By nature we were children of wrath,' Taylor remarks: 'True, we were so when we were dead in sins, and before we were quickened by the Spirit of life and grace. We *were* so; now we *are* not. We were so by our own unworthiness and filthy conversation; now we being regenerated by the Spirit of holiness, we are heirs unto God, and no longer heirs of wrath. This, therefore, as appears by the discourse of S. Paul, relates not to our original sin, but to the actual; and of this sense of the word " nature," in the matter of sinning, we have Justin Martyr, or whoever is the author of the questions and

## Note VII. 347

answers *Ad Orthodoxos*, to be witness. For answering those words of Scripture, "There is not any one clean who is born of a woman," and there is none begotten who hath not committed sin; he says, their meaning cannot extend to Christ, for He was not "πεφυκὼς ἁμαρτάνειν—born to sin;" but *he* is '*natura ad peccandum natus*—πεφυκὼς ἁμαρτάνειν," who, by the choice of his own will, is author to himself to do what he list, whether it be good or evil, ὁ κατὰ τὴν αὐθαίρετον προαίρεσιν ἄγων ἑαυτὸν εἰς τὸ πράττειν ἃ βούλεται εἴτε ἀγαθὰ εἴτε φαῦλα.'—p. 29. One who *can* sin, then, is *born* to sin, in Taylor's sense of the phrase; a man being born to sin *means* that he can sin, and no more. But such a meaning is inconsistent with his own previous meaning of the similar phrase, 'By nature children of wrath,' which he understands to mean great and habitual actual sin, or a bad and corrupt course of life; for the power to sin and the fact of sin are not the same thing. Either meaning, however plainly, falls short of the Apostle's. Why should S. Paul say 'by *nature*,' if actual sin was *all* that he meant? The term evidently introduces another idea beyond and in addition to an actual bad course of life.

The modification which Taylor has hitherto proposed of the doctrine of original sin has been rather concerned with its effects than with itself. The particular view of the sin *itself* which he proposes to substitute for the received one is, that it is *imputed* sin, as distinguished from real sin in us. He objects to the idea of our being *parties* to Adam's sin as absurd; but has no objection to a certain imputation of that sin, considered to be his and his only, to us. 'Indeed, my Lord, that I may speak freely in this great question: when one man hath sinned, his descendants and relations cannot possibly by him, or for him, or in him be made sinners really and properly. For in sin there are but two things imaginable, the irregular action and the guilt or obligation to punishment. Now, we cannot be said in any sense to have done the action which another did, and not we; the action is as individual as the person; and Titius may as well be Caius, and the son be his own father, as he can be said to have done the father's action; and therefore we cannot possibly be guilty for it, for guilt is an obligation to punishment for having done it; the action and the guilt are relatives—one cannot be done without the other,—something must be done inwardly or outwardly, or there can be no guilt. But then for the evil of punishment, that may pass further than the action. If it passes upon the innocent it is not a punishment to them, but an evil inflicted in right of dominion; but yet by reason of the relation of the afflicted to him that hath sinned, to him it is a punishment. But if it passes upon others that are not innocent, then it is a punishment to both; to the first principally; to the descendants or relatives for the other's sake, his sin being *imputed* so far.'— p. 379. 'There is no necessity to affirm that we are sinners in Adam any more than by imputation.'—p. 378.

Taylor considers this view of imputation as a middle one between the received and the Pelagian view of original sin. 'I do not approve of that gloss of the Pelagians that in Adam we are made sinners by imitation, and much less of that which affirms that we are made so properly and formally. But made sinners signifies used like sinners, so as justified signifies treated like just persons; in which interpretation I follow S. Paul, not the Pelagians.'—p. 383.

But what is gained toward reconciling the doctrine of original sin with our natural ideas, by substituting the *imputation* of Adam's sin for sin *in* Adam? If it is contrary to reason that a man should be a party to sin committed before he was born, it is contrary to justice that a sin in which he was no partaker should be imputed to him, and that he should be punished for it. It is true, he says, 'If the evil of punishment passes upon the *innocent*, it is not a punishment to them, but an evil inflicted by right of *dominion*, and therefore Rabbi Simeon Barsema said well, that "When God visits the vices of the fathers upon the children—*jure Dominii, non pœnæ utitur*—He uses the right of empire not of justice."' The result of this distinction is, that God, in cases of punishment for imputed sin, inflicts no more evil than He has a right to inflict where there is no sin in the case. But if on such a ground the imputation of sin is reconciled with our idea of justice, what becomes of the idea itself of *imputation*? There is evidently no real imputation *of*, no punishment *for*, another's sin, and therefore this whole mode of representing original sin falls to the ground. Taylor says, 'By reason of the relation of the afflicted to him that sinned, to him it is a punishment.' Why so? Whether a certain evil is a punishment depends on the ground on which it is inflicted. If it is inflicted on the ground of guilt, actual or imputed, it is punishment; if it is inflicted simply *jure Dominii*, on the ground of that right which the Maker of the world has over the lives and fortunes of His creatures, it is not punishment, but Providence. But Taylor is still unwilling to abandon the idea of punishment, and he suggests a *form* of punishment which, he thinks, is not liable to any charge of injustice. 'In Adam we are made sinners, that is, treated ill or afflicted, though ourselves be innocent of that sin, *which was the occasion of our being used so severely for other sins, of which we were not innocent.*'—p. 4. God inflicts pain upon us, then; which pain is *punishment*, because such pain is greater than it would have been but for Adam's sin; we are not punished *for* Adam's sin, but we are, in consequence of Adam's sin, punished *worse* for *our own* sins. But the difficulty of punishment is not at all lessened by this artifice of attaching the punishment to our own actual sins in the first place, and only charging upon Adam's sin the *increase* of this punishment. Increase of punishment is fresh punishment. Taylor thus oscillates between acknowledging and disowning punishment *for* Adam's sin. He disowns it as inconsistent with justice; he acknowledges it because he cannot wholly deny that something very like it is maintained in Scripture, and he shrinks from wholly giving up the received doctrine. He thus constructs a kind of indirect vicarious punishment, which is inflicted for our own personal sins, but inflicted *more severely* on account of Adam's sin.

Jeremy Taylor falls into all these forced and inconsistent modes of explanation, in consequence of the fundamental misapprehension with which he starts as to the sense and mode in which the truth of original sin is held. Had he perceived properly that it was and professed to be a mysterious as distinguished from an intelligible truth, he would have seen that all these charges of injustice against the doctrine were erroneous, and these consequent attempts at a modification of it superfluous and unnecessary. The profession of a mystery disarms the opposition of reason; for what has reason to object to in that which it does not understand? What has reason before it in such a case? One who holds the doctrine in this sense can hold it in its greatest strictness, without the slightest collision with reason or justice, and is spared this vain struggle with Scripture.

## NOTE VIII. p. 35.

THE doctrine of predestination in Scripture is not uncommonly interpreted in such a way as to represent that doctrine, not as opposed to any counter truth of freewill, but as itself harmonising and coinciding with it. Predestination and election are interpreted to mean predestination and election to privileges or means of grace, which depend on freewill for their cultivation. But this is certainly not the natural sense of the words in Scripture. In the text Matt. xx. 16, 'Many are called but few chosen,' or elect; '*elect*' evidently means elect to eternal life itself, and not merely to the opportunity of attaining it. The same may be said of Matt. xxiv. 22: 'For the elect's sake those days shall be shortened,' the elect being evidently here the saints, the good, those who will be saved, not those who have merely been admitted into the Christian Church and the means of obtaining salvation, many of whom being wicked men and enemies of God, God would not 'for their sakes' perform this special act of mercy. On

Acts xiii. 48, 'As many as were ordained to eternal life believed,' the remark is obvious that that to which men are said to be 'ordained' (which is the same as elect or predestinated) is expressly 'eternal life.' In Eph. i. 4, 'According as He hath chosen us in Him, before the foundation of the world, that we should be holy,' the election is not to the power but to the fact of holiness. And the next verse sustains this obvious sense: 'Having predestinated us unto the adoption of children by Jesus Christ to Himself,' adoption always implying in the epistles sanctity. So 2 Tim. i. 9 : 'Who hath saved us and called us with an holy calling, not according to our works, but according to His own purpose and grace which was given us in Christ before the world began,' obviously speaks of actual holiness and actual salvation, not the mere opportunity of them, as the effect of predestination. And generally it is evident that the terms elect, predestinated, adopted, justified, saints, all refer to the same state and the same class; and that plainly the state and the class of actually holy men who will certainly be saved, as the necessary consequence and reward of such holiness.

The 8th and 9th chapters, however, of the Epistle to the Romans, furnish the most powerful, and because the most powerful the most controverted, evidence for the meaning of predestination as being predestination to eternal life itself, and not merely certain means of grace enabling men to obtain it. In the 8th is the passage: 'We know that all things work together for good to them that love God, to them who are the called according to His purpose. For whom He did foreknow (know before as His own with determination to be for ever merciful unto them—*Hooker, Appendix* to bk. v. vol. ii. p. 751). He also predestinated to be conformed to the image of His Son, that He might be the first born among many brethren. Moreover, whom He did predestinate, them He also called, and whom He called, them He also justified, and whom He justified them He also glorified.' Here it is expressly said that those who are predestinated are predestinated, not to the opportunity of conformation to the image of

Christ, but to that conformation itself, to actual justification, and to actual glory in the world to come.

The 9th chapter has the passage: 'For the children being not yet born, neither having done any good or evil, that the purpose of God according to election might stand, not of works, but of Him that calleth, it was said unto her, the elder shall serve the younger. As it is written, Jacob have I loved, but Esau have I hated. What shall we say then? Is there unrighteousness with God? God forbid. For He saith to Moses, I will have mercy on whom I will have mercy, and I will have compassion on whom I will have compassion. So then it is not of him that willeth, nor of him that runneth, but of God that sheweth mercy. For the Scripture saith unto Pharaoh, even for this same purpose have I raised thee up, that I might show My power in thee, and that My name might be declared throughout all the earth. Therefore hath He mercy on whom He will have mercy, and whom He will He hardeneth. Thou wilt say then unto me, Why doth He yet find fault? for who hath resisted His will? Nay, but, O man, who art thou that repliest against God? Shall the thing formed say unto him that formed it, Why hast thou made me thus? Hath not the potter power over the clay, of the same lump to make one vessel unto honour, and another unto dishonour? What if God, willing to shew His wrath, and to make His power known, endured with much long-suffering the vessels of wrath fitted to destruction. And that He might make known the riches of His glory on the vessels of mercy, which He had afore prepared unto glory.'

Here it is expressly said that some persons are from all eternity objects respectively of the Divine love and the Divine wrath, which love and which wrath involve respectively eternal 'glory,' and 'destruction' (v. 22, 23). All the attempts to explain this passage as meaning only that some persons are predestined to higher and others to lower means of grace, appear to violate its plain and natural meaning. It is not indeed necessary to suppose that the contrast between Jacob and Esau, as individual men, is that of one finally saved to another finally condemned; but it is no less clear that the Apostle uses them as *types* of these two respective classes, and that the argument of the passage has reference to man's eternal end, good or bad; for 'glory' and 'destruction' cannot mean only higher and lower spiritual advantages.

Archbishop Whately indeed raises an ingenious objection to the predestinarian interpretation of the image of the potter and the clay, and remarks, 'We are in His hands, say these predestinarians, as clay in the potters', " who hath power of the same lump to make one vessel to honour and another to dishonour," not observing in their party eagerness to seize an easy apparent confirmation of their system, that this similitude, as far as it goes, rather makes against them, since the potter never makes any vessel for the express purpose of being broken and destroyed. This comparison accordingly agrees much better with the view here taken. The potter according to his arbitrary choice makes of the same lump one vessel to honour and another to dishonour—*i.e.* some to nobler and others to meaner uses, but all to some use; none with a design that it should be cast away and dashed in pieces. Even so the Almighty, of His own arbitrary choice, causes some to be born to wealth or rank, others to poverty or obscurity, some in a heathen, and others in a Christian country; the advantages and privileges bestowed on each are various.'—*Essay* 3, *On Election.* But to extract thus an argument from the general nature of an image used in Scripture is to forget that Scripture, in making use of images, only adopts them in such respects as it uses them, such respects as answer the particular purpose in hand; it does not necessarily adopt the whole image. What we have to do with, then, is not the image itself, but the image *as used by* Scripture. Now, it is true that a potter never makes a vessel for destruction; but some vessels are certainly in this passage spoken of as 'fitted to destruction,' others as 'prepared unto glory;' of which destruction and glory the cause is plainly put further back than their own personal conduct,—viz. in a certain Divine love and wrath, before either side had done any actual good or evil,—'The children being not yet born, neither having done any good or evil, it is written, Jacob have I loved, but Esau have I hated.' And were a predestination to privileges all that was meant by the passage—that some are born to wealth or rank, others to poverty or obscurity, some in a heathen and others in a Christian country, what ground would there be for raising the objection? 'Thou wilt say then unto me, Why doth He yet find fault, for who hath resisted His will?' It is evident that this is a complaint against the Divine justice, or an objection to the Apostle's doctrine just before laid down, on the ground that it contradicts that Divine attribute. But how could a mere inequality in the dispensing of religious privileges provoke such a charge, except from a positive infidel? Inequality is a plain fact of God's visible providence, and could never support a charge of injustice, except the objector were willing to go the further step of denying a Divine creation and providence altogether on account of this fact. The objector here plainly means to say this: How can it be just that a man should be the object of Divine wrath before he has done anything to deserve it? That he should be incapacitated for obtaining the qualifications necessary for eternal life, and then blamed because he has not got them? 'Why doth he find fault, for who hath resisted His will?' Why does God condemn the sinner, when His own arbitrary will has incapacitated him for being anything else but a sinner?

At the same time I am ready to admit, that there is ground for saying that a milder sense of reprobation does *come in*, in this passage, along with the stronger one; and that language *is* used expressive rather of the modified than of the extreme doctrine of predestination. It is at any rate doubtful whether 'honour' and 'dishonour' do not mean higher and inferior good rather than positive good and evil. The use of the words in 2 Tim. ii. 20.— 'In a great house there are not only vessels of gold and silver, but also of wood and earth, and some to honour and some to dishonour'—would seem to attach the former meaning to them. And if so, *so far as* this language goes, the Apostle expresses a modified doctrine of predestination rather than an extreme one, or predestination to unequal advantages, rather than to positive good and evil. But whether this is so or not, such a sense of predestination only obtains so far as the language which expresses it goes. The stronger sense of predestination, as predestination to positive good and evil, is the main and pervading one in the passage; and this sense must not be lost sight of because there may be a milder sense too in which the doctrine is asserted. It is characteristic of S. Paul to slide from one meaning to another; and just as a counter doctrine altogether to that of predestination is put forth in *other* passages of Scripture, so the *same* passage may be more or less contradictory, and contain its own balance. But if the milder meaning of predestination is there, it must not be thought that the stronger meaning is therefore not there too; or supposed that *all* that this passage means is a predestination to unequal privileges and advantages.

There is another mode of interpreting predestination in Scripture, so as to make the doctrine agree with the truth of freewill; viz. that of allowing predestination to be to eternal salvation itself, but with the qualification that it is caused by the Divine foresight of the future good life of the individual. But this qualification is opposed to the plain meaning of those passages of Scripture in which this doctrine is set forth. These passages obviously represent predestination as a predestination of the individual *to* a good life, as well as to the reward of one, to the means as well as to the end; thus making a good life the *effect* of predestination, and not the cause or reason of it. 'He hath chosen us before the foundation of the world that we should be holy' .... 'predestinated us to be conformed to the image of His Son.'

But the ninth chapter of Romans, just quoted, supplies the most decisive answer to this qualification of the doctrine of predestination; it being expressly said there that the purpose of God according to election is antecedent to any differences of life and conduct between one man and another; that it is formed while the children are yet unborn, and have done neither good nor evil; that it is not of works, but of Him that calleth; and that it is not of him that willeth or of him that runneth, but of God that showeth mercy; that it is clay of *the same lump* of which some vessels are made to honour, and others to dishonour.

Jackson, among other commentators, interprets the predestination maintained in this passage in this way, viz. as predestination in consequence of foreseen good works. But in thus interpreting it he endeavours at the same time by an argument more ingenious than substantial, to explain his own interpretation as *not* being such an interpretation as this; and tries to show that he does *not* base predestination upon foreseen good works. He says, predestination is in consequence not of any foreseen works of the law, but the foreseen work of *faith*; which work of faith being a renunciation of the works of the law cannot tself be called a work. He interprets the Apostle's assertion that election is not in consequence of any 'willing or running' of the man himself, in this way, viz. that this expression applies to works of the Jewish law only, and not to works of faith; to the self-willed and self-dependent kind of good works, which are not really good as not proceeding from a spiritual state of mind; not to the true spiritual temper. The work of faith, he says, is 'an *opus quo renunciamus*, the formal act by which all works must be renounced,' and so not properly a work : '*fides justificat non qua opus sed relative*—is essentially included in the act of justification; not included in the universality of works, which are excluded from justification.' And the 'fallacy' of calling such an act a work he expresses thus : 'If such divines as urge it most should come into our pervices and apply it to matters there discussed, thus—

> 'Omne visibile est coloratum :
> Omnis color est visibilis : *ergo*
> Omnis color est coloratus,—

I hope a meaner artist than this nursery (God be praised !)

hath any, would quickly cut off their progress with a distinction of *visibile ut quod, et visibile ut quo*, and show that the major, though universally true of every subject or body that may be seen, did not nor could not comprehend colour by which they are made visible, and by whose formal act they are denominated *colorata*. The fallacy of the former objection drawn into mood and figure is the same, but more apparent.

'Every will or work of man must be utterly renounced from the act of justification or conversion:

'But to deny ourselves and renounce all works is a work:

'*Ergo*, This work must be excluded from the suit of mercy, as no way available.'—Vol. ix. p. 442.

But such a distinction as this applied to works as a ground of the Divine election is inadmissible. The work of faith is a work; not in such an ambiguous sense as that in which colour is a visible thing, but substantially and correctly. It is a humble, self-renouncing act. It is the fundamental act of the Christian life. If election, then, is in consequence of this foreseen work of faith, it is in consequence of good works, which it is plainly said by S. Paul not to be.

Jackson borrows his explanation from Origen, who *implies* the same distinction between 'carnal works' and other works, as the ground of Jacob's election. 'Quod si vel Isaac vel Jacob pro his meritis electi fuissent a Deo *quæ in carne positi* acquisierant, et per *opera carnis* justificari meruissent, posset utique meriti eorum gratia ad posteritatem carnis quoque pertinere. Nunc vero cum electio eorum non ex operibus facta sit, sed ex proposito Dei, et ex vocantis arbitrio, promissionum gratia non in filiis carnis impletur, sed in filiis Dei.'—In Rom. ix. 11. vol. iv. p. 613. Thus Jackson: 'Had not this purpose of God been revealed before the children had been born, Jacob's posterity would have boasted that either their father Jacob or his mother Rebecca had better observed those rites and customs wherein they placed righteousness than Isaac or Esau had done; and that God upon these motives had bestowed the birthright or blessing upon Jacob before

Esau.'—Vol. ix. p. 436. There is considerable confusion here, and Origen seems to slide from works not carnal to no works at all as the ground of election; though the former idea in the main prevails. Origen's main view of the ground of election is foreseen good character.—Vol. iv. p. 616.

Jackson explains the similitude of the potter and the clay on the same principle: 'That it was marred in the first making was the fault of the clay.'—Vol. ix. p. 462. But is this said in Scripture? On the contrary, it is said that all the clay was of the same lump, and therefore the difference of the Divine design did not arise from any difference in the clay. Origen makes in the same way a difference in the clay, though the very phrase *eadem massa*, which he accepts, as he is obliged to do, from the Apostle, refutes it. 'Videns Deus puritatem ejus, et potestatem habens ex eadem massa facere aliud vas ad honorem aliud ad contumeliam, Jacob quidem *qui emundaverat seipsum* fecit vas ad honorem; Esau vero cujus animam *non ita puram nec ita simplicem videbat*, ex eadem massa fecit ad contumeliam.'—In Rom. ix. vol. iv. p. 616.

With the explanation of foreseen goodness, however, as the ground of election, Jackson couples the other mode of reconciling the passage with freewill; viz. that of election to means and opportunities. 'The Apostle imagineth such a potter as the wise man did, that knows a reason why he makes one vessel of this fashion, another of that, why he appoints this to a *base use, that to a better*.'—P. 462.

Hooker's explanation of the passage (given in a recently discovered and edited writing, made an appendix to Ecclesiastical Polity, bk. v.) makes, like Origen's and Jackson's, a difference in the clay, though he will not at the same time allow that the Divine Justice *requires* this reason for its own defence. 'Suppose (which is yet false) that there were nothing in it, but only so God will have it,—suppose God did harden and soften, choose and cast off, make honourable and detestable, whom Himself will, and that without any cause moving Him one way or other, —are we not all in His hands as clay? If thus God did deal, what injury were it? How much less now, when they on whom His severity worketh *are not found like the clay* without form, as apt to receive the best shape as any other, but are *in themselves and by their own disposition* fashioned for destruction and for wrath.'—*Keble's Ed.* vol. ii. p. 748. Now, of this explanation the first part undoubtedly adheres to the natural meaning of the passage in S. Paul more faithfully than the latter, which diverges from it; mankind being plainly represented by S. Paul as being like clay of the same lump, previous to election, and any difference of disposition in them, in this previous state, so far from being asserted, being expressly denied. Indeed, as Jansen says, if S. Paul meant foreseen goodness as the ground of election, he would not have silenced the complainer by a reference to God's inscrutable will, but would have given this simple and intelligible answer to his objection. But *non isto nititur cardine.—De Grat. Christi,* p. 347.

On the whole, that which is commonly called the Calvinistic sense, appears to be the natural sense of these passages of Scripture; and the Calvinistic use of them should be met, not by denying this sense, and explaining away the natural meaning of the language, but by opposing to them other passages of Scripture which speak equally plainly of man's freewill. I may add, that perhaps more has been made by many of the text in S. James than it will exactly bear, and that, though proving difficulty, this text does not prove *so much* difficulty in those parts of S. Paul's Epistles as many would maintain. These epistles were certainly addressed to the whole Church, and were meant to be understood by men of average intelligence who applied their attention properly. Their predestinarian meaning in parts is, on the whole, clear and decided; and the reason why their meaning is thought by many to be so very obscure and difficult to get at, is that they will not acknowledge this predestinarian meaning to be the true one. These interpreters create difficulties for themselves by rejecting the natural meaning of passages, and then lay the difficulty on the passages.

## NOTE IX. p. 46.

THE first work of Pelagius referred to in the controversy, is his letter to Paulinus, which appears to have been written about A.D. 405, during his stay at Rome.—*Benedictine Editor's Preface*, c. 1. But Augustine's doctrinal bias had clearly asserted itself some years before, in the book *De Diversis Quæstionibus ad Simplicianum*, which came out A.D. 397; and had evidently commenced as early as the book *De Libero Arbitrio*, which he began to write A.D. 388. In his Retractations (l. 1. c. 9.) he refers to this early treatise, with which the Pelagians taunted him as contradicting his later ones on the subject of freewill, and shows that, though not consistently brought out, the germ of his ultimate system was to be found in parts of that treatise. He refers particularly to the scheme of the two kinds of Divine gifts laid down in l. 2. cc. 18, 19; according to which both those which did and those which did not admit of a bad use (*virtutes* and *potentiæ*) were alike gifts of God. The explanation which he gives in the Retractations of some of the statements favourable to freewill in the other treatise may be far-fetched; but such a view as this is evidently agreeable to his later doctrine. Nor is Augustine at all a pertinacious interpreter of his early writings in the sense of his later ones. Consistency has less charm for him than development as a writer and thinker; and he dwells on the changes he has gone through with the satisfaction of one who believes his later notions to be a great improvement in depth and acuteness upon his earlier ones.

To these two earlier treatises may be added the Confessions, written A.D. 400. A celebrated dictum in this book —*da quod jubes, et jube quod vis*—was the first apparent stimulus to the speculations of Pelagius, whom it greatly irritated. 'Pelagius ferre non potuit, et contradicens aliquanto commotius, pene cum illo qui illa commemoraverat litigavit.'—*De Dono Perseverantiæ*, n. 53. Neander says: 'Since Augustine had completed his doctrinal system on this particular side more than ten years before the opinions of Pelagius excited any public controversy, it is clear that opposition to Pelagius could not have influenced him in forming it. With more propriety may it be said that opposition to such doctrines as those of Augustine, or to the practical consequences which, through misconstruction or abuse, were derived from such doctrines, had no small share in leading Pelagius to form such a system as he did.' —*Church History*, vol. iv. p. 312.

## NOTE X. p. 52.

SUNT alii [Pelagiani] tam validis testimoniis non audentes resistere; ideoque dant Deo primitias extrinsecas gratiæ et fidei, ac bonorum similium, sed hominibus gratiam ipsam et fidem cum cæteris bonis hujusmodi. Dicunt enim Deum semper prævenire pulsando, et excitando ad gratiam, fidem, et ad bona similia, et hominem subsequi aperiendo et consentiendo, et hoc ex propriis viribus per seipsum, juxta illud Apoc. 3: 'Ecce sto ad ostium, et pulso: si quis audierit vocem meam, et aperuerit mihi januam, introibo ad illum, et cœnabo cum illo, et ipse mecum.' Hi autem faciunt Deum suæ gratiæ publicum venditorem, hominesque emptores. Dicunt enim eum sicut mercatorem pauperculum clamare, et pulsare ad januas, et ad ostia singulorum; aperienti vero pro sua apertione gratiam suam dare, quod tamen verius commutare, seu vendere diceretur. Faciunt quoque Deum scriptorem pauperculum et conductitium suam operam publicantem, et pro pretio parvulo, pro apertione et cœna, aperientium nomina in libro vitæ scribentem; sicque gratia ex præcedentibus operibus nostris erit. . . . Homo non potest aperire nec consentire in talibus ex seipso, sed voluntate Divina, quod et probant auctoritates superius allegatæ. Nemo potest venire ad me, nisi Pater meus traxerit illum. Secundúm istos tamen homo licet pulsatus a Deo, non habens adhuc patrem, aperiendo pulsanti, verius traheret ad se Patrem. . .

## Note X.

Et licet sic pulsat nihil dat nobis, sed nos aperientes damus sibi consensum, contra illud Apostoli, Quis prior dedit illi, et retribuetur ei? Itane hæc positio tribuit nobis quod melius est et majus, Deo vero quod deterius est et minus: quis enim dubitaverit aperire melius et utilius nobis esse quam pulsare, cum pulsare sine apertione, non prosit sed obsit.—*Bradwardine, De Causa Dei*, l. 1. c. 38.

Sentiebant ergo Pelagiani uno omnes consensu, tantas esse vires in naturali libertate, bonique et mali possibilitate constitutas, ut quæcunque tandem a rebus sive extrinsecus irruentibus, sive intrinsecus se commoventibus, vel cogitationes phantasiæque moverentur vel animi desideria motusque cierentur, quicquid tandem sive homines, sive Angeli, sive Dæmones, *adeoque Spiritus ipse sanctus* suaderet, et suggereret, quicunque vel pietatis vel iniquitatis motus inciderent, quibuscunque passionum bonarum auris animus propelleretur, vel malarum fluctibus procellisque turbaretur, nihil de suo imperii principatu domina illa libertas amitteret; sed plenissima discernendi potestate penes vim rationis ac voluntatis permanente, sola fieret ad malum bonumque suasio ac provocatio; nutus vero probandi vel improbandi, utendi et repellendi, in illa naturalis indifferentiæ libertate ac naturali possibilitate persisteret.—*Jansen, De Hær. Pel.* l. 2. c. 3.

Nihil verius de tali possibilitate divino adjutorio munita dici potuit, quam id quod Pelagius dixit: 'Quod possumus omne bonum facere, dicere, cogitare, illius est qui hoc posse donavit, qui hoc posse adjuvat: quod vero bene vel agimus vel loquimur vel cogitamus nostrum est quia hæc omnia vertere in malum possumus.' Quibus verbis adjutorium possibilitatis explicuit. Vigilantissime quippe et perspicacissime vidit (quod ego sæpius supra modum admiratus sum Scholasticos eruditissimos acutissimosque viros non agnoscere) quod sicut usus cujuslibet facultatis sive oculi externorumque sensuum, sive facultatis progressívæ, sive intellectus, sive voluntatis, noster est, hoc est, ad nostræ voluntatis indifferentem flexum et nutum referri debet, non ad Deum, quatenus solam facultatem dedit; ita quoque cujuslibet adjutorii concursus, sive naturalis sive gratuiti, etiamsi esset tantæ præstantiæ adjutorium quantam vel angelica cogitatio comminisci posset, imo etiamsi esset vel ipsa essentia Dei per modum speciei ad sui visionem, vel per modum gratiæ ad sui amorem concurrentis, similiter prorsus noster sit; si videlicet sic solam possibilitatem adjuvet, et usus ejus et non usus in libero relinquatur arbitrio.—*Jansen, De Gratiâ Christi*, l. 2. c. 9.

Hanc ergo mentem Pelagianorum cum prospectam haberet Augustinus, quod quicquid motuum vel Deus vel Diabolus in voluntate suscitaret, isti dominativæ voluntatis potestati subderent, non fuit sollicitus utrum gratiam legis atque doctrinæ, sive revelationem sapientiæ, sive exemplum Christi, sive remissionem peccatorum, sive habitus bonos, sive succensiones ac desideria voluntatis assererent; sed generalissime prophanum eorum dogma quo solum possibilitatem adjuvari gratia censebant, *ubicunque vel qualemcunque ponerent gratiam*, velut exploratum errorem Scripturisque contrarium jugulat. . . . Quamvis enim in gratiam legis plerumque magis propendere videretur, non satis tamen certum erat Augustino quam gratiam tam vario magnificorum verborum strepitu Pelagius tunc defenderet, cum nunc legem, nunc doctrinam, nunc sapientiæ revelationem, nunc exemplum Christi, nunc peccati remissionem, *nunc voluntatum succensionem, nunc desideria a Deo suscitata celebraret.* Fatetur hanc suam incertitudinem passim toto libro Augustinus. . . . Itaque ut omnis erroribus istis latebra clauderetur, sub *qualibet*, et *qualilibet*, et *ubicumque* constituta gratia sua in eos tela dirigit. . . . Nimirum quia utrobique Augustinus quamlibet, qualemlibet, ubilibet constitutam gratiam quisque tueatur, si solam possibilitatem voluntatis et actionis adjuvet, eum sanæ et Apostolicæ et Evangelicæ doctrinæ violatæ reum facit.—*Jansen, De Gratia Christi*, l. 2. c. 10.

## NOTE XI. p. 54.

AUGUSTINE'S view on this subject is comprehended under the following heads:—

1. No one of the human race can be without sin absolutely or from the first, all being born in sin. 'Qui omnino nullum peccatum *habuerit*, habiturusve sit, prorsus nisi unum Mediatorem Dei et hominum Jesum Christum, nullum vel esse vel fuisse vel futurum esse certissimum est.' —*De Pecc. Merit. et Remiss.* l. 2. n. 34. 'Non legitur sine peccato esse nisi Filius hominis.'—*De Perfect. Just.* n. 29. See too *De Pecc. Merit. et Remiss.* l. 1. n. 56, 57.

2. Though all men are in sin to begin with, there is the possibility of attaining to a sinless state in this life; but this possibility is through the Divine grace or power, and by a miraculous exertion of that power. 'Et ideo ejus perfectionem etiam in hac vita esse possibilem, negare non possumus, quia omnia possibilia sunt Deo, sive quæ facit sola sua voluntate, sive quæ cooperantibus creaturæ suæ voluntatibus a se fieri posse constituit. Ac per hoc quicquid eorum non facit, sine exemplo est quidem in ejus operibus factis; sed apud Deum et in ejus virtute habet causam qua fieri possit, et in ejus sapientia quare non factum sit.'—*De Spiritu et Litera*, n. 7. 'Ecce quemadmodum sine exemplo est in hominibus perfecta justitia, et tamen impossibilis non est. Fieret enim si tanta voluntas adhiberetur quanta sufficit tantæ rei. Esset autem tanta, si et nihil eorum quæ pertinent ad justitiam nos lateret, et ea sic delectarent animum, ut quicquid aliud voluptatis dolorisve impedit, delectatio illa superaret: quod ut non sit, non ad impossibilitatem, sed ad judicium Dei pertinet.' —*Ibid.* n. 63. 'Sed inveniant isti, si possunt, aliquem sub onere corruptionis hujus viventem, cui jam non habeat Deus quod ignoscat. . . . . Sane quemquam talem, si testimonia illa divina competenter accipiant, prorsus invenire non possunt; nullo modo tamen dicendum, Deo deesse possibilitatem, qua voluntas sic adjuvetur humana, ut non solum justitia ista quæ ex fide est, omni ex parte modo

perficiatur in homine, verum etiam illa secundum quam postea in æternum in ipsa ejus contemplatione vivendum est. Quandoquidem, si nunc velit in quoquam etiam hoc corruptibili induere incorruptionem, atque hic inter homines morituros eum jubere vivere minime moriturum, ut tota penitus vetustate consumpta nulla lex in membris ejus repugnet legi mentis, Deumque ubique præsentem ita cognoscat, sicut sancti posteà cognituri sunt; quis demum audeat affirmare, non posse? Sed quare non faciat quærunt homines, nec qui quærunt se attendunt esse homines.'—*Ibid.* n. 66.

3. While he thus admits the possibility, he denies the fact that any man has attained to a sinless state in this life: 'Si autem quæratur utrum sit, esse non credo. Magis enim credo Scripturæ dicenti. Ne intres in judicium,' &c.—*De Pecc. Merit. et Remiss.* l. 2. n. 8. 'Hic fortasse respondeas, ista quæ commemoravi *facta non esse* et fieri potuisse, opera esse divina; ut autem sit homo sine peccato, ad opus ipsius hominis pertinere, idque opus esse optimum, quo fiat plena et perfecta et ex omni parte absoluta justitia: et ideo non esse credendum, neminem vel fuisse, vel esse, vel fore in hac vita qui hoc opus impleverit, si ab homine impleri potest. Sed cogitare debes quamvis ad homines id agere pertineat, hoc quoque munus esse divinum, atque ideo non dubitare opus esse divinum.'—*De Spir. et Lit.* n. 2. 'Si omnes illos sanctos et sanctas, cum hic vixerunt, congregare possemus, et interrogare utrum essent sine peccato, quid fuisse responsuros putamus? Utrum hoc quod iste dicit, an quod Joannes Apostolus. Rogo vos, quantalibet fuerit in hoc corpore excellentia sanctitatis, si hoc interrogari potuissent, nonne una voce clamassent, "Si diximus quia peccatum non habemus nos ipsos decipimus, et veritas in nobis non est." An illud humilius responderent fortasse quam verius? Sed huic jam placet, et recte placet, "laudem humilitatis in parte non ponere falsitatis." Itaque hoc si verum dicerent, haberent peccatum, quod, humiliter quia faterentur veritas in eis esset: si autem hoc mentirentur, nihilominus haberent peccatum, quia veritas in eis non esset.'—*De Nat. et Grat.* n. 42. He

reserves, however, the liberty to except the Virgin Mary from this general assertion: 'De qua, propter honorem Domini, nullam prorsus, cum de peccatis agitur, haberi volo quæstionem.'

4. To assert that there have been persons in this life who have attained to the sinless state, though an error, is an error as to a fact rather than a doctrine, and a venial one. 'Quinetiam si nemo est aut fuit, aut erit, quod magis credo, tali puritate perfectus; et tamen esse aut fuisse aut fore defenditur et putatur, non multum erratur, nec perniciose cum quadam quisque benevolentia fallitur: si tamen qui hoc putat seipsum talem esse non putet, nisi revera ac liquido talem se esse perspexerit.'—*De Spir. et Lit.* n. 3. 'Utrum in hoc seculo fuerit, vel sit, vel possit esse aliquis ita juste vivens, ut nullum habeat omnino peccatum, potest esse aliqua quæstio inter veros piosque Christianos. Posse tamen esse certe post hanc vitam quisquis ambigit desipit. Sed ego nec de ista vita volo contendere. Quanquam enim mihi non videatur aliter intelligendum quod scriptum est, "Non justificabitur in conspectu tuo omnis vivens," et siqua similia: utinam tamen possit ostendi hæc testimonia melius aliter intelligi.' —*De Nat. et Grat.* n. 70.

5. Augustine thinks that the subjection of mankind to the law of sin works mysteriously in the Divine scheme for good. 'Idcirco etiam sanctos et fideles suos in aliquibus vitiis tardius sanat, ut in his eos minus, quam implendæ ex omni parte justitiæ sufficit, delectet bonum. . . . Nec in eo ipso vult nos damnabiles esse sed humiles.'—*De Pecc. Merit. et Remiss.* l. 2. n. 33. This very imperfection is in a sense, he thinks, as leading to humility, part of the perfection of human virtue. 'Ex hoc factum est, virtutem quæ nunc est in homine justo, perfectam hactenus nominari, ut ad ejus perfectionem pertineat etiam ipsius imperfectionis et in veritate cognitio, et in humilitate confessio. Tunc enim est secundum hanc infirmitatem pro suo modulo perfecta ista parva justitia, quando etiam quid sibi desit intelligit. Ideoque Apostolus et imperfectum et perfectum se dicit.'—*Contra Duas*, Ep. l. 3. n. 19. 'Deserit

aliquando Deus ut discas superbus non esse. Quidam traduntur Satanæ ut discant non blasphemare.'—*De Nat. et Grat.* n. 32. Pelagius ridicules the idea that *peccatis peccata curantur*.

## NOTE XII. p. 79.

MR. COLERIDGE, in his Aids to Reflection, p. 272, strongly objects to the received doctrine of original sin, as involving the injustice of punishing one man on account of the sin of another; in the place of which, he substitutes (p. 278) a *rationale* of original sin, in which he rests that doctrine, upon the principle of cause and effect; asserting that all evil action implies an evil in the will as the cause of it, which anterior evil, when pushed backward and backward indefinitely, becomes original evil in the will, or original sin. 'Whatever resists and, as a positive power, opposes this (the moral law) in the will, is evil. But an evil in the will is an evil will; and as all moral evil is of the will, this evil will must have its source in the will. And thus we might go back from act to act, from evil to evil, *ad infinitum*, without advancing a step.' This anterior evil in the will, then, regarded as mysterious, independent of time and intelligible succession, is, he argues, original sin. 'Let the evil be supposed such as to imply the impossibility of an individual referring it to any particular time at which it might be conceived to have commenced, or to any period of his existence at which it was not existing. Let it be supposed, in short, that the subject stands in no relation whatever to time, can neither be called *in* time or *out of* time, but that all relations to time are as alien and heterogeneous in this question as the relations and attributes of space (north or south, round or square, thick or thin) are to our affections and moral feelings. Let the reader suppose this, and he will have before him the precise import of the scriptural doctrine of original sin.'

It is evident that, according to this *rationale*, Adam as first created had original sin, and had a corrupt nature as truly as any of his posterity. For the first sinful act of man is as open as any other to this reasoning from effect to cause, from an evil act to an evil will, and from an evil will to a source of evil in the will or original sin: so that Adam's sin in Paradise was the effect of original sin in him, or a corrupt nature, only differing from other sins in being the first effect. 'The corruption of my will may very warrantably be spoken of as a consequence of Adam's fall, even as my birth of Adam's existence; as a consequence, *a link in the historic chain of instances, whereof Adam was the first.* But that it is on account of Adam, or that this evil principle was *à priori* inserted or infused into my will by the will of another—which is indeed a contradiction in terms, my will in such a case being no will,—*this* is nowhere asserted in Scripture explicitly or by implication. It belongs to the very essence of the doctrine, that in respect of original sin *every* man is the adequate representative of *all* men. What wonder, then, that where no outward ground of preference existed, the choice should be determined by outward relation, and that the first *in time* should be taken as the diagram?' —p. 283.

Such being the *rationale* of original sin substituted by Mr. Coleridge for the received doctrine of original sin as the consequence of the sin of Adam, which he rejects on the ground of its opposition to reason, my remark is this —that I cannot think it philosophical in any writer to overthrow a whole received language, *professing* to express an incomprehensible mystery, on such a ground. Contradictory language, or language opposed to reason, is the only one in which mysteries and incomprehensible truths can be expressed; if they could be expressed in consistent language, they would not be mysteries. Moreover, the writer professes that he can only substitute other inconsistent language for that which he rejects. Mr. Coleridge admits the absolute inconsistency of an original evil in the will with the will's self-determination; yet, because he thinks both of these to be truths, he adopts a language which contains them both, as the only mode of expressing ' an acknowledged mystery, and one which, by the nature of the subject, must ever remain such.'—p. 277. What is the improvement, then, in consistency, in *his* language upon the received language? While, on the other hand, the received language, by attributing the fall to an act of freewill only, which no evil in the will preceded, expresses an important truth that sin is not fundamental in, but only accidental to, human nature; a truth which Mr. Coleridge's language of original evil in the will, so far from expressing, rather contradicts.

The same remark may be made on Mr. Coleridge's objection to the received doctrine of the atonement as a *satisfaction* for sin; which he rejects on the same ground as he does the received doctrine of original sin, viz., its opposition to our natural idea of justice. ' Let us suppose, with certain divines, that the varied expressions of S. Paul are to be literally interpreted: *ex. gr.* that sin is, or involves, an infinite debt (in the proper and law-court sense of the word debt),—a debt owing by us to the vindictive justice of God the Father, which can only be liquidated by the everlasting misery of Adam and all his posterity, or by a sum of suffering equal to this. Likewise, that God the Father, by His absolute decree, or (as some divines teach) through the necessity of His unchangeable justice, had determined to exact the full sum, which must therefore be paid either by ourselves or by some other in our own name and behalf. But, besides the debt which all mankind contracted, in and through Adam, as a *homo publicus*, even as a nation is bound by the acts of its head or its plenipotentiary, every man (say these divines) is an insolvent debtor on his own score. In this fearful predicament the Son of God took compassion on mankind, and resolved to pay the debt for us, and to satisfy the Divine justice by a perfect equivalent. . . . .

' Now, as your whole theory is grounded on a notion of *justice*, I ask you, Is this justice a *moral* attribute? But morality commences with, and begins in the sacred distinction between thing and person: on this distinction all law human and divine is grounded; consequently, the law of justice. If you attach any meaning to the term justice, as applied to God, it must be the same to which you refer when you affirm or deny it of any other personal agent—save only, that in its attribution to God you speak of it as unmixed and perfect. For if not, what *do* you mean? And why do you call it by the same name? I may, therefore, with all right and reason, put the case as between man and man. For should it be found irreconcilable with the justice, which the light of reason, made *law* in the conscience, dictates to *man*, how much more must it be incongruous with the all-perfect justice of God! . . . .

'A sum of 1,000*l.* is owing from James to Peter, for which James has given a bond. He is insolvent, and the bond is on the point of being put in suit against him, to James's utter ruin. At this moment Matthew steps in, pays Peter the thousand pounds and discharges the bond. In this case, no man would hesitate to admit, that a complete *satisfaction* had been made to Peter. Matthew's 1,000*l.* is a perfect equivalent for the sum which James was bound to have paid, and which Peter had lent. *It is the same thing:* and this is altogether a question of *things*. Now, instead of James's being indebted to Peter for a sum of money, which (he having become insolvent) Matthew pays for him, we will put the case, that James had been guilty of the basest and most hard-hearted ingratitude to a most worthy and affectionate mother, who had not only performed all the duties and tender offices of a mother, but whose whole heart was bound up in this her only child—who had foregone all the pleasures and amusements of life in watching over his sickly childhood, had sacrificed her health and the far greater part of her resources to rescue him from the consequences of his follies and excesses during his youth and early manhood, and to procure for him the means of his present rank and affluence—all which he had repaid by neglect, desertion, and open profligacy. Here the mother stands in the relation of the creditor: and here too we will suppose the same generous friend to interfere, and to perform with the greatest tenderness and constancy all those duties of a grateful and affectionate son, which James ought to have performed. Will 'this satisfy the mother's

## Note XII.

claims on James, or entitle him to her esteem, approbation, and blessing? Or what if Matthew, vicarious son, should at length address her in words to this purpose: "Now, I trust, you are appeased, and will be henceforward reconciled to James. I have satisfied all your claims on him. I have paid his debt in full: and you are too just to require the same debt to be paid twice over. You will therefore regard him with the same complacency, and receive him into your presence with the same love, as if there had been no difference between him and you. For I have *made it up*." What other reply could the swelling heart of the mother dictate than this? "O misery! and is it possible that *you* are in league with my unnatural child to insult me? Must not the very necessity of *your* abandonment of your proper sphere form an additional evidence of *his* guilt? Must not the sense of your goodness teach me more fully to comprehend, more vividly to feel the evil in him? Must not the contrast of your merits magnify his demerit in his mother's eye, and at once recall and embitter the conviction of the canker-worm in his soul?"

'If indeed by the force of Matthew's example, by persuasion, or by additional and more mysterious influences, or by an inward co-agency, compatible with the existence of a personal will, James should be led to repent; if through admiration and love of this great goodness gradually assimilating his mind to the mind of his benefactor, he should in his own person become a grateful and dutiful child—*then* doubtless the mother would be wholly satisfied! But then the case is no longer a question of *things*, or a matter of *debt* payable by another.'—*Aids to Reflection*, p. 322.

But is not Mr. Coleridge fighting the air, when he objects, on these grounds, to the received doctrine of the atonement as a *satisfaction* for sin? It is quite true that such a doctrine is opposed to our natural idea of justice, as well as to the truth of common reason, that one *person* cannot be a substitute for another in moral action. But who does not acknowledge this contrariety? Does not the most devout believer *profess* to hold this doctrine as a *mystery*, and not as a truth of reason, or an intelligible truth? And if he holds it as such, how can he be charged with holding anything unreasonable? How can an assertion be called contrary to reason, when we do not know what its *meaning*, *i.e.* the thing asserted in it, *is?* And how, therefore, can the maintaining of such an unknown truth be unreasonable? The Christian only believes that there *is* a truth connected with this subject, which in the present state of his capacities he cannot understand, but which, on the principle of accommodation, is expressed in revelation in this form, as that mode of expressing it which is practically nearest to the truth.

## NOTE XIII. p. 84.

THE connection of this present state of sin and suffering with some great original transgression was too deeply laid down in Scripture to offer an easy explanation to the Pelagians. One main solution, however, of such passages was given; viz. that they referred to a connection not of descent, but example, that the sin of Adam was fatal as an imitated, not as a transmitted sin. But such an interpretation obviously fell short of the meaning of Scripture, nor was it improved by the details of the application. The Pelagian comment on the great passage in the Epistle to the Romans, that 'by one man sin entered into the world, and death by sin; and so death passed upon all men, for that all have sinned,' opposed to the received doctrine of transmitted sin; first, the expression 'one man,' which sufficed, it was said, for the view of example, whereas both the man and the woman were necessary for transmission;[1] secondly, the distinction that '*death* passed upon all men,' not sin; and, thirdly, the ground of actual sin, as distinguished from original, 'for that all have sinned.' But the first of these objections was futile; the second was overruled by other texts of Scripture which made death the consequence of sin; and the third can only at most be allowed a balancing, not a disproving weight. The Pelagian was, indeed,

[1] Op. Imp. l. 2. c. 47. 64.; l. 3. c. 85.

the better construer of the Greek words, which our translation with him renders into 'for that,' and not with S. Augustine into 'in whom.'[1]  But though this particular clause, thus translated, refers to a ground of actual sin, not of original, or sin 'in Adam,' as S. Augustine understood it; the reference to actual sin does not destroy the previous reference to original, at the beginning of the verse. The previous assertion is plain and decisive, that 'by one man sin entered into the world;' though the mystery of original sin must still be held together with the truth of nature that God only punishes men 'for that' they themselves 'have sinned.'

It was equally vain in a comment on the text that 'the judgment was from one offence to condemnation, but the free gift was of many offences unto justification,' to attempt to negative the unity of the sin mentioned in the preceding clause by the plurality in the next; and to argue, that if one sin had been the source of the general sinfulness of mankind, it would have been written 'from *one* offence,' not 'from *many* offences unto justification.'[2] The unity of the source is not inconsistent with plurality in the proceeds from it. To interpret 'many' again to mean many offences of one and the same person was gratuitous,[3] though convenient for a coveted inference, that the state out of which a man was raised at justification was contemplated here only as a state of personal, not of original sin.

No candid interpreter, again, of the text, 'As by the offence of one judgment came upon all men to condemnation; even so by the righteousness of One the free gift came upon all men unto justification of life,' would allow its obvious force to be negatived by the remark that, as all mankind do not attain to justification, the universality ascribed to the effect of Adam's sin in the first clause is destroyed by the necessarily limited sense of universality, as applied to justification, in the next.[4] Where the weight

[1] Op. Imp. l. 2. c. 63.
[2] Ibid. c. 105.
[3] 'Doce parvulos multis obnoxios esse criminibus.'—Ibid. c. 114.
[4] 'Si Christus salvarit universos, Adam quoque universis nocuisse fingatur.'—Op. Imp. l. 2. c. 136. Augustine answers, 'Qui propterea omnes liberare dictus est etiam ipse, quoniam non liberat quenquam *nisi*

of Scripture goes plainly in one direction, these minute verbal criticisms on dependent and subordinate clauses, ought not to be allowed to interfere with it.

From the passage in the Epistle to the Romans the Pelagian passed to that in the First Epistle to the Corinthians, 'As in Adam all die, even so in Christ shall all be made alive' (1 Cor. xv. 22.); and his interpretation was the same, that whether death was understood here of natural or of moral death, *i.e.*, sin, Adam was only put forth as the sample, not as the root of it; an interpretation which he confirmed by a reference to the succeeding text, 'As we have borne the image of the earthly we shall also bear the image of the heavenly;' as if this explained the preceding one in the sense of an actual imitation of Adam, not of any transmitted guilt or penalty from him.'[1]

The curse, at the commencement of the book of Genesis, received a double explanation; first, as imposing no new suffering on man; and, secondly, as imposing it, if it did impose it, only for the warning, and not for the punishment of posterity.[2] The Pelagian observed that sorrows were '*multiplied*' on the woman, as if they had *existed* before;[3] and that Adam, again, on whom the curse imposed labour, had laboured before in the Garden of Eden;[4] and that as a matter of fact labour was not the universal penalty, because it was not the universal lot of man. The sentence of death was even more boldly dealt with; and when the Pelagian had inferred from the text, 'For dust thou art, and unto dust shalt thou return,' that this event rested upon a physical ground anterior to man's transgression, he proceeded to observe that the announcement of it at that time was not intended as a severe, but as a consolatory

---

ipse.'—Op. Imp. l. 2. c. 136.

[1] 'Sicut omnes, *i.e. multi* Adæ imitatione moriuntur, ita omnes, *i.e.* multi Christi imitatione salvantur.' —Ibid. l. 6. c. 31.

[2] 'Ut commemoratione primi peccati, afflictio succedanea his, quos reos non fecerat, imitationis malæ indicet cautionem.'—Ibid. c. 27.

[3] Augustine: 'Multiplicabo, multas eas esse faciam. Poterat multiplicare quæ non erant.'—Op. Imp. l. 6. c. 26.

[4] 'Quid ei novum accidisse credimus, si sentiret sudorem.'—Ibid. c. 27.

one—a promise of relief from the trials and pains of life.[1] But S. Augustine appealed to the evident meaning of the curse as a judicial sentence, inflicting a punishment in consequence of man's sin which did not exist before it:[2] he appealed to a larger sense of labour than the narrow one of his opponent;[3] and he showed to the Pelagian the unavoidable inference from his explanation of the sentence of death, that man was wiser after his transgression than he was before it. For if death awaited him before his sin, as the lot of nature, the only difference which the curse, in announcing the event to him, made was, that it gave him the knowledge of it.'[4]

## NOTE XIV. p. 85.

JULIAN the Pelagian interprets Adam being created good as meaning merely that he was created with freewill, or the power to do good; Augustine interprets it as meaning that Adam was created with a good disposition or formed habit, and rejects the Pelagian meaning as a false one, for the plain reason that to be able to be good is not the same as to be good; whereas, Adam was made *good*. He admits, indeed, that in a certain sense, a nature which is able not to sin is a good nature: 'Bonum conditum Adam non ego tantum nec tu, sed ambo dicimus. Ambo enim dicimus bonam esse naturam quæ possit non peccare.'—*Op. Imp.* l. 6. c. 16. But this sense is put aside as insufficient. 'Quid est ergo quod nunc dicis; "Bonus Deus bonum fecit hominem," *si nec bonus nec malus est, habendo liberum arbitrium quod in eo Deus fecit?* . . . Et quomodo verum est, "*Fecit Deus hominem rectum.*"—Eccl. vii. 29. *An rectus erat non habens voluntatem bonam, sed ejus possibilitatem?* Ergo et pravus erat non habens voluntatem pravam, sed ejus possibilitatem. . . . Ita fit, ut per tuam mirabilem sapientiam, nec Deus fecerit rectum hominem; *sed qui rectus posset esse si vellet.*'—L. 5. c. 57.

[1] Op. Imp. l. 6. c. 27.
[2] 'Imo, inquis et damnatus est, et nihil ei accidit novi. Hic risum tenere difficile est.'—L. 6. c. 27.
[3] L. 2. c. 28.
[4] L. 6. c. 27.

Adam being created good, then, meant that he was created with a positive goodness, or a good habit of mind. Such a habit S. Augustine expresses by the term *bona voluntas*, *voluntas* meaning an established bias or inclination, or what we call character. 'Sed, inquis, "Ideo potuit oriri voluntas mala, ut oriri posset et bona." Quasi non cum bona voluntate factus sit vel angelus vel homo. Factus est rectus, sicut dixit Scriptura.—Eccl. vii. 29. Non ergo quæritur unde in illo potuerit oriri bona voluntas, cum qua factus est; sed unde mala cum qua factus non est. Et tu dicis, non attendens quid dicas "Ideo potuit oriri voluntas mala, ut oriri posset et bona:" et hoc putas ad naturam liberi arbitrii pertinere, ut possit utrumque et peccare scilicet et non peccare; *et in hoc existimas hominem factum ad imaginem Dei,* cum Deus ipse non possit utrumque.'—L. 5. c. 38. 'Quis enim ferat, si dicatur talis factus, quales nascuntur infantes? Illa itaque perfectio naturæ quam non dabant anni, sed sola manus Dei, non potuit nisi habere voluntatem aliquam, eamque non malam. Bonæ igitur voluntatis factus est homo . . . *neque enim nisi recta volens rectus est quisquam.*'—L. 5. c. 61.

Julian objects to this implanted *voluntas* on the free-will ground, pronouncing it absurd that a man can be *made* good; on the ground that goodness implied, in its very nature, choice and exertion of the will. 'Est natura humana bonum opus Dei : est libertas arbitrii, id est, possibilitas vel delinquendi vel recte faciendi, bonum æque opus Dei. Utrumque hoc homini de necessario venit. Sed voluntas *in* his exoritur non *de* his. *Capacia* voluntatis sunt quippe, non plena.'—*Op. Imp.* l. 5. c. 56. 'Est ergo ista possibilitas, quæ nomine libertatis ostenditur, ita a sapientissimo constituta Deo, ut sine ipsa non sit, quod per ipsam esse non cogitur.'—c. 57. Augustine replies: 'Ut video, nec bonam voluntatem vis tribuere naturæ, quando est homo primitus conditus: quasi non potuerit Deus hominem facere voluntatis bonæ.'—c. 61.

Augustine's *bona voluntas* only seems to express in a different form the traditional view of the Church from the first, as contained in the writings of the earlier fathers. Bishop Bull, in his discourse on the State of Man before the Fall, quotes their principal statements on the subject. They all take for their basis the scriptural truth, that Adam was made in the image of God; and they commonly interpret this to mean that the soul of Adam had a certain indwelling of the Holy Spirit in it. Tatian, the pupil of Justin Martyr, speaks of 'the familiarity and friendship' of the Spirit with Adam in his created state: τῆς σὺν αὐτῷ διαίτης—τοῦ πνεύματος τοῦ δυνατωτέρου, whom he also calls ἡ Λόγου δύναμις.—*Contra Græcos*, c. 7. Irenæus says: 'Spiritus commixtus animæ unitur plasmati' (l. 5. c. 6.); and also speaks of the robe of sanctity which Adam had from the Spirit: 'quam habuit a Spiritu sanctitatis stolam.'—L. 3. c. 23. Tertullian speaks of the Spirit of God which Adam received by inspiration: 'Spiritum quem tunc de afflatu ejus acceperat.'—*De Baptismo*, c. 5. Clemens Alexandrinus speaks of 'the characteristical propriety of the Holy Spirit superadded' to the nature of Adam: προσγινόμενον ἁγίου πνεύματος χαρακτηριστικὸν ἰδίωμα.—Strom. l. 6. c. 16. Athanasius speaks of God imparting to our first parents the power of His own Word: μεταδοὺς αὐτοῖς καὶ τῆς τοῦ ἰδίου Λόγου δυνάμεως.—*De Incar. Verb.* tom. i. c. 3. Basil speaks of the 'assession of God, and conjunction with him (Adam) by love—ἡ προσεδρεία τοῦ θεοῦ, καὶ ἡ διὰ τῆς ἀγάπης συνάφεια.'— *Homil. quod non Deus est Auctor Peccat.* Cyril speaks of 'that Spirit which formed him (Adam) after the Divine image, and was, as a seal, secretly impressed on his soul— τὸ πρὸς θείαν εἰκόνα διαμορφοῦν αὐτὸ, καὶ σημάντρου δίκην ἀποῤῥήτως ἐντεθειμένον.'—7. *Dialog. de Trin.* This familiar abode of the Spirit in the first man, and the character and seal stamped by the Spirit upon him, evidently imply a certain *disposition* of mind or holy habit which was formed in him, as Cyprian (*De Bono Patientiæ*) actually expresses it, interpreting the Divine image as involving virtues—*virtutes*.

NOTE XV. p. 102.

Thus Justin Martyr says of the human race: ὁ ἀπὸ τοῦ Ἀδὰμ ὑπὸ θάνατον καὶ πλάνην τὴν τοῦ ὄφεως ἐπεπτώκει, παρὰ τὴν ἰδίαν αἰτίαν ἑκάστου αὐτῶν πονηρευσαμένου.— *Dial. cum Tryph.* c. 88. παρὰ here signifying not *besides* (*præter*) but by reason of *sua propria cujusque culpa*, the latter half of this sentence gives the natural truth— viz., that the individual sins by the exercise of his own freewill; as the former gives the revealed, that the individual sins in consequence of the sinfulness of the race. One sentence of Tatian's joins the two in the same way: ζῆθι τῷ θεῷ τὴν παλαιὰν γένεσιν παραιτούμενος· οὐκ ἐγενόμεθα πρὸς τὸ ἀποθνήσκειν, ἀποθνήσκομεν δὲ δι' ἑαυτούς.— *Contra Græc.* c. 11. The 'old birth' is the mysterious, the 'δι' ἑαυτοὺς,' the obvious and conscious cause of sin. So far the fathers only follow the precedent of Scripture, which puts the two grounds together, as in Rom. v. 12., ' As by one man sin entered into the world and death by sin; and so death passed upon all men, *for that* all have sinned;' death being referred in the first part of the sentence to the sin of Adam, in the last to each man's actual sins. Again, several fathers speak of infants as innocent beings: 'Quid festinat innocens ætas ad remissionem peccatorum.'—*Tertullian De Bapt.* c. 18. 'Ἐλθόντες εἰς τόνδε τὸν κόσμον ἀναμάρτητοι.'—*Cyril of Jerusalem, Cat.* iv. 13. ' Τὸ ἀπειρόκακον νήπιον . . μὴ δεόμενον τῆς ἐκ τοῦ καθαρθῆναι ὑγιείας, ὅτι μηδὲ τὴν ἀρχὴν τὴν νόσον τῇ ψυχῇ παρεδέξατο . . . τὸ μήτε ἐν ἀγάθῳ, μήτε ἐν κάκῳ εὑρισκόμενον.'—*Gregory Nyss.* (De iis qui præmature abripiuntur).. But Hagenbach is precipitate in concluding from the passage in Cyril, that ' Cyril of Jerusalem assumed that men are born in a state of innocence' (*History of Doctrines*, v. i. p. 315.); *i.e.* if he means by this that Cyril denied original sin. It is a truth of reason and nature, that infants are innocent beings, which may be asserted, as it must be by every rational person, without prejudice to the mysterious truth of their guilt as descendants of Adam. Tertullian, who asserts it, is at the same time acknowledged as one of those fathers who have most strongly asserted the doctrine of original sin; and Scripture itself asserts both, saying of children, that 'of such is the kingdom of heaven,' while at the same time it declares, that 'in Adam all die.' Chrysostom again denies that one man can be responsible for another man's sin: τὸ μὲν γὰρ ἕτερον δι' ἕτερον κολάζεσθαι οὐ σφρόδρα δοκεῖ λόγον ἔχειν. —*Hom.* X. *in Rom.* But this is a simple truth of reason which nobody can deny, and the assertion of it is quite consistent with holding the mystery of our guilt in Adam. All the early fathers, moreover, assert strongly the freewill of even fallen man, his προαίρεσις ἐλεύθερα, αὐτεξούσιον. But this runs side by side with their assertion of his 'captivity' and 'corruption,' as another part of the whole truth.

The case of Clement of Alexandria is perhaps peculiar, though too much should not be made of particular expressions, like the ones just quoted, found in him. In combating, indeed, the Gnostic doctrine of our evil nature, he uses arguments which would equally tell against the doctrine of original sin. He denies that any one can be evil but by his own personal act: λεγέτωσαν ἡμῖν ποῦ ἐπόρνευσεν τὸ μεννηθὲν παιδίον, ἢ πῶς ὑπὸ τὴν τοῦ Ἀδὰμ ὑποπέπτωκεν ἀρὰν τὸ μηδὲν ἐνεργῆσαν;—*Strom.* 1. 3. c. 16. He describes, again, sin after the fall, as if it were only a repetition, and not an effect of sin at the fall: εἷς γὰρ ὁ ἀπατεὼν ἄνωθεν μὲν τὴν Εὔαν, νῦν δὲ ἤδη καὶ τοὺς ἄλλους ἀνθρώπους εἰς θάνατον ὑποφέρων.—*Ad Gentes,* vol. 1. p. 7. But Hagenbach is precipitate in concluding that Clement 'rejects the doctrine of original sin, properly so called,' simply on the strength of such passages as these.—*History of Doctrine,* v. 1. p. 173. Augustine himself has a similar passage exactly to the one just quoted: 'Etiam nunc in unoquoque nostrum nihil aliud agitur, cum ad peccatum quisque delabitur, quam tunc actum est in illis tribus, serpente, muliere, et viro. —*De Genesi contra Man.* l. 2. c. 14. Such expressions are no more than what common sense justifies and obliges, and are quite consistent with belief in the other truth. But Clement, though he asserts sin to be 'natural,' τὸ γὰρ ἐξαμαρτάνειν πᾶσιν ἔμφυτον καὶ κοινόν (*Pæd.* l. 3. c. 12), (his language, however, seeming to express here universal rather than original sin), certainly seems to explain away the passage in the Psalms, 'in sin hath my mother conceived me,' interpreting it to refer to sinful custom or habit, not to sinful nature (*Strom.* l. 3. c. 16.), though at the same time it must be remarked, that he is relieving the passage of a Gnostic meaning, according to which sin was inherent in natural generation as such, and not opposing the Catholic. Jeremy Taylor gives a somewhat similar explanation with less excuse. 'The words are a Hebraism, and signify nothing but an aggrandation of his sinfulness, and are intended for a high expression, meaning that 'I am wholly and entirely wicked.'—Vol. ix. p. 27. On the whole, though Clement, in common with all the early fathers, is a lenient *interpreter* of the doctrine of original sin, and though such passages as these have not such counterbalancing ones in his writings as they have in those of other fathers, these passages are no test of his belief on the subject.

## NOTE XVI. p. 114.

Τοὺς δὲ (unbaptised infants, or those who by accident died without baptism) μήτε δοξασθήσεσθαι, μήτε κολασθήσεσθαι περὶ τοῦ δικαίου κριτοῦ, ὡς ἀσφραγίστους μὲν ἀπονήρους δὲ, ἀλλὰ παθόντας μᾶλλον τὴν ζημίαν ἢ δράσαντας. οὐ γὰρ ὅστις οὐ κολάσεως ἄξιος ἤδη καὶ τιμῆς· ὥσπερ ὅστις οὐ τιμῆς ἤδη καὶ κολάσεως.—*Gregory Naz. Orat.* 40. v. i. p. 653. Gregory of Nyssa formally discusses the question of the future condition of those who die as infants, without reference to their being or not baptised (v. ii. p. 749); which, in distinction to the ground taken by some, that they do not *deserve* so much happiness as the mature good, he maintains to turn, not so much upon any difference of claim, as of natural aptitude and capacity for happiness. Οὐκ ἔστιν εἰπεῖν κυρίως ἀντίδοσιν τῶν εὐβεβιωκότων γενέσθαι τὴν τῆς ζωῆς μετουσίαν καὶ τιμωρίαν τὸ ἔμπαλιν. Ἀλλ' ὅμοιόν ἐστι τῷ κατὰ τοὺς ὀφθαλμοὺς ὑποδείγματι τὸ λεγόμενον. Οὐδὲ γὰρ τῷ κεκαθαρμένῳ τὰς ὄψεις ἔπαθλόν τι φαμὲν εἶναι καὶ πρεσβεῖον τὴν τῶν ὁρατῶν κατανόησιν, ἢ τῷ νοσοῦντι τὸ ἔμπαλιν καταδίκην τινὰ τὸ μὲ μετέχειν τῆς ὁρατικῆς ἐνεργείας· ἀλλ' ὡς ἀναγκαίως ἔπεται τῷ κατὰ φύσιν διακειμένῳ τὸ βλέπειν, τῷ τε ἀπὸ πάθους παρενεχθέντι τῆς φύσεως, τὸ μὴ ἐνεργεῖν τὴν ὅρασιν· τὸν αὐτὸν τόπον καὶ ἡ μακαρία ζωὴ συμφυής ἐστι καὶ οἰκεῖα τοῖς κεκαθαρμένοις τὰ τῆς ψυχῆς αἰσθητήρια. Upon this principle he proceeds to argue that the happiness of infants in a future state will be in proportion to their capacity for it, which will be lower than that of those who have lived virtuously as mature men; that it will be analogous to their happiness in this life, which is of the simpler and unconscious kind. Καθάπερ γὰρ θηλῇ καὶ γάλακτι ἡ πρώτη τῶν νηπίων ἡλικία τιθυνουμένη ἐκτρέφεται· εἶτα διαδέχεται ταύτην κατάλληλος ἑτέρα τῷ ὑποκειμένῳ τροφή, οἰκείως τε καὶ ἐπιτηδείως πρὸς τὸ τρεφόμενον ἔχουσα, ἕως ἂν ἐπὶ τὸ τέλειον φθάσῃ· οὕτως οἶμαι καὶ τὴν ψυχὴν διὰ τῶν ἀεὶ κατ' ἀλλήλων τάξει τινὶ καὶ ἀκολουθίᾳ μετέχειν τῆς κατὰ φύσιν ζωῆς, ὡς χωρεῖ καὶ δύναται τῶν ἐν τῇ μακαριότητι προκειμένων καταλαμβάνουσα. . . . . . . Ἡ δὲ ἄγευστος τῆς ἀρετῆς ψυχὴ, τῶν μὲν ἐκ πονηριὰς κακῶν, ἅτε μήτε τὴν ἀρχὴν συνενεχθεῖσα τῇ τῆς κακίας νόσῳ, διαμένει ἀμέτοχος τῆς ζωῆς ἐκείνης· τὴν Θεοῦ γνῶσίν τε καὶ μετουσίαν τοσοῦτον μετέχει παρὰ τὴν πρώτην, ὅσον χώρει τὸ τρεφόμενον.—Augustine maintained a middle state, in his earlier theological life. —Dicunt enim : quid opus est ut nasceretur qui antequam iniret ullum vitæ meritum excessit e vita ? Aut qualis in futuro judicio deputabitur, cui neque inter justos locus est, quoniam nihil recte fecit ; neque inter malos, quoniam nihil peccavit ? Quibus respondetur : ad universitatis complexum, et totius creaturæ vel per locos vel per tempora ordinatissimam connexionem, non posse superfluo creari qualemcunque hominem, ubi folium arboris nullum superfluum creatur ; sed sane superfluo quæri de meritis ejus qui nihil meruerit. Non enim metuendum est ne vita esse potuerit media quædam inter recte factum atque peccatum, et sententia judicis media esse non possit inter præmium et supplicium.—*De Lib. Arb.* l. 3. c. 23.

## NOTE XVII. p. 121.

IN the first of the following passages all wickedness, in the second extreme wickedness, is referred to original sin; in the third, different degrees admitted in evil, are accounted for by different degrees of original sin; in the fourth and fifth these degrees in evil appear as the additions of the individual to original sin, though in what precise sense they leave uncertain.

(1.) 'Ad iram quippe Dei [in consequence of original sin] pertinet justam, quicquid cæca et indomita concupiscentia faciunt libenter mali.'—*Enchiridion,* c. 27. (2.) ' Omnes ex eadem massa perditionis et damnationis secundum duritiem cordis sui et cor impenitens, quantum ad ipsos pertinet, thesaurizant sibi iram in die iræ, quo redditur unicuique secundum opera sua.'—*Contra Julianum Pelagianum,* l. 5. c. 4. (3.) ' Veruntamen tacitum non est quod erat eorum malitia naturalis; quæ quidem omnium hominum, sed in aliis minor, in aliis major est: sicut corpora corruptibilia sunt omnium, sed alias animas minus, alias plus gravant, pro diversitate judiciorum Dei, occultorum quidem, sed sine ulla dubitatione justorum.'—*Opus Imp. Contra Julianum,* l. 4. c. 128. (4.) ' Hi ergo qui non pertinent ad istum certissimum et felicissimum numerum pro meritis justissime judicantur. Aut enim jacent sub peccato, quod originaliter generatim traxerunt, et cum illo hæreditario debito hinc exeunt, quod non est regeneratione dimissum; aut per liberum arbitrium alia insuper addiderunt; arbitrium, inquam, liberum sed non liberatum; liberum justitiæ, peccati autem servum, quo volvuntur per diversas noxias cupiditates, alii magis, alii minus; sed omnes mali.'—*De Correptione et Gratiâ,* c. 13. (5.) ' Si autem male vivunt de suo male vivunt, vel quod originaliter traxerunt, vel quod insuper addiderunt. Sed si vasa sunt iræ, quæ perfecta sunt ad perditionem, quæ illis debita redditur, sibi hoc imputent, quia ex ea massa facta sunt, quam propter unius peccatum, in quo omnes peccaverunt, merito Deus justeque damnavit.'—*Ep.* 194. c. 6.

Jansen interprets S. Augustine as making the whole mass of actual sin in the world the simple effect and development of original. 'Positivæ reprobationis causa... peccata omnia cum quibus morituri sunt, etiam originale peccatum. Nam ex illius suppliciis quicquid peccatorum a reprobatis perpetratum est accessu liberæ voluntatis, fluxit . . . ut proinde illa tota suppliciorum concatenatio, usque ad damnationem in ignem æternam, radicaliter et mediate in peccati originalis meritum referenda videatur. Immediate tamen prima pœnarum istarum promeretur secundam, et ita deinceps, donec ultima tandem, velut præcedentium complementum, inferatur.'—*De Gratiâ Christi*, p. 1019.

## NOTE XVIII. p. 123.

'ET propterea conantur parvulis non baptizatis innocentiæ merito salutem ac vitam æternam tribuere ; sed, quia baptizati non sunt, eos a regno cœlorum facere alienos : nova quadam et mirabili præsumptione, quasi salus ac vita æterna possit esse præter Christi hæreditatem, præter regnum cœlorum. . . . Profecto illi quibus Sacramentum defuerit in eis habendi sunt qui non credunt Filio ; atque ideo, si hujus inanes gratiæ de corpore exierint, sequetur eos quod dictum est, " Non habebunt vitam sed ira Dei manet super eos." Unde hoc, quando eos clarum est peccata propria non habere, si nec originali peccato teneantur obnoxii.'—*De Peccat. Merit. et Rem.* l. 1. c. xx.

'Quia ergo de ovibus ejus non esse incipiunt parvuli nisi per baptismum ; profecto, si hoc non accipiunt, peribunt.'—*Ibid.* c. xxvii.

'Quemadmodum enim omnes omnino pertinentes ad generationem voluntatis carnis non moriuntur nisi in Adam in quo omnes peccaverunt : sic ex his omnes omnino pertinentes ad regenerationem voluntatis spiritus non vivificantur nisi in Christo, in quo omnes justificantur. Quia sicut per unum omnes ad condemnationem, sic per unum omnes ad justificationem. Nec est ullus medius locus ut possit esse nisi cum diabolo, qui non est cum Christo. Hic et ipse Dominus volens auferre de cordibus male credentium istam nescio quam medietatem, quam conantur quidam parvulis non baptizatis tribuere, ut quasi merito innocentiæ sint in vita æterna, sed quia non sunt baptizati non sint cum Christo in regno ejus, definitivam protulit ad hæc ora obstruenda sententiam, ubi ait: "Qui mecum non est, adversum me est." Constitue igitur quemlibet parvulum: si jam cum Christo est, ut quid baptizatur? Si autem, quod habet veritas, ideo baptizatur ut sic cum Christo, profecto non baptizatus non est cum Christo, et, quia non est cum Christo, adversus Christum est.'—*Ibid.* c. xxviii.

'Unde fit consequens ut, quoniam nihil agitur aliud, cum parvuli baptizantur, nisi ut incorporentur ecclesiæ, id est, Christi corpori membrisque associentur; manifestum est eos ad damnationem, nisi hoc eis collatum fuerit, pertinere. Non autem damnari possent, si peccatum utique non haberent. Hoc quia illa ætas nulla in vita propria contrahere potuit, restat intelligere vel, si hoc nondum possumus, saltem credere, trahere parvulos originale peccatum.'—*Ibid.* l. 3. c. iv.

'Absit ut causam parvulorum sic relinquamus, ut esse nobis dicamus incertum, utrum in Christo regenerati, si moriantur parvuli, transeant in æternam salutem; non regenerati autem transeant in mortem secundam; quoniam quod scriptum est, "Per unum hominem peccatum intravit in mundum, et per peccatum mors; et ita in omnes homines pertransiit," aliter recte intelligi non potest: nec a morte perpetua quæ justissime est retributa peccato, liberat quenquam pusillorum atque magnorum, nisi ille qui propter remittenda et originalia et propria nostra peccata mortuus est, sine ullo suo originali et proprio peccato. Sed quare illos potius quam illos? Iterum atque iterum dicimus, nec nos piget, "O homo, tu quis es qui respondeas Deo?"'—*De Dono Perseverantiæ*, c. xii.

'Sed ut id quod dicimus alicujus exempli manifesta-

## Note XVIII.

tione clarescat, constituamus aliquos ab abliqua meretrice geminos editos, atque ut ab aliis colligerentur, expositos: horum sine baptismo expiravit unus, alius baptizatus. . . . Quid restat quantum ad baptizatum attinet, nisi gratia Dei quæ vasis factis in honorem gratis datur; quantum autem ad non baptizatum, ira Dei, quæ vasis factis ad contumeliam pro ipsius massæ meritis redditur?'—*Contra Duas Ep. Pel.* l. 2. c. vii.

'Ac per hoc, quia nihil ipsi male vivendo addiderunt ad originale peccatum, potest eorum merito dici in illa damnatione minima pœna, non tamen nulla. Quisquis autem putat diversitatem futuram non esse pœnarum, legat quod scriptum est, "Tolerabilius erit Sodomæ in die judicii, quam illi civitati." Non ergo a deceptoribus inter regnum et supplicium medius locus quæratur infantibus; sed transeant a diabolo ad Christum, hoc est, a morte ad vitam, ne ira Dei maneat super eos.'—*Ep.* 184. c. 1.

'Respondeat quid de illo futurum sit, qui, nulla sua culpa non baptizatus, ista fuerit temporali morte præventus. Si non putamus esse dicturum quod innocentem Deus, nec habentem originale peccatum ante annos quibus habere poterat proprium, æterna morte damnabit; cogitur itaque respondere quod Pelagius in ecclesiastico judicio, ut aliquo modo catholicus pronuntiaretur, anathematizare compulsus est, infantes, etiamsi non baptizentur, habere vitam æternam: hac enim negata, quid nisi mors æterna remanebit?' —*Ep.* 186. c. viii.

'Primus hic error aversandus ab auribus, exstirpandus a mentibus. Hoc novum in ecclesia, prius inauditum est, esse vitam æternam præter regnum cœlorum, esse salutem æternam præter regnum Dei. Primo vide, frater, ne forte hic consentire nobis debeas, quisquis ad regnum Dei non pertinet, eum ad damnationem sine dubio pertinere. Venturus Dominus, et judicaturus de vivis et mortuis, sicut evangelium loquitur, duas partes facturus est, dextram et sinistram. Sinistris dicturus, *Ite in ignem æternam, qui paratus est Diabolo et angelis ejus;* dextris dicturus, *Venite benedicti Patris mei, percipite regnum quod vobis paratum est, ab origine mundi.* Hac regnum nominat, hac cum diabolo damnationem. Nullus relictus est medius locus, ubi ponere queas infantes. De vivis et mortuis judicabitur: alii erunt ad dextram, alii ad sinistram: non novi aliud. Qui inducis medium, recede de medio, sed noli in sinistram. Si ergo dextra erit, et sinistra, et nullum medium locum in Evangelio novimus; ecce in dextra regnum cœlorum est, *Percipite*, inquit, *regnum*. Qui ibi non est in sinistra est. Quid erit in sinistra? *Ite in ignem œternum*. In dextra ad regnum, utique æternum; in sinistra in ignem æternum. Qui non in dextra, procul dubio in sinistra: ergo qui non in regno, procul dubio in igne æterno. Certe habere potest vitam æternam qui non baptizatur? Non est in dextra, id est, non erit in regno. Vitam æternam computas ignem sempiternum? Et de ipsa vita æterna audi expressius, quia nihil aliud est regnum quam vita æterna. Prius regnum nominavit, sed in dextris; ignem æternum in sinistris. Extrema autem sententia, ut doceret quid sit regnum, et quid sit ignis sempiternus—*Tunc*, inquit, *abibunt isti in ambustionem œternam; justi autem in vitam œternam*.

'Ecce exposuit tibi quid sit regnum, et quid sit ignis æternus; ut quando confitearis parvulum non futurum in regno, fatearis futurum in igne æterno.'—*Serm.* 294, c. iii.

## NOTE XIX. p. 131.

HOOKER states S. Augustine's doctrine of predestination as the doctrine 'that the whole body of mankind in the view of God's eternal knowledge lay universally polluted with sin, worthy of condemnation and death; that over the mass of corruption there passed two acts of the will of God, an act of favour, liberality, and grace, choosing part to be made partakers of everlasting glory; and an act of justice, forsaking the rest and adjudging them to endless perdition; these vessels of wrath, those of mercy; which mercy is to God's elect so peculiar, and to them and none else (for their number is definitely known, and can neither be increased nor diminished), to them it allotteth immortality and all things thereunto appertaining; them it predestinateth, it calleth, justifieth, glorifieth them; it poureth voluntarily that spirit into their hearts, which spirit so given is the root of their very first desires and motions tending to immortality; as for others on whom such grace is not bestowed, there is justly assigned, and immutably to every of them, the lot of eternal condemnation.'— *Appendix* to bk. v. Keble's edition, p. 730.

Another statement, a little further on, not so much *of* Augustine's doctrine as professing to be founded upon it, is somewhat less rigid: 'To proceed, we have seen the general inclination of God towards all men's everlasting happiness, notwithstanding sin; we have seen that the natural love of God towards mankind was the cause of appointing or predestinating Christ to suffer for the sins of the whole world—we have seen that our Lord, who made Himself a sacrifice for our sins, did it in the bowels of a merciful desire that no man might perish—we have seen that God, nevertheless, hath found most just occasion to decree the death and condemnation of some—we have seen that the whole cause why such are excluded from life *resteth altogether in themselves*—we have seen that the natural will of God being inclined toward all men's salvation, and His occasioned will having set down the death but of some in such condemnation, as hath been shewed, it must needs follow that of the rest there is a determinate ordinance proceeding from the good pleasure of God, whereby they are, and have been before all worlds, predestinated heirs of eternal bliss—we have seen that in Christ, the Prince of God's elect, all worthiness was foreseen; that in the elect angels there was not foreseen any matter for just indignation and wrath to work upon; that in all other God foresaw iniquity, for which an irrevocable sentence of death and condemnation might most justly have passed over all: for it can never be too often inculcated that touching the very decree of endless destruction and death, God is the Judge from whom it cometh, but man the cause from which it grew. Salvation contrariwise, and life proceedeth only both from God and of God. We are receivers through grace and mercy, authors through merit and desert we are not, of our own salvation. In the children of perdition we must always remember that of the Prophet, "Thy destruction, O Israel is of thyself;" lest we teach men blasphemously to cast the blame of all their misery upon God. Again, lest we take to ourselves the glory of that happiness, which, if He did not freely and voluntarily bestow, we should never be made partakers thereof, it must ever, in the election of saints, be remembered, that to choose is an act of God's good pleasure, which presupposeth in us sufficient cause to avert, but none to deserve it. For this cause, whereas S. Augustine had some time been of opinion that God chose Jacob and hated Esau, the one in regard of belief, the other of infidelity, which was foreseen, his mind he afterwards delivered thus: "*Jacob I have loved;* behold what God doth freely bestow. *I have hated* Esau ; behold what man doth justly deserve."—p. 737.

There is some departure here from the rigour of the real Augustinian language, though no positive inconsistency with the Augustinian doctrine. The modification is given by suppression ; 'We have seen,' he says, 'that the whole cause why such are excluded from life resteth *altogether in themselves.*' S. Augustine would say this, but he would explain at the same time that this cause in man himself was not foreseen personal sin, but original sin. Hooker suppresses this interpretation, and leaves men's actual foreseen sins as the cause, according to the natural meaning of his phrase, of their exclusion from the decree of predestination to life.

A third statement of the doctrine of predestination reverts to a stricter line. 'It followeth, therefore—1. That God hath predestinated certain men, not all men; 2. That the cause moving Him hereunto was not the foresight of any virtue in us at all; 3. That to Him the number of His elect is definitely known ; 4. That it cannot be but their sins must condemn them to whom the purpose of His saving mercy doth not extend; 5. That to God's foreknown elect final continuance in grace is given ; 6. That inward grace whereby to be saved is deservedly not given unto all men; 7. That no man cometh unto Christ, whom

God by the inward grace of the Spirit draweth not; 8. And that it is not in every one, no, not in any man's mere ability, freedom, and power, to be saved; no man's salvation being possible without grace. Howbeit, God is no favourer of sloth, and therefore there can be no such absolute decree touching man's salvation, as on our part includeth no necessity of care and travail, but shall certainly take effect, whether we ourselves do wake or sleep.'—p. 752. The difference between this statement and the Lambeth Articles consists in an omission and insertion, softening the general effect of the language, while the substantial ground is the same. Thus the first Lambeth Article *mentions* reprobation, which the first article of this statement does not; but reprobation is *implied* in it. Again, the 7th Lambeth Article says, ' Gratia salutaris non tribuitur universis hominibus qua servari possint, si voluerint.' Hooker inserts after ' is not given,' ' *deservedly*,' which softens the effect, though the desert may be admitted by the most rigid predestinarian in the shape of original sin. There is a real difference between the two statements of doctrine, in the omission in Hooker's of the doctrine of assurance, which is asserted in the Lambeth document.

## NOTE XX. p. 234.

IN the controversy in the Gallican Church, on the subject of predestination, which arose out of the doctrinal statements of Gotteschalcus; which was conducted by Hinckmar, archbishop of Rheims, on the one side, and Remigius, archbishop of Lyons, on the other, and which produced the Councils of Quiercy and Valence; neither side appears to have sifted the question to its foundation, or to have understood its really turning points; and there is, accordingly, a good deal of arbitrary adoption and arbitrary rejection of language on both sides; a good deal of reliance on distinctions without a difference, that is to say, on words. The doctrinal statement of Gotteschalcus embraces the following five points.—*Usher's Gotteschalci Historia*, p. 27.

' 1. Ante omnia secula, et antequam quicquam faceret

a principio Deus quos voluit prædestinavit ad regnum, et quos voluit prædestinavit ad interitum.

'2. Qui prædestinati sunt ad interitum salvari non possunt, et qui prædestinati sunt ad regnum perire non possunt.

'3. Deus non vult omnes homines salvos fieri, sed eos tantum qui salvantur: et quod dicit Apostolus " Qui vult omnes homines salvos fieri," illos dicit omnes qui tantummodo salvantur.

'4. Christus non venit ut omnes salvaret; nec passus est pro omnibus, nisi solummodo pro his qui passionis ejus salvantur mysterio.

'5. Postquam primus homo libero arbitrio cecidit, nemo nostrum ad bene agendum, sed tantummodo ad male agendum, libero potest uti arbitrio.'

This statement of doctrine is substantially Augustinian, and nothing more; and Remigius approves of it as a whole, making an exception against the 5th proposition; respecting the meaning of which he must have been under some mistake, for the language expresses no more than what is necessarily involved in the doctrine of original sin. With this exception, he maintains this doctrinal statement to be supported, '*uno sensu uno ore*,' by the fathers and the Church, and appeals to the undisputed authority of Augustine in their favour—'*Beatissimi patris Augustini ab omni semper ecclesia venerabiliter recepti et usque in finem seculi recipiendi*,' explaining the text 'Qui vult omnes homines salvos fieri,' apparently contradicted in the 3rd proposition, according to Augustine's interpretation: (1.) ' Ut omnes homines *omnia hominum genera* accipiamus :' (2.) ' non quod omnes salventur, sed quod *nemo nisi* miserationis ejus voluntate salvetur.' On the 4th he says: ' Si inveniantur aliqui patrum qui etiam pro impiis in sua impietate permansuris Dominum crucifixum dicant;' if they can prove it out of Scripture well, if not, ' quis non videat potiorem illam esse auctoritatem, quæ et tam evidenti ratione et tam multiplici Scripturarum attestatione firmatur? . . . . Si autem placet, propter pacem, non renuatur. . . . . Nihil tamen definiatur.'—p. 34.

The Council of Quiercy (Concilium Carisiacense) sum-

## Note XX. 391

moned by Hinckmar, condemned the opinions of Gotteschalcus, and published a counter statement of doctrine, which placed the doctrine of predestination upon a ground of foreknowledge: '*Secundum præscientiam suam* quos per gratiam prædestinavit ad vitam elegit ex massa perditionis. Cæteros autem quos justitiæ judicio in massa perditionis reliquit, perituros præscivit, sed non ut perirent prædestinavit.'—p. 67. There is nothing in the language of this proposition to which the most rigid predestinarian might not subscribe; but Remigius interprets the *præscientia* as the foreknowledge of the individual's good life, and as implying the resting of the doctrine of predestination on that ground: 'Quod manifeste contrarium est Catholicæ fidei. Quia Omnipotens Deus in electione eorum quos prædestinavit, et vocavit ad vitam æternam, non eorum merita præscivit.' On the subject of the Divine will to save all mankind the Council decreed: 'Deus omnipotens omnes homines sine exceptione vult salvos fieri, licet non omnes salventur,' to which proposition Remigius opposes the fact of the heathen world, the damnation of which he considers to be a point which has been decided by the Church. The same question was taken up by the Council in another form; viz. whether Christ did or did not *suffer for all men*, which it decided in the affirmative. 'Christus Jesus Dominus noster, sicut nullus homo est fuit vel erit cujus natura in illo assumpta non fuerit, ita nullus est fuit vel erat homo pro quo passus non fuerit; licet non omnes passionis ejus mysterio redimantur.' On this argument Remigius remarks: 'Quod dicitur quod nullus homo est fuit vel erit cujus natura in Christo assumpta non fuerit. . . . . Susceptio illa naturæ humanæ in Christo non fuit ex necessitate originis, sed ex potestate et gratia et misericordia et dignatione suscipientis. Quia ergo ista tam divina et singularis generatio hominis Christi non aliqua naturali necessitate, sed sola ejus potestate et gratia et misericordia facta est; *sic* per omnes generationes caro ejus descendit; *sic* ex eis veraciter natus verus homo factus est *ut quod ei placuit miserendo, et sanando, et redimendo inde assumeret, quod autem non placuit reprobaret.*'—

p. 79. The argument is, that our Lord's assumption of human nature being itself a condescension, and special dispensation, has a particular limited scope, according to the Divine pleasure, and only brings Him, as possessing this nature, into communion with a certain portion of those whom this nature includes, and is only beneficial to this portion.

The controversy, which is thus substantially between the Augustinian and the Semi-Pelagian doctrines, exhibits, however, much confusion, and is encumbered by false distinctions. A great deal is made of the question of the *duplex prædestinatio*. Hinckmar admitting a predestination to life eternal, refuses to admit a predestination to punishment, and insists on the distinction between *leaving men* in their sinful state, of which punishment will be the consequence, and ordaining men to such punishment. 'Quosdam autem, sicut præscivit, non ad mortem neque ad ignem prædestinavit, *sed in massa peccati et perditionis juste deseruit*, a qua eos prædestinatione sua (*i.e.* gratiæ præparatione) occulto sed non injusto judicio nequaquam eripuit.'—p. 93. But the most rigid predestinarian would not object to this statement. There is no real distinction between abandoning men to a certain state, of which punishment will be the consequence, and ordaining them to that punishment. The only distinction which would make a difference, respects the nature of this sinful state, to which men are abandoned, whether it is original sin or their own personal perseverance in sin. The abandonment of a certain portion of mankind to the state of sin in which they are born, is predestinarian reprobation, whether we express it as abandonment to sin, or as ordaining to punishment. Remigius exposes the irrelevancy of this distinction: 'Mirum valde est quomodo negare contendunt eum æternam ipsorum damnationem prædestinasse, quos jam ab ipso mundi exordio, cum primus homo peccavit, et omne humanum genus ex se propagandum unam massam damnationis et perditionis fecit, manifeste dicant in eadem massa damnationis et perditionis justo Dei judicio deputatos et derelictos. Quid est enim massa damnationis et perditionis ab initio mundi divino judicio effecta, nisi eodem divino judicio æternæ damnationi et perditioni destinata et tradita ?'—p. 93.

Hinckmar insists again on the Augustinian definition of predestination as *gratiæ præparatio* (p. 94.), as favouring his denial of any *prædestinatio damnationis;* to which Remigius replies, that a predestination to life did not exclude the predestination to punishment. It is obvious that the whole of this discussion is verbal, and is not concerned with the real grounds and substance of the controversy.

## NOTE XXI. p. 267.

I SEE no substantial difference between the Augustinian and Thomist, and the Calvinist doctrine of predestination. S. Augustine and Calvin alike hold an eternal Divine decree, which, antecedently to all action, separates one portion of mankind from another, and ordains one to everlasting life and the other to everlasting punishment. That is the fundamental statement of both; and it is evident, that while this fundamental statement is the same, there can be no substantial difference in the two doctrines. This statement is the sum and substance of the doctrine of predestination: and therefore if Augustine and Calvin agree in this statement, it may be pronounced *in limine* idle to talk of any real difference between their respective doctrines on this subject. Let persons only consider what this statement is, and what it necessarily involves, and they must see it is impossible that there can be any real distinction of doctrine on the particular subject of predestination, after this statement has been agreed in by the two. Those who suppose that S. Augustine differs from Calvin in his doctrine of predestination, do not really know the doctrine which S. Augustine held on the subject, and suppose it to be different from what it was. They suppose it to be a qualified doctrine of predestination to privileges and means of grace; or they have some general idea that S. Augustine did not hold such a doctrine as Calvin held—an assumption which settles to begin with the question for them.

But if Augustine's doctrine was the one which has been here stated to be his, and if it was expressed in the above fundamental statement, it must be seen immediately that it is the same as Calvin's doctrine.

And the identity of the two doctrines thus apparent at first sight, and from the fundamental statement by which they are expressed, will appear further from the cautions and checks by which each guards the doctrine. We may be referred to various cautions and checks which S. Augustine and his followers in the schools appended to the doctrine of predestination; from which it will be argued that the doctrine was not the same as the Calvinistic one. But it will be found on examination that Calvin has just the same cautions and checks.

The checks and cautions, which S. Augustine and his followers in the schools appended to their doctrine of predestination, were substantially these two: that God was not the author of evil; and that man had *will*, and was, as having a will, responsible for his own sins. The doctrine of predestination was relieved from two consequences which appeared to follow from it. If God is the sole author and cause of our goodness, how is He not the author and cause of our sin too? If we are bound to refer the one to Him, why not the other? The doctrine thus led to the consequence that God was the author of evil. This consequence, then, was cut off by a formal check, accompanied with more or less of argument, that God was not the author of evil. In the same way the doctrine of predestination, maintaining sin as necessary, led to the result that man was not responsible for his sins. This consequence then was cut off, as the former was, by a formal check, also accompanied by more or less of argument—that man had a will, that he sinned with this will or willingly, and that sinning willingly he was responsible for his sins.

But this whole check to the doctrine of predestination, viz. that man is responsible for his own sins, and not God, is appended to that doctrine by Calvin just as much as it is by Augustine. Indeed, no one who professed to be a Christian could teach the doctrine without such a check. No

## Note XXI.

Christian of any school could make God the author of evil, or say that sin was not blameworthy.

First, Calvin protests generally against *fatalism*; *i.e.* any doctrine that denies *contingency*, and asserts all events to take place according to a certain fixed and inevitable order, which could not have been otherwise: 'Vetus ista calumnia fuit, qua se Augustinus injuste fuisse gravatum alicubi conqueritur: nunc obsoletam esse decebat. Certe hominibus probis et ingenuis, si modo iidem docti sint, valde indigna est. Qualis fuerit Stoicorum imaginatio, notum est. Fatum suum texebant ex Gordiano causarum complexu: in quem cum Deum ipsum involuerant, fabricabant aureas catenas, ut est in fabulis, quibus Deum vincirent, ut subjectus esset inferioribus causis. Stoicos hodie imitantur astrologi, quibus fatalis ex stellarum positu dependet rerum necessitas. Valeant igitur cum suo fato Stoici: nobis libera Dei voluntas omnium sit moderatrix. *Sed contingentiam tolli ex mundo valde absurdum est.* Omitto quæ in Scholis usitatæ sunt distinctiones. Quod afferam simplex, meo judicio, et minime coactum erit, deinde ad vitæ usum accommodatum. Sic evenire necesse est quod statuit Deus, ut tamen neque præcise neque suapte natura necessarium sit. Exemplum in Christi ossibus familiare habeo. Christum corpus habuisse prorsus nostro simile Scriptura testatur. Quare fragilia illi ossa fuisse fateri nemo sanus dubitabit. Sed alia mihi videtur ac separata quæstio, an ullum os ejus frangi potuerit. Nam integra omnia et illæsa manere, quia fixo Dei decreto ita statutum erat, necessario oportuit. Nec vero quod a receptis loquendi formis de necessitate secundum quid et absoluta, item consequentis et consequentiæ abhorream, ita loquor; sed ne quæ lectoris argutia impediat, quin agnoscat vel rudissimus quisque verum esse quod dico. . . . Ac memoria tenendum est, quod ante posui, ubi Deus per medias et inferiores causas virtutem suam exerit, non esse ab illis separandam. Temulenta est ista cogitatio: decrevit Deus quid futurum sit; ergo curam et studium nostrum interponere supervacuum est. Atqui, cum nobis quid agendum sit, præscribat, et virtutis suæ organa nos esse velit; fas nobis est ne putemus separare quæ ille conjunxit. . . . Ergo quantum ad futurum tempus, quia nos adhuc rerum eventus latent, perinde ad officium suum intentus esse quisque debet, ac si nihil in utramvis partem constitutum foret. Vel ut magis proprie loquar, talem in omnibus quæ ex Dei mandato aggreditur, successum sperare debet, ut in rebus sibi incognitis *contingentiam cum certa Dei providentia conciliet.* . . . Hac voce pius vir se divinæ providentiæ organum constitui agnoscet. Hac eadem promissione fretus, alacriter ad opus se accinget, quia persuasus erit, non fortuitam se operam in aere jacere. . . . Invocationem adeo non impedit, ut potius stabiliat. . . . Non sequitur quin rerum adversarum culpam vel ignavia nostra, vel temeritas, vel incogitantia, vel aliud vitium merito sustineat.'—*De Prædestinatione*, vol. x. p. 725.

Here is the doctrine of the schools respecting mediate and secondary causes; that events take their character from the causes that produce them, and are necessary or contingent, according as their causes are the one or the other. Calvin refers in the passage to the distinctions of the schools, with which he says he does not disagree; and his statement is only another form of that of Aquinas: 'Deus omnia movet secundum eorum conditionem; ita quod ex causis necessariis per motionem divinam sequuntur effectus ex necessitate, ex causis autem contingentibus sequuntur effectus contingentes.' *Supra*, p. 254. He protests against indolence or carelessness in temporal or spiritual matters, as a wholly illegitimate result to fasten on his doctrine; and says that people must *act* as if events were contingent, and not suppose that, because events are foreordained, that therefore they are foreordained without the necessary means to bring them about; which means lie in our own conduct and course of action.

Thus, while maintaining the Divine infallible decree of predestination, he protests against men making that decree their starting point, and putting it in prior order to action, in their own ideas and thoughts about themselves: '*Neque ego sane ad arcanam Dei electionem homines ablego, ut inde salutem hiantes expectent:* sed recte ad Christum pergere jubeo, in quo nobis proposita est salus; quæ alioqui in Deo abscondita lateret. Nam quisquis planam fidei viam non ingreditur, illi Dei electio nihil quam exitialis erit labarynthus. . . . *Hinc minime faciendum est exordium, quid de nobis ante mundum conditum Deus statuerit;* sed quid de paterno ejus amore nobis in Christo sit patefactum, et quotidie per evangelium Christus ipse prædicet. Nihil altius nobis quærendum, quam ut Dei filii simus.'—Vol. x. p. 708.

After this protest against fatalism, Calvin proceeds to acknowledge a true *will* in man; that he acts willingly and without constraint; and that consequently the blame of his sins rests entirely upon himself; and that to charge God with the authorship of them is impiety and blasphemy. The ground he takes is strictly Augustinian: 'Voluntas, quia inseparabilis est ab hominis natura, *non periit;* sed pravis cupiditatibus devincta fuit, ut nihil rectum appetere queat.'—*Instit.* l. 2. c. 2. s. 12. 'Non voluntate privatus est homo quum in hanc necessitatem se addixit, sed voluntatis sanitate. . . . Si liberam Dei voluntatem in bene agendo non impedit, quod necesse est illum bene agere: si diabolus, qui nonnisi male agere potest, voluntate tamen peccat; quis hominem ideo minus voluntarie peccare dicet, quod sit peccandi necessitati obnoxius? Hanc necessitatem quum ubique prædicet Augustinus, dum etiam invidiose Cœlestii cavillo urgeretur, ne tum quidem asserere dubitavit—"Per libertatem factum est ut esset homo cum peccato: sed jam pœnalis vitiositas subsequuta ex libertate fecit necessitatem." Ac quoties incidit ejus rei mentio, non dubitat in hunc modum loqui, de necessaria peccati servitute. Hæc igitur distinctionis summa observetur, hominem, ut vitiatus est ex lapsu, *volentem quidem peccare, non invitum nec coactum: affectione animi propinquissima*. . . . Augustino subscribens Bernardus ita scribit, "Solus homo inter animalia liber: et tamen, interveniente peccato, patitur quandam vim et ipse, sed a voluntate non a natura, *ut ne sic quidem ingenita libertate privetur.* Quod enim voluntarium etiam liberum."

Et paulo post—"Ita nescio quo pravo et miro modo ipsa sibi voluntas, peccato quidem in deterius mutata, necessitatem facit; ut nec necessitas (cum voluntaria sit) excusare valeat voluntatem, nec voluntas (quum sit illecta) excludere necessitatem." Est enim necessitas hæc quodammodo voluntaria.' L. 2. c. 3. s. 5. 'Voluntatem dico aboleri non quatenus est voluntas, quia in hominis conversione integrum manet quod primæ est naturæ; creari etiam novam dico, non ut voluntas esse incipiat, sed ut vertatur ex mala in bonam.'—L. 2. c. 3. s. 6.

Upon the ground, then, of the existence of this true will in man, he lays the responsibility of sin entirely upon man himself: 'Nego peccatum *ideo minus debere imputari*, quod necessarium est.'—*Instit.* l. 2. c. 4. s. 5. 'Eant nunc qui Deum suis vitiis inscribere audent, quia dicimus naturaliter vitiosos esse homines. . . . A carnis nostræ culpa non a Deo nostra perditio est.'—L. 2. c. 1. s. 10. 'Respondeant, possintne inficiari causam contumaciæ pravam suam voluntatem fuisse. Si mali fontem intra se reperiant, quid vestigandis extraneis causis inhiant, ne sibi ipsi fuisse exitii authores videantur.'—L. 2. c. 5. s. 11. 'Non extrinseco impulsu, sed spontaneo cordis affectu, scientes ac volentes peccarunt.'—*De Præd.* vol. x. p. 709. '*Ad reatum satis superque voluntaria transgressio sufficit.* Neque enim propria genuinaque peccati causa est arcanum Dei consilium, sed aperta hominis voluntas. . . . . Intus mali sui causam quum inveniat homo, quid circuire prodest, ut eam in cœlo quærat? Palam in eo apparet culpa quod peccare voluerit. Cur in cœli adyta perrumpens in labarynthum se demergit? Quanquam ut per immensas ambages vagando, deludere se homines conentur, nunquam ita se obstupefacient, quin sensum peccati in cordibus suis insculptum retineant. Hominem igitur, quem ipsius sui conscientia damnat, frustra absolvere tendit impietas.'—*De Præd.* vol. x. p. 711. 'Neque in Deum transferimus indurationis causam acsi *non sponte propriaque malitia* seipsos ad pervicaciam acuerent.'— p. 727. 'Quum perditis exitium denuntiat Scriptura, causam in æternum Dei consilium minime rejicit, vel transfert; sed *residere in ipsis* testatur. Nos vero non ideo reprobos tradimus destitui Dei Spiritu, ut scelerum suorum culpam in Deum imputent. *Quicquid peccant homines sibi imputent.* Quod si quis subterfugiat, conscientiæ vinculis fortius constringi dico, quam ut se a justa damnatione expediat. . . . Si quis obstrepat, prompta est exceptio, *Perditio tua ex te Israel.* . . . Non audiendi sunt qui procul remotas causas e nubibus accersunt, ut culpæ suæ notitiam, quæ et eorum cordibus penitus insidet, neque occulta latere potest, utcunque obscurent.'— p. 721.

The cautions and checks, then, which Calvin appends to the doctrine of predestination are substantially the same with those we find appended to the doctrine in S. Augustine and the Augustinian schoolmen. Predestination, according to Calvin, is no excuse for spiritual indolence or carelessness; it does not detract at all from man's responsibility, who is as much to blame for his sins upon this doctrine as upon the contrary one; and therefore whether we look to the fundamental statement of the doctrine, or to the checks and cautions with which it is surrounded, the doctrine of Calvin on this subject is seen to be the same as that of S. Augustine.

It is true Calvin condemns the scholastic treatment of this question, and after S. Augustine nobody, except perhaps S. Bernard, seems to satisfy him. But this complaint is qualified. He acknowledges, in the first place, that however their own interpretations of such doctrines may have fallen short, the fundamental doctrines of the schools were Augustinian and orthodox on this question: ' Qui postea secuti sunt, alii post alios in deterius continuo delapsi sunt; donec eo ventum est ut vulgo putaretur homo sensuali tandem parte corruptus. . . . *Interea volitavit illud in ore omnium, naturalia dona in homine corrupta esse, supernaturalia vero ablata.* Sed quorsum tenderet, vix centesimus quisque leviter gustavit. Ego certe si dilucide tradere velim qualis sit naturæ corruptela, *his verbis facile sim contentus.*'—*Instit.* l. 2. c. 2. s. 4. He admits here a certain foundation in the teaching of the schools which was orthodox, though it was overlaid with weak or injurious commentary. In the next place he makes a distinction amongst schoolmen; and while he complains of the refinements of Lombard and Aquinas, regards them as in the main orthodox: '*Longiore intervallo a recentioribus sophistis differo.*'—*Inst.* l. 2. c. 2. s. 6. The *older* commentators he considers to have maintained, though with too little boldness and openness, and with too great an *appearance* of compromise, the Augustinian ground. Thus he complains of Lombard's use of the term *freewill:* 'Ac principalem quidem causam in gratia esse non negant: sed eo tamen contendunt non excludi liberum arbitrium, per quod sit omne meritum. Neque id tradunt posteriores modo sophistæ, sed eorum Pythagoras Lombardus; quem, si cum istis compares, sanum et sobrium esse dicas. Miræ profecto cæcitatis fuit, quum Augustinum toties in ore haberet, non vidisse quanta solicitudine vir ille caverit ne ulla ex bonis operibus gloriæ particula in hominem derivaretur.'—*Instit.* l. 3. c. 15. s. 7. 'Magister sententiarum duplicem gratiam necessariam esse nobis docet, quo reddamur ad opus bonum idonei. Alteram vocat Operantem, qua fit ut efficaciter velimus bonum; Cooperantem alteram quæ bonam voluntatem sequitur adjuvando. In qua partitione hoc mihi displicet, quod dum Gratiæ Dei tribuit efficacem boni appetitum, innuit hominem jam suapte natura bonum quodammodo *licet inefficaciter* appetere. . . . In secundo membro *ambiguitas* me offendit, quæ *perversam genuit interpretationem.* Ideo enim putarunt nos secundæ Dei gratiæ cooperari, quod nostri juris sit primam gratiam vel respuendo irritam facere, vel obedienter sequendo confirmare. . . . *Hœc duo notare obiter libuit, ut videas jam lector, quantum a sanioribus scholasticis dissentiam.* . . . Utcunque, ex hac tamen partitione intelligimus qua ratione liberum dederint arbitrium homini. *Pronuntiat enim tandem Lombardus, non liberi arbitrii ideo nos esse, quod ad bonum vel ad malum vel agendum vel cogitandum perœque polleamus, sed duntaxat quod coactione soluti sumus.* . . . Optime id quidem, sed quorsum attinebat, rem tantulam adeo superbo titulo insignire. . . . . Equidem λογομαχίας abominor, quibus frustra ecclesia fatigatur; sed religiose censeo cavendas eas voces quæ absurdum aliquid sonant, præsertim ubi perniciose erratur. Quotus enim quæso quisque est, qui, dum assignari homini liberum arbitrium audit, non statim concipit illum esse et mentis suæ et voluntatis dominum, qui flectere se in utramvis partem a seipso possit? Atqui (dicet quispiam) sublatum erit hujusmodi periculum, si de significatione diligenter plebs admoneatur. Imo vero cum in falsitatem ultro humanum ingenium propendeat, citius errorem ex verbulo uno hauriet, quam veritatem ex prolixa oratione.'—*Instit.* l. 2. c. 2. ss. 6, 7.

It is evident that Calvin's quarrel with Lombard here is about the use of a word, and not about a substantial point of doctrine. In substantial doctrine he considers they both agree, though he thinks Lombard's distinction of operative and co-operative grace so worded as to tend to mislead, and though he objects to the use of the word *freewill* altogether, which he thinks will always be practically understood by the mass of men in the sense of a self-determining will. He would not object to the word if Lombard's sense could be fastened upon it; but he differs from him as to the expediency of using a term on which it will be so difficult to fasten this meaning, and which will always more readily suggest another and an erroneous one. His disagreement with Lombard is thus of the same kind with the disagreement noticed above, p. 267, with Aquinas, which was concerned with language and mode of statement as distinguished from substantial doctrine.

Calvin's reflections on the schoolmen, then, do not appear to prove any substantial difference on the subject of predestination, grace, and freewill, between himself and the Augustinian portion of the schoolmen. And this conclusion obliges me to notice some remarks of Pascal bearing on this question in the Provincial Letters.

I must admit, then, that I have against me, on this point, the authority of Pascal, who endeavours in the Provincial Letters to prove a strong distinction between the doctrine of Calvin and the Reformers, and the Augustinian and Jansenist doctrine, on the subject of grace and free-will. But I admit it the more readily, for the obvious consideration, that Pascal was not in a position to ackowledge such an identity in the doctrine of the two schools. As an attached member of the Roman communion, he was obliged by his position to disconnect his own and his party's doctrine as much as possible from that of the Reformers, and to make out a wide difference between them. The Jansenists were attacked on all sides as disaffected members of the Roman Church, Reformers in heart, though outwardly Catholics. They disowned and repelled the charge with indignation. But what is the natural, the irresistible disposition of a religious party under such circumstances, with respect to the doctrines upon which such a charge is founded? It is, of course, to make out, in any way they can, a difference between these doctrines and those of the other school, with which their opponents identify them. Under such circumstances, the authority even of Pascal has not, upon the present question, any irresistible weight. And when we come to examine his argument, and the reasons upon which he erects the difference he does between the Augustinian and the Calvinistic doctrine of grace, any weight that we might previously have been inclined to give his conclusion is much diminished.

Every reader of the Provincial Letters will remember the great argumentative clearness and penetration, supported by the keenest irony, with which Pascal proves the identity, under a guise of verbal difference, of the Thomist doctrine of grace with the Jansenist. The Thomist members of the Sorbonne, siding with the Jesuits against the Jansenists, had distinguished their own doctrine of grace from that of the Jansenists by a particular term; to the use of which, though apparently counter to their own Augustinian doctrine, they had by an arrangement consented among themselves, but to which the Jansenists would not consent. This was the term *prochain—proximus*. The Thomists maintained that every Christian had

## Note XXI. 403

the *pouvoir prochain* to obey the Divine commandments, and so attain eternal life; while the Jansenists, admitting the *power* of any Christian to do this, would not admit that this power was *prochain;* the distinction being, that the term *power* of itself, in the Augustinian sense (even supposing *every one* had such power), committed them to no assertion contrary to the exclusive and predestinarian doctrine, which made salvation only really attainable by the elect. For power in the Augustinian sense only means *potestas si vult;* in which sense the admission that all Christians have the power is not at all opposed to the doctrine that only the elect have the *will* given to them to lead that good life on which salvation depends. But the addition of the term '*prochain*' to 'power' seemed to fix on the word power a freewill sense, as distinguished from the Augustinian one; and to imply the admission that every one had the full and complete power, in the natural sense of the term, to attain eternal life,—which was opposed to the predestinarian doctrine. The Jansenists, therefore, would not admit the term '*prochain*.' Now it is evident that in this refusal they laid themselves open to a charge of inconsistency; for if they were ready to admit 'power' in an artificial sense, they might have admitted '*prochain*' in an artificial sense too. But Pascal adroitly diverts attention from the inconsistency of the Jansenists in their meaning of the word *power*, to the inconsistency of the Thomists in the meaning they gave to ' power *prochain;*' separating, as the latter did from the Jansenists, on the express ground of this phrase being refused, when they themselves held the phrase in a Jansenist sense—*i.e.* so as to be consistent with the exclusive and predestinarian doctrine: 'Mais quoi! mon père, s'il manque quelque chose à ce pouvoir, l'appelez-vous *prochain?* et direz-vous, par exemple, qu'un homme ait, la nuit, et sous aucune lumière, *le pouvoir de voir?* Ouidà, il l'auroit selon nous, s'il n'est pas aveugle.'—1*st Letter.* It is obvious that in this sense the whole Christian body might have the *pouvoir prochain*, and still not a real and *bonâ fide* power of attaining salvation, which might still be confined to the elect. He thus shows that the Thomists only differed from the Jansenists in the use of a word, and agreed with them in meaning and doctrine. And he proves the same thing in the case of the term '*grâce suffisante*,' which the Thomists admitted while the Jansenists rejected it: 'Mais enfin, mon père, cette grâce donnée à tous les hommes est *suffisante*? Oui dit-il. Et néanmoins elle n'a nul effet *sans grâce efficace*? Cela est vrai, dit-il. Et tous les hommes ont *la suffisante*, continuai-je, et tous n'ont pas *efficace*? Il est vrai, dit-il. C'est-à-dire, lui dis-je, que tous n'ont assez de grâce, et que tous n'en ont pas assez; c'est-à-dire, que cette grâce suffit, quoiqu'elle ne suffise pas; c'est-à-dire, qu'elle est suffisante de nom, et insuffisante en effet.'—*2nd Letter*. The Thomists then admitted the term 'suffisante' in an artificial sense, which enabled them to say that such sufficient grace was given to all, while they really held that sufficient grace, in the natural sense of the word, was only given to the elect. And therefore Pascal shows in this instance again, that the Thomists only differed from the Jansenists upon a word, while they agreed with them in meaning and doctrine.

But the same argument by which Pascal proves that the Thomists of the Sorbonne agreed in doctrine with the Jansenists, proves equally that the Jansenist or Augustinian agreed in doctrine with the Calvinist. The eighteenth Provincial Letter contains a long statement and argument to show that the Jansenist doctrine of efficacious grace differed from the Calvinist: the argument resting upon a particular admission with respect to this grace, which the Calvinists did not make, and the Jansenists did —the admission, viz. that man had *the power to resist* this grace. He raises on this ground a broad distinction between the Jansenists and the Calvinists; that the Jansenists allow freewill, while the Calvinists represent man as moved like an inanimate machine. I will extract at some length from this part of the Letter.

'Vous verriez, mon père, que non-seulement ils tiennent qu'on résiste effectivement à ces grâces faibles, qu'on appelle excitantes ou inefficaces, en n'exécutant pas le bien qu'elles nous inspirent, mais qu'ils sont encore aussi fermes à soutenir contre Calvin *le pouvoir que la volonté a de résister même à la grâce efficace et victorieuse* qu'à défendre contre Molina le pouvoir de cette grâce sur la volonté, aussi jaloux de l'une de ces vérités que de l'autre. Ils ne savent que trop que l'homme, *par sa propre nature, a toujours le pouvoir de pécher et de résister à la grâce*, et que, depuis sa corruption, il porte un fonds malheureux de concupiscence qui lui augmente infiniment ce pouvoir ; mais que néanmoins, quand il plaît à Dieu de le toucher par sa miséricorde, *il lui fait faire ce qu'il veut et en la manière qu'il le veut*, sans que cette infaillibilité de l'opération de Dieu détruise en aucune sorte la liberté naturelle de l'homme, par les secrètes et admirables manières dont Dieu opère ce changement, que saint Augustin a si excellemment expliquées, et qui dissipent toutes les contradictions imaginaires que les ennemis de la grâce efficace se figurent entre le pouvoir souverain de la grâce sur le libre arbitre, et la puissance qu'a le libre arbitre de résister à la grâce ; car, selon ce grand saint, que les papes de l'Église ont donné pour règle en cette matière, Dieu change le cœur de l'homme par une douceur céleste qu'il y répand, qui, surmontant la délectation de la chair, fait que l'homme, sentant d'un côté sa mortalité et son néant, et découvrant de l'autre la grandeur et l'éternité de Dieu, conçoit du dégoût pour les délices du péché qui le séparent du bien incorruptible. Trouvant sa plus grande joie dans le Dieu qui le charme, il s'y porte infailliblement de lui-même par un mouvement tout libre, tout volontaire, tout amoureux ; de sorte que ce lui serait une peine et un supplice de s'en séparer. *Ce n'est pas qu'il ne puisse toujours s'en éloigner, et qu'il ne s'en éloignât effectivement s'il le voulait. Mais comment le voudrait-il, puisque la volonté ne se porte jamais qu'à ce qui lui plaît le plus, et que rien ne lui plaît tant alors que ce bien unique, qui* comprend en soi tous les autres biens ? *Quod enim amplius nos delectat, secundùm id operemur necesse est,* comme dit saint Augustin.—*Exp. Ep. ad Gal.* n. 49.

' C'est ainsi que Dieu dispose de la volonté libre de l'homme sans lui imposer de nécessité, et que le libre arbitre, *qui peut toujours résister à la grâce, mais qui ne le veut pas toujours*, se porte aussi librement qu'infailliblement à Dieu, lorsqu'il veut l'attirer par la douceur de ses inspirations efficaces.

' Ce sont là, mon père, les divins principes de saint Augustin et de saint Thomas, selon lesquels il est véritable que " nous pouvons résister à la grâce," contre l'opinion de Calvin. . . .

' C'est par là qu'est détruite cette impiété de Luther, condamnée par le même concile : "*Que nous ne coopérons en aucune sorte à notre salut, non plus que des choses inanimées.*" . . .

' Et c'est enfin par ce moyen que s'accordent tous ces passages de l'Écriture, que semblent les plus opposés : . . . . . . . . . . que, comme dit saint Augustin, " nos actions sont nôtres, à cause du libre arbitre qui les produit ; et qu'elles sont aussi de Dieu, à cause de sa grâce qui fait que notre arbitre les produit." Et que, comme il dit ailleurs, Dieu nous fait faire ce qu'il lui plaît, en nous faisant vouloir ce que nous pourrions ne vouloir pas : *A Deo factum est ut vellent quod nolle potuissent.*

' Ainsi, mon père, vos adversaires sont parfaitement d'accord avec les nouveaux thomistes mêmes, puisque les thomistes tiennent comme eux, et le pouvoir de résister à la grâce, et l'infaillibilité de l'effet de la grâce, qu'ils font profession de soutenir si hautement, selon cette maxime capitale de leur doctrine, qu'Alvarez, l'un des plus considérables d'entre eux. répète si souvent dans son livre, et qu'il exprime (*Disp.* 72. l. viii. n. 4.) en ces termes : " Quand la grâce efficace meut le libre arbitre, il consent infailliblement ; parce que l'effet de la grâce est de faire *qu'encore qu'il puisse ne pas consentir, il consente néanmoins en effet.*" Dont il donne pour raison celle-ci de saint Thomas, son maître (1. 2. q. 112. a. 3) : " Que la volonté de Dieu ne peut manquer d'être accomplie ; et qu'ainsi, quand il veut qu'un homme consente à la grâce, il consent infailliblement, et même nécessairement, non pas d'une nécessité absolue, mais d'une nécessité d'infaillibilité." En quoi la grâce ne blesse pas " le pouvoir qu'on a de *résister si on le veut;*" puisqu'elle fait seulement qu'on ne veut pas y résister, comme votre père Pétau le reconnaît en ces termes (t. i. *Theol. Dogm.* l. ix. c. 7. p. 602.): " La grâce de Jésus-Christ fait qu'on persévère infailliblement dans la piété, quoique non par nécessité : *car on peut n'y pas consentir si on le veut*, comme dit le concile ; mais cette même grâce fait *que l'on ne le veut pas.*"

'C'est là, mon père, la doctrine constante de saint Augustin, de saint Prosper, des pères qui les ont suivis, des conciles, de saint Thomas, et de tous les thomistes en général. C'est aussi celle de vos adversaires, quoique vous ne l'ayez pas pensé . . . .

' " Pour savoir, dites-vous, si Jansénius est à couvert, il faut savoir s'il défend la grâce efficace à la manière de Calvin, qui nie qu'on ait le pouvoir d'y résister ; car alors il serait hérétique : ou à la manière des thomistes, qui l'admettent ; car alors il serait catholique." Voyez donc, mon père, s'il tient qu'on a le pouvoir de résister, quand il dit, dans des traités entiers, et entre autres au tom. iii. l. viii. c. 20. : " *Qu'on a toujours le pouvoir de résister à la grâce, selon le concile:* QUE LE LIBRE ARBITRE PEUT TOUJOURS AGIR ET N'AGIR PAS, *vouloir et ne vouloir pas, consentir et ne consentir pas, faire le bien et le mal ; et que l'homme en cette vie a toujours ces deux libertés, que vous appelez de contrariété et de contradiction.*" Voyez de même s'il n'est pas contraire à l'erreur de Calvin, telle que vous-même la représentez, lui qui montre, dans tout le chapitre 21., " que l'Église a condamné cet hérétique, qui soutient que la grâce efficace n'agit pas sur le libre arbitre en la manière qu'on l'a cru si longtemps dans l'Église," en sorte qu'il soit ensuite au pouvoir du libre arbitre de consentir ou de ne consentir pas : au lieu que, selon saint Augustin et le concile, *on a toujours le pouvoir de ne consentir pas, si on le veut.*'

www.ingramcontent.com/pod-product-compliance
Lightning Source LLC
Chambersburg PA
CBHW071437300426
44114CB00013B/1468